Essentials of Financial Risk Management

Essentials of Financial Risk Management

Edited by
Zachary Bell

MURPHY & MOORE
www.murphy-moorepublishing.com

Published by Murphy & Moore Publishing,
1 Rockefeller Plaza,
New York City, NY 10020, USA

ISBN: 978-1-63987-205-3

Cataloging-in-Publication Data

Essentials of financial risk management / edited by Zachary Bell.
p. cm.
Includes bibliographical references and index.
ISBN 978-1-63987-205-3
1. Financial risk management. 2. Risk management. 3. Finance. I. Bell, Zachary.
HD61 .E87 2022
658.155--dc23

For information on all Murphy & Moore Publications
visit our website at www.murphy-moorepublishing.com

MURPHY & MOORE

Contents

Preface

Financial risk is the likelihood of losing money on an investment or business venture. Financial risk management is the exercise of protecting the economic value of money or investment in a firm by using financial instruments to manage exposure to operational, market, credit, liquidity, and legal risks. It involves identifying the risk sources, quantifying the exposure, and making a hedging decision. It requires the knowledge of mathematics, statistics, economics and finance. Financial risk management is practiced by risk professionals at accounting firms, banks, insurance companies, consulting firms, asset management companies and regulatory agencies. The objective of this book is to give a general view of the different areas of financial risk management, and its applications. It picks up individual branches and explains their need and contribution in the context of a growing economy. Students, researchers, and finance experts will benefit alike from this book.

Significant researches are present in this book. Intensive efforts have been employed by authors to make this book an outstanding discourse. This book contains the enlightening chapters which have been written on the basis of significant researches done by the experts.

Finally, I would also like to thank all the members involved in this book for being a team and meeting all the deadlines for the submission of their respective works. I would also like to thank my friends and family for being supportive in my efforts.

Editor

1

An Object-Oriented Bayesian Framework for the Detection of Market Drivers

Maria Elena De Giuli [1], **Alessandro Greppi** [2] and **Marina Resta** [3,*]

[1] Department of Economics and Management, University of Pavia, 27100 Pavia PV, Italy; elena.degiuli@unipv.it
[2] Zurich Investment Life, 20159 Milan MI, Italy; alessandro.greppi@it.zurich.com
[3] School of Social Sciences, Department of Economics and Business Studies, University of Genova, 16126 Genova GE, Italy
* Correspondence: resta@economia.unige.it

Abstract: We use Object Oriented Bayesian Networks (OOBNs) to analyze complex ties in the equity market and to detect drivers for the Standard & Poor's 500 (S&P 500) index. To such aim, we consider a vast number of indicators drawn from various investment areas (Value, Growth, Sentiment, Momentum, and Technical Analysis), and, with the aid of OOBNs, we study the role they played along time in influencing the dynamics of the S&P 500. Our results highlight that the centrality of the indicators varies in time, and offer a starting point for further inquiries devoted to combine OOBNs with trading platforms.

Keywords: OOBN; Market Drivers; S&P 500

---

1. Introduction

Object Oriented Bayesian Networks—OOBNs—are hierarchical graphical models that break down the initial commitment into a set of sub-problems, and hence into subgraphs, encoding and representing the states of the world in a probabilistic fashion Koller and Pfeffer (1997). They are generally conceived as a robust alternative to Bayesian Networks (BNs) Pearl (1985): OOBNs, in fact, work best in integrating data from various sources and in considering information at different temporal or spatial resolutions Nagl et al. (2008); furthermore, they overcome several drawbacks of BNs Niedermayer (2008). In fact, BNs tend to perform poorly on high dimensional data Huang et al. (2013), Apollo (2017), and in practical applications BNs can suffer for overfitting Sun and Shenoy (2007). Moreover, it is possible to have more than a BN exactly representing the same joint probability distribution, but with a different direction for some of the edges, thus creating problems to assign the right direction of causation between edges Zhong and Xiao (2017).

Applications of OOBNs span over a variety of fields: from forensic genetics Dawid et al. (2007) to medical diagnosis Nagl et al. (2008), information fusion Sutton et al. (2004), and reliability analysis Langseth and Portinale (2007). However, the potential of OOBNs in finance is still rather unexplored: to the best of the authors' knowledge, in fact, only Mortera et al. (2013) apply OOBNs to model anti-competitive behavior in the market, while Musella and Vicard (2015) analyzes improvement strategies in quality management and customer satisfaction.

Our work contributes to this research trail by illustrating a practical application of OOBNs on the Standard & Poor's 500 (S&P 500) index, exploring the causal relationships between the S&P 500 and a bunch of heterogeneous drivers. The issue is part of a more general debate aimed at highlighting the role played by indicators of various nature on fluctuations of stocks and financial indexes; the problem has raised a big wave of essays so that it is not possible to mention everything; we therefore limit them to some of the most relevant. The seminal work of Fama et al. (1969), for instance, investigates the behavior of securities fluctuations depending on splits; later, Hillmer and Yu (1979) analyzes with a statistical method the market speed of adjustment to new information, while Chen et al. (1986) and Shanken and Weinstein (2006) examine a number of macro-economic variables and their influence on price fluctuations; furthermore, Mian and Sankaraguruswamy (2012) uses a measure of investor's sentiment for evaluating how the stock price reacts to firm-specific news; finally, Gokmenoglu and Fazlollahi (2015) turn the attention on commodities' persistence. The main point arising from this huge literature corpus is that the behavior of securities and financial indexes is the result of the interplay among very different variables.

Our research question concerns then disclosing how OOBNs can be helpful to detect main determinants of the S&P 500 index disentangling the complex ties among them and to suggest a trading behavior: we are going to show that OOBNs make possible representing in the same model aspects that should be generally hard to analyze with more conventional techniques and only at the cost of performing at the same time regressions, statistical analyses or information retrieved by data providers such as Bloomberg (https://www.bloomberg.com/), Factset (https://www.factset.com) or Datastream (https://infobase.thomsonreuters.com). Our conclusion is that the OOBN is a promising statistical technique because it allows for summarizing in a single tool the instances of various sophisticated investigation methods; moreover, it helps at highlighting the different influence of determinants across the years, working well as a thermometer of the investors' attitude to trade on the market.

With respect to the existing literature, our work therefore contributes towards various aspects. First of all, for what pertains the combination between the technique in use and the addressed problem: OOBNs have been never applied to determine the drivers of a financial index, and a fortiori to develop signals for active trading. All in all, the added value of this research is not only in managing complexity and unveiling the determinants of a leading financial index, but also in suggesting a concrete way to address such amount of information towards a practical application.

In line with the above, the rest of the paper is organized as follows. Section 2 is devoted to illustrate materials and methods: it starts by describing the dataset to move then at illustrating basic definitions about Bayesian and Object-Oriented Bayesian Networks; Section 3 discusses the results, and Section 4 provides the conclusions.

2. Materials and Methods

2.1. Data

The S&P 500 is an American stock market index based on the market capitalization of 500 large companies whose common stock is listed on the NYSE (New York Stock Exchange, https://www.nyse.com/) or NASDAQ (National Association of Securities Dealers Automated Quotations, https://www.nasdaq.com/). It is a ratio opposing the sum of the adjusted market capitalization of 500 stocks with an index divisor, which is a proprietary figure developed by Standard & Poor's:

$$\text{S\&P 500} = \frac{\sum_{k=1}^{500} AdjCap_k}{Div}, \tag{1}$$

where $AdjCap_k$, is the adjusted capitalization of the k-th stock ($k = 1, \ldots, 500$), and Div is the divisor, which multiple sources[1] peg at 8.9 billion, and it is adjusted in the case of stock issuance, mergers, change of companies in the S&P 500 amongst other corporate actions, thus ensuring that such events do not significantly alter the value of the index. The constituency and weighting methodology LLC (2013) make the S&P 500 index different from other US stock market indices; furthermore, due to the inclusion

[1] see, for instance: https://www.sharptrader.com/new-to-trading/stock-indices/overview-of-the-sp-500-index/ or https://www.sharptrader.com/new-to-trading/stock-indices/overview-of-the-sp-500-index/.

of companies which covers all areas of the United States and across all industries, it is generally considered an effective representation for the economy as well as a bellwether for the economy.

Provided the relevance of the index, we are aimed at capturing the most relevant ties among the S&P 500 and a bunch of indicators. In choosing them, we follow the approach proposed by Patel et al. (2011) that classifies indicators into a set of investment categories (Value, Growth, Sentiment and Momentum/Technical Analysis—TA) containing all the information needed for the analysis of a market index, both from a quantitative and a qualitative perspective. The complete listings with a short description are provided in Table 1.

Table 1 shows for each indicator the abbreviation employed throughout the paper (Network ID), as well as the block (Investing Area) which the index belongs to (Growth, Value, Sentiment, Momentum and TA). We are also going to provide a short explanation for the variables (referred by their abbreviation) included into our study, divided by area.

Table 1. Indicators list.

Name	Network ID	Investment Areas			
		Growth	Value	Sentiment	Momentum and TA
Gold	GOLD	x			
Unemployment rate	UNEMP	x			
DXY index	DXY	x			
Gross Domestic Product	GDP_G	x			
Wheat	WHEAT	x			
Crude oil	OIL	x			
Copper	COPPER	x			
Price to Cash Flow	PCF		x		
Sales Growth	SALES_G		x		
EBITDA growth	EBITDA_G		x		
Enterprise Value to EBITDA	EV_EBITDA		x		
Price to Book Value	P_BV		x		
Price to Sales	P_S		x		
Earnings price per Share	EPS		x		
EPS growth	EPS_G		x		
Dividend Yield	DVD_YLD		x		
Profit margin	PROFIT		x		
Profit per Sale	PS		x		
Return on Equity	ROE		x		
Ebitda margin	EBITDA_MRG		x		
Implied Volatility in 52 weeks	VOLA52W			x	
VIX	VIX			x	
Relative Strength Index	RSI				x
Rate of change	ROC				x
20 and 50 Moving Average Cross	MA20_50				x
Moving Average Convergence Divergence	MACD				x

Growth

GOLD is the most popular precious metal used as investment, especially in case of rising inflation; UNEMP represents the percentage of the total unemployed labor force actively looking for a job and willing to work. The DXY Index is the weighted geometric mean of the value of the US Dollar against the following currencies: Euro (57.6%), Yen (13.6%), Pound (11.9%), Canadian Dollar (9.1%), Swedish Krona (4.2%), and Swiss Franc (3.6%). GDP includes private and public consumption, government expenditure, investments and the trade balance; it is a measure of the economic activity in a country. WHEAT is an agricultural commodity generally used to hedge against inflation. OIL is an unrefined petroleum product whose price monitors the activity level in the manufacturing sector. COPPER is one of the most versatile industrial metals; cheaper than precious metals, it has wide application in various industries.

Value

All indicators in this investment area are ratios including weighted sums of variables in the financial statements of S&P 500 listed companies. Those variables include: the index level and cash flow (PCF); enterprise values and EBITDA (EV_EBITDA); the index price level and book values (P_BV); the index price level and sales (P_S); dividends per share and the index price level (DVD_YLD); net income and revenues (PROFIT); net income and net sales (PS); earnings and the total amount of shares outstanding in the index (EPS); net income and related shareholders' equity (ROE); EBITDA and revenues (EBITDA_MRG). Finally, PROFIT/EBITDA_MRG/EPS_G monitor the growth of these variables in neighbor periods.

Market Sentiment

VOLA52W is the annual implied volatility (derived from the options prices); VIX is the CBOE[2] volatility index.

Momentum and Technical Analysis

RSI compares the magnitude of recent gains to recent losses. ROC measures the speed at which the index changes over a certain period. MA20_50 considers crossing between a fast (20) and a slow (50) moving average. MACD[3] is the difference between 12 and 26 weeks exponential moving averages, with the 9 weeks moving average as a trigger.

2.2. Preliminary Data Analysis

This study uses weekly data from the S&P 500 index in the period Jan 2000–March 2018, collected from the Bloomberg database.

To limit the influence of abrupt changes in the time series, we applied the Bai–Perron test Bai and Perron (2003) in search for structural breaks. The test assumes to consider a standard linear regression model $\mathcal{M}$:

$$y_t = \mathbf{x}_t' \cdot \mathbf{b} + u_t, \tag{2}$$

where y_t is the dependent variable, $\cdot$ is the dot–product operator, $\mathbf{b}$ and $\mathbf{x}_t$ are the regression coefficients and the regressors vectors, respectively, and u_t the zero mean error term. The Bai–Perron technique checks whether it is reasonable to assume that the coefficients are not constant through time, as there are m breakpoints, where the coefficients shift from one stable regression relationship to a different one, so that (2) is turned into:

$$y_t = \mathbf{x}_t' \cdot \mathbf{b}_i^0 + u_t,\, t = T_{i-1}^0 + 1 \ldots, T_i^0, \tag{3}$$

for $i = 1, \ldots, m+1$, while $T_0^0 = 0$ and $T_{m+1}^0 = T$, with T being the total sample size.

The number of breakpoints is not exogenously given, but it is estimated via a double–check procedure at first aimed at minimizing the Residual Sum of Squares (RSS):

$$\text{RSS}(T_1, \ldots, T_m) = \sum_{j=1}^{m} RSS_j(T_1, \ldots, T_m), \tag{4}$$

with:

$$RSS_j(T_1, \ldots, T_m) = \sum_{t=T_{j-1}+1}^{T_j} \left\{ y_t - \mathbf{x}_t' \cdot \hat{\beta}(\{\hat{T}_i\})_{i=1}^m \right\}^2, \tag{5}$$

[2] Chicago Board of Exchange.

[3] Moving Average Convergence–Divergence.

where $\hat{\beta}(\{\hat{T}_i\})$ denotes the estimates based on the given m-partition $(T_1, \ldots, T_m)$. The reliability of the number m of breaks is then checked by minimizing the Bayesian Information Criterion (BIC) of M Schwarz (1978):

$$\text{BIC} = k \ln T - 2 \ln \hat{L}, \tag{6}$$

where $\hat{L} = p(y|\hat{\vartheta}, M)$ is the value of the likelihood function of the model $\mathcal{M}$, with parameters $\hat{\vartheta}$ for the observed time series y; T is the sample size and k is the number of parameters estimated by the model.

Table 2 shows the RSS and the BIC associated to the number of breakpoints m varying from 0 to 3; a visual inspection is also provided in Figure 1: all the computations have been done within the R[4] framework using the library *strucchange*.

Table 2. RSS and BIC scores for the Bai–Perron test.

	$m = 0$	$m = 1$	$m = 2$	$m = 3$
RSS	118,462,323	30,094,169	26,358,449	23,555,096
BIC	13,040	11,834	11,730	11,643

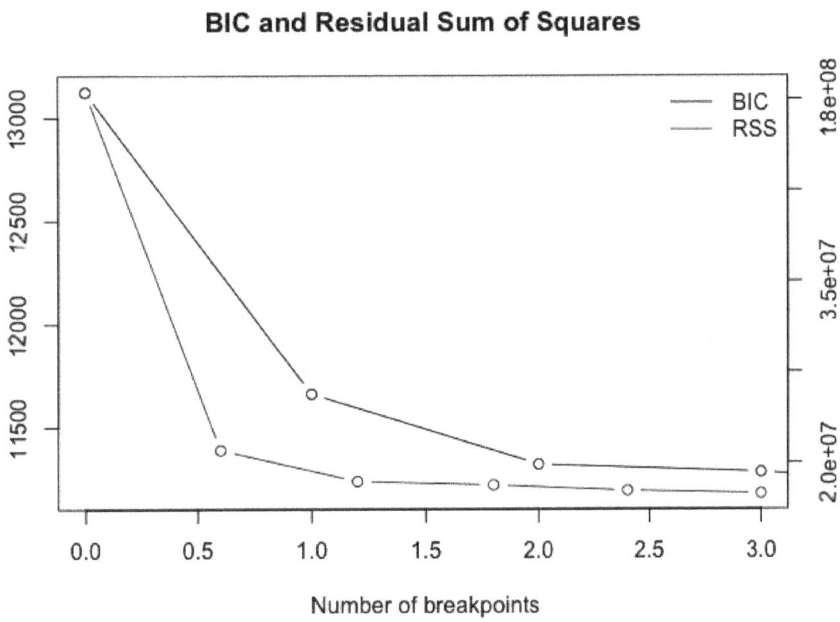

Figure 1. Behavior of the RSS and BIC varying the number of breakpoints from 0 to 3.

We highlight preliminarily that the existence of structural breaks was monitored obeying to various instances. From one hand, in fact, we are aware of considering a time frame (from 2000 to 2018) with various changes in the market dynamics, induced by events such as the 9/11 facts, the subprime crisis, the Lehman Brothers default, to give some examples. However, we also agree with the position of the econometrician Rob J. Hyndman[5] claiming that, in general, it is better talking about evolutionary changes, which can be misidentified as structural changes due to the use of these tests. Overall, these considerations led us to set at $m = 3$ the maximum number of breakpoints to test for, as an acceptable compromise between the need of documenting abrupt changes in the dynamics of the observed time series and the need of avoiding misapplication errors.

---

4 https://cran.r-project.org/.
5 https://robjhyndman.com/hyndsight/structural-breaks/.

The lowest values of both the RSS and BIC correspond to $m = 3$, thus suggesting the presence of three breaks and hence four regimes, as highlighted in Figure 2 representing the behavior of the S&P 500 from January 2000 to March 2018 with breaks evidenced by vertical dashed lines.

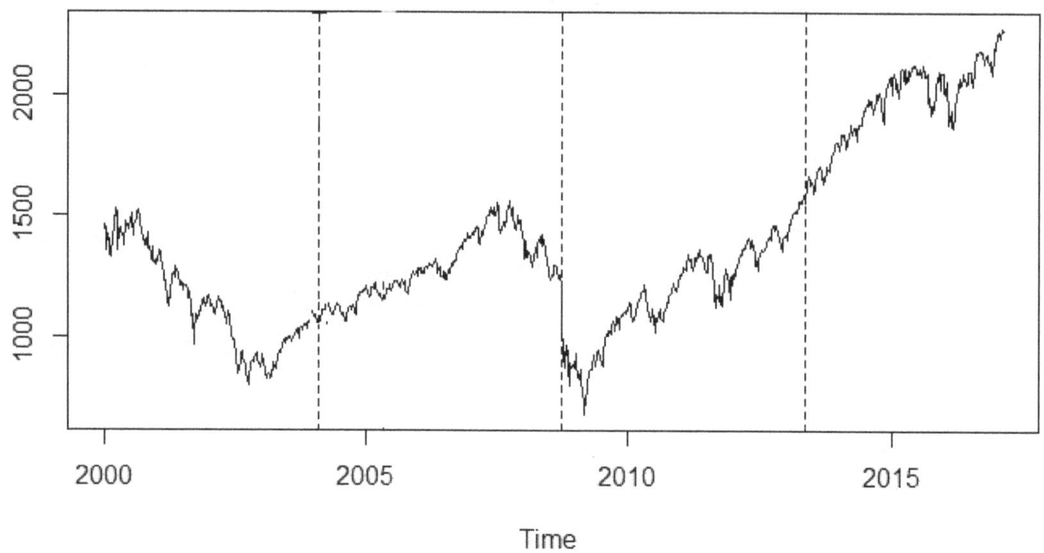

Figure 2. Structural breaks in the S&P 500 time series.

These conclusions are also supported by the values in Table 3 showing the significance at the 99% confidence level of the regression coefficients on the S&P 500 assuming the existence of four segments of the data, corresponding to the breaks identified by the Bai–Perron procedure.

Table 3. Regression coefficients with three breakpoints: the label *** indicates significance of the test values at the 99% level of confidence.

	Estimate	Std. Error	t-Value	$Pr(>\|t\|)$
Intercept	7.0269	0.0089	790.648	$< 2 \times 10^{-16}$ ***
segment2	0.0917	0.0112	8.177	8.92×10^{-16} ***
segment3	0.5204	0.0146	35.741	$< 2 \times 10^{-16}$ ***
segment4	0.7667	0.0147	52.211	$< 2 \times 10^{-16}$ ***

Breaks correspond to the beginning of years 2004, 2009 and to the ending of 2013. We divided our dataset accordingly: basic statistics for each period are reported in Table 4. In detail, we show for each time-slice the reference id (ID), the initial and final date (First and End), the length of the block of data, and a set of basic statistics: Mean, Median, Minimum (Min) and Maximum (Max) values observed in the period, Standard deviation (Std), first and third quantile (1stQ, 3rdQ).

The values in Table 4 combined to the graphical inspection of the index (see Figure 2) suggest the existence of up and down phases in the S&P 500. The challenge we are going to address is testing to which extent the OOBN is helpful at (i) correctly identifying them and (ii) develop trading suggestions towards the right direction, i.e., buying when an uptrend starts, selling when prices begin to slow down, or maintain the position when the price moves up and down without a leading direction (sideward movements)

Table 4. Main statistics for the observed block on the S&P 500.

Time-Slice	ID	First	End	Length	Mean	Median	Min	Max	Std	1st Q	3rd Q
2000–2004	TS1	03/01/00	02/02/04	215	1145.0989	1125.1700	800.5800	1527.4599	201.2463	988.8201	1316.8900
2004–2009	TS2	09/02/04	16/03/09	267	1251.6363	1261.4899	683.3800	1561.8000	176.3480	1161.5150	1387.0599
2009–2013	TS3	23/03/09	16/12/13	248	1295.5064	1287.0899	815.9400	1818.3199	228.7867	1116.9075	1414.6950
2013–2018	TS4	23/12/13	19/03/18	222	2165.6753	2092.2600	1782.589	2872.8701	249.4976	1990.3999	2347.5125

2.3. Methodology

The Bayesian Network (BN) is a valuable tool in constructing and understanding relations among elements of a problem under uncertainty; however, there can be situations where its use can be impractical or even ineffective: we have already highlighted in Section 1 that this can be the case of complex problems, involving too many variables, as well as when it is necessary to represent a hierarchy of dependencies. This is typical for time series models where a certain structure is replicated over time so that links between random variables in different time slices are established.

Going to the heart of the issue, our research question involves all the underlined aspects, as we consider twenty-six variables which potentially can influence the S&P 500 (complexity) whose behavior can be mutually affected (hierarchical effect); furthermore, the S&P index varies over time (time-slice effect). In the paper, we discuss how to overcome these issues with the aid of Object Oriented Bayesian Networks (OOBNs).

We want also to point out that the proposed application of the OOBN within the financial context is not a mere exercise in style, but it is fully justified as in the specialized literature Benjamin-Fink and Reilly (2017) OOBNs are claimed capable to analyze the following scenarios: (i) known hierarchy and full observability, (ii) known hierarchy and partial observability, (iii) unknown hierarchy and full observability, or (iv) unknown hierarchy and partial observability. The discussed application falls in case (iii) and thus it makes appropriate referring to the OOBN. Nevertheless, BNs and OOBNs are strictly related. An OOBN acts as a meta-network linking a number of BNs.

From a formal viewpoint, a BN is a a Directed Acyclic Graph (DAG) with nodes representing random variables and arcs expressing the probabilistic dependencies between variables. A BN is therefore fully described by the following elements:

- the graph structure $\mathcal{G} = (\mathcal{V}, \mathcal{E})$, where $\mathcal{V} = \{v_1, v_2, \ldots, v_n\}$ is the set of vertexes, and $\mathcal{E}$ is the set of directed edges;
- a finite probability space $(\Omega, \mathcal{A}, \mathcal{P})$, where Ω is the probability space, $\mathcal{A}$ is a σ–algebra on Ω and $\mathcal{P}$ a measure on Ω, such that: $\mathcal{P}(\Omega) = 1; \mathcal{P}(\emptyset) = 0$, and $\mathcal{P}(A) \leq \mathcal{P}(B)$, if $A \subseteq B$;
- a set of random variables defined on $(\Omega, \mathcal{A}, \mathcal{P})$, one for each node of the graph whose conditional probability distributions express the strengths of dependency relations between the random variable and its parent connection on the graph:

$$p(v_1, v_2, \ldots, v_n) = \prod_{k=1}^{n} p(v_k | \mathcal{G}(v_k)). \tag{7}$$

In this way, it is possible to define for the graph a set of Conditional Probability Tables (CPT) representing the mutual relationships between nodes and parent nodes. Nodes without any parent have a very simple CPT, given by the prior probability distribution of the node itself. In the remaining cases, the CPT represents all the node's joint probability, as given in (7).

An example of CPT is provided in Tables 5 and 6, where we examine the case of two variables x and y that can assume three states: 0, 1, and 2.

Table 5. Joint probability distribution for two variables x and y that can assume three states: 0, 1 and 2.

	$x=0$	$x=1$	$x=2$	$P(y)$
$y=0$	1/11	1/11	2/11	4/11
$y=1$	2/11	1/11	1/11	4/11
$y=2$	1/11	1/11	1/11	3/11
$P(x)$	4/11	3/11	4/11	1

The cells show the probability of a particular combination of x and y values. The first column sum is the marginal probability that $x = 0$. If we want to find the probability that $y = 0$ given that

$x = 0$, we must compute: $1/11 \div 4/11 = 1/4$. Likewise, from the same column, we can compute the probability that $y = 1$ when $x = 0$, that is: $2/11 \div 4/11 = 1/2$, and the probability that $y = 2$ when $x = 0$: $1/11 \div 4/11 = 1/4$. Working in a similar way with the piece of information in the third and fourth column, we can also find the conditional probabilities for y equalling 0; 1 and given that $x = 1$ and $x = 2$, respectively. The result is the table of conditional probabilities for y, provided in Table 6.

Table 6. Conditional Probability Table for two variables x and y that can assume three states: 0, 1 and 2.

	$x = 0$	$x = 1$	$x = 2$
$P(y = 0 \mid x)$	1/4	1/3	2/4
$P(y = 1 \mid x)$	2/4	1/3	1/4
$P(y = 2 \mid x)$	1/4	1/3	1/4
Sum	1	1	1

With respect to the BN formalism, OOBNs go one step further. The rationale of the OOBN resides in decomposing the complex problem into simpler sub-problems (classes) that can be modeled via BNs linked one to each other into an upper hierarchical structure. The transfer of information is enabled by inference nodes which form interface nodes. Every BN fragments serves as a class, while fragments resulting from instantiating these classes are named objects Nielsen and Jensen (2007). With respect to the BN, then, the OOBN offers a richer paradigm.

An example of an OOBN based on Langseth and Nielsen (2003) is presented in Figure 3.

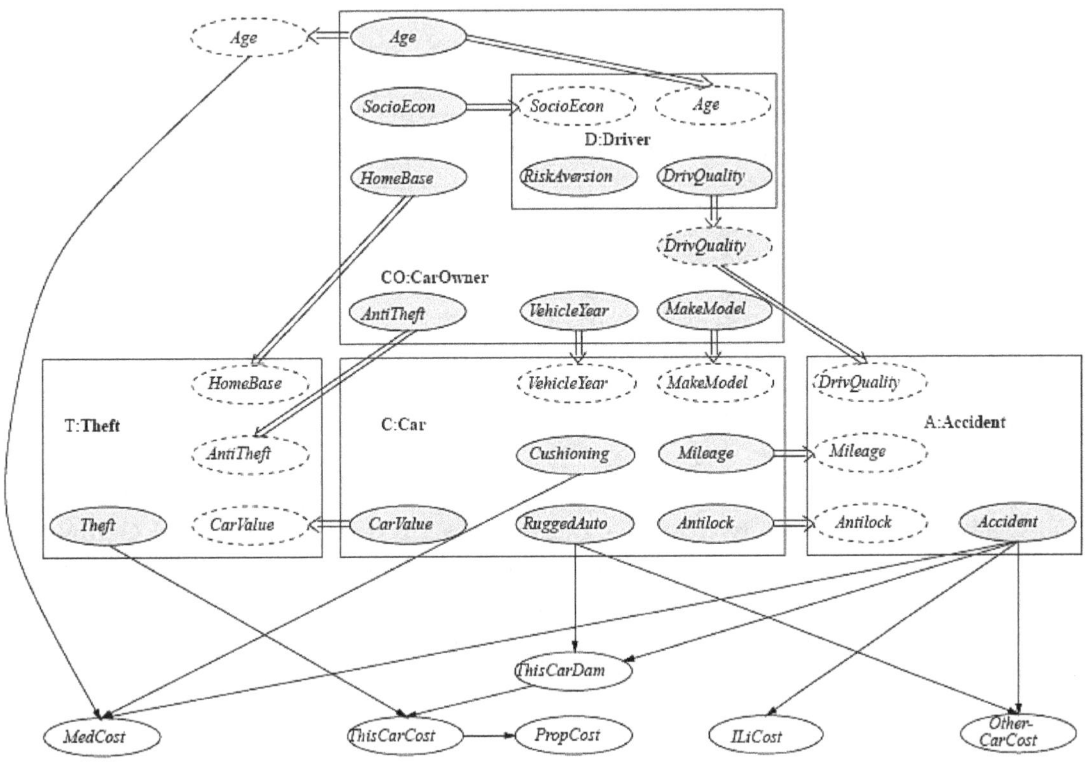

Figure 3. A representation of the insurance network with Object–Oriented Bayesian Networks. Source: (Langseth and Nielsen 2003).

The model introduces six classes: Insurance, Theft, Accident, Car, Car owner and Driver, which can be seen as describing different (abstract) entities in the domain. For instance, the class Car describes the properties associated with a car; the nodes *Cushioning, Mileage, CarValue, RuggedAuto* and *Antilock* are the nodes also used outside the class hence, they occur as output nodes, whereas *Vehicle year* and *Make model* are input nodes and *Airbag* is a normal node. In a similar fashion, the class Driver models the driving features of a car owner. In the insurance context, driving characteristics are an integral part of the notion of a car owner and an instantiation of Driver is therefore encapsulated in the class CarOwner. The class Insurance encapsulates the corresponding instantiations of the other classes. It is worth noticing the active use of reference links: for example, there are two CarValue nodes in the OOBN: C.CarValue is defined in C:Car, but as C.CarValue is a parent of T.Theft, it is imported into T:Theft using an input node (which is named T.CarValue). The reference link between these two nodes shows that it is the same random variable that is used in both situations.

Training an OOBN is typically divided into two distinct stages. The first stage creates the structure of the network: the hierarchical structure maximizing the data likelihood is usually drawn with the Chow–Liu procedure Chow and Liu (1968), while the NPC algorithm Steck (2001) helps in limiting inconsistencies among the set of conditional independence and dependence statements derived from the dataset and in choosing the most suitable model for the problem. The model construction is completed by estimating the conditional probability tables from the data with the EM (Expectation–Maximization) algorithm Lauritzen (1996). More details about the EM algorithms are provided in Appendix A.

3. Simulation and Results

3.1. Experiment Design

For each time-slice, we used earlier 90% of the data to build the OOBN, while the remaining 10% was used later to test the derived trading signals. Labels, first and ending together with the length of each block of data are reported in Table 7.

Table 7. Labels and length of each block of data employed in the trials.

ID	First	End	Length (in Weeks)
$L-TS_1$	03/01/00	01/09/03	215
$T-TS_1$	08/09/03	02/02/04	21
$L-TS_2$	09/02/04	01/09/08	240
$T-TS_2$	08/09/08	16/03/09	27
$L-TS_3$	23/03/09	17/06/13	223
$T-TS_3$	24/06/13	16/12/13	25
$L-TS_4$	23/12/13	09/10/17	200
$T-TS_4$	16/10/17	19/03/18	22

For the examined data, we alternated between two stages: **OOBN learning (OOBN-L)**, in which an OOBN is built based on the twenty-six indicators described in Section 2, and **OOBN towards trading (OOBN-T)**, in which the probability derived in the first stage is employed to develop a trading signal. The steps of the procedure are described in the following rows: note that Steps 3 and 4 were done using the Hugin Expert software[6], any other computation was done using R (version 3.5.2, R Development Core Team, GPL license) and Microsoft Excel (version 2018).

1. Set $i = 1$.
2. Select $L - TS_i$.
3. **(OOBN–L)** Build the OOBN using the Chow–Liu procedure combined to the NPC algorithm.
4. **(OOBN–L)** Derive the CPT for each node with the EM procedure and the related probability for the S&P 500 of going up (1), down (2) or side-ward (0) and extract the highest.

[6] https://www.hugin.com/.

5. **(OOBN-L)** If the highest probability for the S&P 500 is associated to the up state, then put the signal $s_t = 1$ and buy; if highest probability for the S&P 500 is associated to the down state, then set $s_t = -1$ and sell; otherwise, set $s_t = 0$ and maintain the position.
6. **(OOBN-T)** Select $T - TS_i$ and compute the time-series of log-returns:

$$r_k = \log p_{k+1} - \log p_k, \tag{8}$$

for $k = 1, \ldots, n-1$, where n is the length of $T - TS_i$.

7. **(OOBN-T)** For each price level in $T - TS_i$:

   (*a*) Evaluate:

$$s_t \times r_k. \tag{9}$$

   (*b*) Compute the sign of (9):

$$sgn_k = signum(s_t \times r_k). \tag{10}$$

   (*c*) Compute:

$$\hat{r}_k = sgn_k \, r_k. \tag{11}$$

8. **(OOBN-T)** With the time series: $\widehat{T - TS_i} = \{\hat{r}_k\}$ check the goodness of the trading signals with the bundle of performance measures provided in Table 8.
9. Set $i = i + 1$ and go to Step 2.

Table 8 shows the performance measures used to asses the goodness of the trading signals in each period. Their selection is driven by the choices documented in Dempster et al. (2001) and Resta (2009). To ease the readability of the table, please note that all the performance measures assume working on time-series of length $v = n - 1$ whose corresponding mean value is denoted by $\hat{\mu}$; when necessary, it has been made use of the indicator function:

$$\mathbf{1}_k = \begin{cases} 1, r_k \times \hat{r}_k > 0, \\ 0, r_k \times \hat{r}_k \leq 0. \end{cases} \tag{12}$$

Finally, the annualisation factor is set equal 52, as we are working with weekly observations.

Table 8. Indicators employed to evaluate the performance of the trading signals.

Performance Measure	Abbreviation	Formula
% Correct Directional Change	%CDC	$\%CDC = \frac{1}{v-1}\sum_{k=1}^{v} \mathbf{1}_k$
Annualized return	AR	$AR = 52 \times \frac{1}{v-1}\sum_{k=1}^{v} \hat{r}_k$
Annualized volatility	AV	$AV = \sqrt{52}\sqrt{\frac{1}{v-1}\sum_{k=1}^{v}(\hat{r}_k - \hat{\mu})^2}$
Sharpe Ratio	SR	$SR = AR/AV$
Number of Up periods	NUP	$NUP = card\{\hat{r}_k > 0\}$
Number of Down periods	ND	$ND = card\{\hat{r}_k \leq 0\}$
Average gain in up periods	AG	$AG = \frac{1}{NUP}\sum_{k=1}^{v} \mathbf{1}_k \times r_k$
Average loss in down periods	AL	$AL = \frac{1}{ND}\sum_{k=1}^{v}(1 - \mathbf{1}_k) \times r_k$
Average gain/loss ratio	AGL	$AGL = AG/AL$

3.2. Discussion

Every computation was made within the Windows environment on an Intel i7 processor. The computational time spent by the Hugin Expert software in developing each OOBN in the paper is equal on average to six minutes and includes maximizing the data likelihood with the Chow–Liu procedure and the NPC algorithm to limit inconsistencies among the set of conditional independence and dependence statements and estimating the conditional probability tables from the data with the EM algorithm. However evaluating the efficiency of the procedure as well as discussing the computational complexity of the OOBN go beyond the scopes of the paper. The interested reader can refer to more specialized texts in literature, such as: Liu et al. (2016) and Galia (2004).

Moving to the discussion, Figure 4 visualizes the results for the first time segment, illustrating its meaning and relevance: comments on the OOBN refer to $L - TS_1$, while remarks on the trading signal refer to $T - TS_1$. Similar considerations apply for other examined periods so that the conclusion we draw now can be extended to them in a straightforward manner.

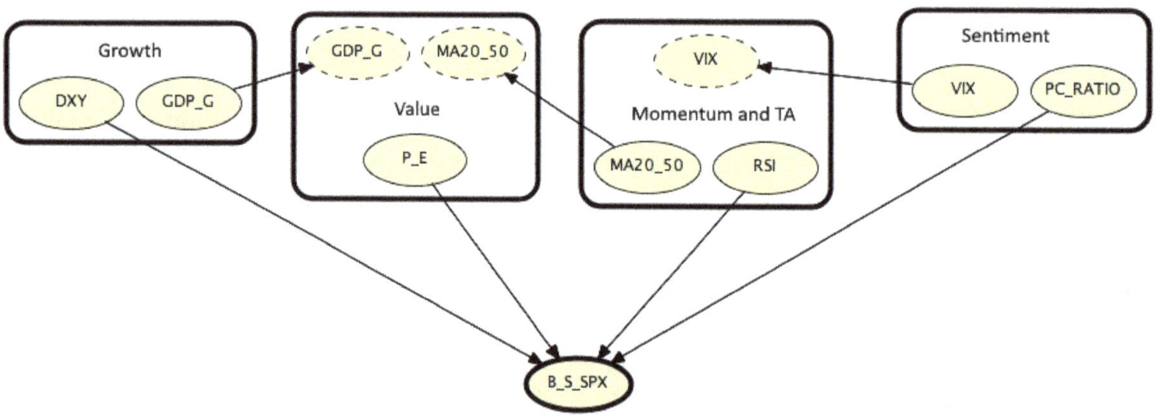

Figure 4. OOBN on the S&P 500 time series during the first time-slice.

From Figure 4, we may see as B_S_SPX is conditioned by four instance nodes belonging to the classes indicated in Section 2; in detail, the output nodes are: DXY (Growth), P_E (Value), RSI (Momentum and TA) and PC_Ratio (Sentiment). Besides Growth and Value classes communicate via the node GDP_G that is a parent node within the Value class; MA20_50 is the bridge between Value and Momentum/TA, which in turn is connected to the Sentiment group by the VIX.

From this representation, one can appreciate the simplicity of the final hierarchy that hides the intricacy of ties existing among the variables: Figure 5 unveils the structure of these complex relationships for each object.

From Figure 5, we observe that there is a BN inside each class of the OOBN presented in Figure 4. Analyzing the ties inside of those BNs, it is possible to get additional insights about the final aspect of the OOBN. To motivate this assertion, we discuss the case of the BN inside the Growth class: clearly similar considerations can be extended to the other classes. More in detail, the behavior of GOLD directly affects all the nodes in the Growth class (Figure 5a), while the opposite happens to WHEAT that is directly conditioned by any node inside the class. Other *big influencers* are DXY and OIL, directly insisting on four over six nodes of the class; among the greatest *followers*, on the other hand, we find COPPER and GDP_G on which insist five on six nodes. The fact that DXY is an instance node in the OOBN in Figure 4 is probably due to the sensitivity in changes of the other nodes in the class, as shown in Figure 6 with the aid of tornado plots comparing the relative importance of the class nodes. In detail, we simulate the sensitivity of each variable to a $\pm 20\%$ change in the values of the remaining ones, putting them in order from the highest to the lowest response. To make an example, looking at Figure 6a, we may observe the response of GDP_G with respect to $\pm 20\%$ fluctuations of the other variables, appearing on the left-hand side of the plot: the sensitivity is at the highest level with DXY;

nevertheless, it is maintained at high level also with respect to changes in the variables UNEMP, OIL, GOLD and COPPER, while it is notably lower with WHEAT. Similar considerations can be applied to the other tornado plots.

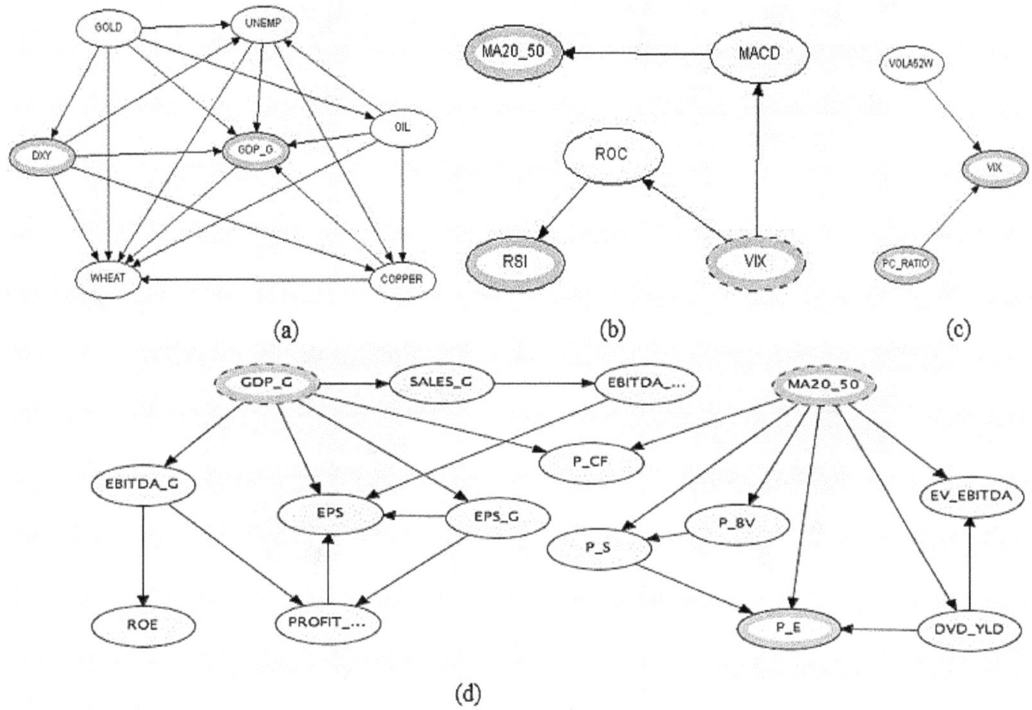

Figure 5. Unveiling the complexity in the S&P 500 drivers. From top to bottom and from left to right, the BN defining the ties among growth (**a**); momentum/technical analysis (**b**); sentiment (**c**); and value indicators (**d**)

Moreover, in the light of the results in Figures 5 and 6, the driving role of DXY with respect to the S&P 500 becomes more understandable.

Overall, disclosed information is multipurpose. First, it aids at revealing the hierarchy of ties in the market in a very simplified way: the main point is that, from the set of dependency among 26 indicators, we extract only four output nodes driving the index. This has notable implications when deriving the CPT for the S&P 500, as it is necessary to address 4×3 instead of 26×3 probabilities for each state.

Furthermore, with respect to the remarks done for the Growth class, we have also highlighted the existence of a richest network of relations behind those drivers. Second, we are going to show that this information can be managed to operate buy/sell/neutral actions on the S&P 500, and hence to simulate the impact on the index of changes in its drivers.

Table 9 examines the role of outputs on the S&P 500 in the four regimes and adds some clues to understand the overall direction of the index, as explained in previous rows. Here, the dependency structure for the S&P 500 index (B_S_SPX) is built under the rationale that the drivers should move either towards the same direction or not, thus suggesting an overall direction of the index, coded by numbers: In-trend (1), Reversal (2) or Sideward (0). In more detail, In-trend is connected to a bullish stage, with increasing price levels from a week to another; the opposite happens in the presence of Reversal, while Sideward is generally associated with uncertainty in the market, with prices moving in a lateral fashion, i.e., sometimes up and sometimes down, without any defined trend.

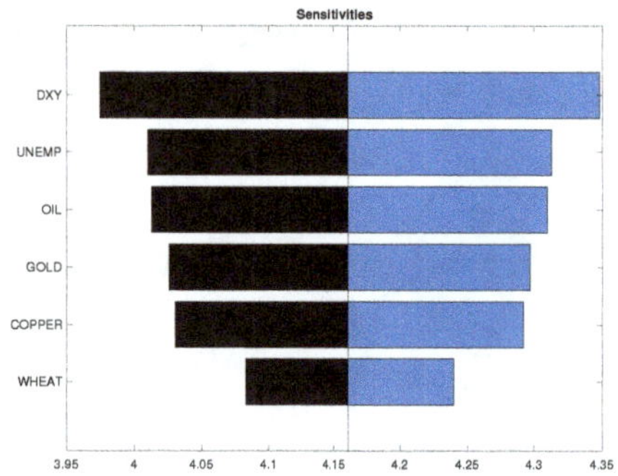

(**a**) GDP_G

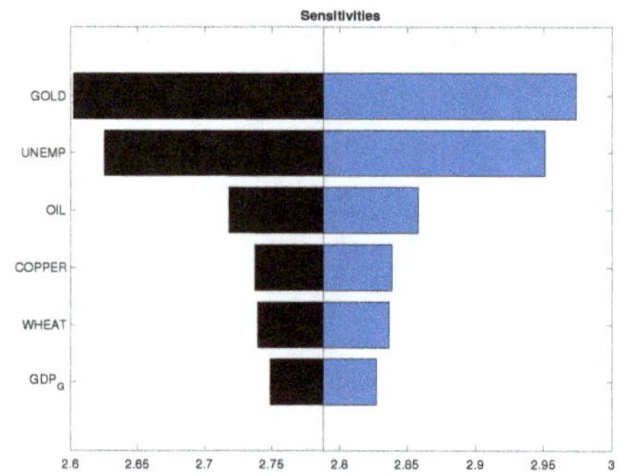

(**b**) DXY

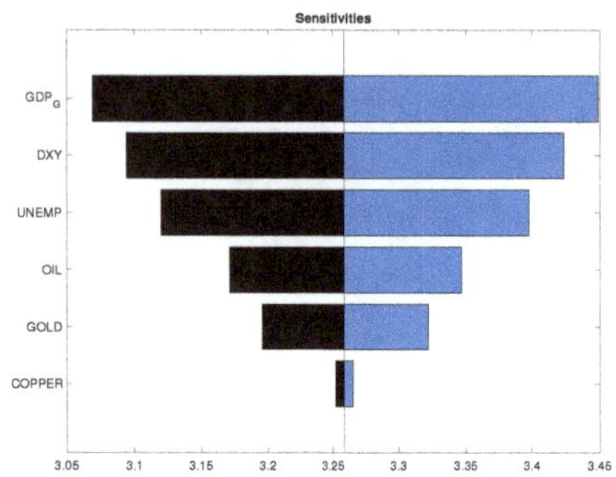

(**c**) WHEAT

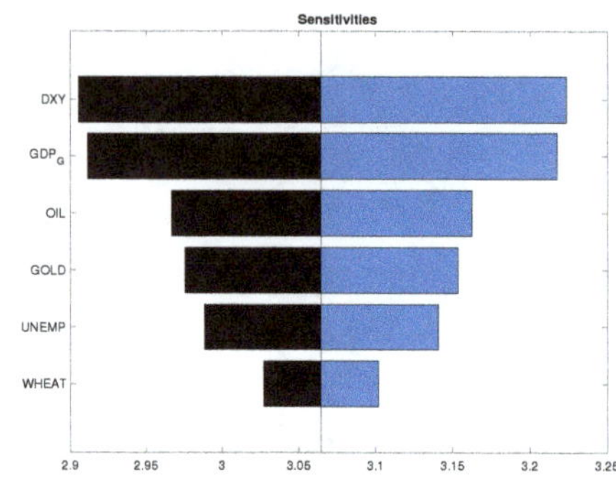

(**d**) COPPER

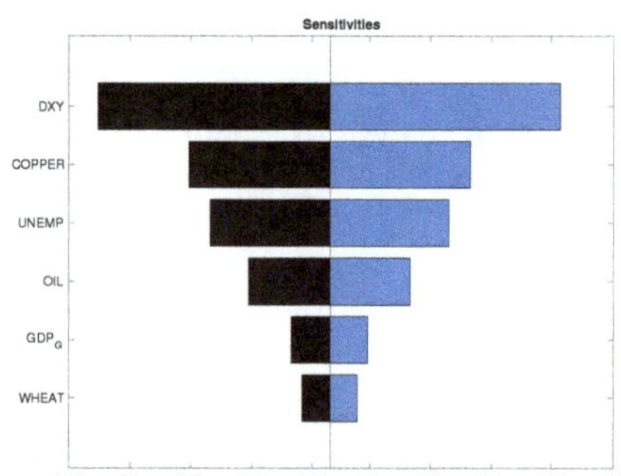

(**e**) GOLD

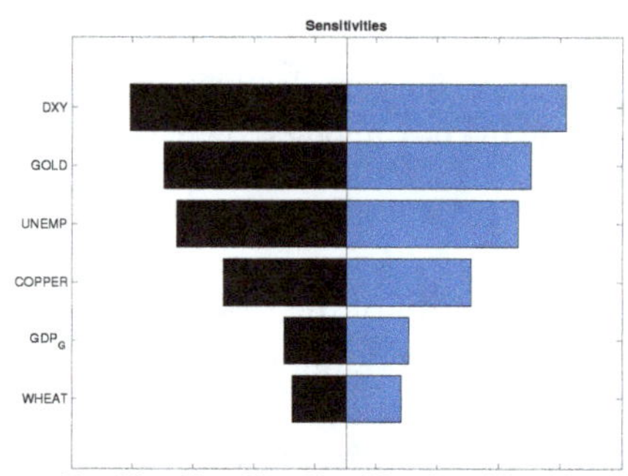

(**f**) OIL

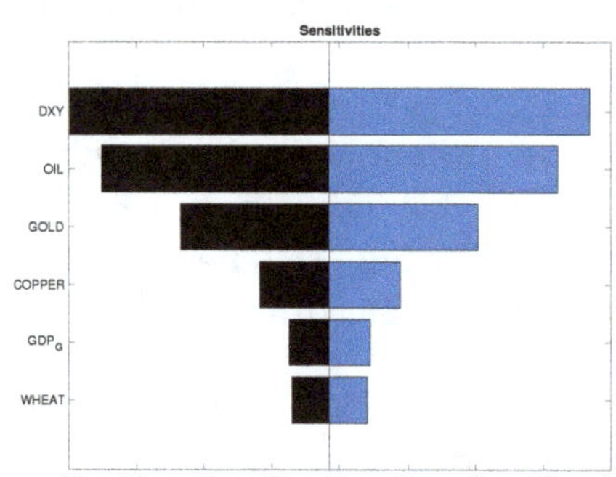

(**g**) UNEMP

Figure 6. Tornado plots for the nodes in the Growth class. From top to bottom and from left to right, the plot shows the sensitivity of each variable (node) to changes in the other within the class.

Table 9. Relations among instance nodes and S&P 500 during the four regimes. The bottom row shows the overall impact on the S&P 500. Numbers code the behavior in the market: In-Trend (1), Reversal (2), and Sideward (0). Corresponding probability is given between brackets.

	$L-TS_1$	$L-TS_2$	$L-TS_3$	$L-TS_4$
DXY	1 (46.15)	1 (42.48)	2 (38.76)	1 (40.73)
P_E	2 (51.39)	1 (38.14)	1 (35.83)	1 (37.06)
RSI	1 (39.68)	1 (48.10)	2 (41.15)	1 (41.76)
PC_Ratio	1 (41.35)	2 (39.66)	1 (43.36)	2 (40.59)
Overall	1 (38.12)	2 (42.93)	1 (43.09)	2 (43.49)

The overall impact of the drivers varies in time. During the first period, three output nodes on four agree in suggesting an in-trend position (1). Moving from the first to the second period, we have again three indicators over four aligned towards in-trend, but the final decision is for a Reversal (2), this, in our opinion, testifying the major influence of the PC_Ratio over the remaining indexes. The same occurs in the fourth regime. The situation in the third regime is different from other ones, as we have two drivers suggesting to stay in-trend and two indicating the opposite. In this perfect balancing situation, the final decision (1) is kept according to the suggestions of Value and Sentiment indicators. These remarks therefore suggest the prominent role played by Sentiment indicators.

To support these conclusions, we examined the performance of a trading system inspired by the results discussed in Table 9, through the trail described in Section 3.1. Results are reported in Table 10.

Table 10. Performance values of the trading signals in the test datasets.

Performance Measure	$T-TS_1$	$T-TS_2$	$T-TS_3$	$T-TS_4$
%CDC	0.8421	0.4	0.7391	0.7
AR	0.2148	0.4409	0.1912	0.2139
AV	0.0283	0.1113	0.0280	0.0385
SR	7.5949	3.9609	6.8179	5.558
NUP	16	10	17	14
ND	4	16	7	7
AG	0.0052	0.022	0.0052	0.0062
AL	0.0082	0.0205	0.0049	0.0082
AGL	0.6321	1.0749	1.0562	0.7505

The results in Table 10 highlight a very good performance of the trading system based on the OOBNs: with the exception of $T-TS_2$, in fact, the %CDC is sensitively over 60%, with peaks over 80% in the case of $T-TS_1$. Indeed, the performance of all the indicators are aligned to %CDC and confirm the satisfactory behavior of the trading system. A possible explanation for the results in the second testing period can be probably retrieved in observing that $T-TS_2$ includes weeks where the 2008 financial crisis was at its very blooming stage. The Average Volatilty (AV) values seem supporting this conclusion.

Furthermore, we provided in Table 11 the comparison of the performance among the Buy and Hold (B&H), the näive and (Näive) and the OOBN-based (OOBN-b) strategies. B&H is a passive investment strategy for which the investor buys stocks and holds them for the whole period regardless of fluctuations in the market with no concern for short-term price movements and technical indicators. The Näive is a strategy assuming to buy in uptrend periods and to sell during downtrends. The performance was computed as:

$$perf = \prod_{k=1}^{v}(1 + r_k|_{strategy}). \quad (13)$$

Here, $r_k|_{strategy}$ is the log-return r_k in the B&H case, while we have $r_k|_{strategy} = \hat{r}_k$ as defined in (11) for the OOBN-b; finally, when dealing with the näive strategy, it is: $r_k|_{strategy} = 1 + r_k$ during uptrend periods and $r_k|_{strategy} = 1 + (-1)\, r_k$ when the time series goes downtrend. In practice, (13) evaluates the convenience of investing each unit capital at the rate $r_k|_{strategy}$ for each week of the testing period.

Table 11. Comparison of the performance among the Buy and Hold (B&H), the Näive and the OOBN-based (OOBN-b) strategies.

	B&H	Näive	OOBN-b
$T - TS_1$	1.0507	1.0507	1.0858
$T - TS_2$	0.7989	1.2208	1.2418
$T - TS_3$	1.0548	1.0548	1.0919
$T - TS_4$	1.0283	0.9707	1.0897

We can note that the performance of the OOBN-b strategy is always higher than both the B&H and the Näive. This is true also during the downtrend periods $T - TS_2$ and $T - TS_4$ when B&H and Näive, respectively, poorly performed. This evidence then supports the idea that the OOBN can be successfully combined with trading systems.

4. Conclusions

The study shows how Object-Oriented Bayesian Networks (OOBNs) can be employed to combine both qualitative and quantitative information of the market and to manage a large amount of information. Our results give an insight about the evolution of the market in a quite simplified way despite of the complexity of ties behind. In addition, our results open the room for a general remark and three interesting scenarios. For what concerns the remark, we have observed the mutant role of the indicators, although, in the examined cases, the Sentiment driver seems playing a prominent role in influencing the overall behavior of the S&P 500. Turning to the scenarios, the probability associated with each state makes it possible to develop what-if cases, as discussed in our results; moreover, the interplay among output nodes and the S&P 500 suggests the possibility of developing trading systems based on the OOBNs responses. To conclude, the use of dedicated software, such as Hugin Expert, which is able to manage both discrete and continuous variables, makes room enough to further developments, such as including a larger variety of explicative variables to refine both the technique and the overall results.

Author Contributions: M.E.D.G. worked at Section 1, and checked the overall soundness of the paper with particular emphasis on Section 2.3, Alessandro Greppi made computation with the Hugin Expert Software and Marina Resta worked at Sections 1 and 2, at the experimental design (Section 3) and for commenting the results. Conclusions were shared by all the authors.

Funding: : This research received no external funding.

Acknowledgments: The authors want to thank the anonymous referees for their comments and suggestions.

Conflicts of Interest: The authors declare no conflict of interest.

Appendix A. The Expectation–Maximization Algorithm

Consider the statistical model which generates a set $\mathbf{X}$ of observed data, a set of unobserved latent data or missing values $\mathbf{Z}$, and a vector of unknown parameters $\boldsymbol{\theta}$, along with a likelihood function

$L(\boldsymbol{\vartheta};\mathbf{X},\mathbf{Z}) = p(\mathbf{X},\mathbf{Z}|\boldsymbol{\vartheta})$; then, the maximum likelihood estimate (MLE) of the unknown parameters is determined by maximizing the marginal likelihood of the observed data:

$$L(\boldsymbol{\vartheta};\mathbf{X}) = p(\mathbf{X},\boldsymbol{\vartheta}) = \int p(\mathbf{X},\mathbf{Z}|\boldsymbol{\vartheta})d\mathbf{Z}. \tag{A1}$$

Expectation–maximization (EM) is an approach used to find the MLE of the marginal likelihood. The intuition behind EM is an old one: alternate between estimating the unknowns and the hidden variables: EM alternates between performing an expectation (E) step, which computes an expectation of the likelihood by including the latent variables as if they were observed, and a maximization (M) step, which computes the maximum likelihood estimates of the parameters by maximizing the expected likelihood found on the E step. The parameters found on the M step are then used to begin another E step, and the process is repeated. In detail:

1. Choose an initial estimate of $\boldsymbol{\vartheta}$.
2. (**E-step**) Compute the auxiliary Q–function $Q(\boldsymbol{\vartheta},\bar{\boldsymbol{\vartheta}}) = E_{\mathbf{Z}|\mathbf{X},\boldsymbol{\vartheta}}[logL(\boldsymbol{\vartheta};\mathbf{X},\mathbf{Z})]$ based on $\boldsymbol{\vartheta}$.
3. (**M-step**) Compute $\hat{\boldsymbol{\vartheta}} = arg\max Q(\boldsymbol{\vartheta},\bar{\boldsymbol{\vartheta}})$ to maximize the auxiliary Q–function.
4. Set $\boldsymbol{\vartheta} = \bar{\boldsymbol{\vartheta}}$ and repeat from **Step 2** until convergence.

References

Apollo, Magdalena. 2017. Prognostic and diagnostic capabilities of OOBN in assessing investment risk of complex construction projects. *Procedia Engineering* 196: 236–43. [CrossRef]

Bai, Jushan, and Pierre Perron. 2003. Computation and analysis of multiple structural change models. *Journal of Applied Econometrics* 18: 1–22. [CrossRef]

Benjamin-Fink, Nicole, and Brian K. Reilly. 2017. A road map for developing and applying objec-oriented bayesian networks to "WICKED"problems. *Ecological Modelling* 360: 27–44. [CrossRef]

Chen, Nai-Fu, Richard Roll, and Stephen A. Ross. 1986. Economic forces and the stock market. *The Journal of Business* 59: 83–403. [CrossRef]

Chow, C., and Cong Liu. 1968. Approximating discrete probability distributions with dependence trees. *IEEE Transactions on Information Theory* 14: 462–67. [CrossRef]

Dawid, A. Philip, Julia Mortera, and Paola Vicard. 2007. Object-Oriented Bayesian Networks for Complex Forensic DNA Profiling Problems. *Forensic Science International* 169: 195–205. [CrossRef]

Dempster, Michael, Tom W. Payne, Yazann Romahi, and G. W. P. Thompson. 2001. Computational learning techniques for intraday FX trading using popular technical indicators. *IEEE Transactions on Neural Networks* 12: 744–54. [CrossRef]

Fama, Eugene F., Lawrence Fisher, Michael C. Jensen, and Richard Roll. 1969. The Adjustment of Stock Prices to New Information. *International Economic Review* 10: 1–21. [CrossRef]

Galia, Weidl. 2004. Adaptive risk assessment in complex large scale processes with reduced computational complexity. Paper presented at 9th International Conference on Industrial Engineering Theory, Applications & Practice, Auckland, New Zealand, November 27–30.

Gokmenoglu, Korhan K., and Negar Fazlollahi. 2015. The Interactions among Gold, Oil, and Stock Market: Evidence from S&P500. *Procedia Economics and Finance* 25: 478–88.

Hillmer, Steven C., and P. L. Yu. 1979. The market speed of adjustment to new information. *Journal of Financial Economics* 7: 321–45. [CrossRef]

Huang, Shuai, Jing Li, Jieping Ye, Adam Fleisher, Kewei Chen, Teresa Wu, and Eric Reiman. 2013. A Sparse Structure Learning Algorithm for Gaussian Bayesian Network Identification from High-Dimensional Data. *IEEE Transactions on Pattern Analysis and Machine Intelligence* 35: 1328–42. [CrossRef] [PubMed]

Koller, Daphne, and Avi Pfeffer. 1997. Object-Oriented Bayesian Networks. Paper presented at Thirteenth Conference on Uncertainty in Artificial Intelligence (UAI '97), Providence, RI, USA, August 1–3, pp. 302–13.

Langseth, Helge, and Thomas D. Nielsen. 2003. Fusion of Domain Knowledge with Data for Structural Learning in Object Oriented Domains. *Journal of Machine Learning Research* 4: 339–68.

Langseth, Helge, and Luigi Portinale. 2007. Bayesian networks with applications in reliability analysis. In *Bayesian Network Technologies: Applications and Graphical Models*. Hershey: IGI Global, pp. 84–102.

Lauritzen, Steffen L. 1996. *Graphical Models*. Wotton-under-Edge: Clarendon Press.

Liu, Quan, Ayeley Tchangani, and François Peres. 2016. Modelling complex large scale systems using object oriented Bayesian networks (OOBN). *IFAC-PapersOnLine* 49: 127–32. [CrossRef]

Standard & Poor's Financial Services LLC staff. 2013. *S&P Indices Index Mathematics Methodology*. New York: The McGraw-Hill Companies, Inc.

Mian, G. Mujtaba, and Srinivasan Sankaraguruswamy. 2012. Investor Sentiment and Stock Market Response to Earnings News. *The Accounting Review* 87: 1357–84. [CrossRef]

Mortera, Julia, Paola Vicard, and Cecilia Vergari. 2013. Object-Oriented Bayesian Networks for a decision support system for antitrust enforcement. *The Annals of Applied Statistics* 7: 714–38. [CrossRef]

Musella, Flaminia, and Paola Vicard. 2015. Object-oriented Bayesian networks for complex quality management problems. *Quality & Quantity* 49: 115–33.

Nagl Sylvia, Matt Williams, and Jon Williamson. 2008. Objective Bayesian Nets for Systems Modelling and Prognosis in Breast Cancer. In *Innovations in Bayesian Networks*. New York: Springer International, pp. 131–67.

Niedermayer, Daryle. 2008. An Introduction to Bayesian Networks and Their Contemporary Applications. In *Innovations in Bayesian Networks-Theory and Applications*. New York: Springer International, vol. 156, pp. 117–30.

Nielsen, Thomas Dyhre, and Finn V. Jensen. 2007. *Bayesian Networks and Decision Graphs*. New York: Springer.

Patel, Pankaj, Souheang Yao, Ryan Carlson, Abhra Banerji, and Joseph Handelman. 2011. *Quantitative Research—A Disciplined Approach*. Technical Report. Zurich: Credit Suisse Equity Research.

Pearl, Judea. 1985. Bayesian Networks: A Model of Self-Activated Memory for Evidential Reasoning. Paper presented at 7th Conference of the Cognitive Science Society, Irvine, CA, USA, August 15–17, pp. 329–34.

Resta, Marina. 2009. Seize the (intra)day: Features selection and rules extraction for tradings on high-frequency data. *Neurocomputing* 72: 3413–27. [CrossRef]

Schwarz, Gideon. 1978. Estimating the dimension of a model. *Annals of Statistics* 6: 461–64. [CrossRef]

Shanken, Jay, and Mark I. Weinstein. 2006. Economic forces and the stock market revisited. *Journal of Empirical Finance* 13: 129–44. [CrossRef]

Steck, Harald. 2001. Constrained—Based Structural Learning in Bayesian Networks Using Finite Data Sets. Ph.D. thesis, Technical University Munich, Munich, Germany.

Sun, Lili, and Prakash P. Shenoy. 2007. Using Bayesian networks for bankruptcy prediction: Some methodological issues. *European Journal of Operational Research* 180: 738–53. [CrossRef]

Sutton, Charles, Clayton T. Morrison, Paul R. Cohen, Joshua Moody, and Jafar Adibi. 2004. *A Bayesian Blackboard for Information Fusion*. Technical Report. Amherst: Department of Computer Science, Massachusetts University.

Zhong, Hongye, and Jitian Xiao. 2017. Enhancing Health Risk Prediction with Deep Learning on Big Data and Revised Fusion Node Paradigm. *Scientific Programming* 2017: 1901876. [CrossRef]

2

On Double Value at Risk

Wanbing Zhang [1], **Sisi Zhang** [2,†] **and Peibiao Zhao** [1,*,†]

1 School of Science, Nanjing University of Science and Technology, Nanjing 210094, China; zvb950831@163.com

2 Securities Co., Ltd., Beijing 102627, China; icesisi@sina.com

* Correspondence: pbzhao@njust.edu.cn

† These authors contributed equally to this work.

Abstract: Value at Risk (VaR) is used to illustrate the maximum potential loss under a given confidence level, and is just a single indicator to evaluate risk ignoring any information about income. The present paper will generalize one-dimensional VaR to two-dimensional VaR with income-risk double indicators. We first construct a double-VaR with (μ, σ^2) (or (μ, VaR^2)) indicators, and deduce the joint confidence region of (μ, σ^2) (or (μ, VaR^2)) by virtue of the two-dimensional likelihood ratio method. Finally, an example to cover the empirical analysis of two double-VaR models is stated.

Keywords: double-VaR; joint confidence region; (μ, VaR^2)

MSC: 91B30

---

1. Introduction

In the early 1990s, the international economic and financial consultancy G30 published the report "derivatives practices and principles" based on the research on financial derivatives, and then proposed Value at Risk (VaR) model to measure the market risk. JP Morgan Bank then launched the VaR risk measurement and control model. Since VaR is accurate and comprehensive to the application of risk measurement and makes up the deficiency of Markowitz mean-variance model, it is generally welcomed by the international financial community, including regulatory authorities, and has become a standard to manage and control financial risk. Furthermore, VaR is widely used to measure credit risks and trading risks.

The biggest benefit of VaR is the ability to critically analyze risk through systematic analysis. The organization can control the front end and back end of the business by calculating VaR to understand the financial risks it faces and establish an independent risk management mechanism.

However, VaR also has its own limitations. Mausser and Rosen (1999) put forward the most obvious limitations of VaR: it does not provide absolute maximum loss value, which can only be expected in a certain confidence level. Another drawback of VaR is that when the calculation is based on historical data, the future situation of any event should be duplicated or fitted by historical data. However, the reality is that we cannot guarantee the future case of an event is just as old as. In addition, some researchers such as Artzner et al. (1999) criticized the VaR model because it does not meet sub-additivity.

The obvious limitation existing in VaR is that it is only used to illustrate the maximum possible loss for the given conditions and is only a single index to characterize the risk, which provides less information to users about other information such as income. In practice, what people usually care about is how much profit they can get while taking risks.

Based on the above considerations, we hope to follow the definition of VaR and Markowitz's portfolio theory, and then construct a double-VaR, that is, we will extend one-dimensional single-risk monitoring indicator-VaR to two-dimensional revenue-risk monitoring indicators-VaR (or double-VaR for short).

There is abundant literature about VaR. Here, the main research literature involved in this paper is described briefly as follows.

Duffie and Pan (1997) made a detailed background description of VaR, characteristics, applications, and the entire VaR-system. Beder (1995) used eight different models to calculate VaR values and compare them. Some foreign scholars studied mainly the calculation of VaR, such as Jorion (1996); Linsmeier and Pearson (1996); Duffie and Pan (1997); Engle and Manganelli (1999). Based on different situations, they arrived at many calculation skills such as the variance-covariance matrix method, historical simulation, and Monte Carlo simulation method, and the related characteristics of VaR, etc.

After 1999, there are an increasing number of new VaR models in the financial, industrial, and other different applied areas. Potters and Bouchaud (1999) proposed how to use the normality of asset volatilities to calculate the VaR of nonlinear combination. Some other scholars studying the nature of VaR and other risk measurement methods, such as Artzner et al. (1999), proposed VaR does not meet sub-additivity; Wang (1999) studied the characteristics of dynamic risk measures; Mausser and Rosen (1999) proposed that if a small-probability event happened in the case of loss exceeding the VaR, then VaR models cannot measure the size of potential losses; Chen et al. (2014) studied future cash arbitrage with VaR-portfolio problems; Tang et al. (2018) investigated the no-arbitrage problem with VaR-like arguments; Cong and Zhao (2018; 2019) posed a non-cash risk measure and a generalized non-cash risk measure, respectively, which improved in some sense VaR under the distribution of any random variable that is uncertain. In addition, some scholars extended the classical Markowitz mean-variance model to the mean-VaR model; for instance, Pearson (2002) and Jorion (2007) used these models with constraints to manage the risk-profit for a fund company.

In addition, many scholars have proposed a series of improved calculation methods based on different markets and different assumptions. Berkowitz (1999) proposed a new method for evaluation of VaR. Taylor et al. (2000) proposed to use the t distribution to fit the income sequence; Hu (2012) based their research on the mixed Copula model to study the evaluation value of VaR; Ze-To (2013) used the Heath-Jarrow-Morton model to measure the value of VaR, and pointed out that the model can capture the non-normal income distribution well and can accurately provide the value of VaR; Li et al. (2017) confirmed that using the Bootstrap method to calculate VaR and CVaR can effectively improve the estimation accuracy.

Meanwhile, many foreign scholars have also attached great importance to the empirical applications of VaR. Jackson et al. (1997) studied how to apply VaR into bank reserves. Berkowitz and O'Brien (2002) proposed how to evaluate the transaction risk of commercial banks through the prediction accuracy of the VaR model. Basak and Shapiro (2001) analyzed the optimal dynamic portfolio risks with VaR model.

In the present paper, we will extend one-dimensional single-risk monitoring indicator—VaR—to two-dimensional benefit-risk monitoring indicators—double-VaR.

Firstly, a reasonable definition of two-dimensional VaR (double-VaR) is given. For a better understanding of double-VaR we choose mean μ and variance σ as the parameters to build the first double-VaR model. Thus, for a given confidence level α, one can not only know the scope of asset risks but also can know their income range. Such indicators are better able to make trade-offs to the risk-return of assets.

Secondly, to solve the first model—double-VaR with respect to (μ, σ^2)—we extend the one-dimensional likelihood ratio method to two-dimensional likelihood ratio method, and derive the joint confidence region containing the unknown parameters. Then, we can solve a specific joint confidence region with ideal point method and area minimization method as well as to compare the results of these two methods.

Finally, according to the accuracy theory of VaR we study the double-VaR based on (μ, VaR^2) so that for a given confidence interval we cannot only know the biggest value of possible asset loss but we can also get the gain range. In this situation a better trade-off of the asset is possible.

The organization of the paper is as follows. Section 2 introduces some necessary conditions and terminologies. Section 3 is devoted to constructing double-VaR models with (μ, σ^2) and (μ, VaR^2). Section 4 confirms that the double-VaR models are effective via some examples.

2. Preliminaries

2.1. VaR

2.1.1. Definitions and Basic Descriptions

Definition 1. *The basic meaning of VaR is the maximum potential loss of risk assets under normal market conditions, for a given confidence level α and holding period t. One can describe it as follows*

$$P(\Delta p > VaR) = \alpha$$

where Δp is the loss of risk asset W within the holding period t and VaR is the value at risk under the confidence level α.

Remark 1. *Under a normal market environment and a given confidence level α, let the probability distribution density function of a risky asset value be $f(w)$, the initial value of a risky asset be w_0, the lowest value of a risky asset under a confidence level α be w^* and the yield on holding period t be r, then we have*

$$VaR = E[w] - w^* \tag{1}$$

where $w = w_0(1+r)$ and w^* can be achieved with the following two formulas

$$\alpha = \int_{w^*}^{\infty} f(w)dw \quad or \quad 1-\alpha = \int_{-\infty}^{w^*} f(w)dw \tag{2}$$

In particular, when the distribution of the risk asset yield r is a normal distribution, that is, $r \sim N(\mu, \sigma^2)$, then one can get VaR of the risk asset by the following steps:

Let

$$1-\alpha = \int_{-\infty}^{-\xi^*} \phi(\epsilon)d\epsilon \tag{3}$$

where ϕ is the probability density function of a standard normal distribution. According to (2) and (3), we can get

$$\int_{-\infty}^{-\xi^*} \phi(\epsilon)d\epsilon = \int_{-\infty}^{w^*} f(w)dw = \int_{-\infty}^{r^*} g(r)dr \tag{4}$$

where $g(r)$ is the normal probability density function of the risk asset with yield r. Since one has

$$\int_{-\infty}^{-\xi^*} \phi(\epsilon)d\epsilon = \int_{-\infty}^{w^*} \frac{1}{\sqrt{2\pi}} e^{-\frac{\epsilon^2}{2}} d\epsilon \tag{5}$$

and

$$\int_{-\infty}^{r^*} g(r)dr = \int_{-\infty}^{r^*} \frac{1}{\sqrt{2\pi}\sigma} e^{-\frac{(r-\mu)^2}{2\sigma^2}} dr = \int_{-\infty}^{\frac{r^*-\mu}{\sigma}} \frac{1}{\sqrt{2\pi}} e^{-\frac{1}{2}t^2} dt \tag{6}$$

where $t = \frac{r-\mu}{\sigma}$ and $t \sim N(0,1)$. We arrive here by (4) and (5)

$$r^* = \mu - \sigma\xi^* \tag{7}$$

Substitute (7) into (1), we then have

$$VaR = E[w] - w^* = w_0 + w_0E[r] - (w_0 + w_0r^*) = w_0\sigma\xi^*$$

that is, there holds

$$VaR = w_0\sigma\xi^* \tag{8}$$

More generally, if one considers the time factor for VaR, then the Formula (8) can be written as $VaR = w_0\sigma\xi^*\sqrt{\Delta t}$.

In other words, when the yield on a risk asset follows a normal distribution, VaR measure of the risk is equivalent to the variance measure.

2.1.2. Properties of VaR

VaR has the following properties:

(1) Transformation invariance

For any $c \in \mathbb{R}$ and positive x, there holds $VaR(x + c) = VaR(x) + c$.

(2) Positive homogeneity

For any $c > 0$, there holds $VaR(cx) = cVaR(x)$.

(3) Co-monotonic additivity

For any x, y is co-monotonic, there holds $VaR(x + y) = VaR(x) + VaR(y)$.

(4) First-order stochastic dominance

For x, y, if the first order of x is better than that of y, there holds $VaR(x_1) \leq VaR(x_2)$.

(5) Discontinuity on the confidence level

With respect to the confidence level $1 - \alpha$, VaR is not continuous.

(6) Convexity is not satisfied

This property means that the local minimizer of an optimizing problem with VaR as an objective function is not unique.

(7) Sub-additivity is not satisfied

This means that VaR for a portfolio is not less than the sum of VaR of all risky assets.

3. Double-VaR

3.1. Introduction of Double-VaR

We now chose the mean and variance as two proposed parameters-based on Markowitz's portfolio theory to form a revenue-risk region D. Then we can define VaR-like as follows

$$P\{(\mu, \sigma^2) \in D\} = 1 - \alpha$$

Remark 2. *It is not hard to speculate that the role of the revenue-risk region D in fact is similar to that of VaR. For convenience, we may call the boundary (or partial boundary) of D a double-VaR with respect to indexes μ and σ^2. A detailed definition of double-VaR will be given later.*

Its real economic significance is under the normal market environment and a given confidence level, an area in which the maximum possible loss (expressed by var σ^2) and the benefits (expressed by mean μ) of an asset within a certain time in the future falls.

3.2. Double-VaR Model with Respect to (μ, σ^2)

3.2.1. Two-Dimensional Likelihood Ratio Argument

Chen and Jiang (2017) proposed and studied a high-dimensional likelihood method for normal distribution. However, for the use of the two-dimensional likelihood method for the derivation of the joint confidence domain, we have not found relevant literature. Thus, we innovate based on learning their ideas to solve the two-dimensional joint confidence region for double-VaR problem.

Assume that the total distribution of ξ follows a distribution whose density function is $f(x;\theta)$, where the parameters $\theta = (\theta_1, \theta_2)$ are unknown. For the given sample observations, it is easy to get the likelihood function:

$$L(\theta_1, \theta_2) = L(x_1, x_2, \cdots, x_n; \theta_1, \theta_2) = \prod_{i=1}^{n} f(x_i; \theta).$$

If the maximum likelihood estimation of (θ_1, θ_2) is $(\hat{\theta}_1, \hat{\theta}_2)$ that is, $L(\hat{\theta}_1, \hat{\theta}_2) = \sup_{\theta \in \Theta}(\theta_1, \theta_2)$, Θ is the parameter space of θ, the likelihood ratio can be defined as

$$R = R(x_1, x_2, \cdots, x_n; \theta_1, \theta_2) = \frac{L(\theta_1, \theta_2)}{L(\hat{\theta}_1, \hat{\theta}_2)}.$$

For a given confidence level, the joint confidence region D of the parameter $\theta = (\theta_1, \theta_2)$ can be calculated by R.

When the total $\xi \sim N(\mu, \sigma^2)$, where $(x_1, x_2, \cdots, x_n)$ is a set of sample values and the confidence level is $1 - \alpha$, the joint confidence region of (μ, σ^2) can be gained by the following two-dimensional likelihood ratio, where the unknown parameter is $\theta = (\mu, \sigma^2)$.

In fact, we have known the maximum likelihood estimations of mean μ and variance σ^2 are respectively by $\hat{\mu} = \bar{x}$ and $\hat{\sigma}^2 = s^2 = \frac{1}{n}\sum_{i=1}^{n}(x_i - \bar{x})^2$. Then we get

$$L(\mu, \sigma^2) = (2\pi\sigma^2)^{-\frac{n}{2}} exp\{ -\frac{1}{2\sigma^2}\sum_{i=1}^{n}(x_i - \mu)^2\},$$

$$L(\hat{\mu}, \hat{\sigma}^2) = (2\pi s^2)^{-\frac{n}{2}} exp\{ -\frac{1}{2s^2}\sum_{i=1}^{n}(x_i - \bar{x})^2\}.$$

Next we can get the likelihood ratio

$$R = \frac{L(\theta_1, \theta_2)}{L(\hat{\theta}_1, \hat{\theta}_2)} = (\frac{s^2}{\sigma^2})^{\frac{n}{2}} exp\{ -\frac{1}{2\sigma^2}\sum_{i=1}^{n}(x_i - \mu)^2 + \frac{1}{2s^2}\sum_{i=1}^{n}(x_i - \bar{x})^2\} \tag{9}$$

Since

$$\sum_{i=1}^{n}(x_i - \mu)^2 = \sum_{i=1}^{n} x_i^2 + n\mu^2 - 2\mu\sum_{i=1}^{n} x_i = \sum_{i=1}^{n} x_i^2 + n\mu^2 - 2n\mu\bar{x} = \sum_{i=1}^{n} x_i^2 - n\bar{x}^2 + n(\bar{x} - \mu)^2.$$

Denote by $\frac{\bar{x}-\mu}{\sigma/\sqrt{n}} \triangleq M$ and $\frac{ns^2}{\sigma^2} \triangleq T$, thus we get the following

$$-\frac{1}{2\sigma^2}\sum_{i=1}^{n}(x_i - \mu)^2 = -\frac{1}{2\sigma^2}\sum_{i=1}^{n}(x_i^2 - n\bar{x}^2) - \frac{n}{2\sigma^2}(\bar{x} - \mu)^2 = -\frac{1}{2\sigma^2}\sum_{i=1}^{n}(x_i^2 - n\bar{x}^2) - \frac{1}{2}M^2.$$

Substitute the formula above into (9) and get

$$\begin{aligned} R &= (\frac{T}{n})^{\frac{n}{2}} exp\{-\frac{1}{2\sigma^2}\sum_{i=1}^{n}(x_i^2 - n\bar{x}^2) - \frac{1}{2}M^2 + \frac{n}{2}\} \\ &= (\frac{T}{n})^{\frac{n}{2}}\{-\frac{\sum_{i=1}^{n}(x_i^2 - n\bar{x}^2)T}{2ns^2} - \frac{1}{2}M^2 + \frac{n}{2}\} \\ &= (\frac{T}{n})^{\frac{n}{2}} exp\{-\frac{1}{2}T - \frac{1}{2}M^2 + \frac{n}{2}\} \end{aligned}$$

Since

$$\frac{\partial R}{\partial T} = n^{-\frac{n}{2}}(\frac{n}{2}T^{\frac{n}{2}-1} - \frac{1}{2}T^{\frac{n}{2}})exp\{-\frac{1}{2}T - \frac{1}{2}M^2 + \frac{n}{2}\},$$

and $T \neq 0$, if we let $\frac{\partial R}{\partial T} = 0$, then there holds $T_0 = n$. Since

$$\frac{\partial R}{\partial M} = (\frac{T}{n})^{\frac{n}{2}}(-M)exp\{-\frac{1}{2}T - \frac{1}{2}M^2 + \frac{n}{2}\},$$

and $M \neq 0$. Let $\frac{\partial R}{\partial M} = 0$, we arrive at $M_0 = 0$. For convenience, we denote by

$$\begin{aligned} A &\triangleq \frac{\partial^2 R}{\partial^2 M}|_{(M_0,T_0)} = (\frac{T}{n})^{\frac{n}{2}}(M^2 - 1)exp\{-\frac{1}{2}T - \frac{1}{2}M^2 + \frac{n}{2}\} = -1, \\ B &\triangleq \frac{\partial^2 R}{\partial T \partial M}|_{(M_0,T_0)} = n^{-\frac{n}{2}}(\frac{n}{2}T^{\frac{n}{2}-1} - \frac{1}{2}T^{\frac{n}{2}})(-M)exp\{-\frac{1}{2}T - \frac{1}{2}M^2 + \frac{n}{2}\} = 0, \\ C &\triangleq \frac{\partial^2 R}{\partial^2 T}|_{(M_0,T_0)} = n^{-\frac{n}{2}} exp\{-\frac{1}{2}T - \frac{1}{2}M^2 + \frac{n}{2}\}[(\frac{n}{2}T^{\frac{n}{2}-1} - \frac{1}{2}T^{\frac{n}{2}})(-\frac{1}{2}) \\ &+ \frac{n}{2}(\frac{n}{2} - 1)T^{\frac{n}{2}-2} - \frac{n}{4}T^{\frac{n}{2}-1}] = -\frac{1}{2n}. \end{aligned}$$

It is obvious that there holds

$$AC - B^2 = \frac{1}{2n} - 0 > 0.$$

By a sufficient condition of two-dimensional extreme points, we can know R has a strict maximum at the point (M_0, T_0). Thus, for the constant C, there exists a region D so that $P\{R \geq C\} = P\{(M,T) \in D\}$. According to the meaning of likelihood ratio, let $P\{R \geq C\} = 1 - \alpha$, then $P\{(M,T) \in D\} = 1 - \alpha$. Since

$$M \sim N(0,1),\ T \sim \chi^2_{n-1},$$

there exist three positive constants a, b and $c(b < c)$, so that

$$P\{(M,T) \in D\} = P\{|M| \leq a, b \leq T \leq c\} = P\{|\frac{\bar{x} - \mu}{\sigma/\sqrt{n}}| \leq a, b \leq \frac{ns^2}{\sigma^2} \leq c\} = 1 - \alpha.$$

Since two statistics M, T are *i.i.d*, there holds

$$P\{|\frac{\bar{x} - \mu}{\sigma/\sqrt{n}}| \leq a, b \leq \frac{ns^2}{\sigma^2} \leq c\} = P\{|\frac{\bar{x} - \mu}{\sigma/\sqrt{n}}| \leq a\} \cdot P\{b \leq \frac{ns^2}{\sigma^2} \leq c\} = 1 - \alpha \tag{10}$$

That is

$$(2\Phi(a) - 1)(\chi^2_{n-1}(c) - \chi^2_{n-1}(b)) = 1 - \alpha,$$

where $\chi^2_{n-1}(b)$ is the function value of χ^2_{n-1} distribution whose freedom is $n-1$ at the point b. Arrange (10) and get the joint confidence region of (μ, σ^2) as below

$$\{(\mu,\sigma^2) : \bar{x} - \frac{a\sigma}{\sqrt{n}} \leq \mu \leq \bar{x} + \frac{a\sigma}{\sqrt{n}}, \frac{ns^2}{c} \leq \sigma^2 \leq \frac{ns^2}{b}\} \tag{11}$$

Obviously, there are unknowns a, b, and c in the joint confidence domain under the confidence level required by this paper. Therefore, to find these three unknowns, we can determine the specific joint confidence domain after given n and sample variance.

Definition 2. *Assume that $X \in \mathbb{R}^n$ is a random vector, and (μ, σ^2) are two index parameters, for given confidence level α $(0 \leq \alpha \leq 1)$, one can define double-VaR of $X \in \mathbb{R}^n$ with respect to indexes (μ, σ^2) as*

$$VaR^{\alpha}_{(\mu,\sigma^2)}(X) \triangleq \partial\{(\mu,\sigma^2) : \bar{x} - \frac{a\sigma}{\sqrt{n}} \leq \mu \leq \bar{x} + \frac{a\sigma}{\sqrt{n}}, \frac{ns^2}{c} \leq \sigma^2 \leq \frac{ns^2}{b}\}.$$

In the above definition, a, b, c are unknown. However, in Section 3.2.2, we use the ideal method to find the joint confidence domain. Thus, the unknown parameters a, b, c are solved. We can look up Tables 1 and 2 to find the value of a, b, c.

Remark 3. *Noticing that the joint confidence region (see Figure 1 below) and combining with Markowitz's portfolio theory, the right boundary of the banded region in Figure 1 can be regarded the dobule-VaR, $VaR^{\alpha}_{(\mu,\sigma^2)}(X)$, with (μ, σ^2).*

That is to say, one can have the following two basic understandings:

(1) For a given risk level $\frac{nS^2}{d}$ $(b \leq d \leq c)$, $VaR^{\alpha}_{(\mu,\sigma^2)}(X) \triangleq VaR|^{\alpha}_{\sigma^2}(\mu; X)$ can be regarded as VaR in the sense of Markowitz's portfolio with a given confidence level α;

(2) For a given benefit level $\mu(\geq \bar{x})$, $VaR^{\alpha}_{(\mu,\sigma^2)}(X) \triangleq VaR|^{\alpha}_{\mu}(\sigma^2; X)$ can also be regarded as VaR in the sense of Markowitz's portfolio with a given confidence level α.

3.2.2. Solution to Joint Confidence Region on (μ, σ^2)

We adopt the so-called ideal point method to solve the joint confidence region.

$$\{(\mu,\sigma^2) : \bar{x} - \frac{a\sigma}{\sqrt{n}} \leq \mu \leq \bar{x} + \frac{a\sigma}{\sqrt{n}}, \frac{ns^2}{c} \leq \sigma^2 \leq \frac{ns^2}{b}\}. \tag{12}$$

It is well known that the joint confidence region of (μ, σ^2) is just as (12). It is now we evaluate a, b and c.

Firstly, one can analyze Figure 1 of this joint confidence region of (μ, σ^2) as below:

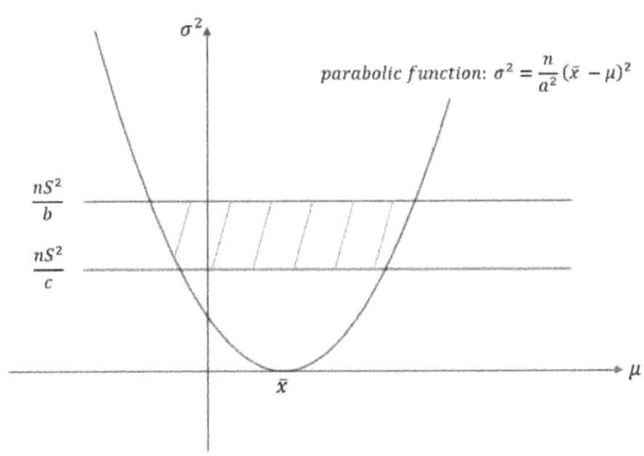

Figure 1. The joint confidence region of (μ, σ^2).

Given the confidence level $1-\alpha$, to minimize the area of this joint confidence region, it implies that if the two straights $\sigma^2 = \frac{ns^2}{b}$ and $\sigma^2 = \frac{ns^2}{c}$ deciding the size of shaded area are closed enough, which shows min $\frac{ns^2}{b}$ and max $\frac{ns^2}{c}$. At the same time, we hope to make the parabolic narrower, that is, one considers the problem: max $\frac{n}{a^2}$ and min $\frac{ns^2}{b}$. The parabolic $\sigma^2 = \frac{n}{a^2}(\bar{x}-\mu)^2$ can be regarded as an effective frontier of Markowitz portfolio in (μ, σ^2)-coordinate system.

Then we need to solve the following optimization model

$$\begin{cases} \max \frac{n}{a^2}, \\ \min \frac{ns^2}{b}, \\ \max \frac{ns^2}{c}, \\ s.t.\ (2\Phi(a)-1)(\chi^2_{n-1}(c) - \chi^2_{n-1}(b)) = 1-\alpha, \\ a, b, c \geq 0. \end{cases} \tag{13}$$

To solve problem (13), we first refer consider three single-objective optimization models, respectively, as follows

$$\begin{cases} \max \frac{n}{a^2}, \\ s.t.\ (2\Phi(a)-1)(\chi^2_{n-1}(c) - \chi^2_{n-1}(b)) = 1-\alpha, \\ a, b, c \geq 0. \end{cases}$$

$$\begin{cases} \min \frac{ns^2}{b}, \\ s.t.\ (2\Phi(a)-1)(\chi^2_{n-1}(c) - \chi^2_{n-1}(b)) = 1-\alpha, \\ a, b, c \geq 0. \end{cases}$$

$$\begin{cases} \max \frac{ns^2}{c}, \\ s.t.\ (2\Phi(a)-1)(\chi^2_{n-1}(c) - \chi^2_{n-1}(b)) = 1-\alpha, \\ a, b, c \geq 0. \end{cases}$$

After knowing n and the variance of samples S^2, these three optimization problems can be simplified as below

$$\begin{cases} \max \frac{1}{a^2}, \\ s.t.\ (2\Phi(a)-1)(\chi^2_{n-1}(c) - \chi^2_{n-1}(b)) = 1-\alpha, \\ a, b, c \geq 0. \end{cases} \tag{14}$$

$$\begin{cases} \min \frac{1}{b}, \\ s.t.\ (2\Phi(a)-1)(\chi^2_{n-1}(c) - \chi^2_{n-1}(b)) = 1-\alpha, \\ a, b, c \geq 0. \end{cases} \tag{15}$$

$$\begin{cases} \max \frac{1}{c}, \\ s.t.\ (2\Phi(a)-1)(\chi^2_{n-1}(c) - \chi^2_{n-1}(b)) = 1-\alpha, \\ a, b, c \geq 0. \end{cases} \tag{16}$$

Now assume that the solutions of these three problems above are respectively denoted by $a = \tilde{a}$, $b = \tilde{b}$, $c = \tilde{c}$. We set $(\tilde{a}, \tilde{b}, \tilde{c})$ and call it an ideal point of (13), but it is obvious that the ideal point is not necessarily a solution to (13). In fact, we want to get the Euclidean distance between this extremum point and the ideal point is as small as possible. That is, we wish to consider the following

$$\begin{cases} \min \sqrt{(a-\tilde{a})^2 + (b-\tilde{b})^2 + (c-\tilde{c})^2}, \\ s.t.\ (2\Phi(a)-1)(\chi^2_{n-1}(c) - \chi^2_{n-1}(b)) = 1-\alpha, \\ a, b, c \geq 0. \end{cases} \tag{17}$$

There is also a point that deserves to be noticed in the theory of probability and statistics when the variance of population is unknown; estimating the mean of population can be divided into two cases:

(1) When the number of sample observations is less than 30, we often choose t distribution to make a parameter estimation of the mean; when the number of sample observations is more than 30, we chose the normal distribution to estimate the parameters. To have a more accurate estimation the number of observations of more than 30 in this article, so we will use the normal distribution to estimate the mean in the process of solving the joint confidence region.

In addition, we notice that freedom n is usually less than 45 in any χ^2 distribution, because when n is more than 45 it is close to a normal distribution $N(n, 2n)$. Thus, this article first studies the case when $30 < n < 45$.

(2) When the number of sample observations is $n > 45$, we will make a further study.

Now we can solve the above optimization problem (17) with fmincon function in MATLAB and get the unknowns a, b, and c when the confidence level is respectively 99%, 95%, and 90% for $30 < n < 45$. By the way, the value zz ($zz = a(b^{-\frac{3}{2}} - c^{-\frac{3}{2}})$) used later is also gained as below Tables 1 and 2.

Table 1. Ideal point method (confidence level is 99% and 95%).

	Ideal Point (Confidence Level: 9			9%) Ideal Point (Confidence Level: 95%)				
n	a	b	c	zz	a	b	c	zz
31	3.6185	13.0228	52.5124	0.0675	3.2248	15.9692	45.8943	0.0402
32	3.6284	13.6810	53.8337	0.0625	3.2340	16.7118	47.1456	0.0373
33	3.6373	14.3476	55.1539	0.0580	3.2427	17.4595	48.3940	0.0348
34	3.6454	15.0216	56.4719	0.0540	3.2510	18.2119	49.6392	0.0325
35	3.6529	15.7018	57.7869	0.0504	3.2590	18.9685	50.8812	0.0305
36	3.6601	16.3877	59.0984	0.0471	3.2666	19.7289	52.1197	0.0286
37	3.6668	17.0785	60.4060	0.0441	3.2740	20.4929	53.3550	0.0269
38	3.6734	17.7739	61.7097	0.0414	3.2812	21.2604	54.5870	0.0253
39	3.6797	18.4736	63.0094	0.0390	3.2882	22.0311	55.8159	0.0239
40	3.6858	19.1774	64.3053	0.0367	3.2949	22.8048	57.0417	0.0226
41	3.6918	19.8851	65.5974	0.0347	3.3015	23.5816	58.2646	0.0214
42	3.6975	20.5965	66.8858	0.0328	3.3079	24.3612	59.4847	0.0203
43	3.7032	21.3115	68.1707	0.0311	3.3141	25.1435	60.7021	0.0193
44	3.7086	22.0299	69.4522	0.0295	3.3202	25.9285	61.9168	0.0183
45	3.7140	22.7516	70.7304	0.0280	3.3261	26.7160	63.1291	0.0175

Table 2. Ideal point method (confidence level is 90%).

n	a	b	c	zz
31	3.0444	17.6622	42.7490	0.0301
32	3.0539	18.4464	43.9610	0.0281
33	3.0629	19.2348	45.1702	0.0262
34	3.0715	20.0270	46.3766	0.0245
35	3.0799	20.8225	47.5800	0.0230
36	3.0879	21.6213	48.7805	0.0217
37	3.0957	22.4231	49.9782	0.0204
38	3.1033	23.2277	51.1732	0.0192
39	3.1106	24.0351	52.3654	0.0182
40	3.1178	24.8451	53.5552	0.0172
41	3.1247	25.6575	54.7424	0.0163
42	3.1314	26.4724	55.9273	0.0155
43	3.1380	27.2895	57.1099	0.0147
44	3.1444	28.1089	58.2902	0.0140
45	3.1507	28.9304	59.4685	0.0134

3.3. Double-VaR Model Based on (μ, VaR^2)

According to the theory of VaR, we will consider the joint confidence region of (μ, VaR^2) is reasonable and significant.

3.3.1. Accuracy Measurement of VaR

By the description in Section 2.1.1, we can know $VaR = w_0\sigma\xi^*$, that is, if the initial value of asset and the confidence level has been known, VaR is only related to standard deviation σ. Because σ is decided by the choice of sample observations there exits statistical errors in the solving of VaR. Different lengths of confidence sections provide different accuracy of VaR. It is very important to get the length of the confidence section.

3.3.2. (μ, VaR^2)-Model

According to the definition of joint confidence region we have

$$P\{(\mu, VaR^2) \in D\} = 1 - \alpha$$

where D is the joint confidence region of (μ, VaR^2) when the confidence level $1 - \alpha$ has been known. In particular, the given confidence level of the joint confidence region of (μ, VaR^2) is not related to the confidence level of VaR itself $1 - \beta$. If the confidence level of VaR is 99% and the confidence level of the joint confidence region of (μ, VaR^2) is 95%, the object studied in this article can be explained as: the return of an asset in one day μ and the biggest 99% loss of VaR are in the area D with the probability 95%.

When the total $\xi \sim N(\mu, \sigma^2)$, $(x_1, \cdots, x_n)$ are a set of sample values and the confidence level is $1 - \alpha$, the joint confidence region of (μ, VaR^2) can be gained by the likelihood ratio method.

In fact, by the argument of maximum likelihood estimations, the mean μ and variance σ^2 are estimated as $\hat{\mu} = \bar{x}, \hat{\sigma}^2 = S^2 = \frac{1}{n}\sum_{i=1}^{n}(x_i - \bar{x})^2$. Since $VaR = w_0\sigma\xi^*$ (where ξ^* is the quantile of standard normal distribution when the confidence level of VaR itself is $1 - \beta$ and ξ^* can be known by checking the corresponding table if β is given), if w_0 and ξ^* are known we can get the maximum likelihood estimation of VaR^2 as below

$$\widehat{VaR}^2 = \widehat{w_0\sigma\xi^*}^2 = (w-0\xi^*)^2\hat{\sigma}^2 = (w_0\xi^*)^2S^2 = (w_0\xi^*)^2\frac{1}{n}\sum_{i=1}^{n}(x_i-\bar{x})^2.$$

Likelihood function is

$$L(\mu,\sigma^2) = (2\pi\sigma^2)^{-\frac{n}{2}}exp\{-\frac{1}{2\sigma^2}\sum_{i=1}^{n}(x_i-\mu)^2\}$$

$$L(\hat{\mu},\hat{\sigma}^2) = (2\pi S^2)^{-\frac{n}{2}}exp\{-\frac{1}{2S^2}\sum_{i=1}^{n}(x_i-\bar{x})^2\}$$

and likelihood ratio is

$$R = \frac{L(\mu,\sigma^2)}{L(\hat{\mu},\hat{\sigma}^2)} = (\frac{S^2}{\sigma^2})^{\frac{n}{2}}exp\{-\frac{1}{2\sigma^2}\sum_{i=1}^{n}(x_i-\mu)^2 + \frac{1}{2S^2}\sum_{i=1}^{n}(x_i-\bar{x})^2\} \tag{18}$$

Similarly, we get the joint confidence region D of (μ, VaR^2) is

$$\begin{aligned}&\{(\mu, VaR^2) : \bar{x} - \frac{a\sigma}{\sqrt{n}} \leq \mu \leq \bar{x} + \frac{a\sigma}{\sqrt{n}}, (w_0\xi^*)^2\frac{nS^2}{c} \leq (w_0\xi^*)^2\sigma^2 \leq (w_0\xi^*)^2\frac{nS^2}{b}\}\\ &= \{(\mu, VaR^2) : \bar{x} - \frac{a\sigma}{\sqrt{n}} \leq \mu \leq \bar{x} + \frac{a\sigma}{\sqrt{n}}, (w_0\xi^*)^2\frac{nS^2}{c} \leq VaR^2 \leq (w_0\xi^*)^2\frac{nS^2}{b}\},\end{aligned} \tag{19}$$

From (18), one can define the so-called double-VaR with respect to (μ, VaR^2) as below.

Definition 3. *Assume that $X \in \mathbb{R}^n$ is a random vector, and (μ, VaR^2) are two index parameters, for given confidence level $\alpha(0 \leq \alpha \leq 1)$, one can define double-VaR of $X \in \mathbb{R}^n$ with respect to indexes (μ, VaR^2) as*

$$VaR^{\alpha}_{(\mu,VaR^2)}(X) \hat{=} \partial\{(\mu, VaR^2) : \bar{x} - \frac{a\sigma}{\sqrt{n}} \leq \mu \leq \bar{x} + \frac{a\sigma}{\sqrt{n}}, (w_0\xi^*)^2\frac{nS^2}{c} \leq VaR^2 \leq (w_0\xi^*)^2\frac{nS^2}{b}\}.$$

whose figure is as Figure 2.

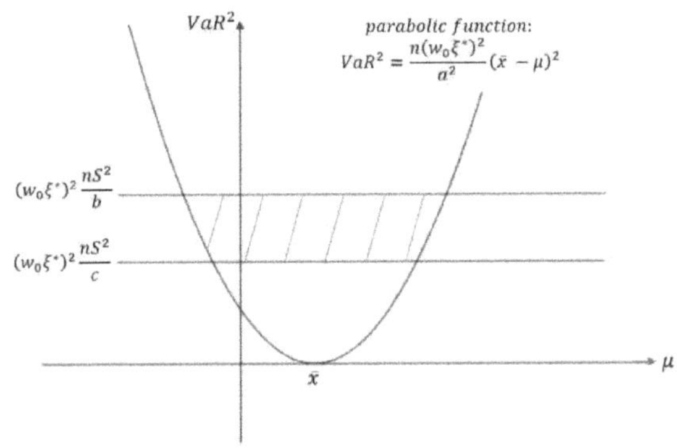

Figure 2. The joint confidence region of (μ, VaR^2).

Remark 4. *Noticing the joint confidence region (see Figure 2) and combining with Markowitz's portfolio theory, the right boundary of the banded region in Figure 2 can be regarded the dobule-VaR, $VaR^{\alpha}_{(\mu,VaR^2)}(X)$, with (μ, VaR^2). That is to say, one can have the following two basic understandings:*

(1) For a given risk level $(w_0\xi^*)^2\frac{nS^2}{d}$ $(b \le d \le c)$, $VaR^{\alpha}_{(\mu,VaR^2)}(X)\hat{=}VaR|^{\alpha}_{VaR^2}(\mu;X)$ can be regarded as VaR in the sense of Markowitz's portfolio with a given confidence level α;

(2) For a given benefit level $\mu(\ge \bar{x})$, $VaR^{\alpha}_{(\mu,VaR^2)}(X)\hat{=}VaR|^{\alpha}_{\mu}(VaR^2;X)$ can also be regarded as VaR in the sense of Markowitz's portfolio with a given confidence level α.

Clearly, we have

$$P\{(\mu, VaR^2) \in D\} = P\{|\frac{\bar{x}-\mu}{\sigma/\sqrt{n}}| \le a, b \le \frac{nS^2}{\sigma^2} \le c\}$$
$$= P\{|\frac{\bar{x}-\mu}{\sigma/\sqrt{n}}| \le a\} \cdot P\{b \le \frac{nS^2}{\sigma^2} \le c\} = 1-\alpha$$

That is, there holds

$$(2\Phi(a)-1)(\chi^2_{n-1}(c)-\chi^2_{n-1}(b)) = 1-\alpha,$$

where $\chi^2_{n-1}(b)$ (or $\chi^2_{n-1}(c)$) is the function value of χ^2 distribution at the point b (or c) when the freedom is $n-1$. Now we solve the unknowns a, b and c by area minimization method.

The area of joint confidence region of (μ, VaR^2) can be calculated by double integrals:

$$\int_{\frac{nS^2\Delta t}{c}}^{\frac{nS^2\Delta t}{b}} \int_{\bar{x}\Delta t+\frac{a\sigma\sqrt{\Delta t}}{\sqrt{n}}}^{\bar{x}\Delta t+\frac{a\sigma\sqrt{\Delta t}}{\sqrt{n}}} d(\mu\Delta t)d(\sigma^2\Delta t) = (\Delta t)^2 \int_{\frac{nS^2\Delta t}{c}}^{\frac{nS^2\Delta t}{b}} \frac{2a\sqrt{\Delta t}\sqrt{\sigma^2}}{\sqrt{n}} d\sigma^2 = \frac{4}{3}nS^3(\Delta t)^4 a(b^{-\frac{3}{2}} - c^{-\frac{3}{2}})$$

Thus, after knowing $n, \alpha, S^2, w_0, \xi^*$, we can solve the joint confidence region of (μ, VaR^2) by the following optimization problem:

$$\begin{cases} \min \frac{4}{3}n(w_0\xi^*)^2 S^3 a(b^{-\frac{3}{2}} - c^{-\frac{3}{2}}) \\ \text{s.t. } (2\Phi(a)-1)(\chi^2_{n-1}(c)-\chi^2_{n-1}(b)) = 1-\alpha \end{cases}$$

Similarly, we can now solve the above optimization problem with fsolve function in MATLAB and get the unknowns a, b, and c when the confidence level is respectively 99%, 95%, and 90% for $30 < n < 45$. By the way, the value zz ($zz = a(b^{-\frac{3}{2}} - c^{-\frac{3}{2}})$) belonging to the area $\frac{4}{3}nS^3a(b^{-\frac{3}{2}} - c^{-\frac{3}{2}})$ is also be gained as below.

At the same time, one can now solve the above optimization problem with fmincon function to solve constrained nonlinear minimization problem in MATLAB and get the unknowns a, b, and c when the confidence level is respectively 99%,95%, and 90% for $n > 45$. Incidentally, the value zz ($zz = a(b^{-\frac{3}{2}} - c^{-\frac{3}{2}})$) belonging to the area $\frac{4}{3}nS^3a(b^{-\frac{3}{2}} - c^{-\frac{3}{2}})$ can also be gained as below.

We can see the result of this model is similar to that under the area minimizing model; then there holds the following:

Theorem 1. *If the confidence levels are respectively 99%, 95%, 90%, $30 < n < 45$. At the same time, the mean $\bar{x}$, the variance S^2 of samples, w_0 and ξ^* have been known. We can inquire of the unknowns a, b, c in Tables 3 and 4 and put them into*

$$\{(\mu, VaR^2) : \bar{x} - \frac{a\sigma}{\sqrt{n}} \le \mu \le \bar{x} + \frac{a\sigma}{\sqrt{n}}, (w_0\xi^*)^2\frac{nS^2}{c} \le VaR^2 \le (w_0\xi^*)^2\frac{nS^2}{b}\}$$

to get the joint confidence region of (μ, VaR^2).

Table 3. Minimizing area method (confidence level is 99% and 95%).

	Min-Area (Confidence Level: 99%)				Min-Area (Confidence Level: 95%)			
n	a	b	c	zz	a	b	c	zz
31	2.9246	14.1512	63.8981	0.0492	2.3414	17.1303	56.5295	0.0275
32	2.9215	14.8181	65.1849	0.0457	2.3384	17.8670	57.7614	0.0256
33	2.9185	15.4917	66.4687	0.0425	2.3356	18.6088	58.9919	0.0239
34	2.9152	16.1680	67.7464	0.0396	2.3328	19.3513	60.2205	0.0224
35	2.9123	16.8527	69.0219	0.0370	2.3301	20.0984	61.4518	0.0210
36	2.9100	17.5339	70.3055	0.0347	2.3279	20.8511	62.6723	0.0198
37	2.9070	18.2239	71.5778	0.0326	2.3255	21.6032	63.8980	0.0186
38	2.9050	18.9163	72.8532	0.0306	2.3233	22.3595	65.1167	0.0176
39	2.9024	19.6137	74.1233	0.0289	2.3212	23.1191	66.3364	0.0166
40	2.9005	20.3139	75.3969	0.0272	2.3192	23.8815	67.5544	0.0157
41	2.8969	21.0252	76.6403	0.0257	2.3175	24.6494	68.7771	0.0149
42	2.8968	21.7419	77.9333	0.0244	2.3155	25.4145	69.9847	0.0141
43	2.8946	22.4362	79.1883	0.0231	2.3137	26.1851	71.2024	0.0134
44	2.8902	23.1570	80.4262	0.0219	2.3121	26.9580	72.4080	0.0128
45	2.8918	23.8752	81.7268	0.0209	2.3105	27.7325	73.6185	0.0122

Table 4. Minimizing area point method (confidence level is 90%).

n	a	b	c	zz
31	2.0457	18.7961	53.0159	0.0198
32	2.0428	19.5671	54.2198	0.0185
33	2.0401	20.3418	55.4228	0.0173
34	2.0375	21.1193	56.6243	0.0162
35	2.0351	21.9005	57.8240	0.0152
36	2.0328	22.6834	59.0225	0.0143
37	2.0307	23.4694	60.2189	0.0135
38	2.0286	24.2587	61.4147	0.0128
39	2.0267	25.0498	62.6071	0.0121
40	2.0248	25.8426	63.7978	0.0114
41	2.0230	26.6392	64.9906	0.0109
42	2.0213	27.4365	66.1760	0.0103
43	2.0197	28.2368	67.3628	0.0098
44	2.0182	29.0392	68.5481	0.0093
45	2.0167	29.8436	69.7319	0.0089

If the confidence level is not in the chart we can get the results by changing parameters in the program.

Theorem 2. *If the confidence levels are respectively 99%, 95%, 90%, $n > 45$. At the same time the mean $\bar{x}$, the variance S^2 of samples, w_0 and ξ^* have been known. We can inquiry the unknowns a, b, c in the Tables 5 and 6 and put them into*

$$\{(\mu, VaR^2) : \bar{x} - \frac{a\sigma}{\sqrt{n}} \leq \mu \leq \bar{x} + \frac{a\sigma}{\sqrt{n}}, (w_0\xi^*)^2\frac{nS^2}{c} \leq VaR^2 \leq (w_0\xi^*)^2\frac{nS^2}{b}\}$$

to get the joint confidence region of (μ, VaR^2).

Table 5. Minimizing area method (confidence level is 99% and 95%).

	Min-Area (Confidence Level: 99%)				Min-Area (Confidence Level: 95%)			
n	a	b	c	zz	a	b	c	zz
46	3.0064	21.7720	78.4073	0.0253	2.3977	27.4369	72.2900	0.0128
47	3.0024	22.4891	79.6858	0.0239	2.3941	28.2136	73.5112	0.0122
48	2.9983	23.2131	80.9560	0.0227	2.3910	28.9950	74.7342	0.0116
49	2.9944	23.9403	82.2217	0.0215	2.3880	29.7792	75.9545	0.0111
50	2.9882	24.6870	83.4624	0.0204	2.3853	30.5680	77.1736	0.0106
60	3.1182	30.7638	87.6602	0.0145	2.3613	38.5214	89.2508	0.0071
70	2.9378	39.7032	108.3873	0.0091	2.3443	46.6338	101.1698	0.0051
80	3.2519	34.5137	108.8108	0.0132	2.3312	54.8651	112.9622	0.0038
90	1.1088	24.1613	27.8069	0.0018	1.0750	24.1328	27.6881	0.0017
100	5.5409	23.9661	26.2147	0.0059	5.5450	23.9705	26.2556	0.0060

Table 6. Minimizing area point method (confidence level is 90%).

n	a	b	c	zz
46	2.0912	30.2984	69.2514	0.0089
47	2.0884	31.1074	70.4505	0.0085
48	2.0857	31.9191	71.6481	0.0081
49	2.0831	32.7310	72.8427	0.0078
50	2.0806	33.5453	74.0353	0.0074
60	2.0598	41.7726	85.8687	0.0050
70	2.0447	50.1308	97.5564	0.0036
80	2.0333	58.5941	109.1282	0.0027
90	1.0479	24.0945	27.5455	0.0016
100	5.5482	23.9796	26.3103	0.0061

4. Empirical Analysis

4.1. Description of Sample Data

This subsection analyzes the sample data from the historical stock quotes in Merchants Bank (600036) of the Sohu securities network. The holding period is a month and there are a total of 40 pieces of data regarding closing prices in the observation period from 23 January 2009 to 27 April 2012. Now we want to predict at a given confidence level the mean and range of risks to China Merchants Bank stock yields at the end of May 2012, that is to solve the joint confidence region of (μ, σ^2).

Here we use the logarithmic gain: $R_t = ln(P_t/P_{t-1})$, where P_t is the closing price of stock at time t. Thus, we can get 39 yields as below Table 7.

Table 7. Sample data year and month closing price yield.

Sample Data			Sample Data			Sample Data		
Y-M	price	yield	Y-M	price	yield	Y-M	price	yield
0901	13.51	-	1001	15.17	−0.173826	1101	12.63	−0.014151
0902	14.27	0.054729	1002	15.90	0.046999	1102	12.87	0.018824
0903	15.93	0.110045	1003	16.28	0.023618	1103	14.09	0.090566
0904	15.50	−0.027364	1004	14.27	−0.131778	1104	14.46	0.025921
0905	16.86	0.084104	1005	13.23	−0.075672	1105	13.91	−0.038778
0906	22.41	0.284563	1006	13.01	−0.016769	1106	13.02	−0.066121
0907	19.64	−0.131939	1007	14.52	0.109809	1107	12.35	−0.052831
0908	13.63	−0.365295	1008	13.54	−0.069879	1108	11.85	−0.041328
0909	14.78	0.081002	1009	12.95	−0.044552	1109	11.06	−0.068993
0910	17.77	0.184237	1010	14.57	0.117869	1110	12.10	0.089870
0911	17.29	−0.027383	1011	13.05	−0.110176	1111	11.21	−0.076399
0912	18.05	0.043017	1012	12.81	−0.018562	1112	11.87	0.057208
-	-	-	-	-	-	1201	12.65	0.063643
-	-	-	-	-	-	1202	12.87	0.017242
-	-	-	-	-	-	1203	11.90	−0.078361
-	-	-	-	-	-	1204	12.20	0.024898

By AVERAGE and VAR function in Excel we can get the MLE: $\bar{x}$ and S^2 of mean μ and variance σ^2 are, respectively, −0.002615 and 0.011898.

4.2. (μ, σ^2)-Model

Effect between Ideal Point Method and the Method of the Smallest

Now we respectively use ideal point method and area minimization method to solve the joint confidence region of at the given confidence level and make a contrast of the results from these two methods.

By checking the corresponding tables when $n = 39$ in this paper we have the following Tables 8 and 9:

Table 8. $n = 39$ (confidence level 99% and 95%).

	Confidence Level 99%				Confidence Level 95%			
Method	a	b	c	zz	a	b	c	zz
ideal point	3.6797	18.4736	63.0094	0.0390	3.2882	22.0311	55.8159	0.0239
Min-area	2.9024	19.6137	74.1233	0.0289	2.3212	23.1191	66.3364	0.0166

Table 9. $n = 39$ (confidence level is 90%).

Method	a	b	c	zz
ideal point	3.1106	24.0351	52.3654	0.0182
Min-area	2.0267	25.0498	62.6071	0.0121

Put these values into the following formula and get the joint confidence region of (μ, σ^2) as below

$$\{(\mu,\sigma^2) : \bar{x} - \frac{a\sigma}{\sqrt{n}} \leq \mu \leq \bar{x} + \frac{a\sigma}{\sqrt{n}}, (w_0\xi^*)^2\frac{nS^2}{c} \leq \sigma^2 \leq (w_0\xi^*)^2\frac{nS^2}{b}\}$$

whose figure is the area enclosed by two horizontal lines and a parabola line

(1) $\alpha = 1\%$ (confidence level is 99%) (Figures 3–5)

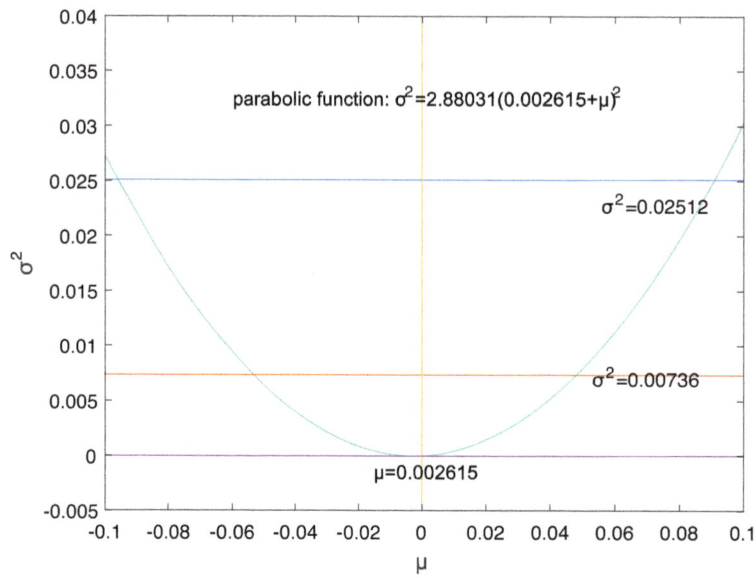

Figure 3. The joint confidence region of (μ, σ^2) by ideal point method.

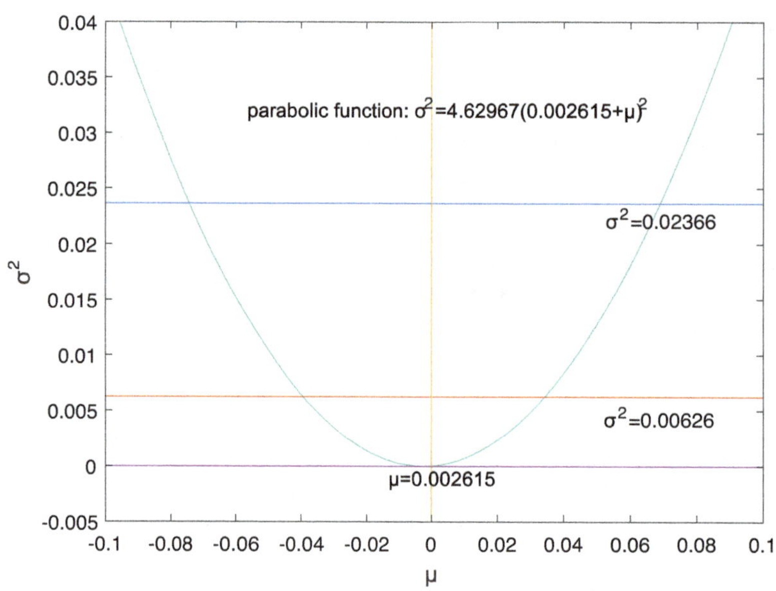

Figure 4. The joint confidence region of (μ, σ^2) by area minimization method.

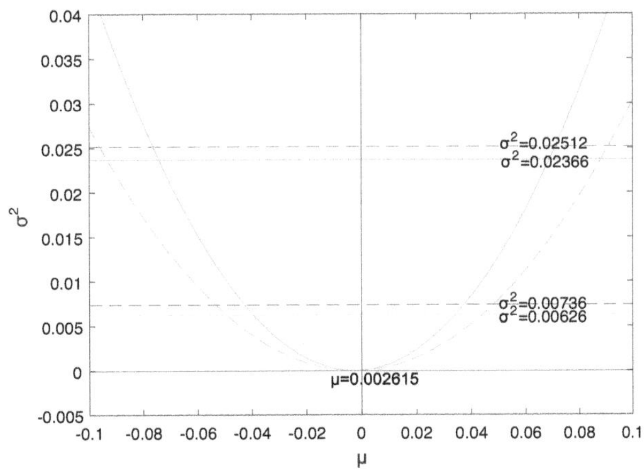

Figure 5. The contrast of two methods.

where the solid line is the result of area minimization method and the broken line is the result of ideal point method.

(2) $\alpha = 5\%$ (confidence level is 95%) (Figures 6–8)

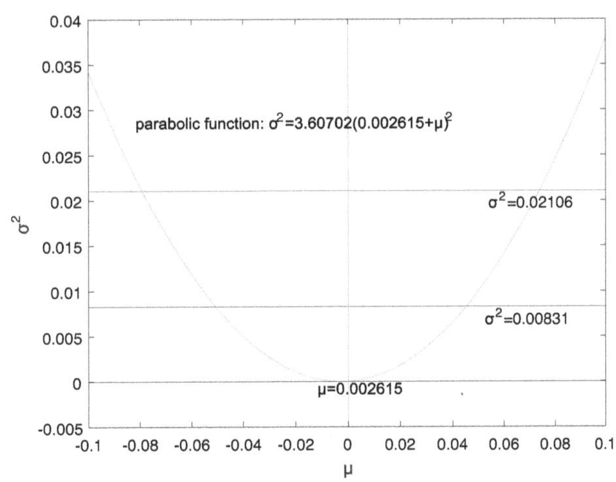

Figure 6. The joint confidence region of (μ, σ^2) by ideal point method.

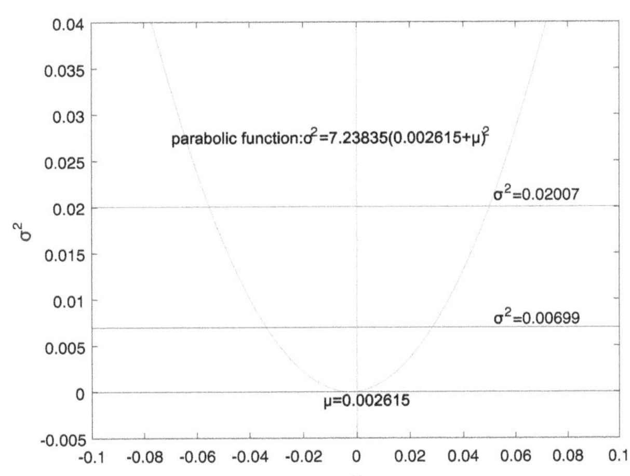

Figure 7. The joint confidence region of (μ, σ^2) by area minimization method.

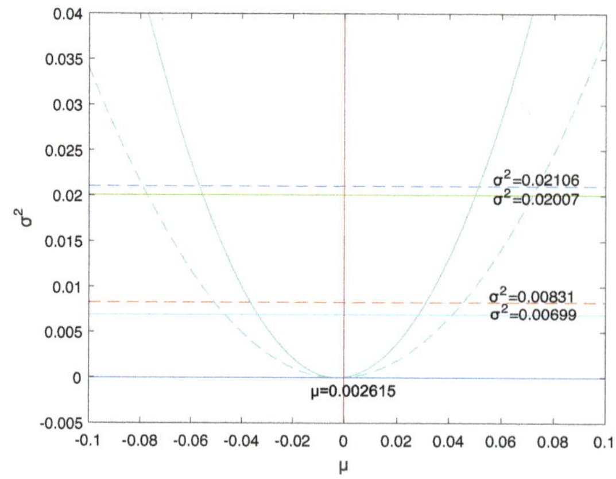

Figure 8. The contrast of two methods.

where the solid line is the result of area minimization method and the broken line is the result of ideal point method.

(3) $\alpha = 10\%$ (confidence level is 90%) (Figures 9–11)

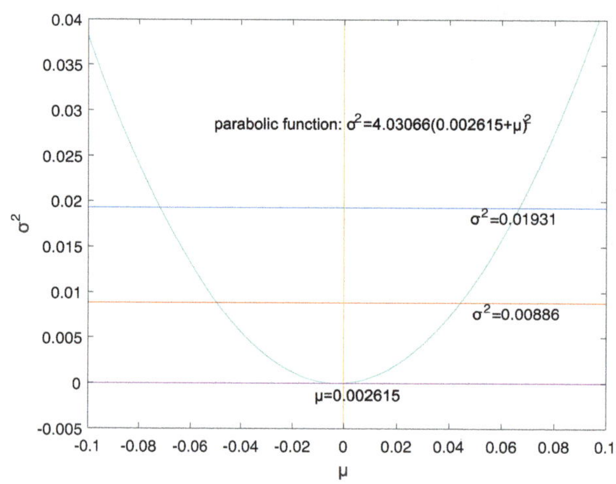

Figure 9. The joint confidence region of (μ, σ^2) by ideal point method.

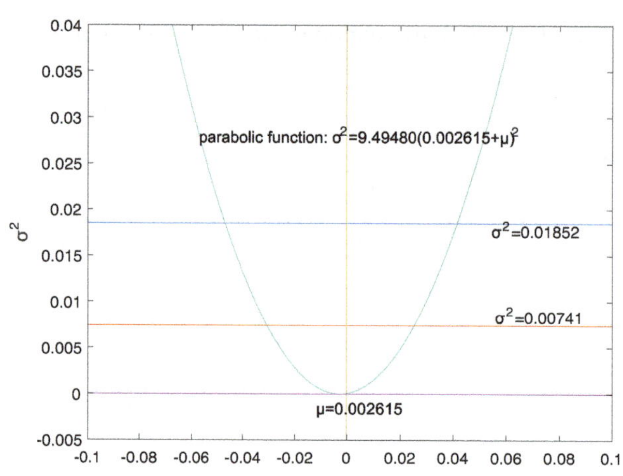

Figure 10. The joint confidence region of (μ, σ^2) by area minimization method.

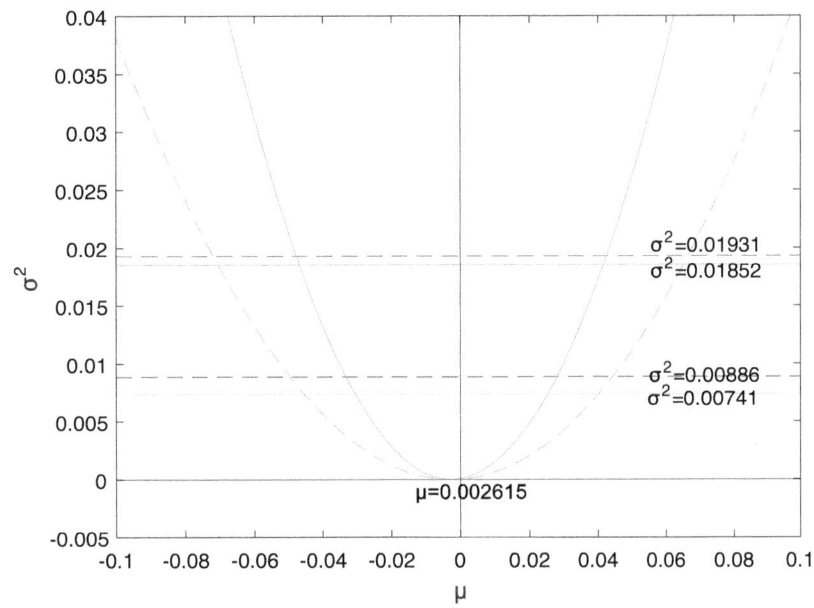

Figure 11. The contrast of two methods.

where the solid line is the result of area minimization method and the broken line is the result of ideal point method.

According to these results, we can know the area by area minimization method is smaller, so at a given confidence level area minimization method has a better effect to solve the joint confidence region of (μ, σ^2).

4.3. (μ, VaR^2)-Model

Suppose a customer buys shares of China Merchants Bank whose initial assets is $w_0 = 1$ and the confidence level of VaR is 95% that is $\xi^* = 1.645$. By Theorem 1 and the corresponding tables we have Table 10 as below.

Table 10. $n = 39$.

α	a	b	c	zz
1%	2.9024	19.6137	74.1233	0.0289
5%	2.3212	23.1191	66.3364	0.0166
10%	2.0267	25.0498	62.6071	0.0121

Put these values into the following formula and get the joint confidence region of (μ, VaR^2) below

$$\{(\mu, VaR^2) : \bar{x} - \frac{a\sigma}{\sqrt{n}} \leq \mu \leq \bar{x} + \frac{a\sigma}{\sqrt{n}}, (w_0\xi^*)^2\frac{nS^2}{c} \leq VaR^2 \leq (w_0\xi^*)^2\frac{nS^2}{b}\}$$

whose figure is the area enclosed by two horizontal lines and a parabola line.

(1) $\alpha = 1\%$ (confidence level is 99%) (Figure 12)

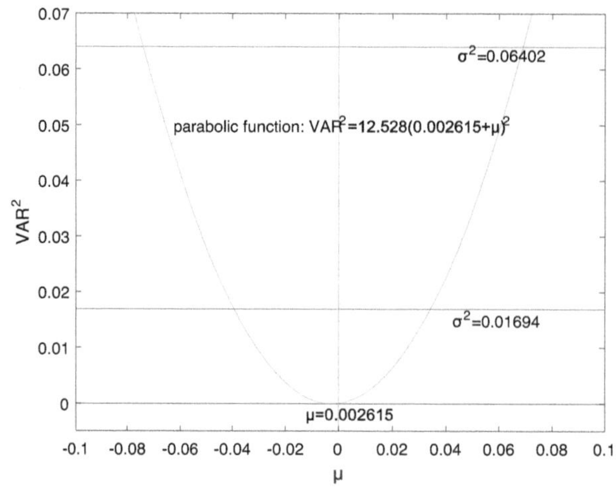

Figure 12. The joint confidence region of (μ, VaR^2) when $\alpha = 1\%$.

(2) $\alpha = 5\%$ (confidence level is 95%) (Figure 13)

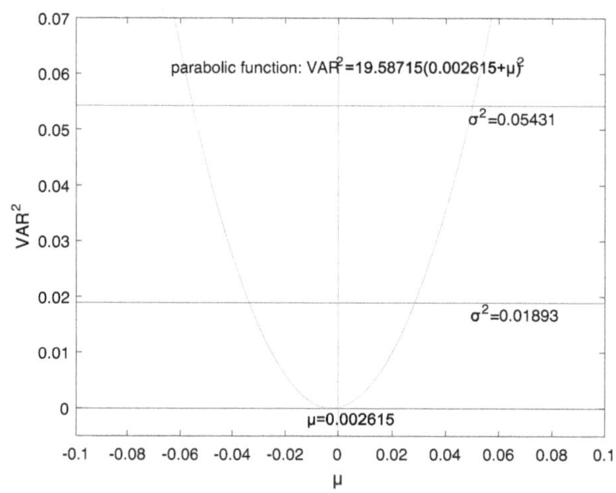

Figure 13. The joint confidence region of (μ, VaR^2) when $\alpha = 5\%$.

(3) $\alpha = 10\%$ (confidence level is 90%) (Figure 14)

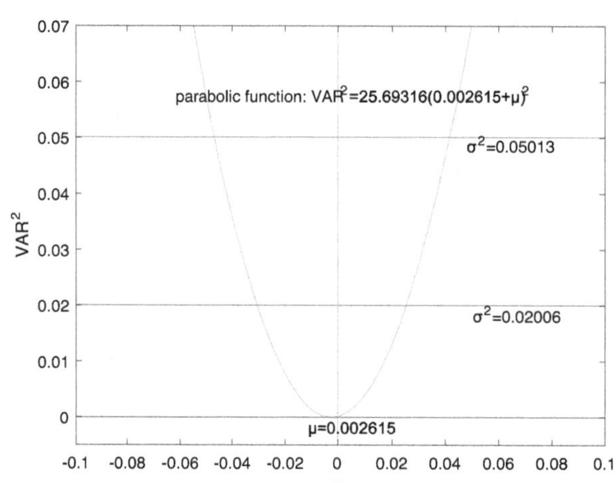

Figure 14. The joint confidence region of (μ, VaR^2) when $\alpha = 10\%$.

5. Conclusions

VaR is just a single indicator value to characterize risk, providing less information to the user, and the risk warning function is too thin. In practice, people often need to know both the benefits they may receive and the risks they are involved with. Therefore, this paper studies and constructs the double VaR according to the definition and research methods of VaR, expanding the one-dimensional single-risk monitoring indicator-VaR into a two-dimensional revenue-risk monitoring indicator.

This paper selects (μ, σ^2) and (μ, VaR^2) as the models of the double-VaR. It shows the risk/maximum loss of an asset at a given time in the future and the area in which the revenue is located. Such indicators can better weigh the risk–return of assets, and deduce the joint confidence region of (μ, σ^2) (or (μ, VaR^2)) by virtue of the two-dimensional likelihood ratio method. Then, the ideal joint method and the area minimization method are used to solve the specific joint confidence domain, and the solution effect of the two methods is compared. The obtained area minimization method is more accurate and better. After the VaR is double-expanded, users can know more information and better evaluate assets and avoid certain financial risks.

In this paper, only the normal distribution is considered in terms of its own knowledge structure and time. In fact, the author has great interest in risk management in the case of market with fat tails and the probability of extreme events, which will have important practical significance. We will discuss this in the next article on VaR.

Author Contributions: All authors contributed equally and significantly to this paper. All authors read and approved the final manuscript.

Funding: This research was supported by the National Natural Science Foundation of China (No. 11871275; No. 11371194) and by a Grant-in-Aid for Science Research from Nanjing University of Science and Technology (2018M640485).

Conflicts of Interest: The authors declare no conflict of interest.

References

Artzner, Philippe, Freddy Delbaen, Jean-Marc Eber, and David Heath. 1999. Coherent measures of risk. *Mathematical Finance* 9: 203–28. [CrossRef]

Basak, Suleyman, and Alexander Shapiro. 2001. Value-at-Risk based risk management: Optimal policies and asset prices. *Review of Financial Studies* 14: 371–405. [CrossRef]

Beder, Tanya Styblo. 1995. VAR: Seductive but dangerous. *Financial Analysis Journal* 51: 12–24. [CrossRef]

Berkowitz, Jeremy. 1999. A Coherent Framework for Stress-Testing. Available online: http://www.federalreserve.gov/pubs/FEDS/1999/199929 (accessed on 28 February 2019).

Berkowitz, Jeremy, and James O'Brien. 2002. How accurate are value-at-risk models at commercial banks. *The Journal of Finance* 57: 1093–111. [CrossRef]

Chen, Huijun, and Tiefeng Jiang. 2017. A Study of Two High-dimensional Likelihood Ratio Tests under Alternative Hypotheses. *Random Matrices: Theory and Applications* 11: 1–21.

Chen, Rongda, Cong Li, Weijin Wang, and Ze Wang. 2014. Empirical analysis on future-cash arbitrage risk with portfolio VaR. *Physica A: Statistical Mechanics and Its Applications* 38: 210–16. [CrossRef]

Cong, Chang, and Peibiao Zhao. 2018. Non-cash risk measure on nonconvex sets. *Mathematics* 6: 186. [CrossRef]

Cong, Chang, and Peibiao Zhao. 2019. Non-cash Risk Measures on weak nonconvex sets. Forthcoming.

Duffie, Darrell, and Jun Pan. 1997. An overview of value at risk. *Journal of Derivatives* 4: 7–49. [CrossRef]

Engle, Robert F., and Simone Manganelli. 1999. CAViaR: Conditional Autoregressive Value at Risk by Regression Quantiles. *Journal of Business and Economic Statistics* 22: 367–81. [CrossRef]

Hu, Ling. 2012. Dependence patterns across financial markets: A mixed copula approach. *Applied Financial Economics* 44: 2462–41. [CrossRef]

Jackson, Patricia, David Maude, and William Perraudin. 1997. Bank capital and value-at-risk. *Journal of Derivatives* 4: 73–90. [CrossRef]

Jorion, Philippe. 1996. Risk2: Measuring the risk in value at risk. *Financial Analysis Journal* 52: 47–56. [CrossRef]

Jorion, Philippe. 2007. *Value at Risk: The New Benchmark for Controlling Market Risk*, 1st ed. Columbus: McGraw-Hill.

Li, Zihe, Jinping Zhang, and Lanlan Feng. 2017. Analysis of Stock Risk Based on VaR and CVaR. *Finance* 7: 257–64.

Linsmeier, Thomas J., and Neil D. Pearson. 1996. Risk Measurement: An Introduction to Value at Risk. Available online: http://www.casact.net/education/specsem99frmgt/pearson2.pdf (accessed on 28 February 2019).

Mausser, Helmut, and Dan Rosen. 1999. Beyond VaR from measuring risk to managing risk. *ALGO Research Quarterly* 1: 5–10.

Pearson, Neil D. 2002. *Risk Budgeting: Portfolio Problem Solving with Value-at-Risk*, 1st ed. Hoboken: John Wiley and Sons.

Potters, Marc, and Jean-Philippe Bouchaud. 1999. Worst Fluctuation Method for Fast Value-at-Risk Estimates. Available online: http://arxiv.org/pdf/cond-mat/9909245.pdf (accessed on 28 February 2019).

Tang, Wanxiao, Fanchao Zhou, and Peibiao Zhao. 2018. Harnack inequality and no-arbitrage analysis. *Symmetry* 10: 517. [CrossRef]

Taylor, Nick, Dick Van Dijk, Philip Hans Franses, and Andre Lucas. 2000. SETS, arbitrage activity, and stock price dynamics. *Journal of Banking and Finance* 24: 1289–306. [CrossRef]

Wang, Tan. 1999. A Class of Dynamic Risk Measures. Available online: http://web.cenet.org.cn/upfile/57263.pdf (accessed on 28 February 2019).

Ze-To, Samuel Yau Man. 2013. Estimating value-at-risk under a Heath-Jarrow-Morton framework with jump. *Applied Economics* 38: 1102–248.

3

Changes of Relation in Multi-Population Mortality Dependence: An Application of Threshold VECM

Rui Zhou [1,*], **Guangyu Xing** [2] **and Min Ji** [3]

1 Department of Economics, University of Melbourne, Parkville, VIC 3010, Australia
2 Manulife-Sinochem, Shanghai 200121, China; stella_gy_xing@manulife-sinochem.com
3 Department of Mathematics, Towson University, Towson, MD 21252, USA; mji@towson.edu
* Correspondence: rui.zhou@unimelb.edu.au

Abstract: Standardized longevity risk transfers often involve modeling mortality rates of multiple populations. Some researchers have found that mortality indexes of selected countries are cointegrated, meaning that a linear relationship exists between the indexes. Vector error correction model (VECM) was used to incorporate this relation, thereby forcing the mortality rates of multiple populations to revert to a long-run equilibrium. However, the long-run equilibrium may change over time. It is crucial to incorporate these changes such that mortality dependence is adequately modeled. In this paper, we develop a framework to examine the presence of equilibrium changes and to incorporate these changes into the mortality model. In particular, we focus on equilibrium changes caused by threshold effect, the phenomenon that mortality indexes alternate between different VECMs depending on the value of a threshold variable. Our framework comprises two steps. In the first step, a statistical test is performed to examine the presence of threshold effect in the VECM for multiple mortality indexes. In the second step, threshold vector error correction model (TVECM) is fitted to the mortality indexes and model adequacy is evaluated. We illustrate this framework with the mortality data of England and Wales (EW) and Canadian populations. We further apply the TVECM to forecast future mortalities and price an illustrative longevity bond with multivariate Wang transform. Our numerical results show that TVECM predicted much faster mortality improvement for EW and Canada than single-regime VECM and thus the incorporation of threshold effect significant increases longevity bond price.

Keywords: multi-population mortality; vector error correction; longevity risk; longevity bond; Wang transform

---

1. Introduction

According to a recent report by World Health Organization (2015), global life expectancy raised dramatically from 64 years in 1990 to 71 years in 2013. The global aging trend is primarily attributed to greater consciousness of healthy lifestyles, development of new medicines, and improvement of health systems in many countries. Milidonis and Efthymiou (2017) identified causation from wealth to mortality improvement in Asia-Pacific countries and revealed that mortality improvements appear faster in more developed than less developed countries. Although increased life expectancy is desirable for individuals, this global trend poses significant financial burdens to social security systems, annuity providers, and pension plan sponsors. As a result, hedging of longevity risk has become an important issue which has attracted much discussion in recent years.

In general, longevity risk hedge can be categorized into customized hedge or standardized hedge. Examples of customized hedge include buy-in, buy-out, and customized longevity swap. Tailored to the hedger's longevity exposure, customized hedge is effective in transferring longevity risk. However, customized hedge is very illiquid and has long maturity. Alternatively, standardized hedge links the payoff of longevity securities to a broad longevity index. It is more transparent and liquid, but less effective due to the difference between the population associated with the hedger's longevity exposure and that underlying the longevity index. The first standardized longevity hedge, which took place in January 2008, is a q-forward contract written on mortality rates of 65-year-old males from England and Wales (EW) between J. P. Morgan and the U.K. pension fund buy-out company Lucida. More recently, Swiss Re launched the Kortis longevity bond to hedge the divergence in mortality improvement between EW and the United States.

Standardized longevity hedge often involves the mortality rates of multiple populations. For example, the Longevity Divergence Index of the Kortis bond depends on the mortality rates of male populations in both EW and the United States. Modeling the mortality dependence of the two populations is crucial for generating accurate forecasts of future Longevity Divergence Index values. The promotion of standardized longevity hedge in recent years has motivated research in multi-population mortality modeling. A comparative study of two-population mortality models can be found in Villegas et al. (2017).

Existing literature in multi-population mortality modeling is often built on the concept of coherence. Originally proposed by Li and Lee (2005), coherent mortality forecasting assumes that the relative mortality rates of any two related populations are mean-reverting; hence, coherent mortality forecasts do not diverge indefinitely over time. The model of Li and Lee (2005) has been adopted by several researchers, including Biffis et al. (2017), Li and Hardy (2011), and Milidonis et al. (2011). Other examples of coherent models include the two-population model proposed by Cairns et al. (2011), the gravity model by Dowd et al. (2011), and the application of vector error correction model (VECM) by Zhou et al. (2014).

Li et al. (2016) criticized that the hypothesis of coherence for being too strong and not always appropriate. A coherent multi-population mortality model may understate the range of possible mortality differentials between two populations. To address this problem, Li et al. (2016) proposed the concept of semicoherence, which is incorporated into mortality forecasts by using a three-regime threshold vector autoregression model. In the middle regime, where the mortality differential between populations does not exceed a specific tolerance corridor, the mortality trajectories of two related populations are allowed to diverge. In the lower and upper regimes, where the mortality differential exceeds the tolerance corridor, mean reversion comes into effect and brings the mortality differential back into the tolerance corridor.

Hunt and Blake (2015), after observing that the relative mortality rates appear to change over time, advocated against the imposing of coherence. They used the the cointegration technique to allow for covariation between mortality rates in the two populations. Cointegration and the resulted vector error correction model (VECM) was introduced by Engle and Granger (1987) to model the long-term tendency of cointegrated variables moving around common stochastic trends, i.e., the long-term equilibrium of cointegrated variables. VECM is essentially a special case of vector autoregressive (VAR) model. VECM has been used in mortality modeling by several other researchers including Kuo et al. (2003), Darkiewicz and Hoedemakers (2004), Lazar (2004), Gaille and Sherris (2011), Yang and Wang (2013), and Zhou et al. (2014).

The existence of cointegration relation has been confirmed among the mortalities of selected countries. The threshold behavior of the VAR model observed by Li et al. (2016) suggests that a fixed relation may be inappropriate for certain countries. However, no existing literature on mortality modeling has yet considered the possibility of changing cointegration relations over time. Changes in the cointegration relation may lead to significant adjustments in the mortality dependence. Therefore, it is essential to incorporate such changes in the multi-population mortality models. Although the threshold VAR used in Li et al. (2016) can accommodate changes in the VAR relation, it does not take cointegration or long-term equilibrium into account. In this paper, we improve on the threshold of Li et al. (2016) by considering threshold VECM (TVECM) proposed by Hansen and Seo (2002), which incorporates both threshold effect and cointegration relation.

In particular, we develop a framework to examine the presence of long-term relation changes and to incorporate these changes into the mortality model. We focus on the equilibrium changes caused by threshold effect, the phenomenon that mortality indexes alternate between different VECMs depending on the value of a threshold variable. We first perform a statistical test to examine the presence of threshold effect in the VECM for multiple mortality indexes. We then apply TVECM to model changes in the cointegration relation. The time series behavior is determined by whether the deviation from the long-term relation is above or below certain threshold values.

For illustrative purposes, we fitted the TVECM model to the mortality rates of EW and Canadian populations. Our statistical test suggests that the relation between EW and Canadian mortalities changes when the deviation from the long-term equilibrium exceeds or fall below certain threshold value; hence, the threshold effect exists. In addition, we used multivariate Wang transform to price an illustrative longevity bond and demonstrate that incorporating changes in the cointegration relation has a significant impact on longevity bond pricing.

The remainder of the paper is organized as follows: Section 2 introduces the dataset and the base mortality model. Section 3 detects and removes outliers in the mortality indexes. Section 4 performs cointegration analysis and estimates VECM. Section 5 introduces TVECM and its estimation. Section 6 applies TVECM in longevity bond pricing. Section 7 presents the conclusion.

2. The Base Mortality Model

2.1. The Lee–Carter Model

The Lee–Carter model, proposed in Lee and Carter (1992), is the most widely used mortality model. It has been recommended for use by the US Bureau of the Census as a benchmark model (Mitchell et al. 2013). The Lee–Carter model is expressed as:

$$\ln(m_{x,t}^{(i)}) = a_x^{(i)} + b_x^{(i)} k_t^{(i)},$$

where (i) represents the ith population; $m_{x,t}^{(i)}$ is the central mortality rate for a life aged x at time t from population (i); $a_x^{(i)}$ represents the stand-alone age-specific parameters describing the average level of mortality at age x; $k_t^{(i)}$ referred to as mortality index, is the time-varying parameter which signifies the general speed of mortality improvement and captures the main time trend for all ages; and $b_x^{(i)}$ is the age-specific parameter that interacts with $k_t^{(i)}$.

Let $D_{x,t}^{(i)}$ and $E_{x,t}^{(i)}$ be the number of deaths and number of exposures-to-risk at age x in year t for population (i). We assume that $D_{x,t}^{(i)}$ follows Poisson distribution with mean equal to $E_{x,t}^{(i)} m_{x,t}^{(i)}$. The loglikelihood for population (i) can be written as

$$LL^{(i)} = \sum_{x,t} D_{x,t}^{(i)} \ln E_{x,t}^{(i)} m_{x,t}^{(i)} - E_{x,t}^{(i)} m_{x,t}^{(i)} - \ln(D_{x,t}^{(i)}!).$$

We maximize the log-likelihood to obtain the parameter estimates of $a_x^{(i)}$, $b_x^{(i)}$, and $k_t^{(i)}$ for each population. To obtain a unique set of parameter estimates, we impose two identification constraints: $\sum b_x^{(i)} = 1$ and $\sum k_t^{(i)} = 0$. Details of the model estimation method can be found in Brouhns et al. (2002). The model estimation can be performed in R using the "fit" function in the "StMoMo" package.

2.2. Data and Estimated Parameters

We used the mortality data of EW and Canadian populations aged 50–89 from 1922 to 2011.[1] The mortality rates were acquired from Human Mortality Database (2017). We use Superscript (1) for EW and Superscript (2) for Canada in the mathematical expressions.

Parameter estimates of the Lee–Carter model of $a_x^{(i)}$ and $b_x^{(i)}$ are depicted in Figure 1. Figure 1a shows that both $a_x^{(1)}$ and $a_x^{(2)}$ increase steadily as the age rises, thus indicating that average mortality rates increase with age. $a_x^{(1)}$ is higher than $a_x^{(2)}$, thereby suggesting that EW population has overall higher mortality rate than Canadian population for the same age group. In Figure 1b, the decreasing trend of $b_x^{(i)}$ suggests that mortality rates at older ages are less sensitive to the changes in $k_t^{(i)}$.

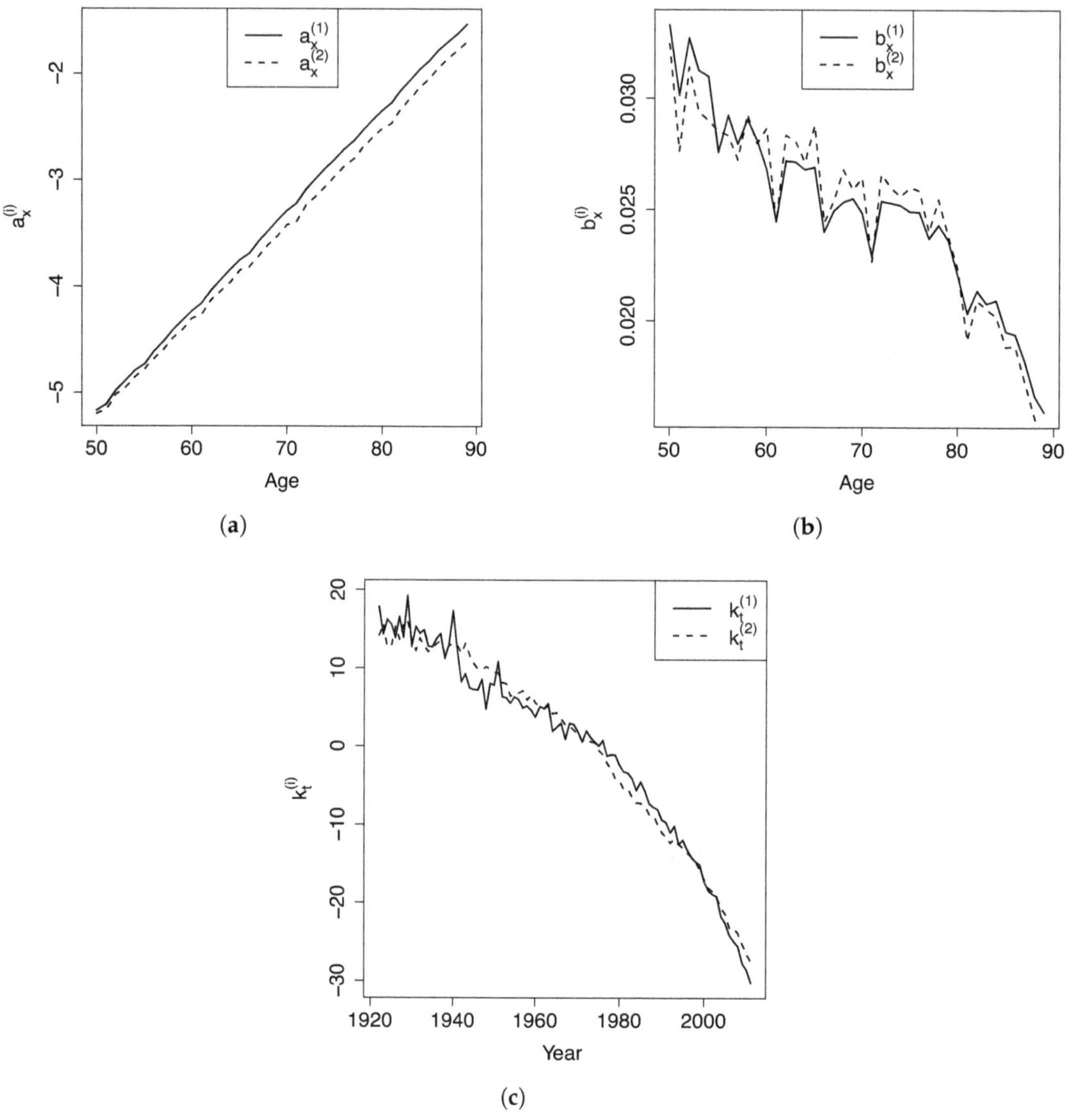

Figure 1. Parameter estimates of the Lee–Carter model using EW and Canadian mortality data. (**a**) Stand-alone age-specific parameters; (**b**) Age-specific parameters that interact with time-varying parameters; (**c**) Time-varying parameters.

[1] EW and Canadian mortality data were intentionally selected to illustrate the occurrence of changing long-term relation. We used a long sample period since our objective was to examine changes of long-term relation. The earliest year in which mortality data are available for both EW and Canadian populations is 1922. The sample age range of 50–89 was chosen due to our focus on longevity risk. Therefore, mortality rates of population close to or in retirement were considered.

Figure 1c plots the estimated time-varying parameters $k_t^{(1)}$ and $k_t^{(2)}$ from 1922 to 2011. Both $k_t^{(1)}$ and $k_t^{(2)}$ generally decline during this sample period, thus implying that mortality rates are decreasing in both regions. The trajectories of $k_t^{(1)}$ and $k_t^{(2)}$, which are very close, cross each other several times over the sample period. Therefore, it is necessary to investigate whether these trajectories share a common trend and to determine how they move around this trend.

3. Removing Additive Outliers

Figure 1c shows that the EW population had mortality rate spikes in 1931 due to the Great Depression, in 1941 due to World War II and, and in 1953 possibly due to the 1952 Great Smog of London. At the same time, members of the Canadian population were not or marginally affected by these one-time events. Outliers in the time series data may significantly affect model identification, estimation, and forecasting (Bovas and Box 1979; Chen and Tiao 1990). In our case, the outliers in $k_t^{(1)}$ may also distort the estimated relation between $k_t^{(1)}$ and $k_t^{(2)}$. Chen and Liu (1993) developed an iterative procedure to detect outliers in univariate time series data and obtain joint estimates of model parameters and outlier effects. In particular, four types of outliers were considered:

- Additive outlier, which causes an immediate and one-time effect on the observed series;
- Temporary change, which produces an initial effect that dies out gradually over time;
- Level shift, which produces an abrupt and permanent step change in the series; and
- Innovative outlier, which produces a temporary effect on stationary time series, but will gradually converge to a permanent effect on non-stationary time series.

For more details about this procedure, readers are advised to read Chen and Liu (1993).

Here, we considered removing only additive outliers, because other types of outliers have impact on mortality for multiple years and may still contain useful information about the relation between the two populations. We used the "tso" function in the "tsoutlier" R package to identify and remove additive outliers with the critical value of 3.5 as the criterion for the determination of outliers. The detected additive outliers are shown in Table 1. Additive outliers only present in $k_t^{(1)}$. The original and outlier-adjusted $k_t^{(1)}$ series are displayed in Figure 2. In the following analysis, $k_t^{(1)}$ represents outlier-adjusted $k_t^{(1)}$ data if not stated.

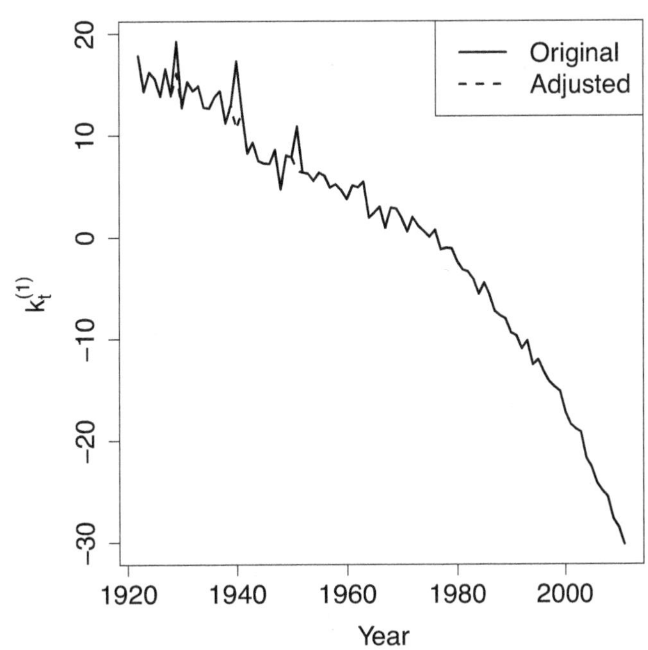

Figure 2. $k_t^{(1)}$ series with additive outliers removed.

Table 1. Detected additive outliers in the time-varying parameter series.

Population	Type	Year	*t*-Value
EW	Additive Outlier	1931	3.54
	Additive Outlier	1942	7.61
	Additive Outlier	1953	4.58
Canada	None		

4. Vector Error Correction Model

4.1. Cointegration

Cointegration is an economic concept that mimics the existence of a long-term equilibrium among an economic time series. A time series y_t is integrated ($I(1)$) if its first difference $\Delta y_t = y_t - y_{t-1}$ is stationary ($I(0)$). If two or more integrated time series have a stationary linear combination, then they are cointegrated. In particular, $k_t^{(1)}$ and $k_t^{(2)}$ are cointegrated if

- $k_t^{(1)}$ and $k_t^{(2)}$ are both $I(1)$ variables; and
- there exists a linear combination with a constant β and $\beta \neq 0$ such that

$$k_t^{(1)} + \beta k_t^{(2)} \sim I(0).$$

When $k_t^{(1)}$ and $k_t^{(2)}$ are cointegrated, they are driven by a common trend and the variations of the two variables are correlated.

4.2. VECM Model

VECM is a special case of vector autoregressive (VAR) model with cointegration relationship taken into consideration. A VAR model with lag order p can be written as

$$\begin{pmatrix} k_t^{(1)} \\ k_t^{(2)} \end{pmatrix} = c + \sum_{i=1}^{p} \Phi_i \begin{pmatrix} k_{t-i}^{(1)} \\ k_{t-i}^{(2)} \end{pmatrix} + \begin{pmatrix} \varepsilon_t^{(1)} \\ \varepsilon_t^{(2)} \end{pmatrix},$$

where c is a 2×1 constant vector, Φ_i is a 2×2 loading matrix for lag i, and $\begin{pmatrix} \varepsilon_t^{(1)} \\ \varepsilon_t^{(2)} \end{pmatrix}$ follows bivariate normal distribution.

A p-order VAR can be written as a $(p-1)$-order VECM, as shown below:

$$\begin{pmatrix} \Delta k_t^{(1)} \\ \Delta k_t^{(2)} \end{pmatrix} = c + \Pi \begin{pmatrix} k_{t-1}^{(1)} \\ k_{t-1}^{(2)} \end{pmatrix} + \sum_{i=1}^{p-1} \Gamma_i \begin{pmatrix} \Delta k_{t-i}^{(1)} \\ \Delta k_{t-i}^{(2)} \end{pmatrix} + \begin{pmatrix} \varepsilon_t^{(1)} \\ \varepsilon_t^{(2)} \end{pmatrix},$$

where Π is a 2×2 long-term loading matrix and Γ_i is a 2×2 short-term loading matrix for lag i.

The rank of Π indicates whether $k_t^{(1)}$ and $k_t^{(2)}$ have a cointegration relationship. If the rank of Π is 0, then there is no long-term equilibrium and the differenced $k_t^{(i)}$ series are stationary. If the rank of Π is full, then the original time series $k_t^{(i)}$ must be stationary. Otherwise, $k_t^{(1)}$ and $k_t^{(2)}$ are cointegrated. Since we only have two time series in our study, the full rank is 2. Cointegration relationship exists only when the rank of Π is equal to 1. In the case that cointegration exists, VECM can be rewritten as follows:

$$\begin{pmatrix} \Delta k_t^{(1)} \\ \Delta k_t^{(2)} \end{pmatrix} = c + \alpha \left(k_{t-1}^{(1)} + \beta k_{t-1}^{(2)} \right) + \sum_{i=1}^{p-1} \Gamma_i \begin{pmatrix} \Delta k_{t-i}^{(1)} \\ \Delta k_{t-i}^{(2)} \end{pmatrix} + \begin{pmatrix} \varepsilon_t^{(1)} \\ \varepsilon_t^{(2)} \end{pmatrix},$$

where α is the 2×1 adjustment coefficient vector and β is the cointegrating value. VECM incorporates both the long-term equilibrium relationship and the short-term relationship. In the long run, the two time series are expected to follow the relationship $k_t^{(1)} + \beta k_t^{(2)} = 0$. If there is deviation from this equilibrium, the error correction term $\alpha(k_t^{(1)} + \beta k_t^{(2)})$ pulls the time series towards the equilibrium. In the short-term, the two time series are affected by their autoregressive terms. We can also allow constant and time trend in the cointegration term. However, we find that these terms are not necessary for our dataset during the process of model building described in the following section.

4.3. Model Building

We used the following procedures to build and estimate VECM:

1. Test if $k_t^{(1)}$ and $k_t^{(2)}$ follow $I(1)$ process.
2. Determine the lag order of VECM.
3. Perform cointegration tests to examine if a cointegration relationship exists.
4. Estimate the VECM with selected lag order.
5. Check residual diagnostics.

We used the Augmented Dickey–Fuller (ADF) test to check whether the two time series are $I(1)$ processes. The null hypothesis of ADF test is that unit roots exist. The existence of unit roots indicates that the tested time series is non-stationary. We expect that the null hypothesis is accepted for the original $I(1)$ process and rejected for the first-order difference of the $I(1)$ process. In other words, we expect $k_t^{(1)}$ and $k_t^{(2)}$ to be non-stationary processes but their first-order differences to be stationary.

Table 2 summarizes the ADF test results for $k_t^{(1)}$, $k_t^{(2)}$, $\Delta k_t^{(1)}$, and $\Delta k_t^{(2)}$. The tests include a drift and use Akaike Information Criteria to select lag order in the test regression. The test statistics for both $k_t^{(1)}$ and $k_t^{(2)}$ have p-value greater than 10%, indicating that we cannot reject the null hypothesis that $k_t^{(1)}$ and $k_t^{(2)}$ are non-stationary at 10% significance level. The test statistics for $\Delta k_t^{(1)}$ and $\Delta k_t^{(2)}$ are both smaller than 1%, suggesting that we reject the null hypothesis at 1% significance level. Therefore, both $\Delta k_t^{(1)}$ and $\Delta k_t^{(2)}$ are stationary. According to the definition of $I(1)$ process, we can conclude that both $k_t^{(1)}$ and $k_t^{(2)}$ are $I(1)$ processes.

Table 2. Augmented Dickey–Fuller test results.

Data	Test Statistic	*p*-Value
$k_t^{(1)}$	3.81	>10%
$k_t^{(2)}$	3.44	>10%
$\Delta k_t^{(1)}$	−8.83	<1%
$\Delta k_t^{(2)}$	−8.15	<1%

To select the lag order for VECM, we first determine the lag order for VAR, and then deduct the order by one for VECM. In the lag order selection for VAR, we consider two criteria: Akaike Information Criteria (AIC), and Bayes Information Criteria (BIC). Since the VAR models are estimated by Ordinary Least Square (OLS) method, AIC and BIC are calculated using the following equations:

$$\begin{aligned} \text{AIC} &= \ln\left|\frac{1}{T}\sum_{t=1}^{T}\varepsilon_t\varepsilon_t'\right| + \frac{2}{T}pK^2, \\ \text{BIC} &= \ln\left|\frac{1}{T}\sum_{t=1}^{T}\varepsilon_t\varepsilon_t'\right| + \frac{\ln(T)}{T}pK^2 \end{aligned}$$

where $\varepsilon_t = [\varepsilon_t^{(1)}, \varepsilon_t^{(2)}]'$, $|X|$ denotes the determinant of a matrix X, T is the sample size, p is the lag order, and K is the dimension of the time series data. The lower the criteria values, the better the goodness of fit.

Table 3 shows that lag order 4 has the lowest AIC, while lag order 2 has the lowest BIC. The two criteria lead to different conclusions since they penalize extra parameters to different extents. It is often believed that AIC selects the model that most adequately describes the data and BIC tries to find the true model among the set of candidates. As a result, the model selected by AIC tends to overfit while the one selected by BIC may underfit. We fit both VECM(1) and VECM(3) one lag less than the corresponding VAR model, and check residual diagnostics to select an adequate model.

Table 3. Lag order selection for VAR model.

Criteria	Lag Order				
	1	**2**	**3**	**4**	**5**
AIC	−0.04	−0.53	−0.57	−0.58	−0.52
BIC	0.13	−0.24	−0.17	−0.07	0.11

Next, we test whether $k_t^{(1)}$ and $k_t^{(2)}$ are cointegrated using the Engle–Granger test. We first perform a linear regression of $k_t^{(1)}$ on $k_t^{(2)}$, and then conduct ADF test on the regression residuals. The estimated linear regression model is shown below:

$$k_t^{(1)} = \underset{(0.1959)}{-0.1574} + \underset{(0.0159)}{0.9863} k_t^{(2)},$$

where the numbers in parentheses are the standard deviations of the estimated parameters. The ADF test on the regression residuals returns a p-value smaller than 5%, indicating that we reject the null hypothesis of the existence of unit roots at 5% significance level. Therefore, the regression residuals are stationary and $k_t^{(1)}$ and $k_t^{(2)}$ are cointegrated. Since the constant term in the regression model is insignificant, we choose not to include a constant in the cointegration term.

Finally, VECM is estimated by the Engle–Granger two-step ordinary least squares (OLS). The estimation can be conducted in R using the "VECM" function in the "tsDyn" package. The first OLS determines the cointegrating value β by a linear regression of $k_t^{(1)}$ on $k_t^{(2)}$, which has been carried out in the cointegration test. Conditioning on the estimated β, the second OLS is performed to obtain other parameters in VECM. VECM can also be estimated by a one-step maximum likelihood estimation (MLE) method. However, in our case, the MLE estimates are very unstable when we use different number of lag orders.

Since AIC and BIC suggest different lag orders, we fit both VECM(1) and VECM(3) and examine the adequacy of the estimated models. Table 4 presents the results of Ljung–Box autocorrelation test for VECM(1) and VECM(3). The p-values for both VECM(1) and VECM(3) are all significantly greater than 5%, thereby indicating autocorrelation has been properly captured by the two models. Table 5 presents the results of univariate and bivariate Doornick–Hansen (DH) normality test for the residuals from VECM(1) and VECM(3). Residuals from VECM(1) fails the bivariate normality test and also the univariate normality test for $k_t^{(2)}$ at 5% significance level. In contrast, residuals from VECM(3) pass all the normality test at 5% significance level. Overall, the residual diagnostics suggest that VECM(3) is more adequate than VECM(1) for our data. Therefore, we use VECM(3) in the following analysis.

Table 4. p-values of Ljung–Box autocorrelation test for VECM.

Model	Lag Order				
	2	4	6	8	10
VECM(1)	0.95	0.21	0.15	0.16	0.12
VECM(3)	0.97	0.30	0.26	0.16	0.20

Table 5. p-values of Doornick–Hansen normality test.

Model	Bivariate	Univariate	
		(1)	(2)
VECM(1)	0.03	0.62	0.01
VECM(3)	0.28	0.68	0.12

The estimated VECM(3) is shown below:

$$\begin{aligned}\begin{pmatrix} \Delta k_t^{(1)} \\ \Delta k_t^{(2)} \end{pmatrix} &= \begin{pmatrix} -0.7820 \\ -0.4041 \end{pmatrix} + \begin{pmatrix} -0.0781 \\ 0.0711 \end{pmatrix} \left(k_{t-1}^{(1)} - 0.9862 k_{t-1}^{(2)} \right) \\ &+ \begin{pmatrix} -0.6308 & 0.2571 \\ 0.0617 & -0.1474 \end{pmatrix} \begin{pmatrix} \Delta k_{t-1}^{(1)} \\ \Delta k_{t-1}^{(2)} \end{pmatrix} \\ &+ \begin{pmatrix} -0.0952 & 0.0230 \\ 0.1046 & -0.0873 \end{pmatrix} \begin{pmatrix} \Delta k_{t-2}^{(1)} \\ \Delta k_{t-2}^{(2)} \end{pmatrix} \\ &+ \begin{pmatrix} -0.0136 & 0.0425 \\ -0.0468 & 0.2245 \end{pmatrix} \begin{pmatrix} \Delta k_{t-3}^{(1)} \\ \Delta k_{t-3}^{(2)} \end{pmatrix} + \begin{pmatrix} \varepsilon_t^{(1)} \\ \varepsilon_t^{(2)} \end{pmatrix}.\end{aligned}$$

The estimated long-term equilibrium is $k_{t-1}^{(1)} - 0.9862k_{t-1}^{(2)} = 0$. The cointegrating value is close to -1, thereby indicating that $k_t^{(1)}$ and $k_t^{(2)}$ are close. However, because of the downward trend in the mortality indexes, the gap between $k_t^{(1)}$ and $k_t^{(2)}$ enlarges over time and $k_t^{(1)}$ and $k_t^{(2)}$ diverge slowly and indefinitely.

When $k_{t-1}^{(1)}$ is larger than $0.9862k_{t-1}^{(2)}$ in year $t-1$, the deviation from the equilibrium is positive. This deviation is multiplied by -0.0781 for $\Delta k_t^{(1)}$ and 0.0711 for $\Delta k_t^{(2)}$, resulting in a reduction of $\Delta k_t^{(1)}$ and increase of $\Delta k_t^{(2)}$ in year t. Therefore, the expected difference between $k_t^{(1)}$ and $0.9862k_t^{(2)}$ in year t narrows. This is how the error correction term forces the two time series to revert to the long-term equilibrium.

5. Threshold Vector Error Correction Model

5.1. TVECM Model

Li et al. (2016) found threshold behavior when modeling multi-population mortality by VAR model, i.e., the time series data follow different VAR models depending on the value of a threshold variable. Since VECM is a special case of VAR model, we are interested in whether threshold effect also presents in VECM and how to incorporate the threshold effect by the threshold VECM (TVEM) model. The difference between TVECM and threshold VAR (TVAR) is that TVECM takes into account cointegration and hence an explicit long-term relation. Although the TVAR model used in Li et al. (2016) implies a mean-reverting mechanism, there is no explicit long-term relation.

Consider a two-regime TVECM in which the threshold variable is the deviation from the long-term equilibrium. Depending on whether the threshold variable exceeds the threshold value, VECM parameters may take different values. This TVECM can be expressed as:

$$\begin{pmatrix} \Delta k_t^{(1)} \\ \Delta k_t^{(2)} \end{pmatrix} = \begin{cases} c_1 + \alpha_1 \left(k_{t-1}^{(1)} + \beta k_{t-1}^{(2)} \right) + \Sigma_{i=1}^{p-1} \Gamma_{1,i} \begin{pmatrix} \Delta k_{t-i}^{(1)} \\ \Delta k_{t-i}^{(2)} \end{pmatrix} + \begin{pmatrix} \varepsilon_t^{(1)} \\ \varepsilon_t^{(2)} \end{pmatrix}, & z_{t-1} > \gamma \\ c_2 + \alpha_2 \left(k_{t-1}^{(1)} + \beta k_{t-1}^{(2)} \right) + \Sigma_{i=1}^{p-1} \Gamma_{2,i} \begin{pmatrix} \Delta k_{t-i}^{(1)} \\ \Delta k_{t-i}^{(2)} \end{pmatrix} + \begin{pmatrix} \varepsilon_t^{(1)} \\ \varepsilon_t^{(2)} \end{pmatrix}, & z_{t-1} \leq \gamma \end{cases}$$

where c_n is the constant vector for regime n; α_n is adjustment coefficient vector for regime n; β is cointegrating value; $\Gamma_{n,i}$ is the AR coefficient for regime n and lag i; $z_{t-1} = k_{t-1}^{(1)} + \beta k_{t-1}^{(2)}$ measures the deviation from the long-term equilibrium; and γ is the threshold value.

Which regime the time series lies in at time t depends on the value of z_{t-1}. If z_{t-1} is higher than the threshold value γ, then the time series switches to the first regime at time t. If z_{t-1} is lower than γ, then it switches to the second regime at time t. When there are more than two regimes, this expression can be easily extended. It is often assumed that there are one or two threshold values for model parsimony corresponding to two or three regimes, respectively.

5.2. Threshold Effect and Model Estimation

We fit the estimated $\{k_t^{(1)}, k_t^{(2)}\}$ by a two-regime TVECM. We do not consider TVECM with higher regimes due to the consideration of model parsimony. The estimation of TVECM model is achieved by minimizing the residual sum of squares using a two-dimensional grid search on β and γ. The estimation can be performed in R using the "TVECM" function in the "tsDyn" package. The estimated model is shown below:

$$\begin{aligned} \begin{pmatrix} \Delta k_t^{(1)} \\ \Delta k_t^{(2)} \end{pmatrix} &= \begin{pmatrix} -1.3482 \\ -0.8089 \end{pmatrix} + \begin{pmatrix} -0.3737 \\ 0.2631 \end{pmatrix} z_{t-1} \\ &+ \begin{pmatrix} -0.4041 & -0.4338 \\ 0.0890 & -0.2212 \end{pmatrix} \begin{pmatrix} \Delta k_{t-1}^{(1)} \\ \Delta k_{t-1}^{(2)} \end{pmatrix} \\ &+ \begin{pmatrix} -0.3235 & -0.3778 \\ -0.0629 & -0.1135 \end{pmatrix} \begin{pmatrix} \Delta k_{t-2}^{(1)} \\ \Delta k_{t-2}^{(2)} \end{pmatrix} \\ &+ \begin{pmatrix} -0.3580 & -0.4661 \\ -0.2245 & 0.3769 \end{pmatrix} \begin{pmatrix} \Delta k_{t-3}^{(1)} \\ \Delta k_{t-3}^{(2)} \end{pmatrix} + \begin{pmatrix} \varepsilon_t^{(1)} \\ \varepsilon_t^{(2)} \end{pmatrix}, \qquad z_{t-1} > -0.0754 \end{aligned}$$

$$\begin{aligned} \begin{pmatrix} \Delta k_t^{(1)} \\ \Delta k_t^{(2)} \end{pmatrix} &= \begin{pmatrix} 0.0354 \\ -0.2738 \end{pmatrix} + \begin{pmatrix} 0.0244 \\ 0.0518 \end{pmatrix} z_{t-1} \\ &+ \begin{pmatrix} -0.5945 & 0.4531 \\ 0.0768 & -0.1493 \end{pmatrix} \begin{pmatrix} \Delta k_{t-1}^{(1)} \\ \Delta k_{t-1}^{(2)} \end{pmatrix} \\ &+ \begin{pmatrix} -0.0602 & 0.5960 \\ 0.2504 & -0.0170 \end{pmatrix} \begin{pmatrix} \Delta k_{t-2}^{(1)} \\ \Delta k_{t-2}^{(2)} \end{pmatrix} \\ &+ \begin{pmatrix} 0.1456 & 0.3559 \\ 0.1018 & 0.0535 \end{pmatrix} \begin{pmatrix} \Delta k_{t-3}^{(1)} \\ \Delta k_{t-3}^{(2)} \end{pmatrix} + \begin{pmatrix} \varepsilon_t^{(1)} \\ \varepsilon_t^{(2)} \end{pmatrix}, \qquad z_{t-1} \leq -0.0754 \end{aligned}$$

where $z_t = k_t^{(1)} - 0.9667 k_t^{(2)}$, and the estimated variance-covariance matrix for the error term is $\begin{pmatrix} 1.0042 & 0.2562 \\ 0.2562 & 0.4512 \end{pmatrix}$.

Before we apply the estimated TVECM, it is important to verify whether the threshold effect is significant in the dataset. We follow Hansen and Seo (2002) and test the presence of threshold effect in $\{k_t^{(1)}, k_t^{(2)}\}$ based on the Lagrange multiplier principle. Asymptotic critical values and p-values of this test are calculated using fixed regressor bootstraps. Under the null hypothesis, there is no threshold effect, so the model reduces to a conventional VECM. Under the alternative hypothesis, the time series data follow a two-regime TVECM. This test can be implemented in R using the "TVECM.SeoTest" function in the "tsDyn" package. Given the cointegrating value of 0.9667, the p-value of the threshold effect test is 0.0272, thereby rejecting the null hypothesis of no threshold effect at 5% significance level.

Since VECM and TVECM are nested models, we also perform a likelihood ratio test to compare their goodness of fit. The test statistics is 2 $\times$ (loglikelihood of TVECM $-$ loglikelihood of VECM), equal to $2(-37.7441 + 59.7507)$. The degree of freedom is (number of parameters in TVECM $-$ number of parameters in VECM), equal to $(34 - 17)$. The p-value of the likelihood ratio test is 0.0003, thereby suggesting that TVECM provides significant improvement over VECM.

As we can see from the estimated model, the threshold value is estimated to be -0.0754 and the long-term equilibrium is $k_t^{(1)} - 0.9667 k_t^{(2)} = 0$. When the deviation is higher than -0.0754, the corresponding adjustment coefficient vector is $\begin{pmatrix} -0.3737 \\ 0.2631 \end{pmatrix}$. If the deviation is below -0.7654, then the corresponding adjustment coefficient vector is $\begin{pmatrix} 0.0244 \\ 0.0518 \end{pmatrix}$.

To understand how error correction works in the TVECM, we consider three cases:

- Case 1: $z_{t-1} > 0$. The time series data are in the upper regime. $k_{t-1}^{(1)}$ is higher than it should be in the long-term equilibrium. Multiplying the deviation by the negative coefficient -0.3737 for EW pulls down $k_t^{(1)}$. At the same time, multiplying the deviation by the positive coefficient 0.2631 for Canada pulls up $k_t^{(2)}$. This adjustment brings $k_t^{(1)}$ and $k_t^{(2)}$ closer to their long-term equilibrium.
- Case 2: $-0.0754 < z_{t-1} \leq 0$. The time series data are still in the upper regime, but $k_{t-1}^{(1)}$ is lower than it should be in the long-term equilibrium. The deviation is multiplied by -0.3737 for EW and 0.2631 for Canada, thereby pulling $k_t^{(1)}$ up and $k_t^{(2)}$ down. The error correction term narrows the deviation again and brings the time series towards their long-term equilibrium.
- Case 3: $z_{t-1} \leq -0.0754$. The process is in the second regime and $k_{t-1}^{(1)}$ is lower than it should be in the long-term equilibrium. The negative deviation is multiplied by 0.0244 for EW and 0.0518 for Canada, thereby pulling both $k_t^{(1)}$ and $k_t^{(2)}$ down. However, $k_t^{(1)}$ is pulled down to a smaller extent which results in a smaller deviation from the long-term equilibrium.

Figure 3 presents the historical process of the deviation z_t in a solid line and the threshold value in a dashed line. During the periods of 1922 to 1940 and 1970 to 1995, the deviation is mostly greater than the threshold value. This indicates that the process is in the upper regime. During 1940–1970 and 1995–2011, the deviation is mostly smaller than the threshold value and hence the process is in the lower regime.

Based on the estimated TVECM model, the reversion to the long-term equilibrium is much faster in the upper regime than it is in the lower regime. Therefore, when experiencing higher mortality than that suggested by the long-term equilibrium, EW population improves their mortality at a faster rate, compared to the Canadian population. Causality analysis employed in Milidonis and Efthymiou (2017) may be used to study the causes of the difference between mortality improvement in the two populations.

Finally, we examine the autocorrelation and normality of the residuals obtained from TVECM. Table 6 shows the result of the Ljung–Box autocorrelation test. The p-values for all the lag orders examined are greater than 5%, thereby indicating no significant autocorrelation in the residuals. We again perform the univariate and multivariate Doornick–Hansen normality test for the residuals. Test results are shown in Table 7. Both multivariate test and univariate test for the residuals pass the normality test at 5% significance level.

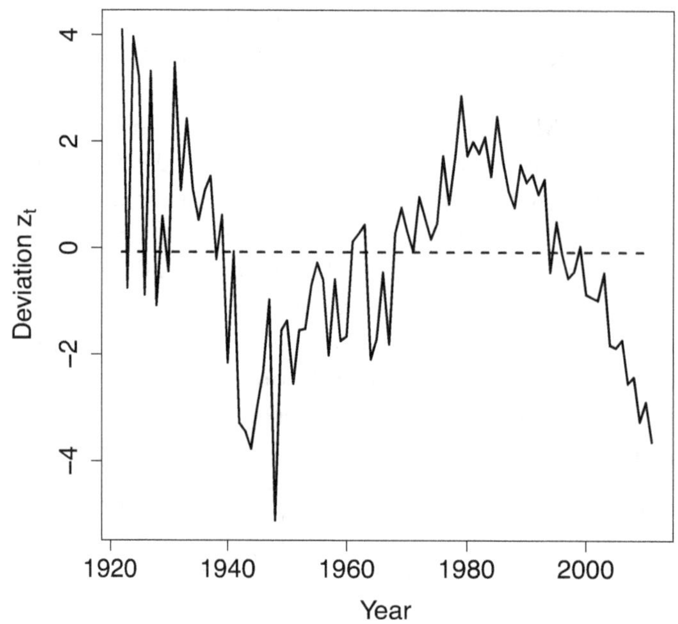

Figure 3. Historical process of deviation z_t.

Table 6. p-values of Ljung–Box autocorrelation test for TVECM.

Model	Lag Order				
	2	4	6	8	10
TVECM	0.98	0.76	0.45	0.33	0.25

Table 7. p-values of Doornick–Hansen normality test for TVECM.

Model	Multivariate	Univariate	
		(1)	(2)
TVECM	0.75	0.59	0.66

5.3. *Comparing Mortality Forecasts of VECM and TVECM*

We simulate the paths of $k_t^{(1)}$ and $k_t^{(2)}$ from year 2012 to 2031 based on the estimated VECM and TVECM model, and determine the 95% prediction intervals. The simulation procedures are shown as follows:

1. Let $t = 2012$. Generate 5000 bivariate normal random vectors as the simulated error terms $\{\varepsilon_t^{(1)}, \varepsilon_t^{(2)}\}$.
2. Calculate the values of $k_t^{(1)}$ and $k_t^{(2)}$ based on the simulated errors for $t = 2012$.
3. Repeat Steps (1) and (2) for $t = 2013, 2014, \ldots, 2031$.

Figure 4a compares the forecasts of $k_t^{(1)}$ obtained from VECM and TVECM. The mean forecasts of $k_t^{(1)}$ using the two models are close from 2012 to 2018, but gradually diverge afterwards. The forecasts from TVECM become lower than those from VECM as the forecast period increases. The prediction interval of TVECM is also smaller than that of VECM, because TVECM explains more variation in the data and hence yields residuals with smaller variance. Figure 4b compares the forecasts of $k_t^{(2)}$ using VECM and TVECM. We again observe that the forecasts of $k_t^{(2)}$ from TVECM are much lower than those from VECM. The prediction interval of TVECM is slightly smaller than that of VECM. Overall, we find that TVECM predicts much faster mortality improvement than VECM for both populations. The mortality improvement pattern predicted by TVECM appears to be more in line with which has been observed in recent years.

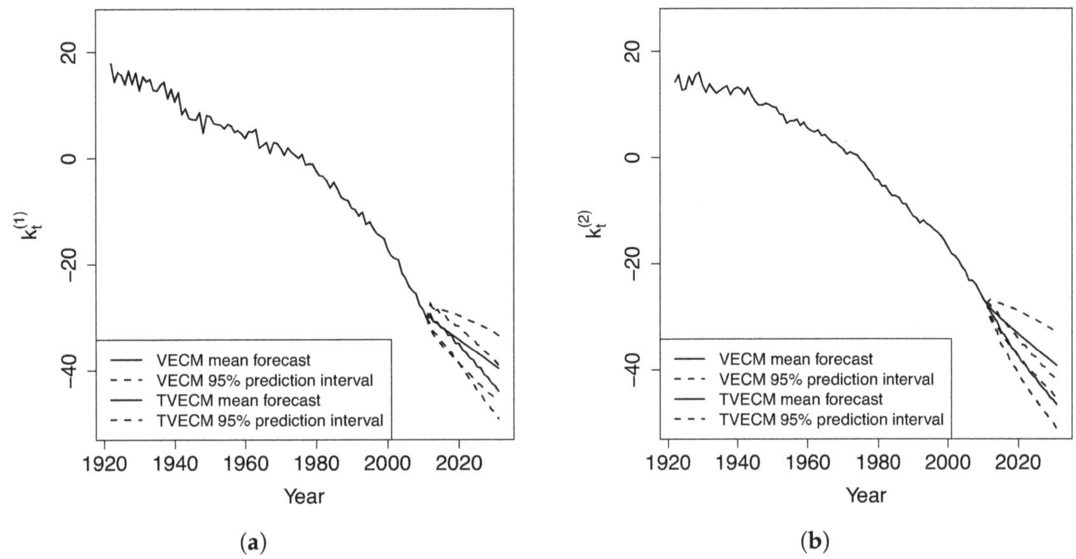

Figure 4. Forecasts of $k_t^{(i)}$ using VECM and TVECM. (**a**) $k_t^{(1)}$; (**b**) $k_t^{(2)}$.

6. Pricing Longevity Bond

6.1. An Illustrative Longevity Bond

In this section, we price an illustrative longevity bond that hedges unexpected mortality improvement associated with EW and Canadian populations. Assume that this bond is issued at the end of 2011 and matures at the end of 2019. The bond issuer has annuity policies in both EW and Canada and annuitants are between age 75 and 85 at the beginning of 2012.

The longevity bond is traded at its face value. It pays quarterly coupon at three-month London Interbank Offered Rate (LIBOR) plus a spread. When the bond matures, the principal will be returned but may be subject to erosion. The principal repayment is associated with the mortality improvement of EW and Canada populations.

Let $\text{Improvement}_x^{(i)}$ be the annual mortality improvement for an individual aged x from population (i). It is defined as

$$\text{Improvement}_x^{(i)} = 1 - \left(\frac{m_{x,2019}^{(i)}}{m_{x,2011}^{(i)}} \right)^{1/8}.$$

The mortality improvement index for population (i) is then defined as

$$MI^{(i)} = \frac{1}{11} \sum_{x=75}^{85} \text{Improvement}_x^{(i)}.$$

The payment of the bond is linked to the weighted average of the mortality improvement (WMI) of the two populations. It is expressed as:

$$WMI = 0.625 MI^{(1)} + 0.375 MI^{(2)}.$$

We set the respective weights of $MI^{(1)}$ and $MI^{(2)}$ at 0.625 and 0.375, because Canadian population size is approximately 60% of EW population size. The principal of the bond is reduced if the realized mortality improvement is higher than a certain threshold value, thereby providing hedge for longevity risk. More specifically, the principal is reduced by a "principal reduction factor" (PRF) given below:

$$PRF = \max\left(\min\left(\frac{WMI - ap}{ap - ep}, 1\right), 0\right),$$

where ap is the point of attachment and ep is the point of exhaustion. There are three possible scenarios for the principal repayment:

1. $WMI < ap$ and $PRF = 0$:
The mortality improvement of EW and Canadian populations is small, and hence the longevity risk exposure is moderate. Full principal will be returned to bond investors.
2. $ap < WMI < ep$ and $PRF = \frac{WMI - ap}{ap - ep}$:
Mortality improvement is significant and the annuity provider suffers loss from its annuity book. The principal of the bond is partially reduced to compensate the loss.
3. $WMI > ep$ and $PRF = 1$:
In this scenario, the mortality improvement is extremely high and the loss on the annuity book is severe. The principal is reduced by 100% to relieve the financial burden of the annuity provider.

We set the point of attachment and point of exhaustion at the 94th and 98th percentile of simulated WMIs based on VECM forecasts. Using these values, the probability of first loss is 6% and the probability of 100% principal reduction is 2%. The point of attachment is 2.23% and the point of exhaustion is 2.52%.

6.2. Risk-Neutral Pricing

Cox et al. (2006), Wang (2007), and Yang and Wang (2013) applied Wang transform to obtain risk-neutral measure and price mortality/longevity-linked securities. We follow this work and apply multivariate Wang transform to TVECM. To obtain the mortality rates under risk-neutral measure, we transform the error term in TVECM. Since the error term follows normal distribution, it is still normally distributed after the multivariate Wang transform. Let $\{\tilde{\varepsilon}_t^{(1)}, \tilde{\varepsilon}_t^{(2)}\}$ be the error term in TVECM under the risk-neutral measure. Using the multivariate Wang transform, we have:

$$\begin{aligned}
\tilde{\varepsilon}_t^{(1)} &= \varepsilon_t^{(1)} + \left(\lambda_\varepsilon^{(1)} + \lambda_\varepsilon^{(2)} \rho_{12}\right) \sigma_1, \\
\tilde{\varepsilon}_t^{(2)} &= \varepsilon_t^{(2)} + \left(\lambda_\varepsilon^{(1)} \rho_{12} + \lambda_\varepsilon^{(2)}\right) \sigma_2,
\end{aligned}$$

where $\lambda_\varepsilon^{(1)}$ and $\lambda_\varepsilon^{(2)}$ are the risk adjustment parameters for the mortality indexes; ρ_{ij} is the correlation between $\varepsilon_t^{(i)}$ and $\varepsilon_t^{(j)}$; and σ_i is the standard deviation of $\varepsilon_t^{(i)}$. After the transform, the mean of $\{\tilde{\varepsilon}_t^{(1)}, \tilde{\varepsilon}_t^{(2)}\}$ becomes $\{(\lambda_\varepsilon^{(1)} + \lambda_\varepsilon^{(2)}\rho_{12})\sigma_1, (\lambda_\varepsilon^{(1)}\rho_{12} + \lambda_\varepsilon^{(2)})\sigma_2\}$ and the variance-covariance matrix remains the same with that of $\{\varepsilon_t^{(1)}, \varepsilon_t^{(2)}\}$. Based on the value of $\lambda_\varepsilon^{(1)}$ and $\lambda_\varepsilon^{(2)}$ and the distribution of $\{\tilde{\varepsilon}_t^{(1)}, \tilde{\varepsilon}_t^{(2)}\}$, we simulate mortality paths and principal repayment of the bond under the risk-neutral measure.

Let x denote the spread over LIBOR. Since the bond is traded at its face value, the spread over LIBOR is the "price" we try to determine. Under the risk-neutral measure, the bond value is calculated as the expected present value of future coupon payments and principal repayment discounted at risk-free interest rate. The bond value is equal to its face value. We assume that the face value is

1 without loss of generality. We use the spot curve for commercial bank liability in England on 31 December 2011[2] as the risk-free interest rate. The three-month LIBOR is set at 0.48%.

To obtain the spread x, we solve the following equation:

$$\sum_{i=\frac{1}{4},\frac{2}{4},\ldots,7\frac{3}{4},8} e^{-ir_i}\left(\frac{0.48\%+x}{4}\right)+[1-E_Q(PRF)]e^{-8r_8}=1$$

where r_i is the yield rate of a i-year commercial bank liability and $E_Q(PRF)$ is the expectation of PRF under the risk-neutral measure. The $E_Q(PRF)$ is calculated as the average of the simulated PRFs under the risk-neutral measure.

6.3. Pricing Results

Cox et al. (2006) found that the market price of risk is 0.1792 for male annuitants and 0.2312 for female annuitants in survivor derivatives. Lin and Cox (2008) discovered that the market price of risk for EIB bond is 0.2408. Therefore, the range of 0.1 to 0.3 is reasonable for the risk adjustment parameters. Table 8 demonstrates the pricing results using VECM and TVECM model when both risk adjustment parameters are set to −0.1, −0.2 and −0.3. Note that the risk adjustment parameters are negative in our case because longevity risk represents the risk of lower than expected $k_t^{(i)}$ and hence a left shift in the error term distribution.

Table 8. E_Q(PRF) and spread over LIBOR.

Model	$\lambda_\varepsilon^{(1)}, \lambda_\varepsilon^{(2)}$	E_Q(PRF)	Spread over LIBOR
VECM	0	0.0356	1.62%
	−0.1	0.0923	2.27%
	−0.2	0.1853	3.33%
	−0.3	0.3249	4.92%
TVECM	0	0.2141	3.65%
	−0.1	0.3097	4.74%
	−0.2	0.4221	6.0%
	−0.3	0.5446	7.42%

We observe that the spread over LIBOR increases with the absolute value of the risk adjustment parameters. A higher absolute value of risk adjustment parameter indicates that bond investors demand higher compensation for taking the same risk and thus a higher quarterly coupon rate.

We also notice that TVECM yields 2.03–2.67% higher spreads than VECM. Recall that TVECM predicts much faster mortality improvement than VECM. There is a higher chance of exceeding the attachment point using TVECM forecasts than using VECM forecasts. As a result, TVECM leads to higher expected principal reduction and also higher coupon rate as compensation to the principal reduction.

7. Conclusions

Our analysis shows that a long-term equilibrium exists between the mortality indexes of EW and Canadian populations. This relation can be captured using VECM, which incorporates an adjustment coefficient and a cointegrating value to revert the time series toward their long-term relation.

However, we also find that threshold effect exists in the VECM, i.e., the time series data follow different VECMs depending on the value of a threshold variable. Therefore, we further consider TVECM to incorporate the threshold effect. In TVECM, the threshold variable is set to the level of

[2] Downloaded from http://www.bankofengland.co.uk/statistics/Pages/yieldcurve/archive.aspx.

deviation from the long-term equilibrium. When comparing the forecasts of mortality index between TVECM and VECM, we find TVECM yields lower mean mortality forecasts and narrower prediction intervals. The mortality improvement pattern predicted by TVECM is more in line with that observed in recent years, in contrast with VECM.

Finally, we price an illustrative longevity bond that hedges the longevity risk for an annuity provider that operates in both EW and Canada. Due to the higher mortality improvement forecasts, the coupon rates required by bond investors based on the TVECM forecasts are much higher than those based on the VECM forecasts. Capturing the changes in the long-term relation has a significant impact on the longevity bond price.

By allowing regime switching, TVECM can capture potential changes in the dependence structure, and hence the flexibility. The VECM in each regime is estimated using the portion of mortality data that belong to the corresponding regime, thereby more accurately representing the mortality dynamics in that regime. In contrast, single-regime VECM assumes that mortality dependence remains unchanged over the sample period. Parameter estimates of single-regime VECM are obtained utilizing the entire dataset. When change of mortality dependence occurs in the historical data, the estimates of the single-regime VECM cannot fully reflect the new mortality dynamics. Therefore, the mortality forecasts using single-regime VECM are less consistent with most recent mortality trend.

Furthermore, TVECM is a nonlinear model while single-regime VECM is linear. Since we observe some curvature in the estimates of $k_t^{(1)}$ and $k_t^{(2)}$, it is expected that the nonlinear TVECM is more suitable for modeling the pair. Since the nonlinear model can capture the acceleration of mortality improvement in the past few decades, TVECM predicts faster mortality improvement than VECM. As a result, longevity risk pricing using TVECM is more conservative compared to VECM, as shown in the pricing of the illustrative longevity bond. For similar reasons, we should also expect higher prices for annuity portfolios using TVECM than single-regime VECM.

We note that the presence of threshold effect is data dependent. For example, there is insignificant threshold effect in the mortality dependence of Canadian and US populations. If we switch to different sample period or sample age range, we might also arrive at different results. Therefore, it is important to test the presence of threshold effect before applying TVECM to mortality data.

When performing residual diagnostics, we observe non-normality caused by outliers in EW mortality. Identifying and removing outliers in time series was extensively studied by Chen and Liu (1993). In future work, we are interested in studying how the removal of outliers affects the long-term relation and the longevity bond pricing. Another venue of future work is to simplify the estimated TVECM. One of the drawbacks of TVECM is the large number of parameters. Given that the sample size of mortality data is relatively small, the large number of parameters introduces great parameter uncertainty. Therefore, it is important to explore various techniques to reduce the model parameters.

Author Contributions: Conceptualization, R.Z. and G.X.; Methodology, R.Z., G.X., and M.J.; Validation, M.J.; Formal Analysis, R.Z. and G.X.; Data Curation, G.X.; Writing—Original Draft Preparation, G.X.; Writing—Review and Editing, R.Z. and M.J.; and Supervision, R.Z.

Funding: This research received no external funding.

Conflicts of Interest: The authors declare no conflict of interest.

References

Biffis, Enrico, Yijia Lin, and Andreas Milidonis. 2017. The Cross-Section of Asia-Pacific Mortality Dynamics: Implications for Longevity Risk Sharing. *Journal of Risk and Insurance* 84: 515–32. [CrossRef]

Bovas, Abraham, and George E. P. Box. 1979. Bayesian analysis of some outlier problems in time series. *Biometrika* 66: 229–36.

Brouhns, Natacha, Michel Denuit, and Jeroen K. Vermunt. 2002. A Poisson log-bilinear regression approach to the construction of projected lifetables. *Insurance: Mathematics and Economics* 31: 373–93. [CrossRef]

Cairns, Andrew J. G., David Blake, Kevin Dowd, Guy D. Coughlan, and Marwa Khalaf-Allah. 2011. Bayesian stochastic mortality modelling for two populations. *Astin Bulletin* 41: 29–59.

Chen, Chung, and Lon-Mu Liu. 1993. Joint estimation of model parameters and outlier effects in time series. *Journal of the American Statistical Association* 88: 284–97.

Chen, Chung, and George C. Tiao. 1990. Random level-shift time series models, ARIMA approximations, and level-shift detection. *Journal of Business and Economic Statistics* 8: 83–97.

Cox, Samuel H., Yijia Lin, and Shaun Wang. 2006. Multivariate exponential tilting and pricing implications for mortality securitization. *Journal of Risk and Insurance* 73: 719–36. [CrossRef]

Darkiewicz, Grzegorz, and Tom Hoedemakers. 2004. *How the Co-Integration Analysis Can Help in Mortality Forecasting*. DTEW Research Report 0406. Belgium: DTEW.

Human Mortality Database. 2017. University of California, Berkeley (USA), and Max Planck Institute for Demographic Research (Germany). Available online: www.mortality.orgorwww.humanmortality.de (accessed on 18 September 2017).

Dowd, Kevin, Andrew J. G. Cairns, David P. Blake, Guy Coughlan, and Marwa Khalaf-Allah. 2011. A gravity model of mortality rates for two related populations. *North American Actuarial Journal* 15: 334–56. [CrossRef]

Engle, Robert F., and Clive W. J. Granger. 1987. Co-integration and error correction: Representation, estimation, and testing. *Econometrica* 55: 251–76. [CrossRef]

Gaille, Séverine, and Michael Sherris. 2011. Improving longevity and mortality risk models using common stochastic long-run trends. *The Geneva Papers on Risk and Insurance Issues and Practice* 36: 595–621. [CrossRef]

Hansen, Bruce E., and Byeongseon Seo. 2002. Testing for two-regime threshold cointegration in vector error-correction models. *Journal of Econometrics* 110: 293–318. [CrossRef]

Hunt, Andrew, and David Blake. 2015. Identifiability, Cointegration and the Gravity Model. Working Paper. Available online: https://www.pensions-institute.org/workingpapers/wp1505.pdf (accessed on 28 September 2017).

Kuo, Weiyu, Chenghsien Tsai, and Wei-Kuang Chen. 2003. An empirical study on the lapse rate: The cointegration approach. *Journal of Risk and Insurance* 70: 489–508. [CrossRef]

Lazar, Dorina. 2004. On forecasting mortality using the Lee-Carter model. Paper presented at 3rd Conference in Actuarial Science & Finance in Samos, Lesvos, Greece, September 2–5.

Lee, Ronald D., and Lawrence R. Carter. 1992. Modeling and forecasting US mortality. *Journal of the American Statistical Association* 87: 659–71.

Li, Johnny Siu-Hang, Wai-Sum Chan, and Rui Zhou. 2016. Semi-coherent multi-population mortality modeling: The impact on longevity risk securitization. *Journal of Risk and Insurance* 84: 1025–65. [CrossRef]

Li, Johnny Siu-Hang, and Mary R. Hardy. 2011. Measuring Basis Risk in Longevity Hedges. *North American Actuarial Journal* 15: 177–200. [CrossRef]

Li, Nan, and Ronald Lee. 2005. Coherent mortality forecasts for a group of populations: An extension of the Lee-Carter method. *Demography* 42: 575–94. [CrossRef] [PubMed]

Lin, Yijia, and Samuel H. Cox. 2008. Securitization of catastrophe mortality risks. *Insurance: Mathematics and Economics* 42: 628–637. [CrossRef]

Milidonis, Andreas, and Maria Efthymiou. 2017. Mortality leads and lags. *Journal of Risk and Insurance* 84: 495–514. [CrossRef]

Milidonis, Andreas, Yijia Lin, and Samuel H. Cox. 2011. Mortality Regimes and Pricing. *North American Actuarial Journal* 15: 266–89. [CrossRef]

Mitchell, Daniel, Patrick Brockett, Rafael Mendoza-Arriaga, and Kumar Muthuraman. 2013. Modeling and forecasting mortality rates. *Insurance: Mathematics and Economics* 52: 275–85. [CrossRef]

Villegas, Andrés M., Steven Haberman, Vladimir K. Kaishev, and Pietro Millossovich. 2017. A comparative study of two-population models for the assessment of basis risk in longevity hedges. *Astin Bulletin* 47: 631–79. [CrossRef]

Wang, Shaun. 2007. Normalized exponential tilting: Pricing and measuring multivariate risks. *North American Actuarial Journal* 11: 89–99. [CrossRef]

World Health Organization 2015. World health statistics 2015. Available online: https://apps.who.int/iris/bitstream/handle/10665/170250/9789240694439_eng.pdf;jsessionid=3810364FBAED15910EAA9D7E531F9A32?sequence=1 (accessed on 28 September 2017).

Yang, Sharon S., and Chou-Wen Wang. 2013. Pricing and securitization of multi-country longevity risk with mortality dependence. *Insurance: Mathematics and Economics* 52: 157–69. [CrossRef]

Zhou, Rui, Yujiao Wang, Kai Kaufhold, Johnny Siu-Hang Li, and Ken Seng Tan. 2014. Modeling period effects in multi-population mortality models: Applications to Solvency II. *North American Actuarial Journal* 18: 150–67. [CrossRef]

4

Modelling Recovery Rates for Non-Performing Loans

Hui Ye * and Anthony Bellotti *

Department of Mathematics, Imperial College London, London SW7 2AZ, UK
* Correspondence: hui.ye16@alumni.imperial.ac.uk (H.Y.); a.bellotti@imperial.ac.uk (A.B.)

Abstract: Based on a rich dataset of recoveries donated by a debt collection business, recovery rates for non-performing loans taken from a single European country are modelled using linear regression, linear regression with Lasso, beta regression and inflated beta regression. We also propose a two-stage model: beta mixture model combined with a logistic regression model. The proposed model allowed us to model the multimodal distribution we found for these recovery rates. All models were built using loan characteristics, default data and collections data prior to purchase by the debt collection business. The intended use of the models was to estimate future recovery rates for improved risk assessment, capital requirement calculations and bad debt management. They were compared using a range of quantitative performance measures under K-fold cross validation. Among all the models, we found that the proposed two-stage beta mixture model performs best.

Keywords: recovery rates; beta regression; credit risk

---

1. Introduction

In Basel II, an internal ratings-based (IRB) approach was proposed by the Basel Committee in 2001 to determine capital requirements for credit risk (Bank for International Settlements 2001). This IRB approach grants banks permission to use their own risk models or assessments to calculate regulatory capital. Under the IRB approach, banks are required to estimate the following risk components: probability of default (PD), loss given default (LGD), exposure at default (EAD) and maturity (M) (Bank for International Settlements 2001). Since Basel II's capital requirement calculation depends heavily on LGD, financial institutions have put more emphasis on modelling LGD in recent years. Unlike the estimation of PD, which is well-established, LGD is not so well-understood and still subject to research. Improving LGD modelling can help financial institutions assess their risk and regulatory capital requirement more precisely, as well as improving debt management.

LGD is defined as the proportion of money financial institutions fail to collect during the collection period, given the borrower has already defaulted. Conversely, Recovery Rate (RR) is defined as the proportion of money financial institutions successfully collected minus the administration fees during the collection period, given the borrower has already defaulted. Equations (1) and (2) give formal definitions of RR and LGD, respectively:

- Suppose individual i has already defaulted on a loan, let EAD_i be the exposure at default for this individual i.
- Let A_i be the administration costs (e.g., letters, phone calls, visits, lawyers and legal work) incurred for individual i.
- Let R_i be the amount recovered for individual i.

Then,

$$\text{Recovery Rate} = \frac{R_i - A_i}{EAD_i} = \frac{\sum \text{Collections} - \sum \text{Admin Fee}}{\text{Outstanding Balance at Default}} \tag{1}$$

and

$$\text{Loss Given Default} = 1 - \text{Recovery Rate} = 1 - \frac{R_i - A_i}{EAD_i} \tag{2}$$

RR mainly lies in the interval [0, 1] and typically has high concentrations at the boundary points 0 and 1. It is possible for RR to be negative if recoveries are less than administration costs, $A_i > R_i$, and greater than 1 if recoveries exceed exposure plus administration costs, $R_i > EAD_i + A_i$. Typically, however, RR is truncated within the interval [0, 1] when developing LGD models.

The main challenge in estimating LGD is the bimodal property with high concentrations at 0 and 1 typically present in LGD empirical distributions, where people either repay in full or repay nothing. For the dataset we used in this study, we found our LGD distribution is actually tri-modal. Therefore, regression models have been studied that specifically deal with this problem. For example, Bellotti and Crook (2012) built Tobit and decision tree models along with beta and fractional logit transformation of the RR response variable to forecast the LGD based on a dataset of 55,000 defaulted credit cards in the UK from 1999 to 2005. They concluded that ordinary least squares regression with macroeconomic variables performed the best in terms of forecast performance. Calabrese (2012) proposed a mixed continuous-discrete model, where the boundary values 0 and 1 are modelled by Bernoulli random variables and the continuous part of the RR is modelled by a Beta random variable. This model is then applied to predict RR of Bank of Italy's loans from 1985 to 1999. The result is compared with Papke and Wooldrige's fractional response model with log-log, logistic and complementary log-log link functions (Papke and Wooldridge 1996) and linear regression. The mixed continuous and discrete model achieves the best performance . Qi and Zhao (2011) applied four linear models, namely ordinary least squares regression, fractional response regression, inverse Gaussian regression, and inverse Gaussian regression with beta transformation, and two non-linear models, namely regression tree and neural network, to model the LGD of 3751 defaulted bank loans and bonds in the US from 1985 to 2008. They concluded that fractional response regression is slightly better than the ordinary least squares regression. Moreover, they reported that non-linear models perform best. Loterman et al. (2012) performed a benchmark study of LGD by comparing twenty-four different models using six datasets extracted from international banks. They concluded that non-linear models, such as neural network, support vector machine and mixture models perform better than linear models.

For this project, we specifically modelled and predicted RR for data from a single European country provided by a debt collection company. Due to reasons of commercial confidentiality and data protection, the debt collection company will remain anonymous and some aspects of the data were also anonymised, including the country of origin. Consequently, the data cannot be made publicly available. We applied some of the models that have already been studied previously and also extended the existing models, proposing a new beta mixture model to improve the accuracy of RR prediction. A good prediction of RR would help the debt collection company to determine collection policy for new debt portfolios. It is important to note that the RR we modelled is different from most RR, as the data only contain positive repayments and no administration fee was recorded. Therefore, all the RRs in our data lie in the range (0, 1] instead of [0, 1]. Figure 1 shows a histogram of RR for the data. We can clearly see that there are modes at 0, 0.55 (approximately) and a high spike at boundary value 1. Since the shape of the empirical RR distribution demonstrates a trimodal feature, it is reasonable to assume that the recovery rate is a mixed type random variable. The multi-modality of RR is a natural consequence of different groups of bad debts being serviced using different strategies; e.g., one strategy may be that some bad debts are allowed to be written off if the debtor paid back some agreed fixed percentage of the outstanding balance. Having outcome RR within $(0, 1]$ motivated the use of the beta regression model and the multi-modal nature of RR motivates the use of a mixture model within this context.

The beta mixture model has been applied successfully within several other application domains. Ji et al. (2005) showed how to apply the beta mixture regression model in several bioinformatics applications such as meta-analysis of gene expression data and to cluster correlation coefficients between gene expressions. Laurila et al. (2011) used a beta mixture model to describe DNA methylation patterns, helping to reduce the dimensionality of microarray data. Moustafa et al. (2018) used a beta mixture model as the basis of an anomaly detection system. Their network data are typically bounded, which suggests a beta distribution, and the use of the beta mixture allowed them to identify latent clusters in normal network use.

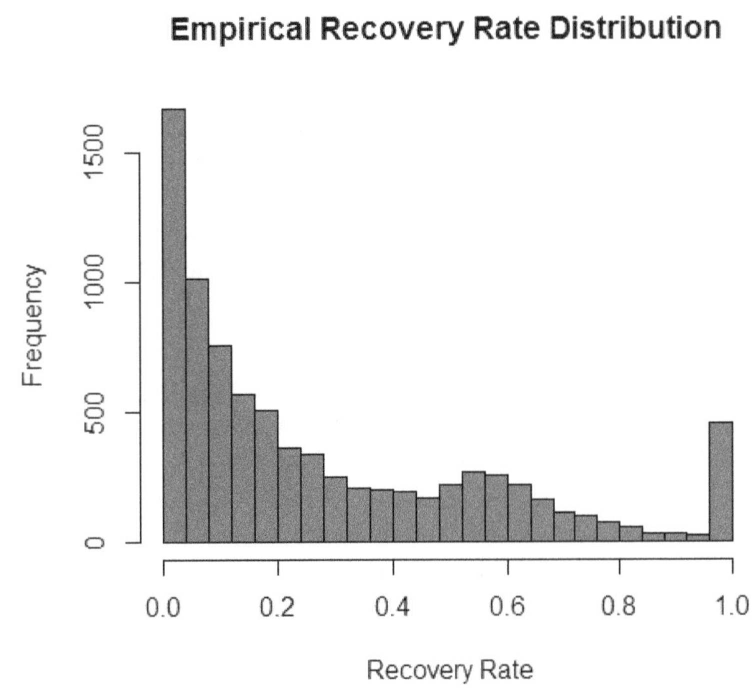

Figure 1. Histogram of recovery rates for 8237 loans after pre-preprocessing described in Section 2. The stack of 1s shows frequency of $RR = 1$, but the stack at 0 shows frequency for small $RR > 0$.

Inspired by Calabrese's mixed continuous-discrete model (Calabrese 2012), we propose a two-stage model composed of:

- A beta mixture model is parameterised by mean and precision based on two sets of predictor variables on the interval of (0, 1) in order to model the two modes located at just after 0 and around 0.55.
- A logistic regression model is used for the mode at boundary value 1.

The above proposed model allows representation of the trimodal feature of the data. The beta mixture component groups the clients into two clusters for RR $<$ 1, based on their personal information, debt conditions and repayment history, which may become useful information for other business analysis and decision-making, and then uses logistic regression to model the third case RR = 1. In addition, we also used linear regression, linear regression with Lasso, beta regression and inflated beta regression to model RR. Model performance was measured by mean squared error, mean absolute error and mean aggregate absolute error under K-fold cross validation.

To our knowledge, this is the first study for estimating RR for portfolios of non-performing loans using a statistical model, and the first use of a beta mixture model for LGD. We also developed a novel procedure for predicting an expected value of outcome from a beta mixture model based on assigning a new observation to one of the clusters in the mixture. The remainder of the article is organised as follows: Section 2 provides a detailed data overview. Section 3 introduces the modelling methodology with great emphasis on the proposed beta mixture model combined with logistic regression model. Section 4 analyses some important features of the models and reports the model performance and Section 5 concludes with key findings and future recommendations.

2. Data

Three datasets were provided by the debt collection company:

Dataset 1 provides 48 predictor variables of personal information including socio-demographic variables, Credit Bureau Score and debt status for 120,699 individuals for loans originating between January 1998 and May 2014 from several different financial institutions. Overall, 97.5% of them have credit card debt and only 2.5% are refinanced credit cards (product = "R"). Partial information was extracted from a Bad Debt Bureau. Each record corresponds to a bad loan and has a unique key Loan.Ref.

Dataset 2 records all the recoveries made by the bank before the debt collection company purchased the debt portfolio. It contains 15 predictor variables about historical collection information, which includes number of calls, contacts and visits made by the bank to collect the debt. It also includes repayments in the format of monthly summary. In total, there are 42,832 individuals' records in Dataset 2, among which only 34,807 individuals can be matched to Dataset 1 by Loan.Ref. Numbers of calls, contacts, visits, repayment and some other monthly activities are aggregated by summing for each loan identified by Loan.Ref.

Dataset 3 records all the recoveries made by the debt collection company after they purchased the debt portfolio from the bank. It includes 12 predictor variables about the ongoing collection information. There are 8281 individuals in total, among which only 8237 individuals are from Dataset 1. Since only positive repayments are recorded, all the recovery rates we calculated are strictly greater than 0. Therefore, in the modelling section, we only focus on the recovery modelling in the interval (0, 1], which is slightly different from the usual RR defined in [0, 1]. The debt collection period recorded in this dataset is from January 2015 to end of November 2016.

Figure 2 shows how the data were joined. There are 8237 data points presented in Dataset 3, but only 7161 individual historical collection information are recorded in Dataset 2. In these cases, there are no historical recoveries by bank, i.e., no calls, contacts, visits or payments for the remaining 1076 individuals. Therefore, a value of 0 was assigned to aggregate recoveries in Dataset 2 for the remaining 1076 individuals. The modified Dataset 2 was then joined to Datasets 1 and 3 by the unique key Loan.Ref and we obtained a table of 8237 data points with 61 variables.

Table A1 gives descriptive statistics for each of the variables in the joined dataset used in the statistical modelling. The predictor variable Pre-Recovery Rate is the bank's RR before the debt portfolio was purchased. The minimum value is −0.130, which is negative due to the substantial amount of administration fee exceeding repayments incurred during the collection period. The predictor variable Credit Bureau Score is a generic credit score provided by a credit bureau.

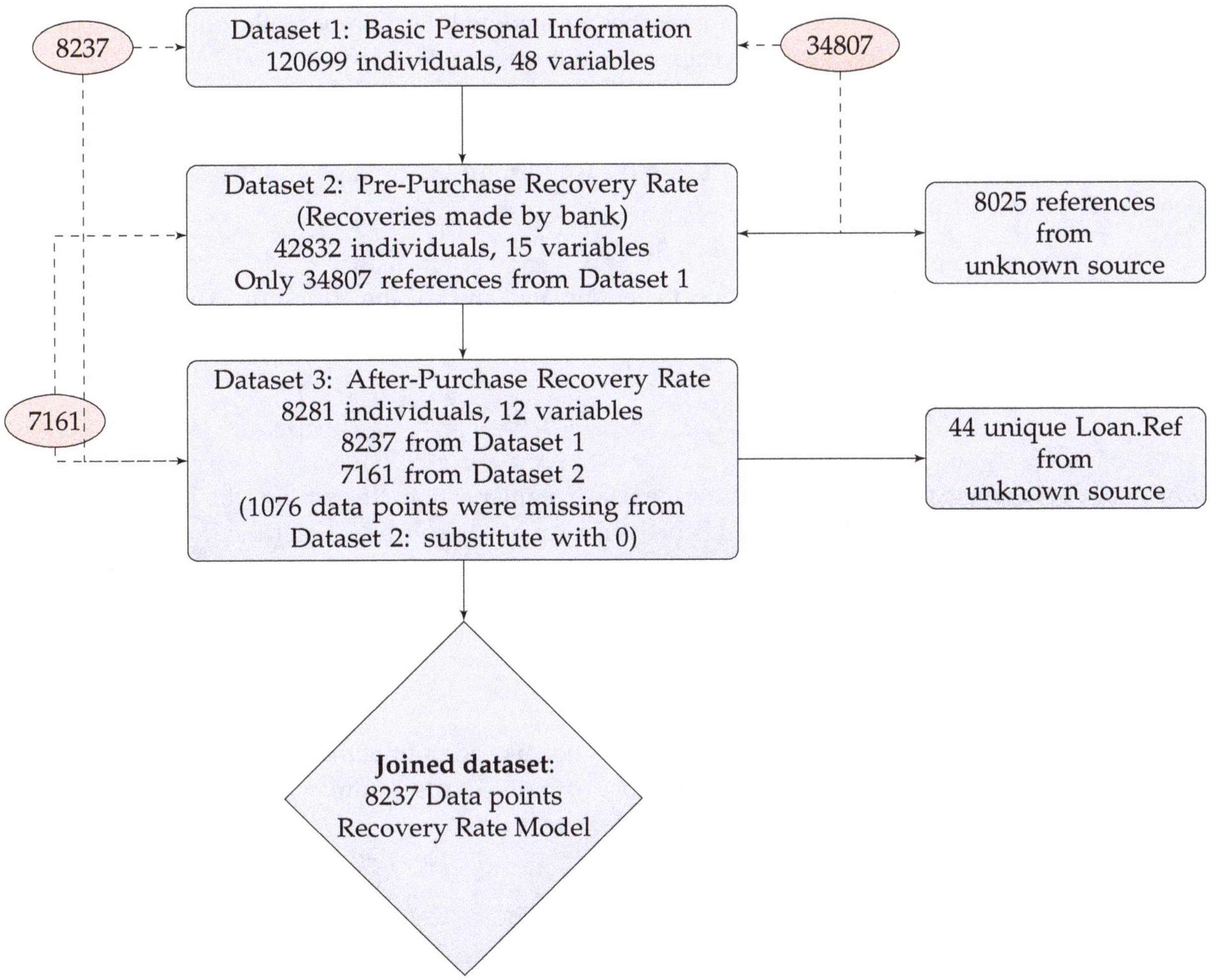

Figure 2. Joining the three datasets.

Recovery Rate Calculation

Since the repayments in Datasets 2 and 3 were recorded in the format of monthly activity summaries, each individual may have several repayments for the same loan. Therefore, we defined the recovery rate as the sum of repayments minus the administration fee (if available) over the original balance of the loan, which is also equivalent to the difference between original balance and ending balance over the original balance. For each individual i, RR is calculated using:

$$\text{Recovery Rate}_i = \frac{\sum \text{Repayments}_i - \text{AdminFee}_i}{\text{Original Balance}_i} = \frac{\text{Original Balance}_i - \text{Ending Balance}_i}{\text{Original Balance}_i} \tag{3}$$

Figure 1 is the empirical RR histogram calculated based on Equation (3), for the 8237 data points after pre-processing. The remaining 112,462 data points not included in the analysis essentially have RR = 0, but we do not know whether they have been serviced or not, thus they were not included in the analysis. Essentially, the goal of our model is to estimate RR computed from Dataset 3 (post-purchase), based on pre-purchase information given in Datasets 1 and 2.

3. Modelling Methodology

We applied various models to estimate RR. In all cases, model performance was measured within a K-fold cross validation framework. We first tried using ordinary least squares linear regression, with and without stepwise backward variable selection using the AIC criterion. In the following sub-sections, we list the other modelling approaches we explored. Let y indicate the outcome variable, recovery rate, and X is a corresponding vector of predictor variables.

3.1. *Linear Regression with Lasso*

We applied linear regression with a Lasso (Least Absolute Shrinkage and Selection Operator) penalty. The model structure is

$$y = \beta_0 + \boldsymbol{\beta}^T X + \epsilon$$

where β_0 and $\boldsymbol{\beta}$ are intercept and coefficients to be estimated and ϵ is the error term. Then, estimation using least squares error with Lasso is given by the optimisation problem on a training dataset of N observations:

$$(\hat{\beta_0}, \hat{\boldsymbol{\beta}}) = \underset{\beta_0, \boldsymbol{\beta}}{\text{argmin}} \left[\frac{1}{N} \sum_{i=1}^{N} \left(y_i - \beta_0 - \boldsymbol{\beta}^T X_i \right)^2 + \lambda \sum_{j=1}^{p} |\beta_j| \right], \tag{4}$$

where $\lambda > 0$ is a tuning parameter controlling the size of regularisation. Regression with Lasso will tend to shrink coefficient estimates to zero and hence is a form of variable selection (Friedman et al. 2010). The value of λ is chosen using K-fold cross validation. For this project, the R packages "lars" (Hastie and Efron 2013) and "glmnet" (Friedman et al. 2010) were used to estimate linear regression with Lasso.

3.2. *Multivariate Beta Regression*

The problem with linear regression is that it does not take account of the particular distribution of RR, which is between 0 and 1. The beta distribution, with two shape parameters α and β, allows us to model RR in the open interval $(0, 1)$:

$$f(y_i; \alpha_i, \beta_i) = \frac{\Gamma(\alpha_i + \beta_i)}{\Gamma(\alpha_i)\Gamma(\beta_i)} y_i^{\alpha_i - 1} (1 - y_i)^{\beta_i - 1}, \quad 0 < y_i < 1, \tag{5}$$

where α, $\beta > 0$ are the shape parameters and $\Gamma(\cdot)$ is the Gamma function. The beta distribution is reparameterised by mean and precision parameters, denoting by μ and ϕ, respectively, following Ferrari and Cribari-Neto (2004), since this parameterisation meaningfully express the expected value and variance:

$$\phi_i = \alpha_i + \beta_i, \quad E(y_i) = \mu_i = \frac{\alpha_i}{\alpha_i + \beta_i}, \quad Var(y_i) = \frac{\mu_i(1 - \mu_i)}{\phi_i + 1}, \tag{6}$$

The reparameterised beta distribution is then

$$f(y_i; \mu_i, \phi_i) = \frac{\Gamma(\phi_i)}{\Gamma(\mu_i \phi_i)\Gamma((1 - \mu_i)\phi_i)} y_i^{\mu_i \phi_i - 1} (1 - y_i)^{(1 - \mu_i)\phi_i - 1}, \quad 0 < y_i < 1, \tag{7}$$

with $0 < \mu_i < 1$ and $\phi_i > 0$. Figure 3a demonstrates three examples of the beta distribution with fixed $\phi = 5$ and different μ. The variance is maximised at $\mu = 0.5$. Figure 3b demonstrates another three examples of beta distribution with fixed $\mu = 0.5$ and different ϕ.

The precision parameter ϕ is negatively correlated with $Var(y_i)$, given a fixed μ. Furthermore, the variance of Y is a function of μ, which enables the regression to model heteroskedasticity. RR is modelled as $y_i \sim \text{B}(\mu_i, \phi_i)$ for $i \in (1, \cdots, N)$ for sample size N. The multivariate beta regression model (Cribari-Neto and Zeileis 2010) is defined as:

$$F_1(\mu_i) = \eta^T X_i = \xi_{1i},$$

$$F_2(\phi_i) = \gamma^T W_i = \xi_{2i},$$

where η is a vector of parameters which needs to be estimated corresponding to predictor variables X and γ is a vector of parameters which needs to be estimated corresponding to predictor variables W.

The predictor variables in W may be the same as in X, or a subset, or contain different variables. For this study, W will have a subset of predictor variables determined using stepwise variable selection. The link function ensures that $\mu_i \in (0,1)$ and $\phi_i > 0$. We applied Logit and Log link function to μ_i and ϕ_i, respectively:

$$\mu_i = \frac{1}{1+e^{-\eta^T X_i}}, \quad \phi_i = e^{-\gamma^T W_i}.$$

With this multivariate beta regression model, η and γ can be estimated by maximum likelihood estimation, where the log-likelihood function is

$$L(\eta,\gamma) = \sum_{i=1}^{N} \Big[\log\Gamma(\phi_i) - \log\Gamma(\mu_i\phi_i) - \log\Gamma((1-\mu_i)\phi_i) + (\mu_i\phi_i - 1)\log y_i + ((1-\mu_i)\phi_i - 1)\log(1-y_i) \Big]. \tag{8}$$

By substituting $\mu_i = F_1^{-1}(\eta^T X_i)$ and $\phi_i = F_2^{-1}(\gamma^T W_i)$ into Equation (8), the log-likelihood is obtained as a function of η and γ. The parameters can be estimated using Broyden–Fletcher–Goldfarb–Shanno (BFGS) quasi-Newton method, which is considered to be the most appropriate method (Mittelhammer et al. 2000; Nocedal and Wright 1999).

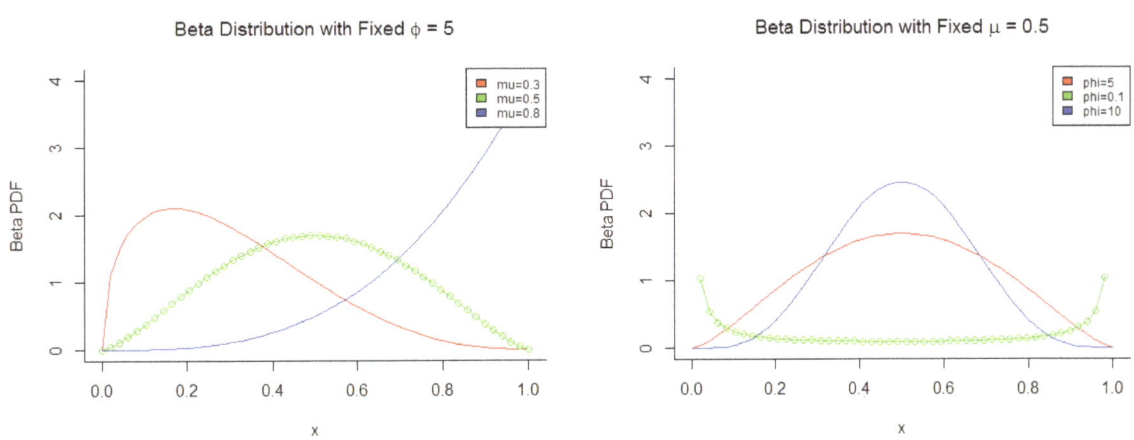

(a) (b)

Figure 3. Beta distribution. (**a**) Beta Distribution with Fixed ϕ; (**b**) Beta Distribution with Fixed μ.

3.3. *Inflated Beta Regression*

The disadvantage of beta regression is that it does not include the boundary values 0 or 1. Therefore, a modification is required before fitting the model. To better represent RR on the boundaries 0 and 1, Calabrese (2012) suggested considering RR as a mixture of Bernoulli random variables for the boundary 0 and 1, and a Beta random variable for the open interval (0, 1). The distribution for this inflated beta regression on [0, 1] is then defined as

$$f_Y(y) = \begin{cases} p_0, & \text{if } y = 0 \\ (1-p_0-p_1) f_B(y;\alpha,\beta), & \text{if } 0 < y < 1 \\ p_1, & \text{if } y = 1 \end{cases} \tag{9}$$

for y $\in [0,1]$, $p_0 = P(y=0)$, $p_1 = P(y=1)$, $0 < p_0 + p_1 < 1$ and $f_B(y)$ is the beta distribution defined in Section 3.2. Moreover, if RR $y \in (0,1]$, i.e., it only inflates at one, as our data do, then the distribution is just

$$f_Y(y) = \begin{cases} (1-p_1)f_B(y;\alpha,\beta), & \text{if } 0 < y < 1 \\ p_1, & \text{if } y = 1 \end{cases} \tag{10}$$

We used maximum likelihood estimation to estimate parameters for Bernoulli random variable and Beta random variables, parameterising the discrete part in the following way (Calabrese 2012):

$$s_i = \frac{p_1}{p_1 + p_0}, \quad d_i = p_0 + p_1,$$

The log-likelihood function is then

$$\begin{aligned} L(s,d,\alpha,\beta) = & \sum_{y_i=0} \log(1-s_i) + \sum_{y_i=0} \log(d_i) + \sum_{y_i=1} \log(s_i) + \sum_{y_i=1} \log(d_i) \\ & + \sum_{0<y_i<1} \log(1-d_i) + \sum_{0<y_i<1} \log(f_B(y;\alpha_i,\beta_i)). \end{aligned} \tag{11}$$

The continuous beta random variables can be parameterised in the same way as described in Section 3.2.

3.4. *Beta Mixture Model combined with Logistic Regression*

Examining the distribution of RR shown in Figure 1, it can be seen that the distribution between 0 and 1 is bimodal. For this reason, we consider a beta mixture model to deal with what appears to be two different groups of recoveries. We propose a two-stage model: beta mixture model combined with logistic regression. The beta mixture model allows us to model the multimodality of RR in the interval (0, 1). This is similar to the two-stage (decision tree) model used by Bellotti and Crook (2012), but with a beta mixture used for regression.

Firstly, RR is classified into ones and non-ones using logistic regression. Secondly, within the non-ones group, a mixture of beta distributions is used to model RR in the range (0, 1). In general, a mixture of beta distribution consists of m components where each component follows a parametric beta distribution. The prior probability of component j is denoted as π_j, where $j \in (1,\cdots,m)$. Let M_j denote the jth component/cluster in the beta mixture model. The beta mixture model with m components is defined as:

$$\begin{aligned} g(y;\mu,\phi) &= \sum_{j=1}^{m} \pi_j f_j(y;X,\mu_j,\phi_j) \\ &= \sum_{j=1}^{m} \pi_j f_j(y;X,W,F_1^{-1}(\eta_j^T X_i),F_2^{-1}(\gamma_j^T W_i)) \\ &= \sum_{j=1}^{m} \pi_j f_j(y;X,W,\eta_j,\gamma_j), \end{aligned}$$

where f_j is the beta distribution corresponding to the jth component with separate parameter vectors η_j and γ_j. The same link functions are used as in Section 3.2. The prior probabilities, π_j, need to satisfy the following conditions:

$$\sum_{j=1}^{m} \pi_j = 1, \quad \pi_j \geq 0.$$

The iterative Expectation-Maximisation (EM) algorithm was used to estimate the parameters of the beta mixture model, as described by (Leisch 2004). In particular, R package "flexmix" (Leisch 2004; Gruen and Leisch 2007, 2008) embedded in R package "betareg" (Cribari-Neto and Zeileis 2010; Gruen et al. 2012) was applied to estimate the model. Figure 4 illustrates the two-stage mixture model as a decision tree.

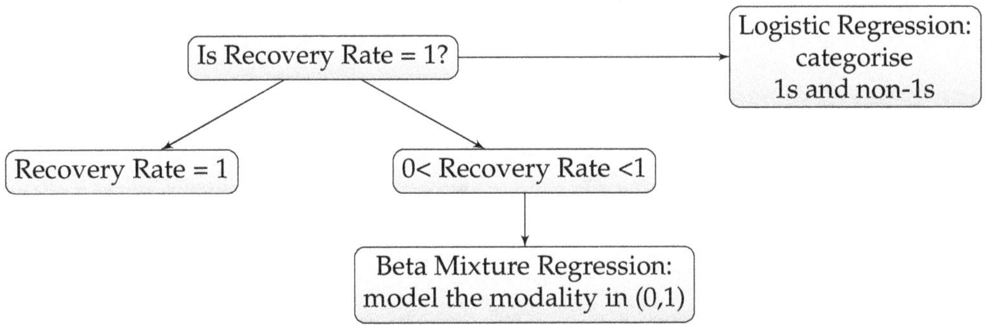

Figure 4. Estimate the expected value of RR using two-stage decision tree model.

The choice of m in the model depends on the number of clusters expected in the data. Based on our analysis of the recoveries for the dataset we used, $m = 2$ was used since this corresponded to the two modes we see in the RR distribution for RR < 1, as shown in Figure 1. If it is not clear how many clusters may exist, approaches based on AIC can be used.

Predictions Using the Beta Mixture Model

Given the beta mixture model, we need to predict the RR for new clients based on their information, i.e., X_{new} and W_{new}. Figure 5 shows a flowchart explaining how to calculate the estimated RR from the beta mixture model. This gives an expected value of RR y conditional on the cluster M_j. Therefore, we need to first identify which cluster the new observation belongs to. Even though the R package "betareg" (Cribari-Neto and Zeileis 2010; Gruen et al. 2012) can compute the conditional expectation for us, it does not identify which cluster the new points should be assigned to. Therefore, we propose a method to do this. In general, there are two feasible approaches to assign a new observation to M_j:

1. Assign the new observation to the cluster that achieves the highest log-likelihood. This is a hard clustering approach, which assigns the observation to exactly one cluster (Fraley and Raftery. 2002).
2. Assign the new observation to each cluster j with probability $P(M_j)$. This is a soft clustering approach, which assigns the observation to a percentage weighted cluster (Leisch 2004).

Decomposing the expected value of y using the Law of Total Expectation, we get

$$E(y \mid x_i) = \sum_{j=1}^{m} P(M_j|x_i)E(y|x_i, M_j) \tag{12}$$

where $E(y|x_i, M_j)$ is calculated from the beta mixture model prediction (refer to Figure 5). We can replace $P(M_j|x_i) = \frac{f(x_i|M_j)P(M_j)}{f(x_i)}$ where $f(x_i) = \sum_{j=1}^{m} f(x_i|M_j)P(M_j)$, to get

$$E(y \mid x_i) = \frac{\sum_{j=1}^{m} f(x_i|M_j)P(M_j)E(y|x_i, M_j)}{f(x_i)} \tag{13}$$

where $P(M_j)$ is the prior probability of belonging to cluster M_j. The density $f(x_i|M_j)$ is estimated using kernel density estimation,

$$\hat{f}(x^{new}) = \sum_{i=1}^{n} \frac{1}{n\prod_{k=1}^{d} h_{i,k}} \prod_{k=1}^{d} K(\frac{x_k^{new} - x_{i,k}}{h_{i,k}})$$

where $K(\cdot)$ is the Gaussian kernel (Azzalini and Menardi 2014) and d is the number of dimensions in data x. In addition, x_i may be high-dimensional, which makes the kernel density estimation computationally expensive. As a remedy, we applied Principal Component Analysis (PCA) to reduce the dimension of x_i, and then kernel density estimation was performed in the reduced dimension space.

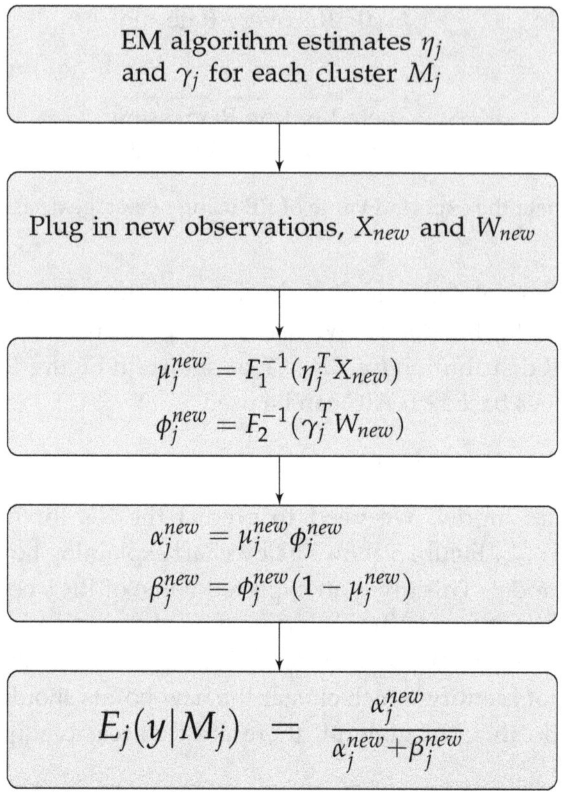

Figure 5. Prediction of RR conditional on each cluster M_j.

Approach 1: Maximum log-likelihood.

Given a new observation x_i, choose j that maximises the density:

$$\arg\max_j \quad \log f(y|x_i, M_j),$$

which is computed using the log-likelihood function. If the objective function is maximised with respect to Cluster M_j, then set

$$P(M_j|x_i) = 1 \text{ and } P(M_k|x_i) = 0 \text{ for all } k \neq j$$

and hence, from Equation (12), the expected value of y is given by $E(y|x_i, M_1)$.

Approach 2: Prior Probability.

Treat $P(M_j)$ as a prior estimated using methods given in Table 1 and use in Equation (13) for soft clustering. By substituting $P(M_j)$ given in Table 1 into Equation (13), we can compute $E(y \mid x)$ for $y \in (0, 1)$.

Table 1. Determining $P(M_j)$ in Approach 2.

Approach 2	$P(M_1)$	$P(M_2)$
π_j prior	Extract π_j from the EM algorithm $\pi_j[1]$	Extract π_j from the EM algorithm $\pi_j[2]$
Prior based on training set cluster size ratio	$\frac{\text{Cluster 1 size}}{\text{Total sample size}}$	$\frac{\text{Cluster 2 size}}{\text{Total sample size}}$
Indifferent Prior	$\frac{1}{2}$	$\frac{1}{2}$

After calculating $E(y \mid x)$ for the interval (0, 1) using the beta mixture model, the boundary 1 needs to be taken into consideration using a logistic regression model. From the decision tree defined in Figure 4, the logistic regression can provide the estimates at the first leaf node: $P(y = 1 \mid X = x)$. Then, the overall expectation of RR $y \in (0, 1]$ is

$$\begin{aligned} E(y \mid x) &= P(y=1 \mid x)E(y \mid x, y=1) \quad + \quad P(0<y<1 \mid x)E(y \mid x, 0<y<1) \\ &= P(y=1 \mid x) \times 1 \quad + \quad (1 - P(y=1 \mid x))\, E(y \mid x, 0<y<1) \\ &= P(y=1 \mid x) \quad + \quad (1 - P(y=1 \mid x))\, E(y \mid x, 0<y<1) \end{aligned} \tag{14}$$

where $E(y \mid x, 0 < y < 1)$ is the predicted RR from the beta mixture model using Approach 1 or 2.

4. Results

The linear model had an adjusted R^2 of 0.69, which was considerably higher than most models of RR (e.g., see Bellotti and Crook (2012); Loterman et al. (2012)), which could be explained by the richness of data, especially collections information. We expected that the linear regression model was misspecified, due to the range of the outcome variable and this is confirmed in the residual vs. fitted plot for the model and a Breusch-Pagan test for heteroscedasticity ($p < 0.0001$).

For the beta mixture model, we used all variables for X, but variable selection for W based firstly on the output of stepwise selection using AIC in linear regression and then on a series of likelihood ratio tests. The result was the selection of four variables for W: pre-recovery rate, post balance, customer payment frequency and credit bureau score. Table 2 shows parameter estimates for η and γ for the two clusters, along with coefficient estimates under standard beta regression in the interval (0, 1) for comparison.

In Table 2, there are "NA" values for some of the p-values in the beta mixture model. This is because the estimation algorithm could not produce reliable standard errors in these cases. We can see that the significance of variables was *diluted* by the two clusters. For instance, credit bureau score was significant in the standard beta regression with a p-value of 0.0022, but in the beta mixture model, it was not significant for either of the clusters, taking a significance level of 5%. The direction of association of coefficient estimates in beta mixture model for both clusters were mostly consistent, where the estimates were significant (at 5% level), although magnitude of association differed. Pre-Recovery Rate for γ component was the only exception to this observation. The model also demonstrated some interesting significant associations between some variables and RR: taking insurance showed higher recoveries and having a record at the bad debt bureau was associated with lower recovery rates. In addition, the recoveries, pre-purchase, were positively correlated with future RR, although total number of calls to customer had a negative association, perhaps because these were difficult customers from whom to collect, hence requiring more intervention.

Table 2. η and γ estimated by EM algorithm. M1 and M2 represent Clusters 1 and 2.

	Beta Mixture Model in (0, 1)				Beta Regression in (0, 1)	
Variables	**M1 Estimate**	**Pr(>∣z∣)**	**M2 Estimate**	**Pr(>∣z∣)**	**Betareg Estimate**	**Pr(>∣z∣)**
η						
(Intercept)	−0.67015	<0.0001	−2.62862	<0.0001	−1.80064	<0.0001
Product R	−0.03376	0.47711	−0.00766	0.59733	0.02270	0.41766
Principal	0.00056	NA	0.00114	NA	0.00081	0.00000
Interest	0.00065	<0.0001	0.00118	NA	0.00097	0.00000
Insurance	0.00082	<0.0001	0.00116	<0.0001	0.00086	<0.0001
Late Charges	0.00042	0.00578	0.00115	<0.0001	0.00072	<0.0001
Overlimit Fees	−0.00105	0.07594	0.00145	<0.0001	0.00018	0.52533
Credit limit	0.00004	NA	−0.00001	NA	−0.00003	<0.0001
Sex = Male	0.03659	0.17453	−0.01412	0.13364	0.00969	0.43796
Marital status =						
Divorced	−0.01175	0.85305	−0.01427	0.47359	−0.03144	0.25840
Married	−0.06356	0.10819	−0.01476	0.16836	−0.03850	0.01957
Single	0.00982	0.83178	0.00695	0.63324	0.00332	0.86926
Widow	−0.14627	0.19497	0.02311	0.51404	−0.03869	0.45314
Other	0.12328	0.17954	−0.03476	0.22384	0.04570	0.24125
Age	−0.00273	0.05378	−0.00038	0.42389	−0.00115	0.07159
Credit Bureau Score	0.00059	0.10337	0.00007	0.07890	0.00038	0.00222
Bureau bad debt	−0.32990	0.01290	-0.06936	<0.0001	−0.24123	0.00000
Cust Payment Freq	0.06530	<0.0001	0.03506	<0.0001	0.05046	<0.0001
Post Balance	−0.00106	NA	−0.00127	NA	−0.00103	0.00000
Total Paid Amount	0.00004	NA	−0.00038	NA	−0.00014	<0.0001
Total Calls	−0.00044	0.00515	−0.00023	0.00275	−0.00032	<0.0001
Total Contacts	−0.00136	0.03257	0.00040	0.08116	−0.00031	0.28402
Bank report Freq	−0.01719	<0.0001	−0.00407	<0.0001	−0.01117	<0.0001
Pre recovery Rate	0.56850	<0.0001	3.63447	<0.0001	2.26212	<0.0001
EmployerNoInfo	−0.04457	0.63820	−0.01277	0.65487	0.03439	0.38375
Total Number	−0.00949	0.16151	−0.00169	0.42951	−0.00776	0.00651
γ						
(Intercept)	1.60514	<0.0001	2.64737	<0.0001	1.45450	0.00000
Pre recovery Rate	0.49096	0.00025	−2.11510	<0.0001	−0.18488	0.01538
Post Balance	0.00039	<0.0001	0.00018	NA	0.00031	0.00000
Cust Payment Freq	0.02949	<0.0001	0.17612	<0.0001	0.07759	0.00000
Credit Bureau Score	−0.00058	0.00458	−0.00033	0.09534	−0.00028	0.01388

Following the procedure in Figure 5, the expected value of RR conditional on Cluster M_j was calculated based on the parameters η and γ estimated in Table 2. Since it was too time consuming to perform kernel density estimation on 29 variables, we reduced the dimension to six by employing PCA analysis, which greatly shortened the running time for two clusters' density estimations. Nevertheless, it is inevitable that information is lost during the dimension reduction process, which may result in weaker estimates. Figure 6 shows histograms of expected value of RR conditional on each jth cluster for the test dataset. The shapes of the two clusters are similar, except Cluster 2 has more estimates in the range 0.2 to 0.6.

Figure 7 shows four histograms of predicted RR corresponding to the four different priors defined in Table 1, in contrast to the true RR. The predicted value of beta mixture model combined with logistic regression model was calculated by applying the formula derived in Equation (14). Models with the different priors performed in a similar way. Importantly, they were all able to model the bimodal nature of the RR. The figure shows that none of the models ewre good at predicting the extreme values of RR close to 0 or 1, but this naturally follows from the fact that these predictions are estimates of *expected values* of RR, through Equation (12), albeit conditional on predictor variables, and thus do not represent the extremes in the distribution well. Further detail can be seen in Figure 8, which shows predicted RR against true RR. The strong correlation between predicted and true RR is clear. However, it is noticeable that, when true RR was around 0.6, the model tended to under-estimate for some observations. This was because the model was not perfect at detecting observations in Cluster 2. This suggests future improvements to the model to enhance its capacity to predict the correct latent cluster.

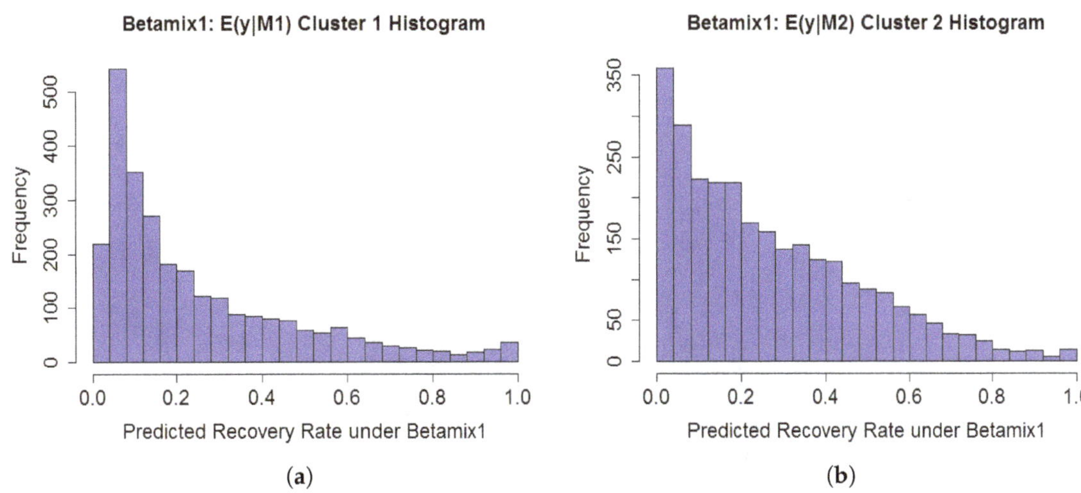

Figure 6. $E(y|M_j, X_{new})$ based on the Test dataset, for the two clusters ($m = 2$). (**a**) $E(y|M_1, X_{new})$; (**b**) $E(y|M_2, X_{new})$.

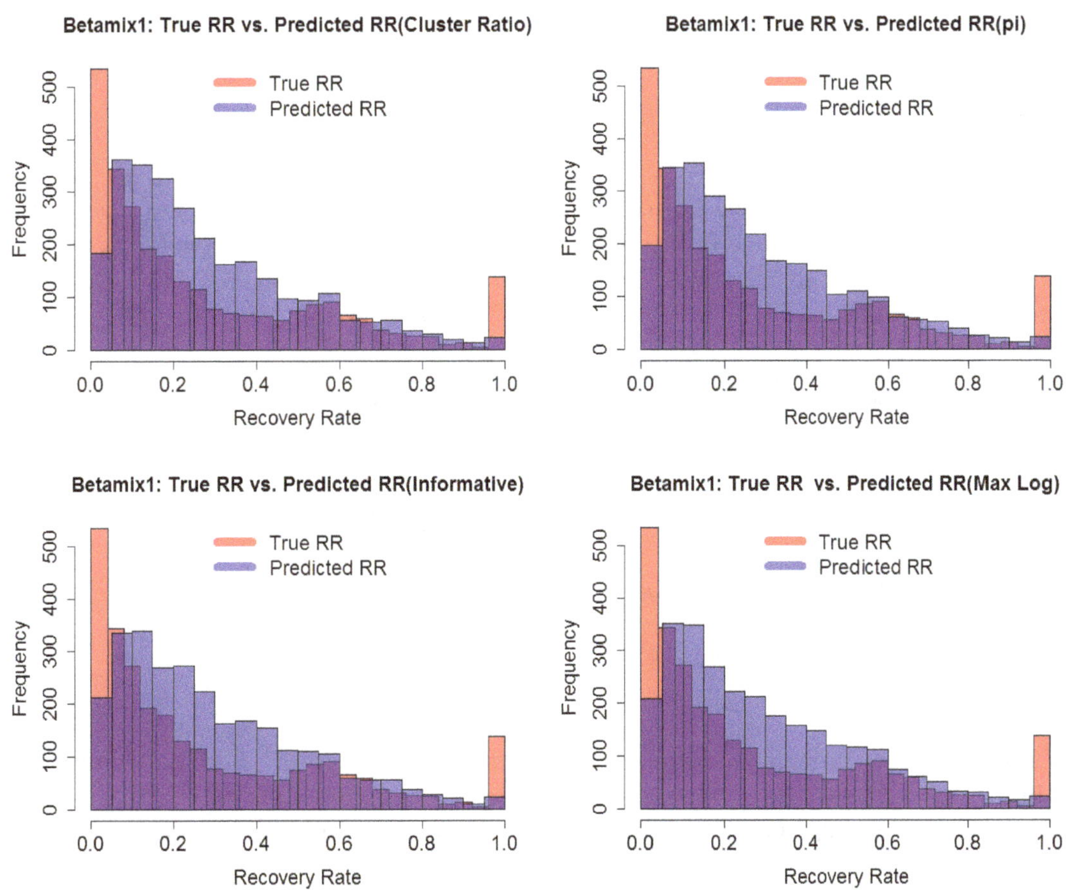

Figure 7. Predicted RR on test data ($n = 2746$) using beta mixture with four different priors, combined with logistic regression.

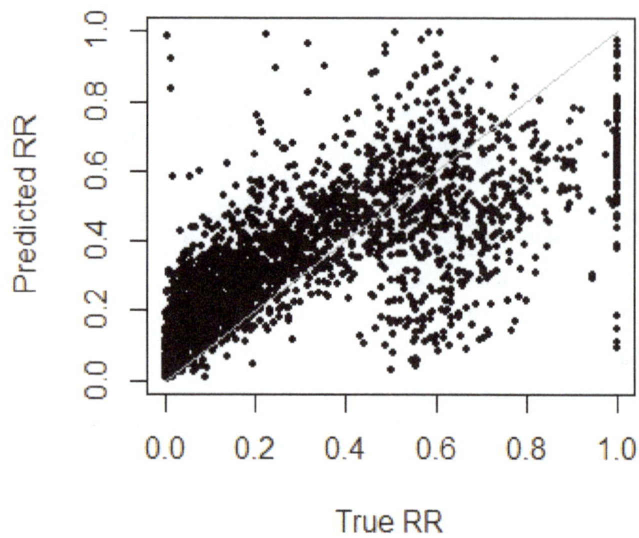

Figure 8. Predicted RR against true RR on test data ($n = 2746$) using beta mixture with the indifferent prior, combined with logistic regression.

Model Performance

Predictive performance was measured using K-fold cross validation with three performance measures popular in the literature on RR estimation: mean squared error (MSE), mean absolute error (MAE) and mean aggregate absolute error (MAAE). Since the sample size (8237) was relatively large and model estimation time was long, $K = 3$ was chosen. Let n be the sample size. Then,

$$MSE = \frac{1}{K}\sum_{k=1}^{K}\frac{1}{n/K}\sum_{i=1}^{n/K}(\hat{y}_{ki} - y_i)^2 = \frac{1}{n}\sum_{k=1}^{K}\sum_{i=1}^{n/K}(\hat{y}_{ki} - y_i)^2,$$

$$MAE = \frac{1}{K}\sum_{k=1}^{K}\frac{1}{n/K}\sum_{i=1}^{n/K}|\hat{y}_{ki} - y_i| = \frac{1}{n}\sum_{k=1}^{K}\sum_{i=1}^{n/K}|\hat{y}_{ki} - y_i|.$$

MAAE is the MAE at segment level (Thomas and Bijak 2015) and defined here as

$$MAAE = \frac{1}{V}\sum_{i=1}^{V}\frac{1}{|S_i|}\left|\sum_{j\in S_i}(y_j - \hat{y}_j))\right|$$

where V is the number of segments expressed as disjoint index sets $S_1, \cdots, S_V$. The segments could express different characteristics, e.g., risk bands. However, for this study, each segment was a different random sample from the test data with approximately the same sample size and jointly exhaustive. We used $V = 100$ since this gave a balance of number of segments approximately equal to number of observations in each segment. MSE, MAE and MAAE are all penalty measures, thus the smaller the value, the better the model. Since the RR is a financial ratio between 0 and 1, the MAE can reflect the size of the error in a more intuitive and direct way. If one is interested in the segment portfolio level, then the MAAE should be used.

All models were trained on the same partitions of data into cross validation folds, to avoid bias being introduced due to different samples. Table 3 shows the results. There was little difference between results for the various linear regressions, with or without variable selection or Lasso penalty, in terms of predictive performance. The last linear model, "excluding Dataset 2", was built without predictor variables from Dataset 2. This showed noticeably worse performance than the other linear models, especially for MAE, which demonstrates that including past recoveries data (i.e., Dataset 2) improved performance. The standard beta regression model, with and without zero-inflation, performed much worse than linear regression, but the beta mixture model with logistic regression gave the best performance on all three measures. The different priors gave slightly different performances but are not very much different, although Approach 1 method for selecting cluster assignment (max log-likelihood) was slightly worse than Approach 2, soft clustering methods.

Table 3. Predictive results using three-fold cross validation.

Model	MSE	MAE	MAAE
Linear Regression			
Linear regression	0.024984	0.114268	0.025894
Stepwise linear regression	0.024752	0.113621	0.025700
Linear regression with Lasso	0.025228	0.114847	0.023739
Linear regression, excluding Dataset 2	0.026822	0.121385	0.026303
Beta regression			
Standard beta regression	0.085630	0.260459	0.161366
Inflated beta regression	0.076650	0.216374	0.048466
Beta mixture model combined with logistic regression			
Max log-likelihood	0.018750	0.095432	0.030629
Prior based on R Flexmix π_j	0.018460	0.091833	0.023991
Prior based on training set cluster size ratio	0.019325	0.092225	0.022594
Indifferent Prior	0.018030	0.092399	0.026298

5. Conclusions

Linear regression, beta regression, inflated beta regression, and a beta mixture model combined with logistic regression were applied to model the recovery rate of non-performing loans. The models' predictive performances were measured using mean squared error, mean absolute error and mean aggregate absolute error under three-fold cross validation. To produce predictions from the beta mixture model, methods of hard and soft clustering were developed and the soft clustering approaches gave marginally better predictive performance. Theoretically, the proposed model, beta mixture model combined with logistic regression model, should be a suitable model to predict recovery rate for this data since it allows us to model the multimodality in the dataset and takes extra consideration of the boundary value. Indeed, we found that it achieved the best results amongst the models. Stepwise linear regression also achieved relatively good performance; however, the normality and homoscedasticity assumptions did not hold. In our experiments, we also found that inclusion of previous collections data boosted predictive performance.

We believe the beta mixture model is useful for modelling RR because it is explaining different servicing strategies. In the case of our study, the cluster with mode around 0.55 is likely expressing those loans for which the debt servicer has agreed with the borrower to repay just a proportion of the outstanding debt. There may be servicing strategies in other bad debt portfolios that could be discovered using a similar mixture model or clustering approach. We developed a technique to predict the correct latent cluster for new observations and this works well. However, results suggest that further work to refine this aspect of the use of the model could yield improved performance.

Author Contributions: Conceptualisation, H.Y. and T.B.; methodology, H.Y. and T.B.; validation, T.B.; investigation and statistical modelling, H.Y.; data analysis, H.Y.; writing—original draft preparation, H.Y..; writing—review and editing, T.B.; and supervision, T.B.

Funding: This research received no external funding.

Acknowledgments: We wish to thank the anonymous debt collection company for use of their data and their expertise, which was essential to understand the meaning and context of the data. We would also like to thank

Tommaso Pappagallo who did preliminary data analysis as part of his MSci project, which was useful in taking this project work forward.

Conflicts of Interest: The authors declare no conflict of interest.

Abbreviations

The following abbreviations are used in this manuscript:

IRB	Internal ratings based
RR	Recovery rate
LGD	Loss given default
PD	Probability of default
EAD	Exposure at default
EM	Expectation-Maximisation (algorithm)
MSE	Mean square error
MAE	Mean absolute error
MAAE	Mean absolute aggregate error

Appendix A

Table A1. Descriptive statistics. $n = 8237$. For numeric variables: min, mean (standard deviation), max. For factors, frequency (%age) for each level. All predictive data is collected prior to servicing.

Variable	Type	Description	Statistics
RR post	numeric	Recovery rate (outcome variable)	0.000508, 0.280 (0.283), 1
Product	factor	Type of loan	C:7468 (90.7%), R:769 (9.3%)
Principal	numeric	Original loan amount	0, 3120 (2330), 15000
Interest	numeric	Interest payments	0, 551 (439), 3380
Insurance	numeric	Insurance fees	0, 42 (84.6), 953
Late charges	numeric	Late charge fees	0, 269 (109), 1470
Overlimit fees	numeric	Over credit limit fees	0, 13.3 (24.6), 315
Creditlimit	numeric	Credit limit	0, 4560 (2660), 13800
Sex	factor	Sex	F:3196 (38.8%), M:5041 (61.2%)
Married	factor	Marriage status	0:1201 (14.6%), D:518 (6.3%), M:3929 (47.7%), O:217 (2.6%), S:2230 (27.1%), W:142 (1.7%)
Age	numeric	Age	1, 48.7 (11.1), 87
DelphiScore	integer	Credit bureau score	0, 298 (138), 443
Bureau Sub 1	factor	Loan is in the servicer's bureau (1 = True)	0: 1520 (18.5%), 1: 6717 (81.5%)
CustPaymentFreq	integer	Customer repayment frequency	1, 7.56 (5.59), 29
Post Balance	numeric	Exposure amount at start of servicing	0, 3130 (2630), 15900
Total paid amount	numeric	Total net paid amount	−275, 1200 (1100), 11200
Total calls	numeric	Total number of calls	0, 104 (106), 911
Total contacts	numeric	Total number of contacts (except calls)	0, 28.5 (26.5), 196
Bankreport Freq	numeric	Bank reporting frequency	0, 11.6 (7.92), 26
Pre recovery rate	numeric	Recovery rate	−0.130, 0.258 (0.217), 2.89
Employer	factor	Employer known	EmployerProvided:8053 (97.8%), NoInfo:184 (2.2%)
Total number	integer	Total number of loan accounts	0, 2.3 (2.43), 68

References

Azzalini, Adelchi, and Giovanna Menardi. 2014. Clustering via nonparametric density estimation: The R package pdfCluster. *Journal of Statistical Software* 57: 1–26. [CrossRef]

Bank for International Settlements. 2001. *The Internal Ratings-based Approach.* Basel: Bank for International Settlements.

Bellotti, Tony, and Jonathan Crook. 2012. Loss given default models incorporating macroeconomic variables for credit cards. *International Journal of Forecasting* 28: 171–82. [CrossRef]

Calabrese, Raffaella. 2012. Predicting bank loan recovery rates with a mixed continuous-discrete model. *Applied Stochastic Models in Business and Industry* 30: 99–114. [CrossRef]

Cribari-Neto, Francisco, and Achim Zeileis. 2010. Beta regression in R. *Journal of Statistical Software* 34: 1–24. [CrossRef]

Ferrari, Silvia, and Francisco Cribari-Neto. 2004. Beta regression for modelling rates and proportions. *Journal of Applied Statistics* 31: 799–815. [CrossRef]

Fraley, Chris, and Adrian E Raftery. 2002. Model-based clustering, discriminant analysis, and density estimation. *Journal of the American Statistical Association* 97: 611–31. [CrossRef]

Friedman, Jerome, Trevor Hastie, and Robert Tibshirani. 2010. Regularization paths for generalized linear models via coordinate descent. *Journal of Statistical Software* 33: 1–22. [CrossRef] [PubMed]

Gruen, Bettina, Ioannis Kosmidis, and Achim Zeileis. 2012. Extended beta regression in R: Shaken, stirred, mixed, and partitioned. *Journal of Statistical Software* 48: 1–25. [CrossRef]

Gruen, Bettina, and Friedrich Leisch. 2007. Fitting finite mixtures of generalized linear regressions in R. *Computational Statistics & Data Analysis* 51: 5247–52.

Gruen, Bettina and Friedrich Leisch. 2008. Flexmix version 2: Finite mixtures with concomitant variables and varying and constant parameters. *Journal of Statistical Software* 28: 1–35. [CrossRef]

Hastie, Trevor, and Brad Efron. 2013. *lars: Least Angle Regression, Lasso and Forward Stagewise.* R package version 1.2. Available online: https://cran.r-project.org/web/packages/lars/lars.pdf (accessed on 18 February 2019).

Ji, Yuan, Chunlei Wu, Ping Liu, Jing Wang, and Kevin R. Coombes. 2005. Applications of beta-mixture models in bioinformatics. *Bioinformatics* 21: 2118–22. [CrossRef] [PubMed]

Laurila, Kirsti, Bodil Oster, Claus L. Andersen, Philippe Lamy, Torben Orntoft, Olli Yli-Harja, and Carsten Wiuf. 2011. A beta-mixture model for dimensionality reduction, sample classification and analysis. *BMC Bioinformatics* 12: 215. [CrossRef] [PubMed]

Leisch, Friedrich. 2004. Flexmix: A general framework for finite mixture models and latent class regression in R. *Journal of Statistical Software* 11: 1–38. [CrossRef]

Loterman, Gert, Iain Brown, David Martens, Christophe Mues, and Bart Baesens. 2012. Benchmarking regression algorithms for loss given default modeling. *International Journal of Forecasting* 28: 161–70. [CrossRef]

Mittelhammer, Ron C., George Judge, and Douglas Miller. 2000. *Econometric Foundations*, 1st ed. Cambridge: Cambridge University Press.

Moustafa, Nour, Gideon Creech, and Jill Slay. 2018. Anomaly Detection System using Beta Mixture Models and Outlier Detection. In *Progress in Computing, Analytics and Networking. Advances in Intelligent Systems and Computing*. Edited by Prasant Kumar Pattnaik, Siddharth Swarup Rautaray, Himansu Das and Janmenjoy Nayak. Singapore: Springer, vol. 710. [CrossRef]

Nocedal, Jorge, and Stephen J. Wright. 1999. *Numerical Optimization*, 1st ed. Berlin: Springer.

Papke, Leslie, and Jeffrey Wooldridge. 1996, 11. Econometric methods for fractional response variables with an application to 401(k) plan participation rates. *Journal of Applied Econometrics 11*, 619–32. [CrossRef]

Qi, Min, and Xinlei Zhao. 2011. Comparison of modeling methods for loss given default. *Journal of Banking & Finance* 35: 2842–55.

Thomas, Lyn, and Katarzyna Bijak. 2015. Impact of Segmentation on the Performance Measures of LGD Models. Available online: https://crc.business-school.ed.ac.uk/wp-content/uploads/sites/55/2017/02/Impact-of-Segmentation-on-the-Performance-Measures-of-LGD-Models-Lyn-Thomas-and-Katarzyna-Bijak.pdf (accessed on 18 February 2019).

5

CEO Overconfidence and Shadow-Banking Life Insurer Performance Under Government Purchases of Distressed Assets

Shi Chen [1], Jyh-Horng Lin [2,*], Wenyu Yao [1] and Fu-Wei Huang [3]

1 School of Economics, Southwestern University of Finance and Economics, Chengdu 611130, China; chenshi@swufe.edu.cn (S.C.); ywy@smail.swufe.edu.cn (W.Y.)
2 Department of International Business, Tamkang University, New Taipei City 25137, Taiwan
3 Department of Management Sciences, Tamkang University, New Taipei City 25137, Taiwan; kwala.wei@mail.tku.edu.tw
* Correspondence: lin9015@mail.tku.edu.tw

Abstract: In this paper, we develop a contingent claim model to evaluate the equity, default risk, and efficiency gain/loss from managerial overconfidence of a shadow-banking life insurer under the purchases of distressed assets by the government. Our paper focuses on managerial overconfidence where the chief executive officer (CEO) overestimates the returns on investment. The investment market faced by the life insurer is imperfectly competitive, and investment is core to the provision of profit-sharing life insurance policies. We show that CEO overconfidence raises the default risk in the life insurer's equity returns, thereby adversely affecting the financial stability. Either shadow-banking involvement or government bailout attenuates the unfavorable effect. There is an efficiency gain from CEO overconfidence to investment. Government bailout helps to reduce the life insurer's default risk, but simultaneously reduce the efficiency gain from CEO overconfidence. Our results contribute to the managerial overconfidence literature linking insurer shadow-banking involvement and government bailout in particular during a financial crisis.

Keywords: profit-sharing life insurance policy; CEO overconfidence; shadow-banking transaction; bailout

---

1. Introduction

The bailout of American International Group (AIG) by the government taking 80% stake on 16 September 2008, was one of the defining moments of the financial crisis (Breitenfellner and Wagner 2010). The bailout was supported because the government perceived the near failure of AIG as too-big-to-fail and was not ready to have AIG fail.[1] The 2008 global financial crisis raises fundamental issues about recapitalizing insurance institutions, particularly from the standpoint of insurer survival. In addition, a growing body of literature examines managerial overconfidence in financial decisions during a financial crisis (e.g., Fahlenbrach and Stulz 2011; Ma 2014; Ho et al. 2016). Our study also places stress on the chief executive officer (CEO) overconfidence. CEOs overestimate the returns on their investment projects and underestimate losses, incurring higher agency costs

---

1 The assistance from the Troubled Asset Relief Program (TARP) changed after the 2008 election. Attention focused on evaluating the financial circumstances of particular large institutions whose financing structure problematic. TARP was created to meet the needs for what the Treasury termed "exceptional assistance" by three large institutions: AIG, Citigroup, and Bank of America because they were "too big to fail" (Calomiris and Khan 2015).

(Heaton 2002; Malmendier and Tate 2005). Berry-Stölzle et al. (2018) provide empirical evidence that CEO overconfidence associated with relatively low loss reserves results in increasing reported earnings. We extend this strand of the literature by examining the impact of the bailout on bankruptcy prediction when CEO overconfidence affecting investment decisions is considered in a life insurance company.[2]

We focus on a life insurance company for two reasons. First, life insurers are the business of providing policyholder protection from risks. Insurance helps economic activities by giving policyholder risk coverage and implicit confidence to make investments that they might otherwise deem too risky (Insurance Europe and Oliver Wyman 2013). Investment returns are an integral part of the life insurance policy itself. In particular, the level of guarantee that can be offered on the profit-sharing life insurance policies is directly affected by the available investments, while the level of participation on existing policies depends on the expected investment performance. A cognitive bias from CEO overconfidence becomes crucial to investment decisions of life insurers.[3] Second, Harrington (2009) examines the role of AIG and its impact on the recent financial crisis. The author argues that the financial authority's perception of AIG as "too big to fail" may have resulted in reducing the market discipline as it gives AIG an inappropriate competitive advantage. However, most previous studies on market structure in the life insurance literature have relied on an assumption of perfect competition.[4] This assumption is not applicable to asset and life insurance policy markets since such markets are always highly concentrated where life insurers set rates and face random asset and policy levels, implicitly consistent with the "too big to fail" argument. Life insurance companies have unique features and provide a great natural laboratory for examining the effect of CEO overconfidence on insurer interest margin management in general. The insurer interest margin, defined as the spread between asset interest rate and guaranteed interest rate in our model, conveys vital information for the efficiency of insurer performance. As the spread is so important to insurer profitability, the issues of how it is optimally determined and how it adjusts to changes in the insurance environment deserve closer scrutiny.

In this paper, we examine the following questions that remain unanswered in the literature. First, what are the most likely effects of CEO overconfidence on the default risk in the shadow-banking life insurance company's equity returns in particular when the optimal insurer interest margin is determined? The existing studies on this topic are largely silent on the optimal insurer interest margin determination. Second, how does the bailout program of buying distressed assets affect the efficiency gain/loss from CEO overconfidence? In this question, our primary emphasis is also the selection of the life insurance company's optimal interest margin, which is generally not addressed in life insurance related work. In light of previous work, the purpose of this paper is to develop a contingent claim model to evaluate the equity and associated default risk of a life insurance company. The developed model of insurer spread behavior integrates the risk of a premature default to the equity return valuation along the line of Grosen and Jørgensen (2002) with managerial overconfidence, shadow insurance, and bailout considerations. The comparative static analyses of the model are investigated to determine the influence of CEO overconfidence on optimal insurer interest margin decisions and further on bankruptcy predictions.

Our contribution to the managerial overconfidence literature is threefold. First, we complement the literature on CEO overconfidence by improving on the perfectly competitive model and studying the dichotomous insurer interest margin determination. Our findings confirm the bankruptcy prediction that the life insurance company's default risk is positively associated with CEO overconfidence at various levels of shadow-banking activity involvement or the bailout program of buying distressed assets. Second, we focus on the bailout program during a financial crisis by

---

2 Hereafter, the terms "insurer" or "life insurer" refer to "life insurance company".

3 The insurance industry is one of the largest institutional investors in Europe (Insurance Europe and Oliver Wyman 2013).

4 For example, see Briys and de Varenne (1994); Grosen and Jørgensen (2002); Chen and Suchanecki (2007); and Ceci et al. (2017). The issue of life insurance settlement presented by Hong and Seog (2018) is an exception.

considering CEO overconfidence and confirming the bankruptcy prediction negatively associated with buying distressed assets at various levels of the cognitive bias from CEO overconfidence and shadow-banking activity involvement. Finally, we also complement the CEO overconfidence literature by elaborating on the issue of the efficiency gain/loss from insurer investment with CEO overconfidence in lieu of CEO rationality. The elaboration allows us to contribute to the topic of CEO overconfidence and financial crisis when the risk of a premature default to the valuation of a life insurance company is considered.

This paper is organized as follows. Section 2 reviews the related literature as a motivation of this study. Section 3 describes the model framework of a life insurance company. Section 4 theoretically discusses optimal decisions and comparative static analyses. Our numerical results are presented in Section 5. Section 6 concludes the paper.

2. Literature and Motivation

This section provides a literature review and presents the motivation of this study. First, in the psychology literature, the theory on managerial overconfidence is based on mis-calibration and the "better-than-average" effect (Alicke 1985; Moore and Healy 2008; Merkle and Weber 2011). Extrapolating from the psychology literature and the overinvestment view, Malmendier and Tate (2005), Goel and Thakor (2008), and Ben-David et al. (2013) argue that overconfident CEOs are convinced of their ability to generate higher returns on their investment projects, resulting in overinvestment. Hirshleifer and Luo (2001) predict that overconfident CEOs overvalue the prospects of borrowers (investors) and underestimate the riskiness of their investments. Adrian and Westerfield (2009) analyze a continuous-time principal-agent model with heterogeneous beliefs. Giat et al. (2009) complement the study of Adrian and Westerfield (2009) and develop a structural model to investigate the effects of asymmetric beliefs and agency conflicts on dynamic principal-agent relationships. By calibrating the model to data on pharmaceutical R&D projects, the authors show that optimism indeed significantly influences project values. Berry-Stölzle et al. (2018) study the relationships between CEO overconfidence and loss-reserving practices in the U.S. property-liability insurance industry. While we also elaborate the issue of managerial overconfidence and overinvestment, our focus on the CEO overconfidence aspects of a life insurer takes our analysis in a different direction.

The second strand is the literature on the channel from which CEOs influence investment. CEOs affect the quality of the information available to the board of directors and investors as well as corporate investment decisions (e.g., Adams and Ferreira 2007). Goel and Thakor (2008) find that the board is likely to end up with a pool of overconfident managers from which to choose a CEO and that moderate degrees of overconfidence actually benefit the shareholders. Dyreng et al. (2010) argue that a CEO can affect tax avoidance by setting the "tone at the top" with regard to the firm's tax activities. This seems to suggest that even if (overconfident) CEOs do not directly influence investment decisions, they influence these decisions that are made by, for example, a CEO or other managers within the firm by having an aggressive personality or by hiring individuals with similar mindsets.[5] A potential issue with using the "tone at the top" argument is that in this particular setting not only do CEOs not directly make the decision, but in many cases investment decisions for life insurers are made external to the firm by investment advisors (e.g., Kim et al. 2017).[6] Our modeling provides a new perspective on how CEO overconfidence affects corporate investment decisions; the introduction of CEO overconfidence into the model makes the life insurers now face a trade-off between risky asset payments and net

[5] We thank an anonymous reviewer whose detailed comments helped us to avoiding ignoring the potential argument of "tone at the top" in the literature.

[6] The investment advisors are common in the life insurance industry and potentially give more thought to how CEO overconfidence translates to investment decisions. We would like to thank an anonymous reviewer for pointing this possibility out to us.

liabilities. Our results provide a useful complement to the argument on the channel from which CEOs influence corporate investment.

The third one is the recent literature on how the life insurance company gets involved in shadow-banking activities.[7] Pozsar et al. (2013) point out that the life insurance company may also get involved in shadow banking activities that take place without direct and explicit access to public sources of liquidity or credit backstops. Life insurers adapted to regulatory policies, and over the years have made extensive use of captive reinsurance or shadow insurance as a way to circumvent stricter reserve requirements and artificially boost risk-based capital ratios; Irresberger and Peng (2017) discuss shadow insurance as a new form of regulatory arbitrage used by U.S. life insurers. Insurance Europe (2014) addresses the most common shadow-banking activities, including insurance securitization, catastrophe bonds, mortgage insurance, and securities lending, in which insurers engage, explaining why they are being undertaken as well as the potential benefits and associated risks. Irresberger and Peng (2017) study shadow insurance usage and capital management in life insurance groups. One of their main findings demonstrates that reinsurance agreements with shadow insurers are used by large and well capitalized insurance groups that deviate from their optimal structure. Our work is related to the literature on shadow-banking engagement on the asset side of the balance sheet where life insurers take some investment risk, in particular considering managerial overconfidence impacting insurer investment decisions.

The fourth is a growing body of literature on government bailout, focusing on the insurance industry. For example, Berry-Stölzle et al. (2014) argue that the government bailout through the Capital Purchase Program to assist U.S. life insurers during the 2008 financial crisis is unnecessary. According to their argument, there is no change in behavior in life insurers' demand for capital during the financial crisis. Niehaus (2014) also concludes that there is no evidence of a differential relationship between life insurers' internal capital flows and their fundamentals during the financial crisis. Barnes (2016) addresses the following crucial question. Did life insurers benefit from TARP or regulatory forbearance during the financial crisis of 2008–2009? An important answer addresses that regulatory forbearance acts as a substitute for the receipt of TARP funds. Lin et al. (2018) investigate how a bank's default risk is affected by distress acquisition. The authors find that the acquirer bank incentivized by the government's purchases of distressed loans under a certain level is likely to proceed with the distress acquisition. Under the circumstances, loan purchase assistance, as such, makes the bank less prone to risk-taking, thereby contributing to the stability of the banking system. Gómez and Ponce (2018) propose a formal model to study the optimal regulation of insurance firms. The authors find that in the absence of systemic risk, the optimal regulation may be implemented by capital regulation and by actuarially fair technical reserve. However, these instruments are not sufficient when insurance companies are exposed to systemic risk. Hsieh et al. (2014) show that before the Sarbanes Oxley Act of 2002 (SOX), companies of overconfident CEOs were more likely than other CEOs to engage in managing earnings through accelerating the timing of cash flow from operations and achieving analyst forecast benchmarks. From a regulatory perspective, their results illustrate that SOX was at least partially successful in curbing some overly aggressive earnings management behaviors. The primary difference between our model and these papers is that we consider the effects of managerial

---

[7] Shadow banking is huge globally, accounting for about 25% of total money transfers between savers and borrowers worldwide. Overviews of the shadow banking system are provided by Pozsar (2008), who catalogues different types of shadow banks and describes the asset and funding flows within the system, and Adrian and Shin (2009), who focus on the role of security brokers and dealers in the system and discuss implications for financial regulation. Gorton and Metrick (2010), and Pozsar et al. (2013) document that the growth of shadow banking has been largely driven by regulatory arbitrage. Plantin (2015) argues that tightening capital requirements may increase shadow banking activities and make banks that not willing to incur adverse selection costs very safe; alternatively, relaxing capital requirements may bring shadow banking activities back in the spotlight of regulation. However, Pozsar et al. (2013) and Jeffers and Baicu (2013) indicate that the interconnections between regular banking and shadow banking activities have negative consequences on financial stability.

overconfidence on insurer interest margin and associated bankruptcy prediction, explicitly considering TARP and shadow insurance during a financial crisis.

3. Model Framework

This section consists of four parts. A few simplifying assumptions are made in the first part. The remaining three parts focus on the valuation of the life insurance company's equity, the efficiency gain/loss from CEO overconfidence, and the bankruptcy prediction.

3.1. Assumptions

We develop a contingent claim model to evaluate the equity of a life insurance company. All economic decisions are made and values are determined with a one-period horizon with two dates, 0 and 1, $t \in [0, 1]$. Since our goal is to demonstrate the distortionary behavior of overconfidence, we are silent on agency problems and assume that the insurer's manager maximizes the shareholder value. The only friction in the model comes from the insurer manager's inflated perception of the insurer investment opportunities. This perception follows Malmendier and Tate (2005).

By applying Grosen and Jørgensen (2002), the equity of the life insurance company can be viewed as a down-and-out call option on the company's earning-asset portfolio where default can occur at any time before the maturity date. The risk of a premature default is introduced, which is most likely to describe the life insurance company in distress. This is the reason that the shareholders of the life insurance company are recognized as the residual claimants on the company's assets after all other liabilities have been met. The strike price of the down-and-out call option is the book value of the company's liabilities when the value of the company's assets is less than the strike price, the company's equity value equals zero. The scenario indicates that shareholders have a limited liability, and if the life insurance company is declared insolvent at $t = 1$, they simply walk away. Under the scenario, life insurance policyholders (also liability holders) receive only what is left. When our model is developed, this story becomes clear.

As in the original work of Grosen and Jørgensen (2002), we assume that at time $t = 0$, the life insurance company owns a capital structure as illustrated in the balance sheet of Table 1. That is, for simplicity, we suppose that the liability holder, also the representative policyholder, whose premium payment at $t = 0$ constitutes the liability of the life insurance company, denoted by $L = \alpha A$ with $0 < \alpha < 1$, and the representative equity holder whose equity is accordingly denoted by $K = (1 - \alpha)A$ form a mutual company, the life insurance company. αA denotes the proportion of the initial assets financed by liabilities, while $(1 - \alpha)A$ denotes that financed by equity. Leverage α is a decision variable of the life insurance company.

Table 1. The life insurance company's balance sheet at $t = 0$.

Assets		Liabilities and Equity	
Assets	A	Liabilities	$L = \alpha A$
		Equity	$K = (1 - \alpha)A$
Total	A	Total	A

In our model, the initial portfolio of assets is assumed to be totally invested in risky assets subject to non-performance. Assets granted by the life insurance company belong to a single homogeneous class of fixed-rate claims with $t \in [0, 1]$. The demand of assets faced by the life insurance company is specified as a downward-sloping function $A(R_A)$ where R_A is the asset interest rate. The assumption of $\partial A / \partial R_A < 0$ implies that the life insurance company exercises some monopoly power in the asset market. Asset market as such is virtually always highly concentrated where the life insurance company sets rates and faces random asset levels. In addition, the investment rationally generates a stochastic future return $(1 + R_A)A$ realized at $t = 1$. The overconfident CEO overestimates future returns by percentage $\alpha_A \geq 0$.[8] This overestimation is due to Choi et al. (2018) that CEO overconfidence noted in mis-calibration and the "better-than-average" effect reveals a tendency in CEOs' overestimation of future payoffs on their investments.[9] Hence, for all levels of investment, the CEO perceives the expected return to be $(1 + R_A)(1 + \alpha_A)A$, with $\alpha_A = 0$ in the benchmark case of a rational CEO.[10] The CEO overconfidence formulated in our model is consistent with the theoretical prediction that overconfident CEOs overestimate the returns on their investment projects (Berry-Stölzle et al. 2018). Results to be derived from our model do not extend to the case where CEO overconfidence may reveal underestimated liabilities on life insurance policies.

Besides CEO overconfidence, the life insurance company in distress is assumed to be willing to participate in the bailout program of buying distressed assets by the government. We focus on the bailout program for a number of reasons.[11] Hoshi and Kashyap (2010) argue that buying distressed assets is an appropriate way to recapitalize financial institutions. However, the authors conclude that the bailout program lacks efficiency since assets cannot be purchased for more than their economic value. The efficiency issue in the bailout program of buying distressed assets will be re-examined based on our developing a contingent claim model to evaluate the equity of a life insurance company. Hoshi and Kashyap (2010) also argue that a distressed financial institution may refuse government bailout if the bailout generates an adverse signal that the institution is expected to have high future losses. Here, this is not the case that we focus on. According to Table 1, the expected repayments from the asset investment at $t = 1$ can be specified as $\theta(1 + R_B)(1 + \alpha_A)A$ in our model, where R_B is the security-market interest rate and θA with $0 < \theta < 1$ at $t = 0$ is the amount of buying distressed assets by the government. The condition of $R_A > R_B$ implies that the purchase of the assets comes at a discount to the book value of θA. The difference between R_A and R_B is the discount, which can be treated as the opportunity cost of bailout participation. The bailout θ is a decision variable of the regulatory authority.

Total assets are financed partly by profit-sharing life insurance policies including two common features: an interest rate guarantee and the contribution principle which entitles the policyholder to a participation in the life insurance company's investment surpluses (Briys and de Varenne 1994). The total payoff to the policyholder of such a life insurance contract at maturity consists of three parts: a guaranteed payment which is the initial premium payment compounded by the interest rate guarantee, a short put option resulting from the fact that the equity holder has a limited liability, and a bonus paying to policyholder a fraction δ of the positive difference of the actual performance of its share in the life insurance company's asset portfolio and the guaranteed amount at maturity (Chen and Suchanecki 2007). Furthermore, our model is assumed to determine the guaranteed interest rate policyholders should require to fully compensate them for the risks they face. The model is also driven by an imperfectly competitive market assumption about life insurance policies

---

8 If we think that CEO labor markets are efficient, we would expect certain types of firms to hire overconfident CEOs and other firms to hire non-overconfident CEOs. Prior studies deal with this. endogeneity (Ho et al. 2016; Berry-Stölzle et al. 2018). Since this perspective can be explored applying the exact same assumption of $\alpha_A > 0$, we believe this issue have no impact on the findings in our study. Another potential issue is that α_A is assumed to be independent to the expected return $(1 + R_A)A$. This assumption ignores the presence of asymmetric adjustment behavior and regime switch under financial turmoil. See Tsagkanos and Siriopoulos (2015) for an analysis on asymmetric effects via threshold cointegration approach.

9 Mis-calibration and the "better-than-average" bias are known to structure CEO overconfidence (e.g., see Merkle and Weber 2011). Miscalibration implies the excessive belief in one's precision, while the "better-than-average" bias implies the tendency to place one's performance and ability as superior to an average peer (e.g., see Moore and Healy 2008; Choi et al. 2018).

10 Malmendier and Tate (2005) develop a CEO overconfidence behavior of a firm with exactly this structure. In addition, our model is limited to the case of overconfidence behavior with overestimated of future payoffs on investments. However, this model is also applicable to the case of underestimated future returns when $\alpha_A < 0$. Since our results show that all the effects of α_A are monotonic, our results can be adapted to situations where α_A is less than zero and within a reasonable range. Adding this complexity affects none of qualitative comparative static results in the paper. The condition that $\alpha_A < 0$ may be used to analyze the assumption of under-confident CEOs. See, for example, Campbell et al. (2011) include a spectrum of confidence (they refer to it as "optimism").

11 As pointed out by Barnes (2016) in previous section, the 2008 financial crisis has witnessed large government bailouts of several life insurance companies worldwide, the most notable being AIG.

(Hong and Seog 2018). Specifically, the supply of life insurance policies faced by the life insurance company is governed by a positive-sloping supply function $L(R) = \alpha(1 + \alpha_A)Ae^R$, where R is the guaranteed rate chosen by the life insurance company. The condition of $\partial L/\partial R > 0$ indicates that the life insurance company conducts some monopoly power in the life insurance contract market.

In addition to balance-sheet insurance activities, we assume that the life insurance company is also involved in shadow-banking entrusted loans permitted by the Gramm-Leach-Bliley Act. This model follows Li and Lin (2016) to frame the entrusted loan transaction.[12] There are entrusted loans made by a trustor (a production firm in general) in the non-financial economy that is run through the life insurance company (the trustee) for legal reasons, but with the company indemnified from the credit risk of the borrowing firm by the trustor.[13] In the model, the fund M at $t = 0$ is lent through the life insurance company to the borrowing firm at an interest rate R_M as instructed by the trustor. The company helps collect $(1 + R_M)M$ at $t = 1$ from the borrowing firm on the behalf of the trustor. The life insurance company charges a commission fee mM, where $m > 0$, for the shadow-banking service as well as the risk burden for the transaction. Note that the life insurance company is not providing the capital for shadow-banking transactions.

3.2. *Equity*

With information about CEO overconfidence, shadow banking, and government bailout, we are ready to develop a contingent claim model along the line of Grosen and Jørgensen (2002). Toward that end, we assume that the market value of the life insurance company's asset portfolio V follows a geometric Brownian motion of the form:

$$\frac{dV}{V} = \mu dt + (\sigma + \frac{\alpha_A \sigma^2}{2})dW, \tag{1}$$

where

$$V = (1 - \theta)(1 + R_A)(1 + \alpha_A)A + (1 + R_M)M,$$

and where V is specified as the non-bailout value of the company's risky-asset repayments in its investments with overconfidence and the entrusted loan repayments in the shadow banking activities. A standard Wiener process is W. V is the expected value with an instantaneous expected rate of return μ and an instantaneous deviation of return $(\sigma + \alpha_A\sigma^2/2)$. More specifically, we argue that there is the potential for overconfident investment in the asset market, perhaps because the life insurance company has gained some inside information as to the quality of its asset portfolio. We adopt a very simple quadratic formulation where the instantaneous deviation raised is given by $(\sigma + \alpha_A\sigma^2/2)$. Here α_A measures the degree of overconfidence in investment in the asset market: the stronger it is, the more risky is overconfident investment relative to the rational case.

The life insurance company seeks to maximize its expected net equity:

$$S = Max\,\{0,\, Min\,[V - X,\, (1 - \delta\alpha)V - (1 - \delta)X]\}, \tag{2}$$

where

$$X = \alpha(1 + \alpha_A)Ae^R - \theta(1 + R_B)(1 + \alpha_A)A + (1 + R_M)M - mM,$$

[12] The goal of Li and Lin (2016) is to explore the role played by bank spread management under capital regulation in the commercial lending and shadow-banking entrusted lending activities. The role played by the trustee in Li and Lin (2016) is assumed to be a bank. This assumption is applicable to a case of a life insurance company permitted by regulation.

[13] Koijen and Yogo (2016) investigate the issue that life insurance companies use reinsurance to move liabilities from regulated companies that sell policies to shadow reinsures. What distinguishes our work from this literature is our focus on the question whether a life insurance company benefits or gets hurt from shadow banking activities on its asset portfolio, specifically including loans and/or entrusted loans.

and where net liabilities X consist of four parts: a guaranteed fixed payment which is the initial premium payment compounded by the interest rate guarantee, a return payment from the bailout asset to the company, a payment to the trustor in the shadow-banking transaction, and a commission fee income. Equation (2) can be rewritten as:

$$S = Max\,[0,\ V - X] - \delta\alpha Max\,[0,\ V - \frac{X}{\alpha}]. \tag{3}$$

The equity position is a hybrid position and its value as of time $t \in [0,\ 1]$ is specified as:

$$S = C(V,\ X) - \delta C(\alpha V,\ X), \tag{4}$$

where the equity S consists of two down-and-out call options: a long down-and-out call on the asset portfolio V with the strike equal to the promised payment X, and a short down-and-out call offsetting exactly the bonus of the liability holder. Both down-and-out call options are specified as follows. The value of $C(V,\ X)$ in Equation (4) is given by a down-and-out call:[14]

$$C(V,\ X) = [VN(b_1) - Xe^{-(R_B-R)}N(b_2)] - [V(\frac{H}{V})^{2\eta}N(b_3) - Xe^{-(R_B-R)}(\frac{H}{V})^{2\eta-2}N(b_4)], \tag{5}$$

where

$$H = \beta X,\ 0 < \beta < 1,$$

$$\eta = \frac{R_B - R}{(\sigma + \alpha_A\sigma^2/2)^2} + \frac{1}{2},$$

$$b_1 = \frac{1}{\sigma + \alpha_A\sigma^2/2}(\ln\frac{V}{X} + (R_B - R) + \frac{(\sigma + \alpha_A\sigma^2/2)^2}{2}),$$

$$b_2 = b_1 - \frac{1}{\sigma + \alpha_A\sigma^2/2},$$

$$b_3 = \frac{1}{\sigma + \alpha_A\sigma^2/2}(\ln\frac{H^2}{VX} + (R_B - R) + \frac{(\sigma + \alpha_A\sigma^2/2)^2}{2}),$$

$$b_4 = b_3 - \frac{1}{\sigma + \alpha_A\sigma^2/2},$$

and where $H = \beta X$ is specified as V that triggers bankruptcy (that is the barrier or knock-out value of the life insurance company), and β is defined as the barrier-to-debt ratio in the premature default mode. $R_B - R$ is the compounded riskless rate of return due to the specification of X. $N(\cdot)$ is the cumulative density function of the standard normal distribution. In Equation (5), the first term $[\cdot]$ on the right-hand side can be interpreted as the value viewed as a standard call option on V at the strike price of X, while the second term $[\cdot]$ can be interpreted as the down-and-in call option, lying dormant until a barrier is breached. Thus, Equation (5) illustrates a barrier option on the asset portfolio with strike equal to the promised payment at any time before the maturity date, called the residual barrier option. Analogously, the specification of $C(\alpha V,\ X)$ is given by:

$$C(\alpha V,\ X) = [\alpha VN(d_1) - Xe^{-(R_B-R)}N(d_2)] - [\alpha V(\frac{H}{\alpha V})^{2\eta}N(d_3) - Xe^{-(R_B-R)}(\frac{H}{\alpha V})^{2\eta-2}N(d_4)], \tag{6}$$

[14] We simplify our discussion by assuming a zero rebate upon failure in the formula for the down-and-out call option in the model.

where

$$d_1 = \frac{1}{\sigma + \alpha_A \sigma^2/2}(\ln \frac{\alpha V}{X} + (R_B - R) + \frac{(\sigma + \alpha_A \sigma^2/2)^2}{2}),$$

$$d_2 = d_1 - \frac{1}{\sigma + \alpha_A \sigma^2/2},$$

$$d_3 = \frac{1}{\sigma + \alpha_A \sigma^2/2}(\ln \frac{H^2}{\alpha V X} + (R_B - R) + \frac{(\sigma + \alpha_A \sigma^2/2)^2}{2}),$$

$$d_4 = d_3 - \frac{1}{\sigma + \alpha_A \sigma^2/2}.$$

3.3. *Efficiency Gain Prediction*

The return and the variance of the life insurance company's equity explicitly taking CEO overconfidence into account reveal the potentially substantial benefits and costs of relationship insurance. A question that arises is the extent to which CEO overconfidence adds efficiency gain/loss to the life insurance company when providing its insurance services. As far as insurer equity risk is concerned, the variance of the life insurance company's return σ_S will then be given by the Ronn and Verma (1986) formula:

$$\sigma_S = \frac{1}{2}(\sigma + \frac{\alpha_A \sigma^2}{2})^2 [\frac{V}{C(V,X)} \frac{\partial C(V,X)}{\partial V} + \delta \frac{\alpha V}{C(\alpha V,X)} \frac{\partial C(\alpha V,X)}{\partial \alpha V}], \tag{7}$$

With information about S in Equation (4) and σ_S in Equation (7), we can now compare the risk/return efficiency gain/loss from CEO overconfidence behavior. We apply Ergungor (2005) and specify the life insurance company's efficiency gain/loss differential as:

$$\Delta E = E(WF) - E(OF), \tag{8}$$

where

$$E(WF) = \frac{S(\alpha_A > 0)}{\sigma_S(\alpha_A > 0)},$$

$$E(OF) = \frac{S(\alpha_A = 0)}{\sigma_S(\alpha_A = 0)},$$

and where $E(WF)$ is defined as the ratio of equity return to equity standard deviation when CEO overconfidence reveals where $\alpha_A > 0$, and $E(OF)$ is also defined as the ratio when CEO rationality reveals where $\alpha_A = 0$ in our model. ΔE in Equation (8) can be viewed as the equity return differential, per unit of standard deviation, that accrues from insurer investment with CEO overconfidence in lieu of CEO rationality. $\Delta E > 0$ can be interpreted as efficiency gain from CEO overconfidence behavior, whereas $\Delta E < 0$ can be interpreted as efficiency loss.

3.4. *Bankruptcy Prediction*

In the following subsection, we illustrate one particular application of Equation (4) to the problem of bankruptcy prediction. We now use the model of Brockman and Turtle (2003) and adapt it to value the default probability in the life insurance company's equity returns. The valuation of Equation (4) implies a risk-neutral default probability over the interval from $t \in [0, 1]$. This default probability consists of the following two parts. The first one is the default probability that the life insurance company's asset portfolio will be less than the book value of the company's liabilities based on $C(V, X)$. In the same way, the second one is the default probability based on the valuation $\delta C(\alpha V, X)$. We can write the default probability as:

$$P = P(V, X) + \delta P(\alpha V, X), \tag{9}$$

where

$$P(V,X)=N(h_1)+e^{h_2}(1-N(h_3)),$$

$$h_1=\frac{1}{\sigma+\alpha_A\sigma^2/2}(\ln\frac{\beta X}{V}-(R_B-R)+\frac{(\sigma+\alpha_A\sigma^2/2)^2}{2}),$$

$$h_2=\frac{2}{(\sigma+\alpha_A\sigma^2/2)^2}((R_B-R)-\frac{(\sigma+\alpha_A\sigma^2/2)^2}{2})\ln\frac{\beta X}{V},$$

$$h_3=-\frac{1}{\sigma+\alpha_A\sigma^2/2}(\ln\frac{\beta X}{V}+(R_B-R)-\frac{(\sigma+\alpha_A\sigma^2/2)^2}{2}),$$

$$P(\alpha V,X)=N(k_1)+e^{k_2}(1-N(k_3)),$$

$$k_1=\frac{1}{\sigma+\alpha_A\sigma^2/2}(\ln\frac{\beta X}{\alpha V}-(R_B-R)+\frac{(\sigma+\alpha_A\sigma^2/2)^2}{2}),$$

$$k_2=\frac{2}{(\sigma+\alpha_A\sigma^2/2)^2}((R_B-R)-\frac{(\sigma+\alpha_A\sigma^2/2)^2}{2})\ln\frac{\beta X}{\alpha V},$$

$$k_3=-\frac{1}{\sigma+\alpha_A\sigma^2/2}(\ln\frac{\beta X}{\alpha V}+(R_B-R)-\frac{(\sigma+\alpha_A\sigma^2/2)^2}{2}).$$

This equation estimates only a risk-neutral default probability and provides a meaningful ranking of the life insurance company according to its susceptibility to failure at various levels of alternative parameters in our model. Our measure of default risk is used to examine the relationship between default risk and insurer equity returns. This measure can be also used to demonstrate the state of financial stability discussed in the later sections.

4. Optimal Decisions and Comparative Static Analyses

This section mainly consists of two parts. The first part examines the solutions to the life insurance company's optimization problem. The second part theoretically considers the effects on the optimal solutions from changes in managerial overconfidence and buying distressed assets of the model.

4.1. Dichotomized Optimal Decisions

In the model, the life insurance company is assumed to set R_A or R to maximize the market value of the life insurer's equity. Partially differentiating the equity function with respect to R_A or R, the first-order conditions for the equity maximization are given by:

$$\frac{\partial S}{\partial R_A}=\frac{\partial C(V,X)}{\partial R_A}-\delta\frac{\partial C(\alpha V,X)}{\partial R_A}=0, \tag{10}$$

$$\frac{\partial S}{\partial R}=\frac{\partial C(V,X)}{\partial R}-\delta\frac{\partial C(\alpha V,X)}{\partial R}=0. \tag{11}$$

Based on assumptions, it is reasonable to believe that the equity function of Equation (4) is strictly concave, at least in the short run, where there are sufficient conditions of $\partial^2 S/\partial R_A^2<0$ and $\partial^2 S/\partial R^2<0$ for optima in a non-simultaneous decision environment. This decision is understood because life insurers do not raise debt to purchase financial assets to cover liabilities towards policyholders (Thimann 2014). It should be noted that while our model is based on the assumption of dichotomy, our results to be derived from our model do not extend to the simultaneous case.

The dichotomized optimal solutions are explained as follows.[15] The first-order condition in Equation (10) determines the optimal R_A where R remains constant. The optimal R_A is determined by the life insurance company where the marginal long position of R_A equals the marginal short position of R_A, the latter being weighted by δ. Alternatively, the first-order condition in Equation (11) determines the optimal R where R_A is fixed. The same pattern as Equation (10) applies. As in the model, asset and liability sides are dichotomized. First, since R is not a choice variable of the life insurance company, examining the impacts of parameters on the optimal insurer interest margin, i.e., the spread between R_A and R, is tantamount to examining that on the optimal R_A. We call such spread behavior asset-side interest margin management. Second, since R_A is not a choice variable, examining the effects of parameters on the optimal insurer interest margin is tantamount to examining that on the optimal R. Similarly, we call such spread behavior liability-side interest margin management. It is recognized that insurer interest margin conveys vital information for the efficiency of the insurance system. Identifying the determinants of insurer interest margin would help to understand changing trends in insurance efficiency and provide implications for the regulatory insurance environment. These results are used in a later subsection when the comparative static effects are analyzed.

4.2. Overconfidence Effects

Here, the importance of CEO overconfidence is emphasized. Our following results address the issue: what are the most likely effects of the CEO overconfidence on the life insurance company's interest margin and default risk? First, to capture the response of the optimal insurer interest margin to a change in CEO overconfidence, one implicitly differentiates Equation (10) with respect to α_A where R remains constant, or Equation (11) with respect to α_A where R_A remains constant, which yields the following:

$$\left.\frac{\partial R_A}{\partial \alpha_A}\right|_{R=\text{constant}} = -\frac{\partial^2 S}{\partial R_A \partial \alpha_A} \Big/ \frac{\partial^2 S}{\partial R_A^2}, \tag{12}$$

$$\left.\frac{\partial R}{\partial \alpha_A}\right|_{R_A=\text{constant}} = -\frac{\partial^2 S}{\partial R \partial \alpha_A} \Big/ \frac{\partial^2 S}{\partial R^2}. \tag{13}$$

Equation (12) depicts the impact on the life insurance company's asset interest rate (and thus the company's asset-side interest margin) from changes in the level of CEO overconfidence. Equation (13) analyzes the impact on the life insurance company's guaranteed interest rate (and thus the company's liability-side interest margin) from changes in the level of CEO overconfidence. Theoretical explanations about both the scenarios will be represented in the next numerical section.

Second, we consider the impact of CEO overconfidence on the default risk in the life insurance company's equity returns. Differentiation of Equation (9) evaluated at the optimal R_A or the optimal R with respect to α_A yields:

$$\left.\frac{dP}{d\alpha_A}\right|_{R=\text{constant}} = \frac{\partial P}{\partial \alpha_A} + \frac{\partial P}{\partial R_A}\frac{\partial R_A}{\partial \alpha_A}, \tag{14}$$

$$\left.\frac{dP}{d\alpha_A}\right|_{R_A=\text{constant}} = \frac{\partial P}{\partial \alpha_A} + \frac{\partial P}{\partial R}\frac{\partial R}{\partial \alpha_A}, \tag{15}$$

where the first term on the right-hand side of Equation (14) can be interpreted as the direct effect, while the second term can be interpreted as the indirect effect. The direct effect demonstrates the change in P due to an increase in α_A, holding the optimal R_A constant. The indirect effect arises because of changed P due to an increase in α_A through every possible optimal state of R_A. Equation (15) depicts the relationship between P and α_A, explicitly considering the adjustment of every possible optimal

---

15 Slovin and Sushka (1983) develop a model of the commercial loan rate where the asset and liability sides of bank operations are assumed to be dichotomized. We employ their conceptual approach to model the optimal solutions of CEO overconfidence issues.

state of R. The same pattern as previously applies. The added complexity of path dependent options, in general, leads to complicated comparative static results of Equations (12)–(15). In the next section, we will calculate these comparative static results numerically to provide intuition.

4.3. Bailout Effects

Buying distressed assets by the government was one of the most important bailout programs during the 2007/2008 global financial crisis. In this subsection, we theoretically show how the bailout program can influence the life insurance company's decision makings. First, to analyze the response of the optimal insurer interest margin to a change in the bailout program of buying distressed assets, one implicitly differentiates Equation (10) with respect to θ where R remains constant, or Equation (11) with respect to θ where R_A remains constant, which gives the following:

$$\left.\frac{\partial R_A}{\partial \theta}\right|_{R=\text{constant}} = -\frac{\partial^2 S}{\partial R_A \partial \theta} / \frac{\partial^2 S}{\partial R_A^2}, \tag{16}$$

$$\left.\frac{\partial R}{\partial \theta}\right|_{R_A=\text{constant}} = -\frac{\partial^2 S}{\partial R \partial \theta} / \frac{\partial^2 S}{\partial R^2}. \tag{17}$$

Second, we examine the impact of buying distressed assets by the government on the life insurance company's default risk. Since the derivation is analogous to that for the CEO overconfidence, we jump to the results:

$$\left.\frac{dP}{d\theta}\right|_{R=\text{constant}} = \frac{\partial P}{\partial \theta} + \frac{\partial P}{\partial R_A}\frac{\partial R_A}{\partial \theta}, \tag{18}$$

$$\left.\frac{dP}{d\theta}\right|_{R_A=\text{constant}} = \frac{\partial P}{\partial \theta} + \frac{\partial P}{\partial R}\frac{\partial R}{\partial \theta}. \tag{19}$$

Third, since changes in the bailout program of buying distressed assets from the insurance company by the government can affect CEO overconfidence behavior, and thus efficiency gain/loss from CEO overconfidence, one differentiates Equation (8) with respect to θ when the optimal R or R_A is constant, giving:

$$\left.\frac{d\Delta E}{d\theta}\right|_{R=\text{constant}} = \frac{\partial \Delta E}{\partial \theta} + \frac{\partial \Delta E}{\partial R_A}\frac{\partial R_A}{\partial \theta}, \tag{20}$$

$$\left.\frac{d\Delta E}{d\theta}\right|_{R_A=\text{constant}} = \frac{\partial \Delta E}{\partial \theta} + \frac{\partial \Delta E}{\partial R}\frac{\partial R}{\partial \theta}. \tag{21}$$

The first term on the right-hand side in Equation (20) can be explained as the direct effect, while the second term can be explained as the indirect effect. The direct effect demonstrates the change in the efficiency gain/loss from CEO overconfidence due to an increase in the buying distressed assets by the government, holding the optimal loan asset interest rate constant. The indirect effect describes the change in the efficiency gain/loss by $A(R_A)$ in every possible optimal state. The same interpretation as previously stated, applies to Equation (21). Again, given the chosen parameter values we will calculate the comparative static results based on Equations (16)–(21) to provide intuition regarding the bailout problems in the next section.

5. Numerical Analysis

According to the overconfidence and bailout effects introduced in the previous section, we can determine the comparative static results through a numerical combination of the parameters. In this section, we first assume some reasonable parameter values for the comparative static analyses. Next, as before, we consider two effects: CEO overconfidence and bailout.

5.1. Numerical Assumptions

The assumed numerical values based on our derived model are demonstrated as follows.

(i) We follow Briys and de Varenne (1994) and assume $65\% \leq \delta \leq 95\%$, and $\sigma = 0.30$ for the numerical analysis in the model.
(ii) Let $(R_A(\%), A)$ faced by the life insurance company change from $(5.50, 300.5)$ to $(6.10, 269)$ due to the downward-sloping assumption.
(iii) Let $(R\ (\%), L)$ change from $(2.25, 285)$ to $(3.75, 347)$ to capture the upward-sloping condition.
(iv) Let the shadow-banking entrusted loans M fluctuate from 60 to 80 with the commission rate of $m = 0.10\%$.
(v) We assume that $R_M = 5.00\%$, and $R_B = 4.00\%$. The condition of $R_A > R_M$ implies that the asset interest rate determined by the life insurance company is greater than the market rate of return from M invested in the financial market. The condition of $R_M > R_B$ reasonably demonstrates a financial environment where the expected rate of return from the risky investment M is greater than the security-market interest rate from buying distressed assets by the government.
(vi) The initial barrier level is assumed to be set $\beta = 0.60$ which are observed from an empirical barrier average estimated by Brockman and Turtle (2003).
(vii) We assume that the degree range of overconfidence is $0.20 \leq \alpha_A \leq 0.45$.
(viii) Let the level of buying distressed assets θ increase from 0.40 to 0.65.

5.2. CEO Overconfidence Analysis

Due to the dichotomized optimization in our analysis, we consider the following two sets of the effects of CEO overconfidence behavior on either asset-side or liability-side interest margin management, and then on its default risk in the life insurance company's equity returns.

The result based on Equation (12) is summarized in the second panel of Table 2 that CEO overconfidence is associated with the low amount of assets at an increased asset interest rate chosen by the life insurance company, resulting in low revenue earnings. Intuitively, as the overconfident CEO of the life insurance company overestimates future investment return (Malmendier and Tate 2005), the life insurance company must now provide a return to a higher behavioral bias base. One way the life insurance company may attempt to augment its total returns is by decreasing its asset investment at an increased asset interest rate. Malmendier and Tate (2005) provide empirical evidence that managerial overconfidence impacts corporate investment decisions. Further, our finding contributes the managerial overconfidence literature: if asset demand faced by the life insurance company is relatively rate-elastic, a lower asset earning is possible at an increased interest margin due to CEO overconfidence. In addition, the computed results based on Equation (14) are demonstrated in the last panel of Table 2 that CEO overconfidence is associated with high default risks. The positive direct effect captures the increase in P due to an increase in α_A, holding the optimal R_A constant. This is because distortion in insurer investment may be a result of CEO overestimating the returns to his/her investment, resulting in increasing the default risk in the life insurance company's equity returns. The negative indirect effect arises because (i) an increase in the CEO overconfidence increases the asset interest rate chosen by the life insurance company, and then (ii) a low amount of asset (and thus a less risky asset) is possible at an increased asset interest rate, yielding a lower level of default risk. Therefore, the negative indirect effect insufficiently offsets the positive direct effect to give a positive response of default risk to an increase in CEO overconfidence. Our result is in large consistent with the empirical findings of Berry-Stölzle et al. (2018).[16]

[16] Berry-Stölzle et al. (2018) examine the relation between CEO overconfidence and earnings management in the U.S. property-ability insurance industry. The authors find that overconfident managers overestimate the returns on their investment projects and underestimate losses, implicitly resulting in increasing the default risk of the insurance companies.

Table 2. Responsiveness of asset-side interest margin (asset interest rate) and default risk to CEO overconfidence degree based on Equations (12) and (14) [1].

	$(R_A(\%), A)$						
α_A	(5.50, 300.5)	(5.60, 300)	(5.70, 299)	(5.80, 297)	(5.90, 293)	(6.00, 285)	(6.10, 269)
				S			
0.20	88.6904	88.7137	88.6163	88.2773	87.4542	85.6613	81.9249
0.25	91.5091	91.5327	91.4309	91.0780	90.2220	88.3579	84.4738
0.30	94.3162	94.3401	94.2339	93.8671	92.9782	91.0433	87.0121
0.35	97.1116	97.1359	97.0253	96.6446	95.7229	93.7173	89.5396
0.40	99.8956	99.9201	99.8050	99.4105	98.4562	96.3802	92.0566
0.45	102.6680	102.6927	102.5732	102.1649	101.1780	99.0319	94.5629
				$\partial R_A/\partial\alpha_A(\%)$			
0.20→0.25	-	0.6034	−3.6332	−5.7463	−6.7994	−7.3230	-
0.25→0.30	-	0.5230	−3.5086	−5.5196	−6.5217	−7.0200	-
0.30→0.35	-	0.4489	−3.3935	−5.3101	−6.2652	−6.7402	-
0.35→0.40	-	0.3805	−3.2868	−5.1161	−6.0277	−6.4811	-
0.40→0.45	-	0.3172	−3.1876	−4.9358	−5.8070	−6.2403	-
				P			
0.20	0.1116	0.1111	0.1106	0.1101	0.1098	0.1097	0.1103
0.25	0.1146	0.1141	0.1135	0.1131	0.1127	0.1126	0.1132
0.30	0.1177	0.1171	0.1165	0.1161	0.1157	0.1156	0.1161
0.35	0.1208	0.1202	0.1196	0.1191	0.1188	0.1187	0.1191
0.40	0.1240	0.1234	0.1228	0.1223	0.1219	0.1218	0.1222
0.45	0.1272	0.1266	0.1260	0.1255	0.1251	0.1249	0.1254
				$dP/d\alpha_A$: total effect (%),R = constant			
0.20→0.25	-	5.9360	5.9304	5.9088	5.8740	5.8210	-
0.25→0.30	-	6.0737	6.0678	6.0464	6.0123	5.9607	-
0.30→0.35	-	6.2055	6.1993	6.1781	6.1446	6.0944	-
0.35→0.40	-	6.3318	6.3253	6.3043	6.2714	6.2225	-
0.40→0.45	-	6.4531	6.4464	6.4256	6.3932	6.3455	-

[1] Parameter values, unless stated otherwise, $\delta = 0.65$, $\sigma = 0.30$, $m = 0.10\%$, $\alpha = 0.95$, $R_M = 5.00\%$, $R_B = 4.00\%$, $\beta = 0.60$, $M = 60$, $\theta = 0.40$, and $R = 2.25\%$. The second-order condition of Equation (10) is consistently confirmed by $\partial^2 S/\partial R_A^2 < 0$. The shaded areas represent the values of S, $\partial R_A/\partial\alpha_A$, P, and $dP/d\alpha_A$ with the optimal $R_A = 5.60\%$. The negative indirect effect, $(\partial P/\partial R_A)(\partial R_A/\partial\alpha_A) < 0$, is insufficient to offset the positive direct effect, $\partial P/\partial\alpha_A > 0$.

Regarding changes in the other two parameters, namely, the shadow-banking transactions and the government's purchases of distressed assets, the positive effect of CEO overconfidence on the default risk in the life insurance company's equity return becomes less significant when the shadow-banking transactions increase (Figure 1), and that when the distressed purchases increase (Figure 2). Our study focuses on the behavioral bias of managerial overconfidence impacting on investment decisions. As the increased shadow-banking transactions conducted by the life insurance company is considered, the company must now provide a return to a lower risk level. Thus, the positive effect of CEO overconfidence on the default risk becomes less significant. The result is understood that shadow insurance could reduce the risk of asset portfolio and thereby improve life insurer performance. Here, we conclude that shadow insurance helps to enhance the survival probabilities. Our conclusion is in large supported by Koijen and Yogo (2016). As an alternative, Figure 2 depicts the relationship between CEO overconfidence and default risk for various levels of the government's distressed purchases. The same pattern previously stated applies. The life insurance company must now provide a return to a larger capital base and a lower risk level when the distressed purchases increase. Again, this reflects the positive effect of managerial overconfidence on the default risk becomes less significant due to efficiently recapitalized the life insurance company by buying distressed assets from its balance sheet.

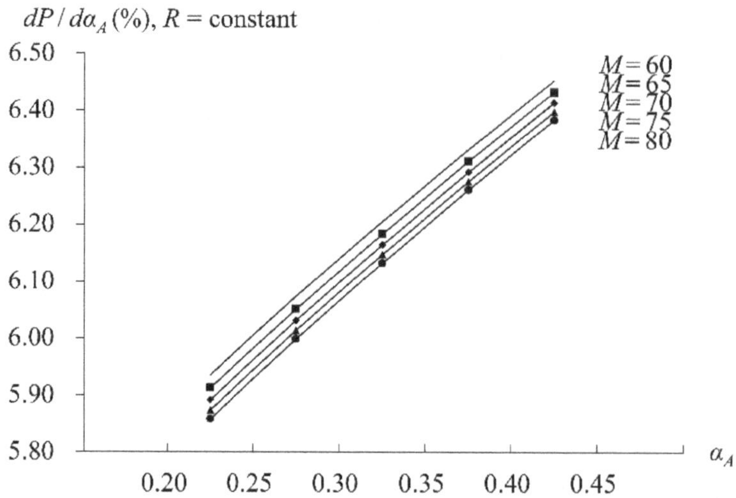

Figure 1. Responsiveness of default risk to overconfidence degree at various levels of shadow-banking transaction based on Equation (14). Parameter values, unless stated otherwise, $\delta = 0.65$, $\sigma = 0.30$, $m = 0.10\%$, $\alpha = 0.95$, $R_M = 5.00\%$, $R_B = 4.00\%$, $\beta = 0.60$, $\theta = 0.40$, and $R = 2.25\%$. All results are valued at the optimal R_A of 5.60%. The negative indirect effect, $(\partial P/\partial R_A)(\partial R_A/\partial \alpha_A) < 0$, is consistently insufficient to offset the positive direct effect, $\partial P/\partial \alpha_A > 0$ at various levels of shadow-banking transaction.

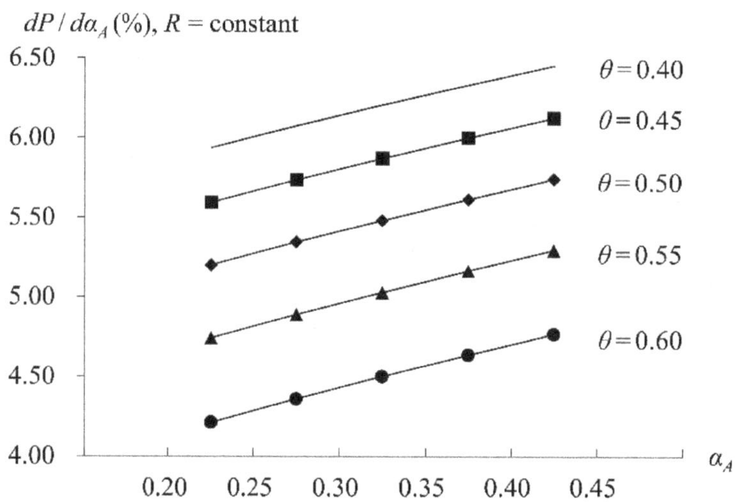

Figure 2. Responsiveness of default risk to overconfidence degree at various levels of buying distressed assets by the government based on Equation (14). Parameter values, unless stated otherwise, $\delta = 0.65$, $\sigma = 0.30$, $m = 0.10\%$, $\alpha = 0.95$, $R_M = 5.00\%$, $R_B = 4.00\%$, $\beta = 0.60$, $M = 60$, and $R = 2.25\%$. All results are valued at the optimal R_A of 5.60%. The negative indirect effect, $(\partial P/\partial R_A)(\partial R_A/\partial \alpha_A) < 0$, is insufficient to offset the positive direct effect, $\partial P/\partial \alpha_A > 0$.

Table 3 demonstrates the following two related overconfidence results when the optimal guaranteed rate decisions of the life insurance company are considered. First, the guaranteed rate of the life insurance contract is increased when the CEO overconfidence becomes stronger. As stated earlier, the overconfident CEO overinvests because of overestimating the returns on his/her investments. One way the life insurance company may attempt to augment its total returns is to increase its life insurance policies at an increased guaranteed rate (and thus a decreased interest margin) since overestimating insurer investment returns are an integral part of the contract itself. Second, we show that the default risk in the life insurance company's equity returns is increased when the CEO overconfidence becomes stronger. The result is understood because overconfidence increases risky investments, directly leading to increasing the default risk. In addition, overconfidence increases the life insurance contracts at an increased guaranteed rate, resulting in increasing cost burden, and hence increasing the default risk in the life insurance company's equity returns. Therefore, we can argue that CEO overconfidence reinforces marginal cost of issuing policies and thereby results in increasing inefficiency. Our result is in large consistent with an empirical finding of Ho et al. (2016).[17] It is important to note that the asset and liability sides of life insurer operations are dichotomized. As mentioned previously, an increase in the CEO overconfidence increases the optimal asset-side interest margin and the default risk of the life insurance company's equity returns (Table 2) and decreases the optimal liability-side interest margin and increases the default risk (Table 3). Our findings provide evidence that managerial overconfidence from a cognitive bias is more likely to impact insurer spread behavior.

Table 3. Responsiveness of liability-side interest margin (guaranteed interest rate) and default risk to CEO overconfidence degree based on Equations (13) and (15) [1].

	$(R\ (\%),\ L)$						
α_A	(2.25, 285)	(2.50, 307)	(2.75, 323)	(3.00, 334)	(3.25, 341)	(3.50, 345)	(3.75, 347)
				S			
0.20	88.5708	93.4583	96.7642	98.7667	99.7374	99.9412	99.6359
0.25	91.3848	96.4723	99.9163	102.0058	103.0230	103.2432	102.9342
0.30	94.1872	99.4741	103.0560	105.2324	106.2963	106.5331	106.2208
0.35	96.9780	102.4638	106.1833	108.4467	109.5573	109.8110	109.4958
0.40	99.7572	105.4415	109.2982	111.6485	112.8061	113.0769	112.7592
0.45	102.5250	108.4071	112.4009	114.8381	116.0427	116.3310	116.0110
				$\partial R/\partial\alpha_A$			
0.20→0.25	-	0.6323	0.5298	0.4216	0.3032	0.1607	-
0.25→0.30	-	0.6068	0.5088	0.4055	0.2926	0.1572	-
0.30→0.35	-	0.5833	0.4894	0.3907	0.2828	0.1539	-
0.35→0.40	-	0.5615	0.4715	0.3769	0.2738	0.1509	-
0.40→0.45	-	0.5412	0.4549	0.3641	0.2654	0.1481	-
				P			
0.20	0.1117	0.1147	0.1184	0.1224	0.1269	0.1316	0.1366
0.25	0.1147	0.1178	0.1215	0.1257	0.1302	0.1351	0.1401
0.30	0.1177	0.1209	0.1248	0.1290	0.1337	0.1386	0.1437
0.35	0.1208	0.1242	0.1281	0.1324	0.1372	0.1422	0.1474
0.40	0.1240	0.1274	0.1314	0.1359	0.1407	0.1458	0.1511
0.45	0.1272	0.1308	0.1349	0.1394	0.1443	0.1495	0.1549
				$dP/d\alpha_A$: total effect (%), R_A = constant			
0.20→0.25	-	6.9302	7.1201	7.2250	7.2593	7.2087	-
0.25→0.30	-	7.0579	7.2425	7.3457	7.3815	7.3361	-
0.30→0.35	-	7.1801	7.3597	7.4613	7.4982	7.4576	-
0.35→0.40	-	7.2972	7.4720	7.5719	7.6099	7.5736	-
0.40→0.45	-	7.4094	7.5797	7.6780	7.7169	7.6846	-

[1] Parameter values, unless stated otherwise, $\delta = 0.65$, $\sigma = 0.30$, $m = 0.10\%$, $\alpha = 0.95$, $R_M = 5.00\%$, $R_B = 4.00\%$, $\beta = 0.60$, $M = 60$, $\theta = 0.40$, and $R_A = 5.50\%$. The second-order condition of Equation (11) is consistently confirmed by $\partial^2 S/\partial R^2 < 0$. The shaded areas represent the values of S, $\partial R/\partial\alpha_A$, P, and $dP/d\alpha_A$ with the optimal $R = 3.50\%$. The positive indirect effect, $(\partial P/\partial R)(\partial R/\partial\alpha_A) > 0$, reinforces the positive direct effect, $\partial P/\partial\alpha_A > 0$.

5.3. *Bailout Analysis*

This subsection considers the following bailout effects on either asset-side or liability-side interest margin management, and then on the default risk in the life insurance company's equity return and the efficiency gain/loss from CEO overconfidence.

[17] Ho et al. (2016) find that overconfident banks experience more severe worsening of stock return performance, along with greater increases in default risk. We argue that their finding may be applicable to life insurance companies since bank and insurance company can be broadly classified as a financial institution.

It is necessary to elaborate on the bailout program of buying distressed assets by the government. Toward that end, we compute Equations (16) and (18). The numerical examples provide intuition. The result of $\partial R_A/\partial\theta < 0$ in Equation (16) observed from the second panel in Table 4 demonstrates that an increase in buying insurer distressed assets by the government increases the amount of assets at a reduced asset interest rate chosen by the life insurance company. This bailout program results in increasing the life insurance company's earning revenues since asset demand faced by the company is rate-elastic. The result implies that bailout helps to decrease the life insurance company's leverage via increasing its core capital ratio, yielding increases to its earning revenues at a reduced interest margin. This explains an important role in discussions of life insurer spread behavior.

Table 4. Responsiveness of asset-side interest margin (asset interest rate) and default risk to buying distressed assets based on Equations (16) and (18) [1].

				$(R_A(\%), A)$			
θ	(5.50, 300.5)	(5.60, 300)	(5.70, 299)	(5.80, 297)	(5.90, 293)	(6.00, 285)	(6.10, 269)
				S			
0.40	88.6904	88.7137	88.6163	88.2773	87.4542	85.6613	81.9249
0.45	83.5083	83.5274	83.4345	83.1176	82.3520	80.6871	77.2203
0.50	78.3158	78.3306	78.2424	77.9478	77.2397	75.7035	72.5074
0.55	73.1096	73.1203	73.0368	72.7646	72.1146	70.7077	67.7837
0.60	67.8854	67.8920	67.8133	67.5639	66.9725	65.6959	63.0459
0.65	62.6366	62.6393	62.5657	62.3394	61.8073	60.6624	58.2891
				$\partial R_A/\partial\theta(\%)$			
0.40→0.45	-	−7.0386	3.7524	9.1416	11.8330	13.1769	-
0.45→0.50	-	−7.5139	4.1159	9.9241	12.8248	14.2724	-
0.50→0.55	-	−8.0377	4.5715	10.8690	14.0137	15.5819	-
0.55→0.60	-	−8.6051	5.1620	12.0380	15.4708	17.1803	-
0.60→0.65	-	−9.1957	5.9607	13.5302	17.3077	19.1845	-
				P			
0.40	0.1116	0.1111	0.1106	0.1101	0.1098	0.1097	0.1103
0.45	0.1067	0.1062	0.1057	0.1053	0.1050	0.1051	0.1057
0.50	0.1012	0.1008	0.1003	0.1000	0.0997	0.0999	0.1007
0.55	0.0951	0.0947	0.0943	0.0940	0.0938	0.0941	0.0951
0.60	0.0883	0.0879	0.0875	0.0873	0.0872	0.0876	0.0888
0.65	0.0805	0.0802	0.0799	0.0797	0.0797	0.0802	0.0817
				$dP/d\theta$: total effect			
0.40→0.45	-	−0.0973	−0.0972	−0.0965	−0.0954	−0.0934	-
0.45→0.50	-	−0.1084	−0.1081	−0.1073	−0.1060	−0.1038	-
0.50→0.55	-	−0.1212	−0.1208	−0.1199	−0.1184	−0.1158	-
0.55→0.60	-	−0.1361	−0.1356	−0.1345	−0.1328	−0.1298	-
0.60→0.65	-	−0.1534	−0.1528	−0.1515	−0.1495	−0.1460	-

[1] Parameter values, unless stated otherwise, $\delta = 0.65$, $\sigma = 0.30$, $m = 0.10\%$, $\alpha = 0.95$, $R_M = 5.00\%$, $R_B = 4.00\%$, $\beta = 0.60$, $\alpha_A = 0.20$, $M = 60$, and $R = 2.25\%$. The second-order condition of Equation (10) is consistently confirmed by $\partial^2 S/\partial R_A^2 < 0$. The shaded areas represent the values of S, $\partial R_A/\partial\theta$, P, and $dP/d\theta$ with the optimal $R_A = 5.60\%$. The positive indirect effect, $(\partial P/\partial R_A)(\partial R_A/\partial\theta) > 0$, is insufficient to offset the negative direct effect, $\partial P/\partial\theta < 0$.

Next, the last panel presents the result of $dP/d\theta < 0$, which can be explained by the direct effect and the indirect effect in Equation (18). The negative direct effect demonstrates decreases in the life insurance company's default risk due to increases in the buying distressed assets by the government. The result is unambiguous because increases in the buying distressed assets by the government makes the life insurance company's assets less risky to invest. In response to this, the reduced investment riskiness results in decreasing the default risk in the life insurance company's equity returns, ceteris paribus. The indirect effect arises when the adjustments of the optimal asset interest rate due to changes in the buying distress assets are explicitly considered. As usual, the sign of this indirect effect is indeterminate. Table 4 provides us with a hunch that the indirect effect evaluated at the optimal R_A

is positive. The rationale is that (i) an increase in the buying distressed assets increases the invested assets at a decrease in asset interest rate, as mentioned previously, and then (ii) the default risk is increased due to an increase in the risky asset investment. The indirect effect becomes positive and works against, but insufficiently, the negative direct effect, yielding the result that life insurer default risk reacts negatively to an increase in the bailout program of buying insurer distressed assets. As a result, we argue that buying distressed assets is an appropriate way to recapitalize the life insurance company from the standpoint of financial stability.[18]

Figure 3 demonstrates the result that the negative effect of the buying of distressed assets by the government on the life insurance company's default risk becomes more significant when the cognitive bias from CEO overconfidence exacerbates. Not surprisingly, the outcries for more bailouts of the life insurance company with the overconfident CEO tend to be greater. The result is understood because managerial overconfidence induces greater overinvestment and incurs higher investment returns (Malmendier and Tate 2005), and hence increases the effect of the bailout on the decreased default risk. The bailout program of buying distressed assets is an appropriate way to assist the life insurance company. Under the circumstances, CEO overconfidence helps to enhance the survival probabilities as well. Figure 4 suggests that the negative effect of the buying of distressed assets on the life insurance company's default risk becomes less significant when the life insurance company increasingly gets involved in the shadow-banking transactions. Under the circumstances, shadow insurance incurs higher default risks.

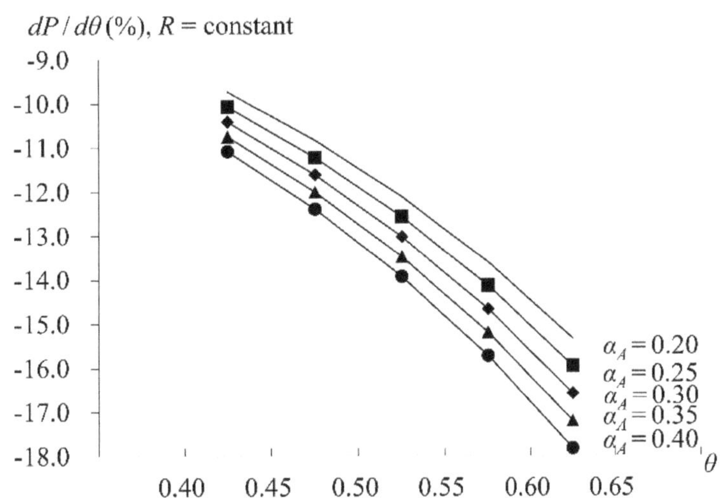

Figure 3. Responsiveness of default risk to buying distressed assets at various levels of CEO overconfidence based on Equation (18). Parameter values, unless stated otherwise, $\delta = 0.65$, $\sigma = 0.30$, $m = 0.10\%$, $\alpha = 0.95$, $R_M = 5.00\%$, $R_B = 4.00\%$, $\beta = 0.60$, $M = 60$, and $R = 2.25\%$. All results are valued at the optimal R_A of 5.60%. The positive indirect effect, $(\partial P/\partial R_A)(\partial R_A/\partial\theta) > 0$, is consistently insufficient to offset the negative direct effect, $\partial P/\partial\theta < 0$ at various levels of CEO overconfidence.

Table 5 depicts two effects of government purchases of distressed assets on the optimal guaranteed rate of the life insurance policy, and further on the default risk in the life insurance company's equity returns when the asset interest rate remained fixed in the dichotomized environment. First, we show that an increase in buying distressed assets by the government decreases the guaranteed rate (and thus increases the interest margin) set by the life insurance company, and therefore leads to less insurance cost burden which increases the equity return. Second, this guaranteed rate decrease also decreases costs which reduces the default risk of equity return (the negative indirect effect in our model). In addition, it is the negative direct effect in our model that a decrease in the default risk due

[18] Hoshi and Kashyap (2010) also conclude the result for distressed banks.

to an increase in buying distressed assets by the government, ceteris paribus. The total negative effect of these two influences can be determined. Overall, the bailout of buying distressed assets induces higher interest margin and incurs lower default risk, thereby contributing to the financial stability.

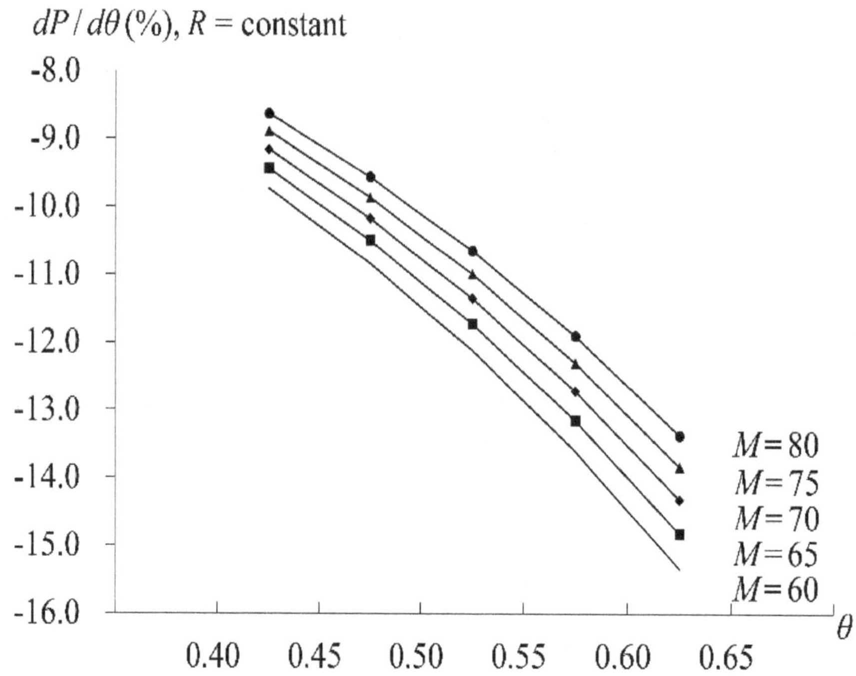

Figure 4. Responsiveness of default risk to buying distressed assets at various levels of shadow-banking transaction based on Equation (18). Parameter values, unless stated otherwise, $\delta = 0.65$, $\sigma = 0.30$, $m = 0.10\%$, $\alpha = 0.95$, $R_M = 5.00\%$, $R_B = 4.00\%$, $\beta = 0.60$, $\alpha_A = 0.20$, and $R = 2.25\%$. All results are valued at the optimal R_A of 5.60%. The positive indirect effect, $(\partial P/\partial R_A)(\partial R_A/\partial \theta) > 0$, is consistently insufficient to offset the negative direct effect, $\partial P/\partial \theta < 0$ at various levels of shadow-banking transaction.

As mentioned previously, Merkle and Weber (2011) argue that overconfident CEOs who overestimate the value of investment projects due to either mis-calibration or "better-than-effect" bias are expected to overinvest. We further argue that there is an efficiency gain from CEO overconfidence in lieu of CEO rationality due to the life insurance company's overinvestment (the upper panel in Table 6). This is because the life insurance company optimally determines the insurer interest margin by exercising some monopoly power in the asset market. Overinvestment returns efficiently allow the life insurance company to have the equity maximization at the optimal interest margin. However, an increase in the buying distressed assets by the government decreases the efficiency gain from CEO overconfidence in the life insurance company's overinvestment (the lower panel in Table 6). Intuitively, when the life insurer company decides to participate in the bailout program of buying distressed assets, the bailout may generate an adverse signal that the life insurance company is expected to have high future losses. Under the circumstances, the overconfident CEO with a less cognitive bias reveals less overinvestment due to the adverse signal realization, which reduces the efficiency gain from CEO overconfidence. As a result, CEO overconfidence induces higher efficiency gain from insurer overinvestment but reduces the efficiency gain when the bailout of buying distressed assets is increased.

Table 5. Responsiveness of liability-side interest margin (guaranteed interest rate) and default risk to buying distressed assets based on Equations (17) and (19) [1].

θ	$(R\ (\%), L)$						
	(2.25, 285)	(2.50, 307)	(2.75, 323)	(3.00, 334)	(3.25, 341)	(3.50, 345)	(3.75, 347)
				$S(R_A = \text{constant})$			
0.40	88.5708	93.4583	96.7642	98.7667	99.7374	99.9412	99.6359
0.45	83.3974	87.9120	90.9577	92.7928	93.6696	93.8338	93.5248
0.50	78.2136	82.3549	85.1406	86.8089	87.5925	87.7181	87.4063
0.55	73.0162	76.7837	79.3095	80.8117	81.5032	81.5915	81.2782
0.60	67.8008	71.1936	73.4597	74.7968	75.3976	75.4501	75.1370
0.65	62.5609	65.5777	67.5843	68.7573	69.2693	69.2883	68.9777
				$\partial R/\partial\theta(R_A = \text{constant})$			
0.40→0.45	-	−1.1789	−0.9982	−0.8111	−0.6126	−0.3884	-
0.45→0.50	-	−1.2706	−1.0740	−0.8702	−0.6536	−0.4079	-
0.50→0.55	-	−1.3788	−1.1628	−0.9386	−0.6998	−0.4273	-
0.55→0.60	-	−1.5087	−1.2684	−1.0187	−0.7518	−0.4452	-
0.60→0.65	-	−1.6686	−1.3968	−1.1137	−0.8102	−0.4585	-
				$P(R_A = \text{constant})$			
0.40	0.1117	0.1147	0.1184	0.1224	0.1269	0.1316	0.1366
0.45	0.1068	0.1097	0.1133	0.1174	0.1219	0.1267	0.1317
0.50	0.1013	0.1041	0.1077	0.1118	0.1163	0.1211	0.1263
0.55	0.0952	0.0979	0.1014	0.1054	0.1100	0.1149	0.1201
0.60	0.0883	0.0908	0.0942	0.0982	0.1028	0.1077	0.1130
0.65	0.0806	0.0829	0.0861	0.0900	0.0945	0.0995	0.1049
				$dP/d\theta$: total effect $(R_A = \text{constant})$			
0.40→0.45	-	−0.1144	−0.1152	−0.1138	−0.1106	−0.1058	-
0.45→0.50	-	−0.1267	−0.1281	−0.1270	−0.1238	−0.1186	-
0.50→0.55	-	−0.1409	−0.1432	−0.1424	−0.1393	−0.1338	-
0.55→0.60	-	−0.1573	−0.1608	−0.1607	−0.1577	−0.1519	-
0.60→0.65	-	−0.1764	−0.1814	−0.1822	−0.1795	−0.1734	-

[1] Parameter values, unless stated otherwise, $\delta = 0.65$, $\sigma = 0.30$, $m = 0.10\%$, $\alpha = 0.95$, $R_M = 5.00\%$, $R_B = 4.00\%$, $\beta = 0.60$, $\alpha_A = 0.20$, $M = 60$, and $R_A = 5.50\%$. The second-order condition of Equation (11) is consistently confirmed by $\partial^2 S/\partial R^2 < 0$. The shaded areas represent the values of S, $\partial R/\partial\theta$, P, and $dP/d\theta$ with the optimal R. The negative indirect effect, $(\partial P/\partial R)(\partial R/\partial\theta) < 0$, reinforces the negative direct effect, $\partial P/\partial\theta < 0$.

Table 6. Responsiveness of efficiency gain from CEO overconfidence to buying distressed assets when asset-side interest margin is considered, Equation (20) [1].

θ	$(R_A(\%), A)$						
	(5.50, 300.5)	(5.60, 300)	(5.70, 299)	(5.80, 297)	(5.90, 293)	(6.00, 285)	(6.10, 269)
				$\Delta E(R = \text{constant})$			
0.40	382.6842	383.4322	383.6164	382.6658	379.4346	371.6220	354.6120
0.45	365.5638	366.2484	366.3970	365.4670	362.3694	354.9185	338.7295
0.50	348.6239	349.2440	349.3552	348.4429	345.4740	338.3754	322.9901
0.55	331.9120	332.4659	332.5374	331.6391	328.7924	322.0341	307.4298
0.60	315.4932	315.9787	316.0076	315.1183	312.3851	305.9513	292.0981
0.65	299.4595	299.8740	299.8561	298.9692	296.3377	290.2065	277.0639
				$d\Delta E/d\theta$: total effect $(R = \text{constant})$			
0.40→0.45	-	−344.2025	−344.3187	−344.8459	−345.1266	−344.3650	-
0.45→0.50	-	−340.6029	−340.7746	−341.4050	−341.8812	−341.4956	-
0.50→0.55	-	−336.0606	−336.3045	−337.0674	−337.7932	−337.8868	-
0.55→0.60	-	−330.2196	−330.5597	−331.4968	−332.5493	−333.2681	-
0.60→0.65	-	−322.5414	−323.0135	−324.1863	−325.6788	−327.2374	-

[1] Parameter values, unless stated otherwise, $\delta = 0.65$, $\sigma = 0.30$, $m = 0.10\%$, $\alpha = 0.95$, $R_M = 5.00\%$, $R_B = 4.00\%$, $\beta = 0.60$, $\alpha_A = 0.20$, $M = 60$, and $R = 2.25\%$. The shaded areas represent the values of ΔE and $d\Delta E/d\theta$ with the optimal R_A. The negative indirect effect, $(\partial\Delta E/\partial R_A)(\partial R_A/\partial\theta) < 0$, reinforces the negative direct effect, $\partial\Delta E/\partial\theta < 0$.

Figure 5 demonstrates that the negative effect of buying distressed assets on the efficiency gain from CEO overconfidence is increased when the shadow-banking activities involved by the life insurance company increase. If we can argue that buying distressed assets, reducing an efficiency gain from CEO overconfidence, is an appropriate way to recapitalize the life insurance company, an increase in the shadow insurance reinforces the appropriateness. Figure 6 states that the negative effect of buying distressed assets on the efficiency gain from CEO overconfidence is decreased when the barrier ratio in the equity valuation increases. The same pattern as before applies. The government is interested in CEO overconfidence as long as the risk of a premature default to the equity valuation of the life insurance company is decreased.

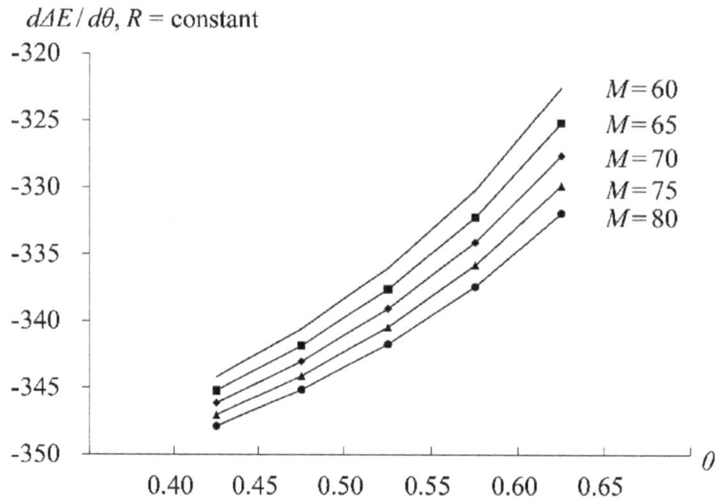

Figure 5. Responsiveness of efficiency gain to buying distressed assets at various levels of shadow-banking transaction based on Equation (20). All results are valued at the optimal R_A of 5.60%. The negative indirect effect, $(\partial\Delta E/\partial R_A)(\partial R_A/\partial\theta) < 0$, consistently reinforces the negative direct effect, $\partial\Delta E/\partial\theta < 0$ at various levels of shadow-banking transaction.

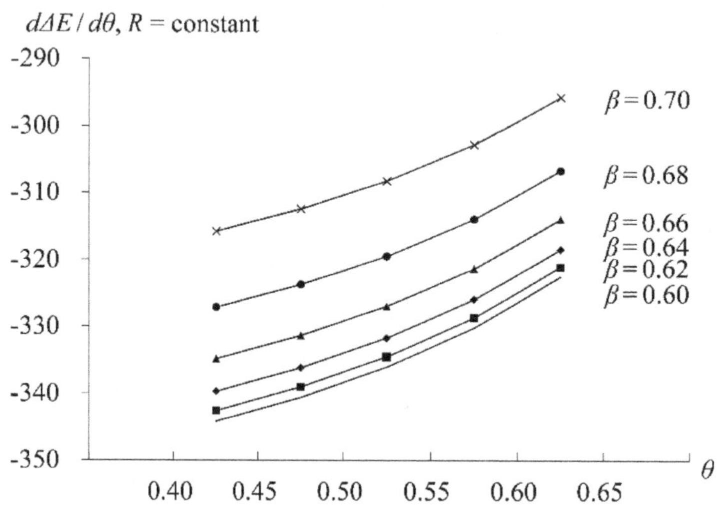

Figure 6. Responsiveness of efficiency gain to buying distressed assets at various levels of barrier based on Equation (20). All results are valued at the optimal R_A of 5.60%. The negative indirect effect, $(\partial\Delta E/\partial R_A)(\partial R_A/\partial\theta) < 0$, consistently reinforces the negative direct effect, $\partial\Delta E/\partial\theta < 0$ at various levels of shadow-banking transaction.

Table 7 demonstrates the case that the optimal guaranteed interest rate of the life insurance policy is determined in a non-simultaneous environment where the optimal asset interest rate chosen by the life insurance company remains constant. We conclude that the life insurance company with the overconfident CEO is more likely to increase efficiency gain from overinvestment than life insurance companies with rational CEO. However, the efficiency gains from CEO overconfidence due to overinvestment is reduced when the bailout program of buying distressed assets increases. The same interpretation as before applies. Note that an increase in the bailout decreases the life insurance policies at a reduced guaranteed rate, yielding increases to the efficiency gain due to overinvestment with CEO overconfidence. This indirect effect is insufficient to offset the negative direct effect to give an overall negative effect of buying distressed assets on the efficiency gain from CEO overconfidence.

Table 7. Responsiveness of efficiency gain from CEO overconfidence to buying distressed assets when liability-side interest margin is considered, Equation (21) [1].

	$(R\,(\%), L)$						
θ	(2.25, 285)	(2.50, 307)	(2.75, 323)	(3.00, 334)	(3.25, 341)	(3.50, 345)	(3.75, 347)
				$\Delta E(R_A = \text{constant})$			
0.40	382.1271	399.4593	409.0159	412.3793	411.0198	406.2966	399.4606
0.45	365.0342	381.1930	389.9318	392.7723	391.1249	386.2899	379.4602
0.50	348.1212	363.1163	371.0382	373.3498	371.4041	366.4444	359.6067
0.55	331.4355	345.2799	352.3864	354.1622	351.9052	346.8041	339.9401
0.60	315.0418	327.7539	334.0481	335.2795	332.6946	327.4307	320.5169
0.65	299.0321	310.6385	316.1261	316.8026	313.8683	308.4133	301.4180
				$d\Delta E/d\theta$: total effect $(R_A = \text{constant})$			
0.40→0.45	-	−447.0598	−419.8383	−403.0517	−394.5667	−392.7941	-
0.45→0.50	-	−443.6601	−415.4157	−398.3368	−390.1077	−389.0221	-
0.50→0.55	-	−439.4267	−409.8815	−392.4324	−384.5324	−384.3285	-
0.55→0.60	-	−434.0668	−402.8217	−384.8895	−377.4238	−378.3831	-
0.60→0.65	-	−427.1525	−393.6093	−375.0231	−368.1493	−370.6963	-

[1] Parameter values, unless stated otherwise, $\delta = 0.65$, $\sigma = 0.30$, $m = 0.10\%$, $\alpha = 0.95$, $R_M = 5.00\%$, $R_B = 4.00\%$, $\beta = 0.60$, $\alpha_A = 0.20$, $M = 60$, and $R_A = 5.50\%$. The shaded areas represent the values of ΔE and $d\Delta E/d\theta$ with the optimal R. The positive indirect effect, $(\partial\Delta E/\partial R)(\partial R/\partial\theta) > 0$, is insufficient to offset the negative direct effect, $\partial\Delta E/\partial\theta < 0$.

6. Conclusions

Guided by the existing theories, this paper theoretically develops the impact of managerial overconfidence on insurer interest margin, and default risk at various levels of shadow-banking transactions conducted by the life insurance company. This paper also investigates the effect of bailout on insurer interest margin, default risk, and efficiency gain/loss from CEO overconfidence at various levels of shadow-banking involvement.

Our two main results are as follows. First, CEO overconfidence raises the default risk in the life insurance company's equity returns regardless of whether asset-side or liability-side interest margin is determined. Shadow-banking activities involved by the life insurance company attenuate the unfavorable effect. Buying distressed assets by the government weakens the effect as well. Second, government bailouts help to reduce the default risk in the life insurance company's equity returns regardless of whether asset-side or liability-side interest margin is determined. However, government bailouts reduce the efficiency gain from CEO overconfidence. If the case is that buying distressed assets is an appropriate way to recapitalize the life insurance company, an increase in the shadow-banking involvement reinforces the appropriateness.

One caveat that should be stressed is that this analysis focuses only on a cognitive bias in which managerial overconfidence impacts insurer investment decisions and does not deal with the many other important areas of the life insurance policies. For example, issues such as managerial overconfidence affecting the guaranteed interest rate and the participation level of the profit-sharing life insurance policies are not considered. While there are significant issues, they can be perhaps understood only when the underlying economic link between life insurance policy issuance and market demand status is made clear. Such concerns are beyond the scope of this research and so are not addressed here. What this research does demonstrate, however, is the important role played by managerial overconfidence in affecting insurer investment decisions and further insurer bankruptcy prediction.

Author Contributions: Conceptualization, J.-H.L.; Data curation, W.Y.; Formal analysis, S.C.; Funding acquisition, S.C.; Investigation, F.-W.H.; Methodology, J.-H.L.; Project administration, J.-H.L.; Resources, F.-W.H.; Software, W.Y.; Writing—review & editing, W.Y.

Funding: This research was funded by National Natural Science Foundation of China, grant number 71603217.

Acknowledgments: We would like to thank three anonymous referees, and the Academic Editor for their comments and suggestions. The usual disclaimer applies.

Conflicts of Interest: The authors declare no conflict of interest.

References

Adams, Renee B., and Daniel Ferreira. 2007. A theory of friendly boards. *Journal of Finance* 62: 217–50. [CrossRef]

Adrian, Tobias, and Hyun Song Shin. 2009. The shadow banking system: Implications for financial regulation. *Financial Stability Review, Banque de France* 13: 1–10. Available online: https://publications.banque-france.fr/sites/default/files/medias/documents/financial-stability-review-13_2009-09.pdf (accessed on 23 February 2019).

Adrian, Tobias, and Mark M. Westerfield. 2009. Disagreement and learning in a dynamic contracting model. *Review of Financial Studies* 10: 3873–906. [CrossRef]

Alicke, Mark D. 1985. Global self-evaluation as determined by the desirability and controllability of trait adjectives. *Journal of Personality and Social Psychology* 49: 1621–30. [CrossRef]

Barnes, Michelle L. 2016. Did life Insurers Benefit from TARP or Regulatory Forbearance during the Financial Crisis of 2008–2009? FRB of Boston Working Paper No. 16-24. Available online: https://ssrn.com/abstract=2917098 (accessed on 29 January 2019).

Ben-David, Itzhak, John R. Graham, and Campbell R. Harvey. 2013. Managerial miscalibration. *Quarterly Journal of Economics* 128: 1547–84. [CrossRef]

Berry-Stölzle, Thomas R., Gregory P. Nini, and Sabine Wende. 2014. External financing in the life insurance industry: Evidence from the financial crisis. *Journal of Risk and Insurance* 81: 529–62. [CrossRef]

Berry-Stölzle, Thomas R., Evan M. Eastman, and Jianren Xu. 2018. CEO overconfidence and earnings management: Evidence from property-liability insurers' loss reserves. *North American Actuarial Journal* 22: 380–404. [CrossRef]

Breitenfellner, Bastian, and Niklas Wagner. 2010. Government intervention in response to the subprime financial crisis: The good into the pot, the bad into the crop. *International Review of Financial Analysis* 19: 289–97. [CrossRef]

Briys, Eric, and François de Varenne. 1994. Life insurance in a contingent claim framework: Pricing and regulatory implications. *Geneva Papers on Risk and Insurance Theory* 19: 53–72. [CrossRef]

Brockman, Paul, and H. J. Turtle. 2003. A barrier option framework for corporate security valuation. *Journal of Financial Economics* 67: 511–29. [CrossRef]

Calomiris, Charles W., and Urooj Khan. 2015. An assessment of TARP assistance to financial institutions. *Journal of Economic Perspectives* 29: 53–80. [CrossRef]

Campbell, T. Colin, Michael Gallmeyer, Shane A. Johnson, Jessica Rutherford, and Brooke W. Stanley. 2011. CEO optimism and forced turnover. *Journal of Financial Economics* 101: 695–712. [CrossRef]

Ceci, Claudia, Katia Colaneri, and Alessandra Cretarola. 2017. Unit-linked life insurance policies: Optimal hedging in partially observable market models. *Insurance: Mathematics and Economics* 76: 149–63. [CrossRef]

Chen, An, and Michael Suchanecki. 2007. Default risk, bankruptcy procedures and the market value of life insurance liabilities. *Insurance: Mathematics and Economics* 40: 231–55. [CrossRef]

Choi, Paul Moon Sub, Chune Young Chung, and Chang Liu. 2018. Self-attribution of overconfident CEOs and asymmetric investment-cash flow sensitivity. *North American Journal of Economics and Finance* 46: 1–14. [CrossRef]

Dyreng, Scott D., Michelle Hanlon, and Edward L. Maydew. 2010. The effects of executives on corporate tax avoidance. *The Accounting Review* 85: 1163–89. [CrossRef]

Ergungor, Ozgur Emre. 2005. The profitability of bank-borrower relationships. *Journal of Financial Intermediation* 14: 485–512. [CrossRef]

Fahlenbrach, Rüdiger, and René M. Stulz. 2011. Bank CEO incentives and the credit crisis. *Journal of Financial Economics* 99: 11–26. [CrossRef]

Giat, Yahel, Steve T. Hackman, and Ajay Subramanian. 2009. Investment under uncertainty, heterogeneous beliefs, and agency conflicts. *Review of Financial Studies* 23: 1360–404. [CrossRef]

Goel, Anand M., and Anjan V. Thakor. 2008. Overconfidence, CEO selection, and corporate governance. *Journal of Finance* 63: 2737–84. [CrossRef]

Gómez, Fabiana, and Jorge Ponce. 2018. Systemic risk and insurance regulation. *Risks* 6: 74. [CrossRef]

Gorton, Gary, and Andrew Metrick. 2010. Regulating the shadow banking system. *Brookings Papers on Economic Activity* 2010: 261–97. [CrossRef]

Grosen, Anders, and Peter Løchte Jørgensen. 2002. Life insurance liabilities at market values: An analysis of insolvency risk, bonus policy, and regulatory intervention rules in a barrier option framework. *Journal of Risk and Insurance* 69: 63–91. [CrossRef]

Harrington, Scott E. 2009. The financial crisis, systemic risk, and the future of insurance regulation. *Journal of Risk and Insurance* 76: 785–819. [CrossRef]

Heaton, James B. 2002. Managerial optimism and corporate finance. *Financial Management* 31: 33–45. [CrossRef]

Hirshleifer, Dice, and Guo Ying Luo. 2001. On the survival of overconfident traders in a competitive securities market. *Journal of Financial Markets* 4: 73–84. [CrossRef]

Ho, Po-Hsin, Chia-Wei Huang, Chih-Yung Lin, and Ju-Fang Yen. 2016. CEO overconfidence and financial crisis: Evidence from bank lending and leverage. *Journal of Financial Economics* 120: 194–209. [CrossRef]

Hong, Jimin, and S. Hun Seog. 2018. Life insurance settlement and the monopolistic insurance market. *Insurance: Mathematics and Economics* 81: 36–50. [CrossRef]

Hoshi, Takeo, and Anil K. Kashyap. 2010. Will the US bank recapitalization succeed? Eight lessons from Japan. *Journal of Financial Economics* 97: 398–417. [CrossRef]

Hsieh, Tien-Shih, Jean C. Bedard, and Karla M. Johnstone. 2014. CEO overconfidence and earnings management during shifting regulatory regimes. *Journal of Business Finance & Accounting* 41: 1243–68. [CrossRef]

Insurance Europe. 2014. *Why Insurers Differ from Banks*. November 5, Brussels: Insurance Europe, Available online: http://www.insuranceeurope.eu/sites/default/files/attachments/Why%20insurers%20differ%20from%20banks.pdf (accessed on 29 January 2019).

Insurance Europe and Oliver Wyman. 2013. Funding the Future: Insurers' Role as Institutional Investors. Available online: www.insuranceeurope.eu (accessed on 3 March 2019).

Irresberger, Felix, and Ying Peng. 2017. Shadow Insurance Usage and Capital Management in Life Insurance Groups. Fox School of Business Research Paper No. 16-022. Available online: https://ssrn.com/abstract=2754489 (accessed on 29 January 2019).

Jeffers, Esther, and Claudia Baicu. 2013. *The Interconnections Between the Shadow Banking System and the Regular Banking System: Evidence from the Euro Area*. CITYPERC Working Paper Series 2013-07; London, UK: Department of International Politics, City University London, Available online: http://openaccess.city.ac.uk/2119/1/CITYPERC-WPS-2013_07.pdf (accessed on 23 February 2019).

Kim, Kyeonghee, J. Tyler Leverty, and Joan T. Schmit. 2017. The effect of investment advisors in the life insurance industry. Working Paper, University of Wisconsin-Madison. Available online: https://bus.wisc.edu/-/media/bus/knowledge-expertise/academic-departments/asrmi/events/2017-2018/kyeongheekim_jobmarketpaper.pdf?la=en (accessed on 23 February 2019).

Koijen, Ralph S. J., and Motohiro Yogo. 2016. Shadow insurance. *Econometrica* 84: 1265–87. [CrossRef]

Li, Xuelian, and Jyh-Horng Lin. 2016. Shadow-banking entrusted loan management, deposit insurance premium, and capital regulation. *International Review of Economics and Finance* 41: 98–109. [CrossRef]

Lin, Jyh-Jiuan, Chuen-Ping Chang, and Shi Chen. 2018. How does distress acquisition incentivized by government purchases of distressed loans affect bank default risk? *Risks* 6: 39. [CrossRef]

Ma, Yueran. 2014. Bank CEO optimism and the financial crisis. Unpublished Working Paper, Harvard University, Cambridge, MA, USA. Available online: http://scholar.harvard.edu/files/yueranma/files/bankoptimism_0.pdf (accessed on 29 January 2019).

Malmendier, Ulrike, and Geoffrey Tate. 2005. CEO overconfidence and corporate investment. *Journal of Finance* 60: 2661–700. [CrossRef]

Merkle, Christoph, and Martin Weber. 2011. True overconfidence: The inability of rational information processing to account for apparent overconfidence. *Organizational Behavior and Human Decision Processes* 116: 262–71. [CrossRef]

Moore, Don A., and Paul J. Healy. 2008. The trouble with overconfidence. *Psychological Review* 115: 502–17. [CrossRef] [PubMed]

Niehaus, Greg. 2014. Managing Capital and Insolvency Risk via Internal Capital Market Transactions: The case of Life Insurers. Available online: https://ssrn.com/abstract=2429024 (accessed on 29 January 2019).

Plantin, Guillaume. 2015. Shadow banking and bank capital regulation. *Review of Financial Studies* 28: 146–75. [CrossRef]

Pozsar, Zoltan. 2008. The Rise and Fall of the Shadow Banking System. *Regional Financial Review* 44: 13–25. Available online: http://wisburg.com/wp-content/uploads/2017/04/sbs.pdf (accessed on 23 February 2019).

Pozsar, Zoltan, Tobias Adrian, Adam Ashcraft, and Hayley Boesky. 2013. Shadow Banking. *Federal Reserve Bank of New York Economic Policy Review* 19: 1–16. Available online: https://www.newyorkfed.org/medialibrary/media/research/epr/2013/0713adri.pdf (accessed on 23 February 2019).

Ronn, Ehud I., and Avinash K. Verma. 1986. Pricing risk-adjusted deposit insurance: An option-based model. *Journal of Finance* 41: 871–95. [CrossRef]

Slovin, Myron B., and Marie Elizabeth Sushka. 1983. A model of the commercial loan rate. *Journal of Finance* 38: 1583–96. [CrossRef]

Thimann, Christian. 2014. How Insurers Differ from Banks: A Primer in Systemic Regulation. SRC Special Paper No 3. Available online: https://ssrn.com/abstract=2502458 (accessed on 29 January 2019).

Tsagkanos, G. Athanasios, and Costas Siriopoulos. 2015. Stock markets and industrial production in north and south of Euro-zone: Asymmetric effects via threshold cointegration approach. *Journal of Economic Asymmetries* 12: 162–72. [CrossRef]

6

Measuring Equity Share Related Risk Perception of Investors in Economically Backward Regions

Ranjit Singh [1] **and Jayashree Bhattacharjee** [2,*]

[1] Department of Management Studies, Indian Institute of Information Technology, Allahabad 211012, India; ranjitsingh@iiita.ac.in

[2] Department of Business Administration, Assam University, Silchar 788011, India

* Correspondence: jayasree.bhattacharjee@gmail.com

Abstract: Risk perception is an idiosyncratic process of interpretation. It is a highly personal process of making a decision based on an individual's frame of reference that has evolved over time. The purpose of this paper is to find out the risk perception level of equity investors and to identify the factors influencing their risk perception. The study was conducted using a stratified random sampling design of 358 investors. It was found that the overall risk perception level of equity investors is moderate and that the main factors affecting their risk perception are information screening, investment education, fear psychosis, fundamental expertise, technical expertise, familiarity bias, information asymmetry, understanding of the market, etc. Considering the above findings, efforts should be made to bring people with a high risk perception to the low risk perception category by providing them with training to handle or manage high-risk scenarios which will help in promoting an equity-investment culture.

Keywords: risk; risk perception; equity investment; risk propensity; factor analysis

---

1. Introduction

Risk is a concept that indicates a potentially negative influence to an asset or some feature of value that may augment from some present process or future event. According to Lopes (1987), "risk refers to situations in which a decision is made whose consequences depend on the outcomes of future events having known probabilities." Thus, it can be expressed as follows:

$$\text{Risk} = \text{Consequences} \times \text{Probability}$$

Risk perception is a personalized ideal that people hold about features and the severity of a risk. Risk perception analyses the opinions of people when they are asked to evaluate hazardous or risky activities, substances, and technologies (Slovic 1987). Risk perception involves peoples' beliefs, attitudes, judgments, and feelings as well as their values—both social and cultural—and dispositions. It plays a prominent role in peoples' decision-making process and thus in the case with the decision to invest in equity shares (Pidgeon et al. 1992). According to Bernstein (1995), the perception of risk throughout the history of any society has reflected the temper of the times of each society, as the emphasis has swung from the instinct to measurements and back. As long as people perceive that they have no control over their characteristics, chance can explain the entire outcome of risk-taking. Then, the experimentation, exploration, and demonstration of that choice are a valid human activity and the aforementioned risk is something to be borne. It is well known that investors do not have control over the return from equity shares and, hence, investments into equity shares are perceived to be risky.

Equity share investments involve a certain degree of risk as the returns expected from the equity shares are not certain. Thus, when going for investments in shares, people try to make proper tradeoffs between risks and return (Fischer and Jordan 2006). Additionally, people are generally risk averse (Kahneman and Tversky 1979). They like to invest where the returns are higher for a given level of risk or risks are least for a given level of return. Risk perception and equity share investments are negatively correlated, indicating that low risk perception will lead to high equity investment (Lennart 2002; Slovic 1987; Milliman and Weber 1997; Singh and Bhowal 2009a; Roszkowski 2010; Veeramani and Karthikeyan 2014). Higher equity investments make people more entrepreneurial and catalyze them to take more risks, leading to the growth of the economy (Singh and Bhowal 2009b).

Risk perception is a vital constituent in several assessments and, hence, psychologists are continuously attempting to find out the best way of measuring risk perception. Singh and Bhowal (2008) established that the risk perception of an individual can be controlled provided that a person is aware of the different aspects of his/her risk perception, as well as the reason for the given risk perception. Therefore, authorities entrusted with the job of framing policies should strive to measure the risk perception of the individuals who manage it and implement the policies (Singh and Bhowal 2006).

Thus, there is a need to manage the risk perception of people (Singh 2009, 2011), which is only possible if it can be measured. Equity-related risk perception among the retail investors is different in economically advanced regions compared to economically backward and geographically remote regions (Deb and Singh 2018). The levels of literacy, income, and available infrastructure in economically backward regions are relatively low compared to those of economically advanced regions (Deb and Singh 2017). For the purposes of this study, the South Assam region of India, consisting of the Cachar, Karimganj, and Hailakandi Districts are chosen as a representative of the economically backward and geographically remote regions. The per capita income and the life expectancy of this region are also lower than the national averages of India (Registrar General 2011).

Southern Assam or Barak Valley (22,244 km^2), which covers almost 30% of Assam's area, is geographically isolated from the main area of the country. Due to infrastructural issues, it is even isolated from Brahmaputra Valley, i.e., the main part of Assam. Up to date, there are no large industries in this valley except for the Cachar Paper Mill (which is on the verge of shutting down), a medium scale cement industry (viz Barak Valley Cement) and some tea estates. There are only two industrial estates in this valley, out of which only one is operational. According to the 2011 census, the literacy rate of this valley is around 77%, which is higher than the state literacy rate of 72.19% and the national literacy rate of 74.04%. Despite the high literacy rate, the per capita income of this valley is much lower in comparison to the state and the national income. According to the 2013–2014 figures, the per capita income of this valley was around Rs. 19,612 (NSDP capita, INR at current prices) compared to the state per capita income of Rs. 44,263 and the national per capita income of Rs. 44,263. People in this valley have faith only in traditional investment avenues such as bank deposits, post office savings, insurances, etc. Their low income does not allow them to invest in risky ventures such as equity. A few years back, a number of share broking houses, as well as a few banks started their operation and, hence, the equity investment culture entered the developing phase in the area. However, due to the poor response from the investors, these broking houses had to close down permanently. Although some banks and the Stock Holding Corporation of India Limited are able to continue their operation due to the compulsory dematerialization of physical shares, there may be certain factors which do not encourage the investors to invest in equity shares, influencing them towards traditional investment avenues instead. Only 0.2% of the populations of this valley have a Demat account (NSDL 2011) compared to the national figure of 1.81%.

Therefore, a study on measuring the risk perception level of investors' in equity shares and the factors influencing the aforementioned risk perception will not only be important but also contemporary in order to understand the current equity investment scenario in this region. In order to measure the risk perception of equity investors, a survey on the basis of a structured questionnaire was given to the retail equity investors. The questionnaire was framed using the variables identified by Singh and Bhowal (2011), Singh (2012), and Deb and Singh (2018) with a five-point scale.

The rest of the paper is organized as follows: Section 2 explains several theories of risk perception, Section 3 discusses the review of the relevant literature, Section 4 states the objectives of the study, Section 5 states the research question of the study, Section 6 deals with the research methodology used in the study, Section 7 describes the analysis and the findings of the study, Section 8 presents the conclusions and policy implications of the study and, finally, Section 9 presents the scope for future research.

2. Theories of Risk Perception

There are various theories of risk perception which have been evolved over a period of time and propounded by various scholars. Some of the theories are briefly mentioned here:

a. Protection Motivation Theory: According to protection motivation theory, people are more likely to protect themselves when they anticipate negative consequences, have the desire to avoid them, and feel they have the ability to take preventive measures. Sheeran et al. (2014) found that enhancing the elements of risk appraisal (such as risk perception and perceived security) has a combined positive effect on changing intentions and behavior towards safety. In the context of equity investment, the practices of putting 'stop-loss' by the equity traders/investors can be explained by this theory. Stop loss order is an order where a trader can make important decisions about cutting losses. Having an idea about equity share investment before investing in equity share (Deb and Singh 2016; Ensuring certainty of income from equity shares (Deb and Singh 2016; Singh and Bhowal 2011; Powers 2009); Facing the hassles of making share market investment (Singh and Bhowal 2011) and Having doubt about the integrity of local agent (Deb and Singh 2016; Singh and Bhowal 2011) are some of the dimensions in equity share investment which are identified from literature review and supports the Protection Motivation Theory.

b. Risk Compensation/Risk Homeostasis Theory: Risk Compensation or Risk Homeostasis Theory states that people tend to take more risks when they feel a greater sense of security. In other words, individuals adjust their level of risk-taking behavior depending on the safety measures that are in place (Wilde 1994). It is observed in the stock market that the financial advisors' advice young people who have a secure family background to have more equity exposure. Requirement of huge sum money for equity investment (Singh and Bhowal 2011; Powers 2009); Ensuring guaranteed income from equity investment (Singh and Bhowal 2011); and Tracking the daily price movements of shares (Deb and Singh 2016; Singh and Bhowal 2011) are a few of the phenomena identified from literature that can be explained by Risk Compensation Theory.

c. Situated Rationality Theory: Situated rationality theory makes the argument that it is erroneous to presume that safe behavior is inherently rational and high-risk behaviors are inherently irrational. In other words, there is likely a rational justification for why people choose to take risks that are more explanatory than assuming that a risk taker is simply crazy or thrill seeking. If the reward of risk-taking is too great, it is often considered rational to take risks. As Finucane et al. (2000) note, the greater the perceived benefit of activity, the lower the perceived risk. The fact that a vast majority of Indian households prefer to invest their money in bank deposits, while less than 10 per cent choose to invest in mutual funds or stocks (Security Exchange Board of India (SEBI), Survey Report, 2017) is testifying of this theory. Lack of confidence among the people regarding time at which equity shares need to be bought and sold (Deb and Singh 2016; Singh and Bhowal 2011; MacCrimmon and Wehrung 1990); Lack of confidence regarding price at which equity shares are to be bought and sold (Singh and Bhowal 2011; MacCrimmon and Wehrung 1990), and Lack of knowledge about grievance redressal mechanism of a company (Deb and Singh 2016; Singh and Bhowal 2011) are some of the facts which testify this theory.

d. Habituated Action Theory: Habituated Action theory argues that engaging in high-risk behavior many times without a negative outcome often decreases the perceived risk associated with this behavior. Those who repeatedly perform a high-risk action without an adverse consequence eventually become desensitized to the risk (Kasperson et al. 1988; Weyman and Kelly 1999). For example, it is observed that people who play on margins in equity investments and have not faced any loss will keep on increasing their margin. Expertise among some people in calculation of income from equity investment (Deb and Singh 2016; Singh and Bhowal 2011; Powers 2009); Information about stock market as an investment avenue (Singh and Bhowal 2011) Education for equity share investment (Deb and Singh 2016; Singh and Bhowal 2010b, 2011), and Existence of coaching/counseling/share investors' forum locally and change in investors' behavior due to this (Singh and Bhowal 2011), etc., testify this theory.

e. Social Action Theory: Social Action theory states that people take a risk because of peer pressure or a general community perception that activity is of low risk. The propensity towards risk can be affected by coworkers' expectations. Individuals confirm to group norms to avoid sanctions (e.g., teasing, bullying) and start to identify with the group and accept group perceptions and behavior (Harding and Eiser 1984). For example, a Muslim community follows Shariah law for investment. Certain actions confirm the social action theory such as the Feeling of becoming a victim of fraud committed by others; De-motivation among investors to invest due to the pattern of change in the price of equity shares (Deb and Singh 2016; Singh and Bhowal 2011); Considering some people's opinion about riskiness of equity investment (Singh and Bhowal 2011); Investors' response to reporting of equity share related scandals in papers (Deb and Singh 2016; Singh and Bhowal 2011; Kahneman and Tversky 1979); Seeing others suffer loss in equity investment (Singh and Bhowal 2011); Lack of/irregular/little information/article/paper in vernacular medium regarding equity share investment (Singh and Bhowal 2011).

f. Social Control Theory: Social Action Theory was first introduced by Hirschi (1969) and states that the connectedness to organizations promotes behavior conformity, which can reduce the probability of high-risk behavior. For example, it is often viewed that people prefer to buy stocks of the companies where they work. (ONGC employees prefer to buy ONGC shares, OIL employees prefer to buy OIL shares and so on). Investors' reaction towards lack of information about the existence of company where investment to be made (Singh and Bhowal 2011); No availability of office of the company locally (Singh and Bhowal 2010a, 2011); Understanding the complex rules and regulation about equity investment (Deb and Singh 2016; Singh and Bhowal 2011; Bhattacharjee and Singh 2017); Complexity in stock market investment (Deb and Singh 2016; Singh and Bhowal 2011), etc., confirm to this theory.

g. Bounded Rational Theory: Bounded rational theory was coined by Simon (1950) and is the idea that in decision making, the rationality of individuals is limited by the information they have, the cognitive limitations of their minds and the finite amount of time they have to make a decision. For example, an investor needs to sell off his stocks immediately due to immediate financial requirement. So, it might not be possible for him to wait for the stock price to be conducive enough to yield him optimum results due to time constraint. Awareness about the complex rules and regulation about equity investment (Singh and Bhowal 2011; Bhattacharjee and Singh 2017); Need of daily monitoring of the share market for investment (Singh and Bhowal 2011); Lack of knowledge about the utilization of equity market information for making decision to invest (Singh and Bhowal 2010b, 2011); Difficulty in monitoring macroeconomic data, financial, and non-financial performance of the company for equity investment (Singh and Bhowal 2011; Fischer and Jordan 2006), Selecting company and type of equity shares for investment (Singh and Bhowal 2011; Fischer and Jordan 2006); and Difficulty in understanding the buying-selling price fixation mechanism of shares (Singh and Bhowal 2011) are some of the aspects of equity investment which can be explained by bounded rationality theory.

Risk perception of a person is the function of his/her internal as well as external environment such as the person's attitude, heredity, environment, upbringings, etc., and therefore, all the theories work collectively in influencing the risk perception of the individual in a mixed way. They are acting collectively and not in isolation; therefore, the scale to measure risk perception is constructed by extracting the variables from each of the theories.

3. Review of the Existing Literature and Research Gap

A detailed and comprehensive literature review was undertaken to understand the facets of the area. The literature relevant to risk perception was studied to know the factors studied by other researchers. Karmakar (2001) opined that the people are in general risk-averse and safety is given the highest priority while taking an investing decision. Purkayastha (2008) revealed that age, salary, and designation do impact the risk appetite of an investor. In reality, investors tend to invest in average-risk mutual funds, irrespective of their demographics and risk tolerance.

Singh and Bhowal (2010a) highlighted that the risk perception of the employees for the shares of their own company share is relatively lower than the risk perception for the shares of other companies. Singh (2009) found that investors perceive mutual funds as relatively less risky than that of direct investment in equity. Roszkowski (2010) stated that the economic crisis of 2008 was said to lower the risk tolerance of the investors. MacCrimmon and Wehrung (1990) conducted a study among the executives to know the characteristics of risk-taking by them and it was found that the most successful executives are the biggest risk takers and most mature executives are the most risk-averse. Lion and Meertens (2005) suggested that risk avoiders and risk takers differ in the extent to which they focus on the worst and best outcomes of the risky activity.

Veeramani and Karthikeyan (2014) concluded that investors' perception of the total investment risk and return determines the capacity of investors and investors prefer less risky investment avenues.

Risk perception can be managed and in order to achieve this, there is a need to measure risk perception (Singh and Bhowal 2008). Sitkin and Pablo (1992) published a paper re-conceptualizing the determinants of risky behavior. Sitkin and Weingart (1995) highlighted the determinants of risky decision-making behavior and the role of risk perceptions. There were studies conducted to design the appropriate measure of risk and to establish a relation between risks and return (Powers 2009). Palmer (1996) and Weber (2001) have focused on the way where people subjectively convert objective risk information (i.e., possible consequences of risky choice options such as mortality rates or financial returns and their likelihood of occurrence) in ways that reflect the impact that these events have on their lives.

MacGregor et al. (1999) and Koonce et al. (2005) in their studies asked financial experts to rate the risks involved in various types of investments. The results of these two studies were comparable, in line with each other, and found that quantitative aspects (probability of loss and volatility) and qualitative aspects (such as worry and anxiety, and knowledge) were both significant predictors of perceived risk.

Duxbury and Summers (2004), Klos et al. (2005), Nosic and Weber (2010), and Veld and Veld-Merkoulova (2008) presented their results of studies using experimental approach which commonly reveal that potential losses arise larger than the volatility of outcomes both for describing risk judgments and predicting investment decisions.

Singh and Bhowal (2011) measured investors risk perception from the perspective of the marketing mix. Singh (2012) studied the risk perception of general investors in respect of their investment in Initial Public Offer (IPO) of shares. Deb and Singh (2018) have used the scale of Singh and Bhowal (2011) to study the risk perception of investors in respect of mutual funds.

From the above discussion, it is seen that there have been many studies on measuring risk and risk perception in several situations and markets, but no attempt has been made to measure the risk perception of retail equity investors from a geographically isolated area such as South Assam. Therefore, in this study, the risk perception of retail equity investors from economically backward region is measured using the parameters used by Singh and Bhowal (2011); Singh (2012); and Deb and Singh (2018).

Based on the above background and gap areas, the present study bridges the gap between the existing literatures to measure the risk perception of retail investors in equity shares belonging to South Assam of India which is relatively isolated from the mainstream of the country. The investigation on the risk perception of the investors from this region will help in knowing the level of risk perception of the investors from a relatively economically backward area. The study is also helpful in framing policy with respect to investment education in the region so that misperception, if any, can be eliminated or reduced.

This paper contributes to the existing literature on risk perception in respect of equity shares in several aspects, for example, the data cover very recent years, up to 2017, which have not been covered in previous studies, and the study is conducted on a geographically and economically isolated area, which has also not been done in the previous studies.

Based on the literature review on risk perception about equity investment, measurement of risk perception and theories of risk perception the following research framework has been proposed as given in Figure 1.

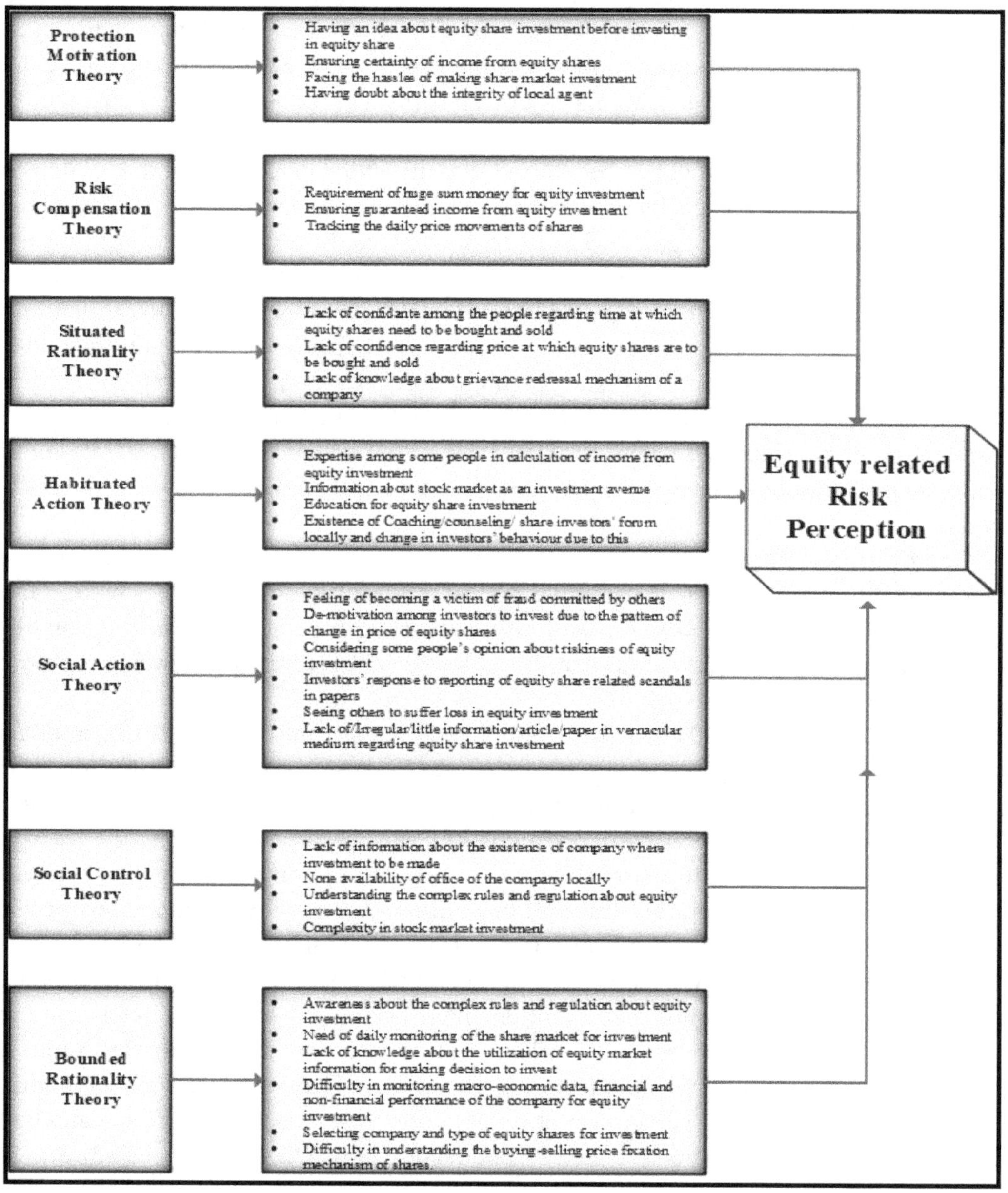

Figure 1. Research framework. Source: Compiled by authors from various sources.

4. Objectives of the Study

The objectives of the present study are as follows:

i. To measure the level of risk perception of investor towards equity share investment;
ii. To identify the factors that influences the risk perception of the equity investors.

5. Research Questions

The following research questions are attempted to be answered in this paper:

i. What is the level of risk perception of the equity investors in India?
ii. What are the variables that affect towards building risk perception of the investors?
iii. Which of the variables are least important in framing the overall level of risk perception of the investors?
iv. What are the factors that affect the risk perception of the investors?

6. Research Methodology

The study was conducted using the following research methodology.

i. Type of Research: The study is descriptive in nature.
ii. The Universe of the Study: For the purpose of the study, the universe consists of the entire individual having demat a/c with National Securities Depository Limited (NSDL) in three districts of Assam, i.e., Cachar, Karimganj, and Hailakandi. There were 7148 demat account holders (as on 31st March 2015) in these three districts.
iii. Sample and Sample unit: The sampling design for this study is stratified sampling. Therefore, at 5% level of significance and 95% confidence level, a sample of 365 investors was obtained. However, seven (7) of them were excluded from the analysis due to incomplete information. Thus, a sample of 358 investors was finally taken into consideration for the study.

The numbers of investors' with demat account holders in Cachar, Karimganj, and Hailakandi districts are 4730, 601, and 1817, respectively. Now with proportional allocation method under stratified sampling technique, a sample of 245, 38, and 75 from Cachar, Karimganj, and Hailakandi districts, respectively, were taken to accomplish the total number of sample size 358.

iv. Data Collection: The study was based on primary data and a structured questionnaire was used to collect the necessary information relevant for our study. However, secondary data was also obtained from relevant sources such as journals, official reports, newspaper, etc., for providing necessary background information of the study area.
v. Development of the Questionnaire: To measure the risk perception, a scale was framed by considering 35 items as mentioned in the research framework given in Figure 1 and Table 1, which are identified from the review of the literature and theories related to risk perception. The details of the items and their source are given in the Table 1.

By applying item–total correlation on the above items, it was found that the item–total correlation value of Item No. 6, Item No. 11, Item No 23, Item No 32, and Item No. 34 was less than 0.2, which means that these items does not correlate very well with the overall score and thus may be dropped. So, a total of 30 items were used for analysis purpose.

For measuring risk perception, the responses to the above-mentioned items were obtained on a five-point Likert scale, where a response of strongly disagree was given a score of 1, which consequently denotes a very low level of risk perception, and response of 5 was given for strongly agree, which denotes a very high level of risk perception. Besides these, there were questions on the demographic and socio-economic profile of the respondents.

Table 1. Details of questionnaire.

Sl. No.	Items	Source(s)
1	Idea about equity share investment	Deb and Singh (2016); Singh and Bhowal (2011)
2	Certainty of income from equity shares	Deb and Singh (2016); Singh and Bhowal (2011); Powers (2009).
3	Difficulty in calculation of income from equity investment	Deb and Singh (2016); Singh and Bhowal (2011); Powers (2009)
4	Awareness about the complex rules and regulation about equity investment	Singh and Bhowal (2011); Bhattacharjee and Singh (2017)
5	Understanding the complex rules and regulation about equity investment	Deb and Singh (2016); Singh and Bhowal (2011); Bhattacharjee and Singh (2017)
6	Requirement of huge sum money for equity investment	Singh and Bhowal (2011); Powers (2009)
7	No guaranteed income from equity investment	Singh and Bhowal (2011)
8	Need of daily monitoring of the share market for investment	Singh and Bhowal (2011)
9	Lack of knowledge about the utilization of equity market information for making decision to invest	Singh and Bhowal (2010b, 2011)
10	Complexity in stock market investment	Deb and Singh (2016); Singh and Bhowal (2011)
11	Hassles of making share market investment	Singh and Bhowal (2011)
12	Likelihood of becoming a victim of fraud committed by others	Deb and Singh (2016); Singh and Bhowal (2011)
13	Difficulty in monitoring macro-economic data for equity investment	Singh and Bhowal (2011); Fischer and Jordan (2006)
14	Difficulty in selecting company for equity investment	Singh and Bhowal (2011); Fischer and Jordan (2006)
15	Difficulty in selecting type of equity shares for equity investment	Singh and Bhowal (2011)
16	Difficulty in monitoring financial performance of a company	Singh and Bhowal (2011); Fischer and Jordan (2006)
17	Difficulty in monitoring non-financial performance of a company	Singh and Bhowal (2011)
18	Difficulty in understanding the buying-selling price fixation mechanism of shares	Singh and Bhowal (2011)
19	Lack of confidence regarding time at which equity shares need to be bought	Deb and Singh (2016); Singh and Bhowal (2011); MacCrimmon and Wehrung (1990)
20	Lack of confidence regarding price at which equity shares are to be bought	Singh and Bhowal (2011); MacCrimmon and Wehrung (1990)
21	De-motivation to invest due to the pattern of change in price of equity shares	Deb and Singh (2016); Singh and Bhowal (2011)
22	Difficulty in tracking the daily price movements of shares	Deb and Singh (2016); Singh and Bhowal (2011)
23	Lack of information about stock market as an investment avenue	Singh and Bhowal (2011)
24	Lack of education for equity share investment	Deb and Singh (2016); Singh and Bhowal (2010b, 2011)
25	Some people's opinion about riskiness of equity investment	Singh and Bhowal (2011)
26	Lack of coaching/counseling/share investors' forum locally	Singh and Bhowal (2011)
27	Lack of information/article/paper in vernacular medium regarding equity share investment	Singh and Bhowal (2011)
28	Irregular information/article/paper in vernacular medium regarding equity share investment	Singh and Bhowal (2011)

Table 1. *Cont.*

Sl. No.	Items	Source(s)
29	Little information/article/paper in vernacular medium regarding equity share investment	Singh and Bhowal (2011)
30	Reporting of equity share scandals in papers	Deb and Singh (2016); Singh and Bhowal (2011); Kahneman and Tversky (1979)
31	Seeing others to suffer loss in equity investment	Singh and Bhowal (2011)
32	Lack of information about the existence of company where investment to be made	Singh and Bhowal (2011)
33	None availability of office of the company locally	Singh and Bhowal (2010a, 2011)
34	Doubt about the integrity of local agent	Deb and Singh (2016); Singh and Bhowal (2011)
35	Lack of knowledge about grievance redressal mechanism of a company	Deb and Singh (2016); Singh and Bhowal (2011)

Source: Compiled by authors from various sources.

vi. Profile of the Respondents

The profile of the respondents is given in Table 2.

Table 2. Demographic and socio-economic profile of the respondents.

Gender of the Investor		
Gender	Frequency	Percent
Male	278	77.7
Female	80	22.3
Total	358	100
Qualification of the Investor		
Qualification	Frequency	Percent
Undergraduate	39	10.9
Graduate	158	44.1
Post Graduate	120	33.5
Others	41	11.5
Total	358	100
Age of the Investor		
Age	Frequency	Percent
18–28 years	83	23.2
28–38 years	106	29.6
38–48 years	74	20.7
48–58 years	64	17.9
58 years and above	31	8.7
Total	358	100
Occupation of the Investor		
Occupation	Frequency	Percent
Service	85	23.7
Business	146	40.8
Housewife	62	17.3
Student	6	1.7
Professionals	12	3.4
Others	47	13.1
Total	358	100

Table 2. *Cont.*

Annual Family Income of the Family		
Annual Family Income	Frequency	Percent
Below 1 lac	54	15.1
1–2 lakhs	56	15.6
2–5 lakhs	119	33.2
5–10 lakhs	77	21.5
10–20 lakhs	45	12.6
20 lakhs and above	7	2
Total	358	100

Source: Compiled from questionnaire.

vii. Data Analysis

To assess the risk perception of equity investors, statistical tests such as mean, standard deviation, etc., are used. Reliability of the scale constructed to measure the equity share related risk perception is tested using Cronbach's alpha. Cronbach's alpha is a measure of internal consistency. A high value of Cronbach's alpha means, the scale is a reliable one and the items are collectively measuring the latent variable. In the considered scale, some of the items were on reverse scaling so as to ensure the accuracy of response (Tavakol and Dennick 2011). The formula for the Cronbach's alpha is given below:

$$\left[\alpha = \frac{N.\bar{c}}{\bar{v} + (N-1)\cdot\bar{c}}\right]$$

Here, N is equal to the number of items, c-bar is the average inter-item covariance among the items and v-bar equals the average variance.

Factors affecting the risk perception of equity investors are extracted using factor analysis. To identify the number of factors that significantly relate to the original variables, the Rotation Sum of Squared Loadings is used that shows the variance and Eigenvalue after rotation. Eigenvalue is the sum of squared factor loadings pertaining to that particular factor and the process uses rotated Eigenvalue to decide the number of significant factors. Each of the components has an Eigenvalue of total variance explained and it explains the variance of that particular component. The same is also expressed in percentage of variance. The method used to get the output is the Varimax rotation.

7. Findings of the Study

The findings of the study are presented in the following paragraphs.

i. Reliability of the Scale

The reliability of the scale prepared to measure risk perception of equity investors was tested using Cronbach's alpha. The value of Cronbach's alpha is 0.881. Cronbach's alpha of more than 0.70 is considered to be a good measure of the reliability of scale (Nunnaly 1978). Thus, in the present study, it can be inferred that the scale is a reliable one and it is actually measuring the latent variable namely risk perception.

ii. Item Statistics

Item statistics of 30 items considered for the scale to measure risk perception in respect of equity shares is given in Table 3.

Table 3. Item Statistics.

Items	Mean	SD
Availability of coaching/counseling/share investors' forum locally	2.4972	1.13697
Understanding about the complex rules and regulation about equity investment	2.6201	0.91721
Seeing others to suffer loss in equity investment	2.6648	0.9133
Irregular information/article/paper in vernacular medium regarding equity share investment	2.6704	0.90301
Likely to become a victim of fraud committed by others	2.7765	0.99596
Reporting of equity share scandals in papers	2.8408	1.03432
Little information/article/paper in vernacular medium regarding equity share investment	2.8464	1.01329
No office of the company locally	2.8603	1.0358
Complexity in market investment	2.8994	1.03494
Lack of knowledge about grievance redressal mechanism of a company	2.919	1.17472
Difficulty in selecting company for equity investment	2.9302	1.06807
No guaranteed income from equity investment	2.9972	1.17989
Daily monitoring of the market	2.9972	1.24459
Difficulty in tracking the daily price movements	3.0084	1.20104
Idea about equity share investment	3.0307	1.18896
Difficulty in monitoring non-financial performance of a company	3.0838	0.98659
Some people's opinion about riskiness of equity investment	3.095	0.99124
Difficulty in monitoring macro-economic data for equity investment	3.1145	1.05892
Difficulty in calculation of income from equity investment	3.1229	1.16508
Pattern of change in price of equity shares de-motivate	3.1508	1.07147
Lack of knowledge about the utilization of equity market information	3.162	1.06984
Certainty of income from equity shares	3.1927	1.19722
Difficulty in monitoring financial performance of a company	3.1927	0.98405
Lack of information/article/paper in vernacular medium regarding equity share investment	3.2235	1.11033
Lack of confidence regarding time at which equity shares need to be bought	3.2374	1.05429
Difficulty in understanding the buying selling price fixation mechanism	3.2737	1.04944
Lack of confidence regarding price at which equity shares are to be bought	3.3073	1.02107
Awareness about the complex rules and regulation about equity investment	3.3101	1.25979
Lack of education for equity share investment	3.419	0.98895
Difficulty in selecting type of equity shares for equity investment	3.4609	0.90587

Source: Compiled from questionnaire.

iii. Scale Construction

The scale considered for this study contains 30 items. Since a score of 5,4,3,2, and 1 was given to the respondents for their response of strongly agree, agree, moderately agree, disagree, and strongly disagree, respectively, the maximum one respondent can score in each of the items is 5. Therefore, the maximum possible score is 150 (30 × 5). Similarly, the minimum one respondent can score in each of the items is 1 and, therefore, the minimum possible score is 30 (30 × 1). The difference between maximum and minimum possible score is 120 (150 − 30). In order to ascertain the risk perception at five levels, this range (120) is divided by 5. It is found to be 24. Adding 24 with 30 (lowest possible score), the very low level of risk perception range (30 − 54) is obtained. Similarly, adding 24 with subsequent value, next higher range is obtained. In Table 4, risk perception score is interpreted.

Table 4. Interpretation of risk perception level score.

30–54	Very low level of risk perception
54–78	Low level of risk perception
78–102	Moderate level of risk perception
102–126	High level of risk perception
126–150	Very high level of risk perception

Source: Compiled by authors.

The mean value of the scale statistics is found to be 90.90 as shown in Table 5, which lies in the interval 78–102, representing a moderate level of risk perception.

Table 5. Scale Statistics.

Mean	Variance	Std. Deviation	*N* of Items
90.9050	231.571	15.21745	30

Source: Compiled from questionnaire.

iv. Overall Risk Perception

The overall risk perceptions of the respondents are calculated by adding their score in the Likert scale, and then its value was interpreted using Table 4. The overall level of risk perception is then presented in Table 6.

Table 6. Overall risk perception level.

Level of Risk Perception	Frequency	Percentage
Very low	5	1.40%
Low	155	43.30%
Moderate	186	52.00%
High	12	3.40%
Very high	0	0.00%

Source: Compiled from questionnaire.

From Table 6, it is clear that the majority on the investors of Barak Valley has a moderate level of risk perception towards equity investment.

v. Factor analysis

In order to perform factor analysis, the first thing to be done is to test the adequacy of the sample considered for the study. To test the adequacy of the collected data from the samples, the Kaiser–Meyer–Olkin (KMO) measure of sample adequacy and Bartlett's test were done on the 358 responses. The KMO and Bartlett's test of sphericity check the redundancy among the variables and whether the variables can be summarized with a small number of factors. Both tests have the same objective of ensuring if the factor analysis can be done efficiently with the original variables. Bartlett's test of sphericity uses the following formula:

$$x^2 = -\left(n - 1 - \frac{2p + 5}{6}\right) \times \ln|R|$$

In the above equation, $|R|$ represents the determinants of correlation matrix and is computed to measure the overall relation with the variables. The value of KMO should be more than 0.5 for a satisfactory factor analysis (Kaiser 1974). Table 7 shows that the KMO value for this study is 0.737, which means sample size is adequate enough to carry out the factor analysis.

Table 7. Kaiser–Meyer–Olkin (KMO) and Bartlett's Test.

Kaiser–Meyer–Olkin Measure of Sampling Adequacy		0.737
Bartlett's Test of Sphericity	Approximate Chi-Square	6268.120
	DF	435
	Sig	0.000

Source: Compiled from questionnaire.

Again, Table 7 shows that the p-value for Bartlett's test of sphericity is 0.000 (which is less than 0.05). This also confirms the data considered for factor analysis is appropriate.

The number of factors is identified on the basis of Eigenvalue. The Eigenvalue for a given factor measures the variance in all the variables which are accounted for by that factor. If the factor has Eigenvalue less than unity, then it is contributing little to the explanation of variances and may be ignored as redundant with more important factors.

From Table 8, it is evident that nine factors have Eigen value more than 1 and these nine factors can explain 73.29% of the total variability. Thus, there are nine components for Principal Component Analysis.

Table 8. Total Variance Explained.

Component	Initial Eigen Values			Extraction Sums of Squared Loadings			Rotation Sums of Squared Loadings		
	Total	% of Variance	Cumulative %	Total	% of Variance	Cumulative %	Total	% of Variance	Cumulative %
1	6.992	23.307	23.307	6.992	23.307	23.307	3.444	11.480	11.480
2	3.533	11.776	35.083	3.533	11.776	35.083	3.026	10.085	21.566
3	2.483	8.276	43.359	2.483	8.276	43.359	3.010	10.034	31.600
4	2.069	6.897	50.256	2.069	6.897	50.256	2.680	8.933	40.533
5	1.867	6.222	56.478	1.867	6.222	56.478	2.299	7.662	48.195
6	1.516	5.054	61.533	1.516	5.054	61.533	2.167	7.224	55.419
7	1.305	4.350	65.883	1.305	4.350	65.883	1.855	6.184	61.602
8	1.147	3.824	69.707	1.147	3.824	69.707	1.841	6.138	67.740
9	1.077	3.589	73.296	1.077	3.589	73.296	1.667	5.555	73.296
10	0.974	3.246	76.542						
11	0.865	2.883	79.424						
12	0.731	2.438	81.862						
13	0.619	2.063	83.926						
14	0.537	1.790	85.716						
15	0.506	1.685	87.401						
16	0.455	1.517	88.918						
17	0.422	1.407	90.325						
18	0.364	1.213	91.538						
19	0.347	1.157	92.695						
20	0.317	1.058	93.753						
21	0.287	0.957	94.710						
22	0.259	0.864	95.574						
23	0.244	0.814	96.388						
24	0.209	0.697	97.085						
25	0.193	0.642	97.727						
26	0.176	0.586	98.313						
27	0.171	0.572	98.885						
28	0.132	0.441	99.325						
29	0.110	0.367	99.692						
30	0.092	0.308	100.000						

Extraction Method: Principal Component Analysis.

Source: Compiled from questionnaire.

The Principal component analysis is used to find that which variables are most strongly correlated with each component, i.e., which of these numbers are large in magnitude. This process helps in identifying the low correlation variables with the component. Table 9 shows the Rotated Component Matrix, where larger correlations are in boldface.

Table 9. Rotated Component Matrix.

	Component								
	1	2	3	4	5	6	7	8	9
Difficulty in monitoring financial performance of a company	**0.827**	0.082	−0.022	0.128	0.138	0.243	0.041	0.041	0.036
Difficulty in monitoring non-financial performance of a company	**0.750**	0.033	0.075	0.194	0.131	0.157	−0.116	0.079	0.045
Difficulty in tracking the daily price movements	**0.680**	−0.142	0.333	−0.027	0.224	−0.075	0.111	0.315	−0.021
Likely to become a victim of fraud committed by others	**0.657**	−0.040	0.146	−0.249	0.110	0.358	−0.017	0.043	0.180
Difficulty in selecting company for equity investment	**0.456**	0.183	−0.059	0.005	−0.228	0.368	0.311	0.140	0.322
Lack of education for equity share investment	−0.083	**0.796**	0.039	−0.001	−0.065	−0.003	0.229	0.082	−0.184
Some people's opinion about riskiness of equity investment	−0.026	**0.771**	0.075	0.327	0.159	0.014	−0.205	−0.038	−0.135
Little information/article/paper in vernacular medium regarding equity share investment	−0.121	**0.613**	0.245	−0.155	0.121	−0.017	0.060	0.230	0.423
Lack of knowledge about the utilization of equity market information	0.332	**0.548**	−0.140	0.145	0.358	−0.025	0.024	−0.077	0.321
No guaranteed income from equity investment	0.398	**0.529**	0.322	0.092	0.069	−0.014	0.034	−0.387	0.142
Seeing others to suffer loss in equity investment	0.310	**0.458**	0.362	0.060	−0.359	0.185	−0.224	0.182	0.040
Understanding about the complex rules and regulation about equity investment	0.230	0.117	**0.811**	0.016	0.062	−0.094	0.073	−0.168	−0.009
Irregular information/article/paper in vernacular medium regarding equity share investment	0.048	0.125	**0.708**	0.085	−0.151	0.271	0.215	−0.053	0.179
Idea about equity share investment	−0.006	0.020	**0.660**	0.470	0.199	−0.047	−0.004	0.162	0.103
Lack of information/article/paper in vernacular medium regarding equity share investment	0.055	0.447	**0.463**	0.350	0.205	0.189	−0.056	0.078	0.193
Daily monitoring of the market	−0.016	0.063	**0.460**	0.061	0.289	0.411	0.010	0.391	0.199
Certainty of income from equity shares	0.047	0.257	0.311	**0.733**	−0.055	0.024	0.181	−0.062	0.319
Difficulty in calculation of income from equity investment	0.025	0.103	0.161	**0.724**	0.013	−0.031	0.319	0.304	0.143
Lack of confidence regarding time at which equity shares need to be bought	0.171	0.038	−0.012	**0.659**	0.055	0.465	0.107	0.037	−0.022
Difficulty in monitoring macro-economic data for equity investment	0.222	0.085	0.279	−0.020	**0.812**	0.067	−0.017	−0.007	0.006
Difficulty in selecting type of equity shares for equity investment	0.310	0.060	−0.173	0.025	**0.778**	0.052	−0.060	0.112	0.014
Awareness about the complex rules and regulation about equity investment	−0.242	0.346	0.353	0.399	**0.553**	0.021	0.192	−0.073	0.033
Pattern of change in price of equity shares de-motivate	0.313	−0.039	0.132	−0.088	0.028	**0.811**	−0.012	0.099	0.089
Lack of confidence regarding price at which equity shares are to be bought	0.217	0.048	−0.018	0.363	0.054	**0.713**	0.123	0.006	−0.026
No office of the company locally	−0.150	−0.077	0.226	0.197	0.051	−0.043	**0.802**	0.040	0.123
Lack of knowledge about grievance redressal mechanism of a company	0.134	0.107	−0.003	0.147	−0.035	0.145	**0.769**	0.078	−0.038
Rare reporting of equity share scandals in papers	0.158	0.184	0.015	0.025	−0.089	0.062	0.042	**0.822**	0.038
Difficulty in understanding the buying selling price fixation mechanism	0.199	−0.179	−0.149	0.345	0.241	0.093	0.143	**0.649**	0.016
Lack of coaching/counseling/share investors' forum locally	0.063	0.016	0.274	0.247	0.005	0.003	−0.046	0.085	**0.747**
Complexity in market investment	0.400	−0.195	−0.058	0.083	0.038	0.250	0.253	−0.096	**0.585**

Source: Compiled from Questionnaire.

Table 10 shows all the components thus identified.

Table 10. Results of Factor Analysis.

Component	Variables Included	Name of the Component
1	• Difficulty in monitoring financial performance of a company, • Difficulty in monitoring non-financial performance of a company, • Difficulty in tracking the daily price movements, • Likely to become a victim of fraud committed by others, • Difficulty in selecting company for equity investment,	Information screening
2	• Some people's opinion about riskiness of equity investment, • Lack of education for equity share investment, • Little information/article/paper in vernacular medium regarding equity share investment, • Lack of knowledge about the utilization of equity market information, • No guaranteed income from equity investment, • Seeing others to suffer loss in equity investment	Investment education
3	• Understanding about the complex rules and regulation about equity investment, • Irregular information/article/paper in vernacular medium regarding equity share investment, • Idea about equity share investment, • Lack of information/article/paper in vernacular medium regarding equity share investment.	Information processing
4	• Certainty of income from equity shares, • Difficulty in calculation of income from equity investment, • Lack of confidence regarding time at which equity shares need to be bought	Fear psychosis
5	• Difficulty in monitoring macro-economic data for equity investment, • Difficulty in selecting type of equity shares for equity investment, • Awareness about the complex rules and regulation about equity investment.	Fundamental Expertise
6	• De-motivation due to pattern of change in price of equity shares, • Lack of confidence regarding price at which equity shares are to be bought.	Technical Expertise
7	• No office of the company locally, • Lack of knowledge about grievance redressal mechanism of a company.	Familiarity bias
8	• Reporting of equity share scandals in papers, • Difficulty in understanding the buying selling price fixation mechanism	Information asymmetry
9	• Lack of coaching/counseling/share investors' forum locally, • Complexity in market investment.	Understanding of Market

Source: Compiled from questionnaire.

8. Conclusions and Policy Implication

It is seen that the overall level of risk perception of the investors towards equity share investment is of moderate level. This is different from the findings of Singh and Bhowal (2010a), where the risk perception level of employees of a large Public Sector Unit was found to be of high level. This shows that the risk perception of people from an economically backward region is relatively lesser than that of people who have very secured source of income. However, this is not reflected in their equity investment. The items such as difficulty in selecting the type of equity shares for equity investment, lack of education for equity share investment, awareness about the complex rules and regulation about equity investment have a relatively high contribution in building the overall level of risk perception towards equity investment. All these variables are directly related to the exposure of the people to the equity market. Exposure to a risky situation influences a person to make an investment in a risky asset

(Krueger 1993). It means their risk perception is relatively favorable for making equity investment (Singh and Bhowal 2009b) but they do not have the necessary exposure to the equity market and hence they are not making an equity investment. Given their moderate level of risk perception, if they are given exposure to the equity market, the equity investment culture in the region can be improved and, consequently, entrepreneurial activities can be accelerated.

The study identifies nine factors which have an impact on investors' risk perception. These are Difficulty in the screening of information, inadequate investment education, inadequate information, Return-related suspicions, Fundamental expertise, and Technical expertise, Familiarity with the company, Information asymmetry, and Inadequate understanding of market.

Thus, it is evident from the findings that most important factor that has an impact on investors' risk perception is difficulty in the screening of information, which is similar with the findings of Fischhoff et al. (1978).

Risk perceptions are exaggerated when vulnerable investors believe that they have difficulty in screening the available information. In such cases, the difficulty is experienced not only by the retail investors but also in the experts, regulators and Government officials who monitor the activity or market. Sachsea et al. (2012) focused on the effects of individual characteristics on financial risk perception. Ricciardi (2004) stated that difficulty in the screening of information might influence an investment professional's risk perception. Pellinen et al. (2011) stated that risk perception increases when investors have more information but they are unable to screen it. Thus, there is a need for proper investment education and training (Singh and Bhowal 2010b).

Perceived risk determines not only the sources of information conferred but also the type of information that has been used by the investor. The same behavior could be observed in the stock market as well because information is a means which allows limiting the uncertainty surrounding the investment situation. Nwezeaku and Okpara (2010) indicates that the level of information asymmetry can be featured by the risk of investing with a privately informed investor. Thus, the less the investors share the same information, the higher will be the level of risk perception towards their decisions in the stock market (Mahmood et al. 2011). Moreover, Wang et al. (2006) specified that good quality of information disclosure could substantially reduce investors' risk perception. Social action theory of risk perception confirms to this behavior.

Information is the first component of protection motivation theory (Rogers 1983). Based on information, an individual identifies prospective threats and potential opportunities. The individual then must assess this information to determine whether or not to engage with that potential opportunity to a given threat.

Familiarity of something comes from exposure. This can be knowledge (Hall 2007), experience (Klein 2008), or types of unconscious priming (Kahneman 2003). This may eventually lead to a comfort, affiliation, or some other type of cognitive bond (Laing and Crouch 2004). Shavit et al. (2016) and Singh and Bhowal (2010a) have also confirmed the presence of familiarity bias.

Social Control theory also stated that connectedness or familiarity to an organization reduces the probability of high risk behavior (Hirschi 1969).

Hodder et al. (2001) and Koonce et al. (2005) documented that changes in the level of investment education can result in an adjustment to their risk perception for a specific activity or situation. Therefore, there is a need for imparting investment education (Singh and Bhowal 2010b) and make them expert in dealing with their own investment decision.

According to Dreyfus (2005), though experts are rational, they have not been able to defend their own actions rationally all the time. Expertise in doing fundamental analysis for making equity investment is also one of the important components of rationality. Rationality is one of the important components of Bounded Rationality theory. However, possessing technical expertise is one of the most essential elements to manage risk as per situated rationality theory. It says that considering the situation in hand, a risk needs to be managed and technical analysis attempt to do the same.

Return-related suspicions can influence the risk perception where investors tend to worry that their investment could be lost (Hira and Mugenda 1999). MacGregor et al. (1999) studied the relationship between fear psychosis and risk perception and found that fear psychosis is a significant indicator of risk perception, and Risk Compensation theory also states that people used to take more risk when they feel more secured.

An investor who has understood the market through his prior experience is likely to use his/her expertise in handling the risk and Habituated Action Theory says the same thing.

Thus, it is seen that the factors affecting risk perception as identified in this study are also linked with the existing theories of risk perception and all the theories are having an influence in building the equity related risk perception of an investors. This finding can be explained with the help of Figure 2 of this paper.

Thus, looking at Figure 2, it is evident that several factors affecting risk perception of equity investors are ultimately related to the several theories of risk perception developed over period of time.

Thus, keeping in mind on the above-mentioned factors, efforts should be made to bring the people with high risk perception to low risk perception category by imparting them training to handle or manage high-risk scenarios (Singh and Bhowal 2009a, 2010c). Once they are brought to low risk perception category or trained to handle and manage the high-risk scenario, then it will be easier for the government to promote equity investment culture amongst the people as well as the same people will act as entrepreneurship–culture initiator and adaptor (Singh 2011). Understanding the risk perception of individuals, policy makers can take steps to improve their risk perception and it will in turn promote better investment culture.

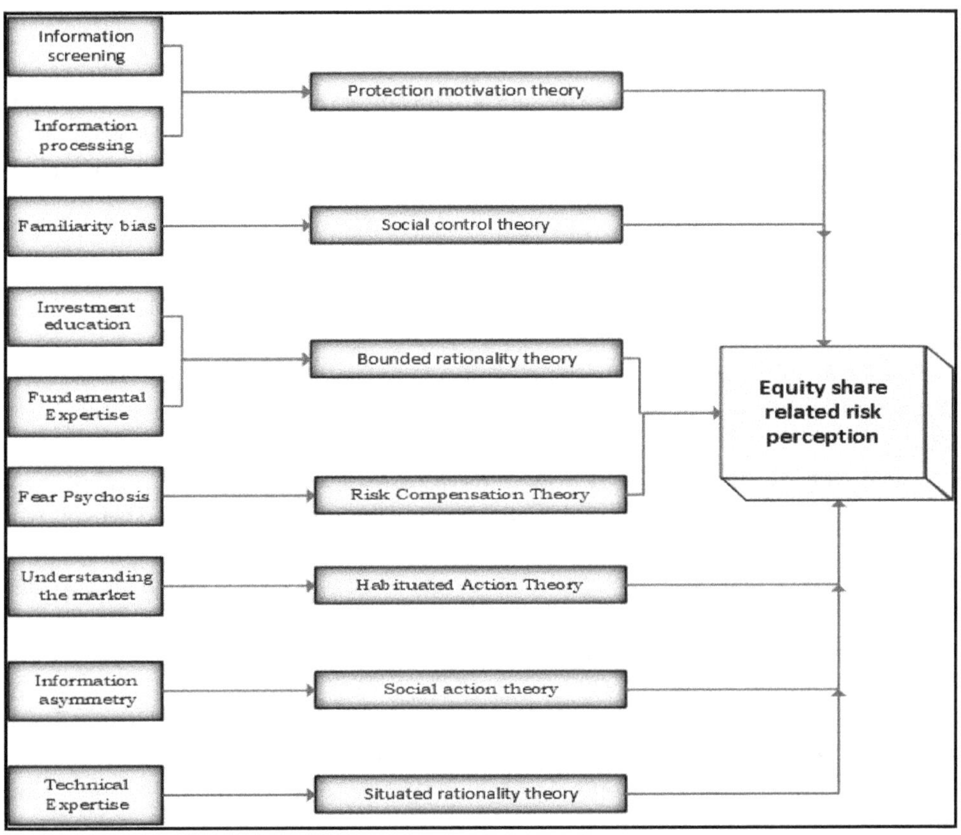

Figure 2. Factors affecting equity related risk perception along with theories. Source: Compiled by the authors from various sources.

9. Scope for Future Research

The present study is confined into the retail equity investors of Barak Valley of Assam only. So, there is a scope that a large-scale research work can be carried out for the entire state of Assam. To know their risk perception level with respect to the different demographic variables and also to find out the impact of risk perception level on actual equity investment, an exploratory study can be carried out.

Author Contributions: Conceptualization, methodology, writing—review and editing, supervision, resources, visualization etc. done by R.S.; Formal analysis, investigation, original draft preparation done by J.B.

Funding: This research received no external funding.

Acknowledgments: The help provided by A. Bhowal, Assam University, Diphu Campus, D. Bhattacharjee, Assam University is greatly acknowledged.

Conflicts of Interest: The authors declare no conflict of interest.

References

Bernstein, Peter. 1995. Risk as a History of Ideas. *Financial Analysts Journal* 51: 7. [CrossRef]

Bhattacharjee, Jayashree, and Ranjit Singh. 2017. Awareness about equity investment among retail investors: A kaleidoscopic view. *Qualitative Research in Financial Market* 9: 310–24. [CrossRef]

Deb, Sujit, and Ranjit Singh. 2016. Impact of Risk Perception on Investors towards their Investment in Mutual Fund. *Pacific Business Review International* 9: 16–23.

Deb, Sujit, and Ranjit Singh. 2017. Influence of Demographic and Socio-economic Variables on Investors' Risk Perception towards Mutual Fund: A Study on Bank Employees of Tripura. *Bank Parikrama* XLI: 94–116.

Deb, Sujit, and Ranjit Singh. 2018. Risk perception dynamics of mutual fund investment decisions. *Iranian Journal of Management Studies* 11: 407–26.

Dreyfus, Hubert. 2005. Overcoming the myth of the mental: How philosophers can profit from the phenomenology of everyday expertise. *Proceedings and Addresses of the American Philosophical Association* 79: 47–65.

Duxbury, Darren, and Barbara Summers. 2004. Financial risk perception. Are individuals variance averse or loss averse? *Economics Letters* 84: 21–8. [CrossRef]

Finucane, Melissa, Ali Alhakami, Paul Slovic, and Stephen M. Johnson. 2000. The affect heuristic in judgments of risks and benefits. *Journal of Behavioral Decision Making* 13: 1–17. [CrossRef]

Fischer, Donald E., and Ronald J. Jordan. 2006. *Security Analysis and Portfolio Management*. New Delhi: Prentice Hall.

Fischhoff, Baruch, Paul Slovic, Sarah Lichtenstein, Stephen Read, and Barbara Combs. 1978. How safe is safe enough? A psychometric study of attitudes towards technological risks and benefits. *Policy Sciences* 9: 127–79. [CrossRef]

Hall, James W. 2007. *New Handbook of Auditory Evoked Responses*. New York: Pearson.

Harding, Christina M., and J. Richard Eiser. 1984. Characterising the perceived risks and benefits of some health issues. *Risk Analysis* 4: 131–41. [CrossRef]

Hira, Tahira K., and Olive M. Mugenda. 1999. The relationships between self worth and financial beliefs, behavior and satisfaction. *Journal of Family and Consumer Sciences* 91: 76–82.

Hirschi, Travis. 1969. A control theory of delinquency. In *Criminology Theory: Selected Classic Readings*. Berkeley: University of California Press, pp. 289–305.

Hodder, Leslie, Lisa Koonce, and Mary Lea McAnally. 2001. SEC Market Risk Disclosures: Implications for Judgement and Decision Making. *Accounting Horizons* 15: 49–70. [CrossRef]

Kahneman, Daniel. 2003. A perspective on judgment and choice: Mapping bounded rationality. *American Psychologist* 58: 697. [CrossRef] [PubMed]

Kahneman, Daniel, and Amos N. Tversky. 1979. Prospect Theory: An Analysis of Decision making Under Risk. *Economatricia* 47: 263–92. [CrossRef]

Kaiser, Henry F. 1974. An Index of Factorial Simplicity. *Psychometrika* 39: 31–36. [CrossRef]

Karmakar, Madhusudan. 2001. Investment Behavior of Household Sectors: A study of a Rural Block in West Bengal. *Journal of Commerce* 54: 1–2.

Kasperson, Roger E., Ortwin Renn, Paul Slovic, Halina S. Brown, Jacque Emel, Robert Goble, and Samual Ratick. 1988. The Social Amplification of Risk: A Conceptual Framework. *Risk Analysis* 8: 177–87. [CrossRef]

Klein, Gary. 2008. Naturalistic decision making. *Human Factors* 50: 456–60. [CrossRef]

Klos, Alexander, Elke U. Weber, and Martin Weber. 2005. Investment decisions and time horizon: Risk perception and risk behavior in repeated gambles. *Management Science* 51: 1777–90. [CrossRef]

Koonce, Lisa, Mary Lea McAnally, and Molly Mercer. 2005. How do investors judge the risk of financial items? *The Accounting Review* 80: 221–41. [CrossRef]

Krueger, Norris F. 1993. The Impact of Prior Entrepreneurial Exposure on Perceptions of New Venture Feasibility and Desirability. *Entrepreneurship Theory and Practice* 18: 5–21. [CrossRef]

Laing, Jennifer, and G. I. Crouch. 2004. Vacationing in space: tourism seeks 'new skies'. In *New Horizons in Tourism: Strange Experiences and Stranger Practices*. Oxford: Oxford University Press, pp. 11–25.

Lennart, Sjoberg. 2002. The Allegedly Simple Structure of Experts' Risk Perception: An Urban Legend in Risk Research. *Science, Technology and Human Values* 27: 443–59.

Lion, Rene, and Ree M. Meertens. 2005. Security or Oportunity: The influence of risk—Taking tendency on risk information preference. *Journal of Risk Research* 8: 283–94. [CrossRef]

Lopes, Lola L. 1987. Between Hope and Fare: The Psychology of Risk. *Advances in Experimental Social Psychology* 20: 255–95.

MacCrimmon, Kenneth R., and Donald A. Wehrung. 1990. Characteristics of Risk Taking Executives. *Management Science* 36: 422–35. [CrossRef]

MacGregor, Donald G., Paul Slovic, Michael Berry, and Harold Evensky. 1999. Perception of financial risk: A Survey Study of Advisors and Planners. *Journal of Financial Planning* 25: 68–86.

Mahmood, Iqbal, H. Ahmad, Abdul Zahid Khan, and Mansoor Anjum. 2011. Behavioral Implications of Investors for Investments in Stock Market. *European Journal of Social Sckiences* 20: 240–47.

Milliman, Richard A., and Elke U. Weber. 1997. Perceived Risk Attitudes: Relating Risk Perception of Risky Choice. *Management Sciences* 42: 123–44.

Nosic, Alen, and Martin Weber. 2010. How Riskily Do I Invest? The Role of Risk Attitudes, Risk Perceptions, and Overconfidence. *Decision Analysis* 7: 282–301. [CrossRef]

NSDL. 2011. NSDL Facts and Figures. Available online: https://nsdl.co.in/about/facts-figs.php (accessed on 15 December 2018).

Nunnaly, Jum C. 1978. *Psychometric Theory*. New York: McGraw Hill.

Nwezeaku, N. C., and G. C. Okpara. 2010. Stock Market Volatility and Information Asymmetry: lessons from Nigeria. *Interdisciplinary Journal of Contemporary Research in Business* 2: 67–79.

Palmer, Christina G. 1996. Risk Perception: An Empirical Study of the Relationship between World View and The Risk Construct. *Risk Analysis* 16: 717–23. [CrossRef]

Pellinen, Antti, Kari Tormakangas, Outi Uusitalo, and Anu Raijas. 2011. Measuring the financial capability of Investors: A case of the customers of mutual funds in Finland. *International Journal of Bank Marketing* 29: 107–33. [CrossRef]

Pidgeon, Nick F., Christopher Hood, David Jones, Barry Turner, and Rose Gibson. 1992. Risk perception. In *Risk Analysis, Perception and Management: Report of a Royal Society Study Group*. London: Royal Society, pp. 89–134.

Powers, Michel. 2009. Rethinking risk and return: Part 1—Novel norms for non-normality? *The Journal of Risk Finance* 10: 101–6. [CrossRef]

Purkayastha, Saptarshi. 2008. Investor Profiling and Investment Planning: An Empiric Study. *The Icfaian Journal of Management Research* 7: 17–40.

Registrar General, India. 2011. *Census of India 2011: Provisional Population Totals-India Data Sheet*. New Delhi: Office of the Registrar General Census Commissioner, India.

Ricciardi, Victor. 2004. *A Risk Perception Primer: A Narrative Research Review of the Risk Perception Literature in Behavioral Accounting and Behavioral Finance*. New York: Golden Gate University.

Rogers, Ronald W. 1983. Cognitive and psychological processes in fear appeals and attitude change: A revised theory of protection motivation. In *Social Psychophysiology: A Sourcebook*. New York: The Guilford Press, pp. 153–76.

Roszkowski, Michael J. 2010. Risk Perception and Risk Tolerance Changes Attributable to the 2008 Economic Crisis: A Subtle but Critical Difference. *Journal of Financial Service Professionals* 64: 42–53.

Sachsea, Katharina, Helmut Jungermanna, and Julia M. Beltingb. 2012. Investment risk—The perspective of individual investors. *Journal of Economic Psychology* 33: 437–47. [CrossRef]

Shavit, Tal, Eyal Lahav, and Mosi Rosenboim. 2016. Don't fare Risk, learn about it: How Familiarity reduces Perceived Risk. *Applied Economics Letters* 23: 1069–72. [CrossRef]

Sheeran, Paschal, Peter R. Harris, and Tracy Epton. 2014. Does heightening risk appraisals change people's intentions and behavior? A meta-analysis of experimental studies. *Psychological Bulletin* 140: 511. [CrossRef] [PubMed]

Simon, Herbert A. 1950. Administrative behaviour. *Australian Journal of Public Administration* 9: 241–45. [CrossRef]

Singh, Ranjit. 2009. Preference for Direct Equity Investment vs. Indirect Equity Investment: A Study on Salaried Investors. *Domain-The Journal of Management* 2: 23–28.

Singh, Ranjit. 2011. Equity investment culture and Entreprenureship- Culture Initiation and Adaptation. *Pacific Business Review International* 4: 66–71.

Singh, Ranjit. 2012. Risk Perception in Initial Public Offer of Shares: A Psychometric Study. *Asia Pacific Journal of Risk and Insurance* 6: 44–56. [CrossRef]

Singh, Ranjit, and Amalesh Bhowal. 2006. Bank employees risk perception as entrepreneurship culture initiator and adopter. In *National Seminar on Global Convergence on Commerce Education*. Shillong: NEHU, vol, vol. 9, November 7.

Singh, Ranjit, and Amalesh Bhowal. 2008. Risk Perception-The Theoretical Kaleidoscope. *Vanijya* 18: 54–63.

Singh, Ranjit, and Amalesh Bhowal. 2009a. Developing Entrepreneurial Culture by Inculcating the Culture of Equity Investment. *Business Vision* 5: 87–99.

Singh, Ranjit, and Amalesh Bhowal. 2009b. Risk perception dynamics and equity share investment behavior. *Indian Journal of Finance* 3: 23–30.

Singh, Ranjit, and Amalesh Bhowal. 2010a. Risk Perception of employees with respect to equity shares. *Journal of Behavioral Finance* 11: 177–83. [CrossRef]

Singh, Ranjit, and Amalesh Bhowal. 2010b. Imparting Investment Education to Employees by Employer: An Expectation-Experience Gap Study. *Amity Management Analyst* 5: 57–65.

Singh, Ranjit, and Amalesh Bhowal. 2010c. Marketing Dimension of Equity related Risk Perception of Employees: Own Company's Shares Vs Other Company's Shares. *Management Insight* 6: 22–36.

Singh, Ranjit, and Amalesh Bhowal. 2011. Development of Marketing Driven Measure of Risk Perception. *The Journal of Risk Finance* 12: 140–52. [CrossRef]

Sitkin, Sim B., and Amy L. Pablo. 1992. Re-conceptualizing the determinants of risky behavior. *The Academy of Management Review* 17: 9–38. [CrossRef]

Sitkin, Sim B., and Laurie R. Weingart. 1995. Determinants of risky Decision-making behaviour: A test of the mediating role of risk perceptions and propensity. *The Academy of Management Journal* 38: 1573–92.

Slovic, Paul. 1987. Perception of Risk. *Science* 236: 280–85. [CrossRef] [PubMed]

Tavakol, Mohsen, and Reg Dennick. 2011. Making sense of Cronbach's alpha. *International Journal of Medical Education* 2: 53–55. [CrossRef] [PubMed]

Veeramani, G., and M. Karthikeyan. 2014. An Analytical Study on Risk Perception and Return for Individual Investment. *Asia Pacific Journal of Research* 1: 4–13.

Veld, Chris, and Yulia Veld-Merkoulova. 2008. The risk perceptions of individual investors. *Journal of Economic Psychology* 29: 226–52. [CrossRef]

Wang, Xiao Lu, Kan Shi, and Hong Xia Fan. 2006. Psychological mechanisms of investors in Chinese Stock Market. *Journal of Economic Psychology* 27: 762–80. [CrossRef]

Weber, Elke U. 2001. Personality and Risk Taking. In *Balteseds International Encyclopedia of Social and Behavioral Sciences*. Bergama: Pergamon, pp. 11274–76.

Weyman, Andrew, and C. J. Kelly. 1999. *Risk Perception and Risk Communication: A Review of Literature*. London: Health and Safety Executive.

Wilde, Gerald. 1994. *Target Risk: Dealing with the Danger of Death, Disease and Damage in Everyday Decisions*. Toronto: Castor & Columba.

7

A Genetic Algorithm for Investment–Consumption Optimization with Value-at-Risk Constraint and Information-Processing Cost

Zhuo Jin [1,*], Zhixin Yang [2] and Quan Yuan [2]

1 Centre for Actuarial Studies, Department of Economics, The University of Melbourne, Melbourne, VIC 3010, Australia
2 Department of Mathematical Sciences, Ball State University, Muncie, IN 47306, USA; zyang6@bsu.edu (Z.Y.); qyuan@bsu.edu (Q.Y.)
* Correspondence: zjin@unimelb.edu.au

Abstract: This paper studies the optimal investment and consumption strategies in a two-asset model. A dynamic Value-at-Risk constraint is imposed to manage the wealth process. By using Value at Risk as the risk measure during the investment horizon, the decision maker can dynamically monitor the exposed risk and quantify the maximum expected loss over a finite horizon period at a given confidence level. In addition, the decision maker has to filter the key economic factors to make decisions. Considering the cost of filtering the factors, the decision maker aims to maximize the utility of consumption in a finite horizon. By using the Kalman filter, a partially observed system is converted to a completely observed one. However, due to the cost of information processing, the decision maker fails to process the information in an arbitrarily rational manner and can only make decisions on the basis of the limited observed signals. A genetic algorithm was developed to find the optimal investment, consumption strategies, and observation strength. Numerical simulation results are provided to illustrate the performance of the algorithm.

Keywords: genetic algorithm; investment; Value-at-Risk; rational inattention

1. Introduction

In this paper, we consider an investment–consumption problem. The decision maker manages the investment and consumption with a long-term perspective. General financial information for each investment class is observable. By analyzing the available financial information, the decision maker dynamically allocates the proportion of each investment class to maximize the utilities of consumptions in the long term. The objective under consideration can be traced back to the framework of Merton's two-asset consumption and investment problem.

Since the financial crisis incurred by the credit risk and the subsequent liquidity risk shocked the banking and insurance system led to a global recession during 2007–2009, regulators and practitioners have paid more attention to risk measurement and management, and numerous techniques have been put forward in the finance and insurance literature. Solvency II, which gradually replaced the Solvency I regime and came into effect on 1 January 2016, is a fundamental review of the capital adequacy regime for the European insurance industry. Value at Risk (VaR) has been widely adopted to quantify and control risk exposure because it is convenient to use. Specifically, it is the maximum expected loss over a finite horizon period at a given confidence level. There are quite a few scholars who have utilized the idea of VaR in the pursuit of deriving optimal risk management strategies (see Yiu 2004; Yiu et al. 2010; Chen et al. 2010; Zhang et al. 2016).

Recent research raises a concern that decision makers generally fail to process all of the information in a rational manner as a result of finite information-processing capability. Under the information-processing constraint, the decision maker can only make decisions through "processed" or "observed" states, which is called "rational inattention". Sim (2003, 2006) introduced the concept of "rational inattention" and claimed that the process of decision-making is subject to the information-processing constraint. Huang and Liu (2007) investigated the optimal portfolio selection strategies under rational inattention constraints. Maćkowiak and Wiederholt (2015) studied the business cycles within the rational inattention framework and developed a dynamic stochastic general equilibrium model. In addition, it costs to observe the signals and filter the necessary variables. It is natural that the decision maker pays to have a better estimation. Andrei and Hasler (2017) studied the investment and consumption strategies under the rational inattention constraint that an observation cost should be paid to observe key economic factors. See Brennan and Xia (2002), Abel et al. (2013), Steiner et al. (2017), and Kacperczyk et al. (2016) for more work on rational inattention.

Similar to Andrei and Hasler (2017), we also investigate the optimization problem with the information-processing cost. To be specific, in our model, one of the parameters that affect the return of the asset is not observable, thus formulating a partially observable problem. The decision maker can only implement the observable signal to estimate the observable factor. By using the Kalman filter Liptser and Shiryaev (2001), an optimization problem of five state variables and three control variables is formulated. However, our control problem is subject to the Value-at-Risk constraint. The decision maker in our framework controls the consumption, investment, and observation strength to maximize the utilities of consumptions under a given Value-at-Risk requirement.

Our work is also different from Andrei and Hasler (2017) in terms of methodology and research focus. For the research objective, Andrei and Hasler (2017) examined the relationships between attention, risk investment, and related state variables dynamically, whereas our work is dedicated to using an innovative method to achieve the optimal strategies. As for the methodology, Andrei and Hasler (2017) derived the Hamilton–Jacobi–Bellman (HJB) equation for its dynamic system and use the Chebyshev collocation method to approximate the solution of the HJB equation with a sum of certain "basis functions" (in their work, the sum of production of Chebyshev polynomials). Finding the coefficients of Chebyshev polynomials requires solving a system of linear equations. However, the dimension of the derived system of linear equations would increase significantly in our framework with the Value-at-Risk restriction. This limitation motivates us to come up with an alternative method to solve our problem of interest.

Note that the approach applied by Andrei and Hasler (2017) represents one typical way to solve a stochastic control problem, and the method falls into the category of dynamic programming. With dynamic programming, one is able to establish connections between the optimal control problem and a second-order partial differential equation called the HJB equation. If HJB is solvable, then the maximizer or minimizer of the Hamiltonian will be the corresponding optimal feedback control. A more detailed discussion of this field of work can be seen in Yong and Zhou (1999) and references therein. It is very likely that there is no explicit solution to the HJB equation because of the complex nature of a lot of dynamic systems. Thus, the search for effective numerical methods attracts the attention of many scholars accordingly. One common approach follows the track of a numerical method of solving partial differential equations (PDEs; see Andrei and Hasler (2017), for example). Most of the time, it requires good analytical properties such as differentiability and continuity for the dynamic system so that the PDE approach is feasible. The Markov-chain approximation method lies on the other side of the spectrum. It also tackles stochastic control problems but does not require particular analytical properties of the system. This method was proposed by Kushner (see Kushner and Dupuis 2001). The basic idea is to approximate the original control problem with a simpler control process (a Markov chain in a finite state space) and the associated cost function for which the desired computation can be carried out. The state space is a "discretization" of the original state space of the control problem. Under certain conditions, one can prove that the sequence of optimal cost functions for the sequence of approximating chains converges to that for the underlying original process as the approximation parameter goes to zero. A potential problem with the Markov-chain approximation method is that one has to handle the solution of optimization in each iteration step, and this could be time-consuming for high-dimension systems. To deviate from the two popular methods mentioned above, we advocate for the use of Genetic Algorithms to solve stochastic control problems to overcome these issues.

A genetic algorithm (GA) is a metaheuristic inspired by the process of natural selection. Essentially, natural selection acts as a type of optimization process that is based on conceptually simple operations of competition, reproduction, and mutation. Genetic algorithms use these bio-inspired operators (selection, crossover, and mutation) to generate high-quality solutions to optimization problems Mitchell (1996). John Holland introduced genetic algorithms in 1960 on the basis of the concept of Darwin's theory of evolution; afterward, his student Goldberg extended the GA in 1989 Sadeghi et al. (2014). A fundamental difference between GAs and a lot of traditional optimization algorithms (e.g., gradient descent) is that GAs work with a population of potential solutions of the given problem. The traditional optimization algorithms start with one candidate solution and move it toward the optimum by updating this one estimate. GAs simultaneously consider multiple candidate solutions to the problem of maximizing/minimizing and iterate by moving this population of candidate solutions toward a global optimum. Because of the high dimensionality of parameters and the dynamic constraints in our dynamic system, we developed a Genetic Algorithm to study the optimal strategies.

Note that in recent years, a lot of machine learning methods (both supervised and unsupervised), such as logistic regression, neural networks, support vector machines, *k*-nearest neighbors, and so on, have been widely used in the field of risk management. These machine learning models are closely related to the problem of optimization since they can be formulated as maximization/minimization of some profit/loss functions. In practical problems, these profit/loss functions tend to be high-dimensional, multi-peak/valley, or may have noise terms, and sometimes they are even discontinuous in some regions. For these situations, a genetic algorithm is a powerful tool for obtaining global optimal solutions. Genetic algorithms have been utilized as optimization methods since the 1980s and 1990s in the field of machine learning (Goldberg and Holland 1988). In many studies, genetic algorithms and machine learning models (such as support vector machines, neural networks) have been used in combination to obtain optimal parameters. On the other hand, machine learning techniques have also been used to improve the performance of genetic and evolutionary algorithms (Zhang et al. 2011).

The contributions of our work are as follows. First, we look at the investment–consumption optimization problem of information cost with the VaR restriction.Second, instead of applying the classical numerical algorithms in which differentiability or continuity assumption is required, we make use of the GA to carry out our analysis. It is very flexible and can handle many types of optimization problems, even if analytical properties such as continuity or differentiability break down. What is more, a lot of numerical algorithms, such as the Markov-chain approximation method, are local optimal algorithms. The GA is a global optimal algorithm instead, and we are thus able to achieve global optimal strategies. Last but not least, the GA is easy to implement and very efficiently handled high-dimensional data.

The rest of the paper is organized as follows. The formulation of the dynamics of wealth inflation, observation processes, and objective functions are presented in Section 2. Numerical examples are provided in Section 3 to illustrate the implementation of the genetic algorithm. Finally, additional remarks are provided in Section 4.

2. Formulation

Let $(\Omega, \mathcal{F}, \mathbb{P})$ be a complete probability space, where $\mathcal{F} = \{\mathcal{F}_t\}_{t\geq 0}$ is a complete and right-continuous filtration generated by a 4-dimensional standard Brownian motion $B_p(t), B_y(t), B_V(t), B_\beta(t)$. $\mathcal{F}_t$ is the filtration containing the information about the financial market and the investor's observation at time t, and $\mathbb{P}$ is a probability measure on Ω. We consider an asset price process motivated by a fully stochastic volatility model,

$$\frac{dP(t)}{P(t)} = [\bar{\mu} + \beta(t)(y(t) - \bar{y})]dt + \sqrt{V(t)}dB_p(t), \tag{1}$$

where $\bar{\mu}$ is the expected average rate of return. $y(t)$ is an observable state variable that represents useful market information, such as the earnings-to-price ratio or a change in trading volumes to predict the future return rate; $\beta(t)$ is the impact coefficient of the state variable $y(t)$ and is an unobservable factor; $V(t)$ represents the stochastic volatility. Specifically, the observable variable $y(t)$ is assumed to follow a diffusion process

$$: dy(t) = \lambda_y(\bar{y} - y(t))dt + \sigma_y(t)dB_y(t). \tag{2}$$

For the volatility $V(t)$, we adopt the stochastic volatility below:

$$dV(t) = \lambda_V(\bar{V} - V(t))dt + \sigma_V\sqrt{V(t)}dB_V(t). \tag{3}$$

The unobservable factor $\beta(t)$, which can be considered to be certain economic variables that cannot be completely observed, is assumed to follow

$$d\beta(t) = \lambda_\beta(\bar{\beta} - \beta(t))dt + \sigma_\beta dB_\beta(t). \tag{4}$$

Note that for variables $y(t)$, $V(t)$, and $\beta(t)$ above, we use $\bar{y}$, $\bar{V}$, and $\bar{\beta}$ to denote the long-term average of variables and use λ_y, λ_V, and λ_β to refer to mean-reversion parameters. These parameters show the rates at which the variables $y(t)$, $V(t)$, and $\beta(t)$ revert to their long-term means in these three mean-reverting processes.

Instead of observing $\beta(t)$ completely, we only have access to the observation of it with noise according to the following dynamics:

$$dO(t) = \beta(t)dt + \frac{1}{\sqrt{\alpha(t)}}dB_o(t), \tag{5}$$

where $B_o(t)$ is a Brownian motion that denotes the observation noises and is independent of $B_p(t)$, $B_y(t), B_V(t), B_\beta(t)$. Note that $\alpha(t)$ is a control variable, which determines the precision of our observations and is used to describe the capacity of observing and processing signals. The more frequently we observe the signals, the more precise information we have on the observation. Similarly, a smaller value of $\alpha(t)$ implies less return predictability.

Note that $\mathcal{F}_t$ is the information set up to time t and contains the realized return of the asset, innovations of predictive variable, changes in the volatilities of stock return, and observed signals. The estimated predictive coefficient is denoted by $\hat{\beta}(t) = \mathbb{E}(\beta(t)|\mathcal{F}_t)$, and its posterior variance is $\nu(t) = E[(\beta(t) - \hat{\beta}(t))^2|\mathcal{F}_t]$. Using the standard filtering results from Liptser and Shiryaev (2001), we are able to get the dynamics of the estimated predictive coefficient $\hat{\beta}(t)$ (filter) and the posterior variance $\nu(t)$ (uncertainty) as below:

$$d\hat{\beta}(t) = \lambda_\beta(\bar{\beta} - \hat{\beta}(t))dt + \frac{\nu(t)(y(t) - \bar{y})}{\sqrt{V(t)}}dB_1(t) + \nu(t)\sqrt{\alpha(t)}dB_4(t). \tag{6}$$

$$d\nu(t)/dt = -[\frac{(y(t) - \bar{y})^2}{V(t)} + \alpha(t)]\nu^2(t) - 2\lambda_\beta\nu(t) + \sigma_\beta^2. \tag{7}$$

So far, all state variables have become observable. We thus obtain a new dynamic system with observed variables satisfying the following dynamics:

$$\begin{cases} \frac{dP(t)}{P(t)} = [\bar{\mu} + \hat{\beta}(t)(y(t) - \bar{y})]dt + \sqrt{V(t)}dB_1(t), \\ dy(t) = \lambda_y(\bar{y} - y(t))dt + \sigma_y(t)dB_2(t), \\ dV(t) = \lambda_V(\bar{V} - V(t))dt + \sigma_V\sqrt{V(t)}dB_3(t), \\ dO(t) = \hat{\beta}(t)dt + \frac{1}{\sqrt{\alpha(t)}}dB_4(t), \end{cases} \tag{8}$$

where $B_1(t), B_2(t), B_3(t)$, and $B_4(t)$ are independent Brownian motions under the investor's observation filtration.

Combining risky assets with a risk-free asset, we can represent the wealth process as:

$$dX(t) = \left[rX(t) + \pi(t)X(t)(\bar{\mu} + \hat{\beta}(t)(y(t) - \bar{y}) - r) - C(t) - \overline{K}(t)\right]dt + \pi(t)X(t)\sqrt{V(t)}dB_1(t), \tag{9}$$

where $C(t)$ is the consumption by a representative investor, consumed at time t; $\pi(t)$ is the risky investment share; r is used to denote the risk-free rate of return; and $\overline{K}(t)$ is the information cost.

Now, we proceed with the introduction of the VaR restriction. Note that with the phenomenal prosperity of financial markets, risk management has recently gained increasing attention from practitioners. Value at Risk has been the standard benchmark for measuring financial risks among banks, insurance companies, and other financial institutions. VaR is regarded as the maximum expected loss over a given time period at a given confidence level and is used to set up capital requirements. VaR constraints have been adopted by many studies on optimization problems to make the model more reasonable. Consistent with Chen et al. (2010), we define the dynamic VaR as follows.

For a small enough $h > 0$, the loss percentage in interval $[t, t+h)$ is defined by

$$\Delta X(t) := X(t)e^{rh} - X(t+h).$$

The above definition tells us that relative loss is defined as the difference between the value yielded at time $t+h$ if we deposit the surplus in a bank account at time t and the surplus at time $t+h$ obtained by implementing reinsurance and investment strategies. e^{rh} can be interpreted as the value of time for one unit of currency after time period h.

For a given probability level $\phi \in (0,1)$ and a given time horizon $h > 0$, the VaR at time t, denoted by $\mathrm{VaR}_t^{\phi,h}$, is defined by

$$\mathrm{VaR}_t^{\phi,h} := \inf\{L \geq 0 : \mathbb{P}(\Delta X^{\phi}(t) \geq L|\mathcal{F}_t) < \phi\}. \tag{10}$$

To proceed, let the control variable $u(t)$ be $u(t) = (C(t), \pi(t), \alpha(t))$ as a triplet of control variables. Let δ be the discount factor. Our objective is to choose consumption $C(t)$, attention to news $\alpha(t)$, and the risky investment share $\pi(t)$ so as to maximize an individual's expected utility of consumption over a given time horizon from t to T conditional on that individual's information set at time t:

$$J(t, x, \hat{\beta}, y, V, v) = \max_{C,\pi,\alpha} \mathbb{E}\left[\int_t^T e^{-\delta(s-t)}U(C_s)ds|\mathcal{F}_t\right] \tag{11}$$

subject to a constant level $R > 0$ of an upper boundary of VaR at all times.

$$\mathrm{VaR}_t^{\phi,h} \leq R \text{ for a given } \phi \text{ and } h. \tag{12}$$

Our interest in this work is the application of a genetic algorithm to solve the optimal investment and consumption strategies in a two-asset model. Compared with some other numerical algorithms,

GA is a global optimization method. Moreover, it does not require the differentiability or even continuity of drift and diffusion of the dynamic process. What is more, it is very robust to a change in parameters and easy to implement (Liu and Zhao 1998).

Originating from Darwinian evolution theory, a genetic algorithm can be viewed as an "intelligent" algorithm in which a probabilistic search is applied. In the process of evolution, natural populations evolve according to the principles of natural selection and "survival of the fittest". Individuals who can more successfully fit in with their surroundings will have better chances to survive and multiply, while those who do not adapt to their environment will be eliminated. This implies that genes from highly fit individuals will spread to an increasing number of individuals in each successive generation. Combinations of good characteristics from highly adapted ancestors may produce even more fit offspring. In this way, species evolve to become progressively better adapted to their environments.

A GA simulates these processes by taking an initial population of individuals and applying genetic operators to each reproduction. In optimization terms, each individual in the population is encoded into a string or chromosome or some float number, which represents a possible solution to a given problem. The fitness of an individual is evaluated with respect to a given objective function. Highly fit individuals or solutions are given opportunities to reproduce by exchanging some of their genetic information with other highly fit individuals by a crossover procedure. This produces new "offspring" solutions (i.e., *children*), which share some characteristics taken from both parents. Mutation is often applied after crossover by altering some genes or perturbing float numbers. The offspring can either replace the whole population or replace less-fit individuals. This evaluation-selection-reproduction cycle is repeated until a satisfactory solution is found. The basic steps of a simple GA are shown below and in the next section, and we define the detailed steps of the GA after a specific example is introduced.

- Generate an initial population and evaluate the fitness of the individuals in the population;
- Select parents from the population;
- Crossover (mate) parents to produce children and evaluate the fitness of the children;
- Replace some or all of the population by the children until a satisfactory solution is found.

3. Numerical Simulation with Genetic Algorithm

3.1. Numerical Example

Andrei and Hasler (2017) investigated the determinants of optimal attention and risky investment share, and they calibrated the parameter of the model. Another major focus of their work concerns the exploration of the relation between the model-implied and empirically measured attention and risky investment. Our focus in this work is quite different, and we aim to shed light on the application of the GA to a constrained stochastic control problem. In this section, we numerically apply the GA to a specific example in order to provide a visualized understanding of optimal attention behavior, consumption, as well as an investor's portfolio selection for maximizing its utility function over time. For the sake of convenience, we used the estimated parameters out of Andrei and Hasler (2017) to proceed with our simulations below. To be more specific,

$$r = 0.0508, \quad \lambda_V = 1.9592, \quad X_0 = 100, \quad \bar{V} = 0.0158,$$

$$\sigma_V = 0.176, \quad \lambda_y = 0.1163, \quad \bar{y} = 0.0686, \quad \sigma_y(t) = \sigma_y = 0.0136,$$

$$\bar{\mu} = 0.0685, \quad \lambda_\beta = 0.2151, \quad \bar{\beta} = 0.0021, \quad \sigma_\beta = 0.9531.$$

$$\begin{cases} \frac{dP(t)}{P(t)} = [0.0685 + \hat{\beta}(t)(y(t) - 0.0686)]dt + \sqrt{V(t)}dB_1(t), \\ dy(t) = 0.1163(0.0686 - y(t))dt + 0.0136dB_2(t) \\ dV(t) = 1.9592(0.0158 - V(t))dt + 0.176\sqrt{V(t)}dB_3(t), \\ dO(t) = \hat{\beta}(t)dt + \frac{1}{\sqrt{\alpha(t)}}dB_4(t), \\ d\hat{\beta}(t) = 0.2151(0.0021 - \hat{\beta}(t))dt + \frac{\nu(t)(y(t) - 0.0686)}{\sqrt{V(t)}}dB_1(t) + \nu(t)\sqrt{\alpha(t)}dB_4(t), \\ d\nu(t)/dt = -[\frac{(y(t) - 0.0686)^2}{V(t)} + \alpha(t)]\nu^2(t) - 0.4302\nu(t) + 0.9531^2. \end{cases} \tag{13}$$

Thus, our corresponding wealth processes can be represented as below:

$$\begin{aligned} dX(t) &= [0.0508X(t) + \pi(t)X(t)(0.0685 + \hat{\beta}(t)(y(t) - 0.0686) - 0.0508) \\ &\quad -\eta(t)X(t) - 0.1\alpha^2(t)X(t)]dt + \pi(t)X(t)\sqrt{V(t)}dB_1(t), \\ X(0) &= 100. \end{aligned} \tag{14}$$

Here, we naturally assume that consumption is a proportion of wealth $C(t) = \eta(t)X(t)$ and that the per unit of wealth information cost function is $\bar{K}(t) = k\alpha^2(t)$. The information cost parameter k is assumed to be $k = 0.1$. Thus, we need to choose the control set $u(t) = (\eta(t), \pi(t), \alpha(t))$ to maximize our utility function. To be specific, we adopted the power utility function $U(C) := \frac{C^{1-\gamma}}{1-\gamma}$ for the simulation, in which we further assume that the value of the aversion parameter is $\gamma = 3$. The time window is assumed to be 60 years. Then, we have

$$J(x, \hat{\beta}, y, V, \nu) = \max \mathbb{E}\left[\int_0^{60} -e^{-0.01t}\frac{C_t^{-2}}{2}dt\right] \tag{15}$$

subject to

$$\text{VaR}_t^{\phi,h} \leq 0.1X(t), \tag{16}$$

where the discount factor takes the value of $\delta = 0.01$ and $\phi = 0.01$. To proceed with our numerical analysis, we used step size $\Delta t = h = 1/2$ and simulated the trajectory 10,000 times. Realizing that relative loss is actually more meaningful since the impact of a \$10,000 loss differs between a billionaire and a junior investor. Therefore, in our example, we did not choose a specific upper bound for the VaR. Instead, we restricted the loss portion to be less than 10% of the wealth to proceed with our simulation, and the constant upper bound of the VaR can be regarded as a special case of our example.

3.2. Implementation of GA

Note that there are a lot of variations of genetic algorithms. To solve our problem of interest, we can use the form along the lines of what Liu and Zhao (1998) suggested in their book. Below are the specifics of the basic steps of our GA.

Step 1: Set parameters $P_c = 0.2$ (probability of crossover), $P_m = 0.1$ (probability of mutation), $N = 30$ (size of population), $b = 0.05$ (the parameter used in the evaluation); set iteration $iter := 0$, $best := 0$.

Step 2: Initialize population $pop(iter) = \{\theta_1, \ldots, \theta_N\}$, which is a population that contains N solutions. In our context, $\theta_i = (\eta_1, \ldots, \eta_{120}, \pi_1, \ldots, \pi_{120}, \alpha_1, \ldots, \alpha_{120})$, η_j, π_j, and α_j $(j = 1, \ldots, 120)$ are three random controls following a uniform distribution $U(0, 1)$. Note that our time window is 60 years and the step size is $1/2$; thus, each control variable can be discretized from $j = 1$ up to $j = 120$.

Step 3: Evaluate $pop(iter) : \{\theta_1, \ldots, \theta_N\}$:

3-1: For each θ_i, plug θ_i into the discretized form of Equation (15).

3-2: Descending sort $\{J(\theta_1), \ldots, J(\theta_N)\}$; for the sake of brevity, we assume $J(\theta_1) \geq J(\theta_2) \geq \cdots \geq J(\theta_N)$. If $best < J(\theta_1)$, then denote the best value as $best = J(\theta_1)$ and store θ_1.

3-3: If the stop criterion $iter = 1000$ is satisfied, output θ_1 and the best value $best$ and stop the genetic algorithm. Otherwise, continue the algorithm.

3-4: Evaluate each θ_i by

$$eval(\theta_i) = b(1-b)^{i-1}.$$

Step 4: Selection:

For $i := 1$ **to** N

4-1: For each θ_i, calculate the cumulative probability q_i

$$\begin{cases} q_0 = 0, \\ q_i = \sum_{j=1}^{i} eval(\theta_j) \quad i = 1, 2, \ldots, N \end{cases}$$

4-2: Generate a random number $r \sim U(0, q_N)$;

4-3: If $q_{i-1} < r \leq q_i$, then choose the ith individual θ_i, and let $\theta_i' \leftarrow \theta_i$;

End For (Here, we can obtain N individuals $\theta_1', \ldots, \theta_N'$).

Step 5: Crossover:

For $i := 1$ **to** N

5-1: Generate a random number $r \sim U(0,1)$;

5-2: Choose θ_i' as a parent if $r < P_c$, and let $V_i \leftarrow \theta_i'$;

End For (Here, we can obtain k ($k \leq N$) parents $V_1, \ldots, V_k$).

5-3: Partition $\{V_1, \ldots, V_k\}$ into $k/2$ pairs randomly $(V_1, V_2), (V_3, V_4), \ldots$ (if k is odd, we can discard an arbitrary one).

5-4: Generate another random number $d \sim U(0,1)$; for each pair (V_i, V_{i+1}), we can get two new individuals by

$$\begin{aligned} X &= dV_i + (1-d)V_{i+1} \\ Y &= (1-d)V_i + dV_{i+1} \\ V_i &\leftarrow X \\ V_{i+1} &\leftarrow Y \end{aligned}$$

5-5: Use $\{V_1, \ldots, V_k\}$ to replace k individuals in $\{\theta_1', \ldots, \theta_N'\}$.

Step 6: Mutation:

For $i := 1$ **to** N

6-1: Generate a random number $r \sim U(0,1)$;

6-2: If $r < P_m$, generate an individual $V_i' = (\eta_1, \ldots, \eta_{120}, \pi_1, \ldots, \pi_{120}, \alpha_1, \ldots, \alpha_{120})$ and let $\theta_i' \leftarrow V_i'$; η_j, π_j, and α_j are three random controls following a uniform distribution $U(0,1)$. Then, let $\theta_i' \leftarrow V_i'$;

End For

Step 7: Now, a new population $\{\theta_1', \ldots, \theta_N'\}$ is obtained. Let $\theta_i \leftarrow \theta_i'$, $iter \leftarrow iter + 1$, and go to Step 3.

Remark 1. *Note that in Steps 2 and 6 above, both θ_i and V_i' refer to the ith generic feasible solution from a population of size N for the optimization problem, and they have different appearances in different contexts.*

In Figures 1 and 2, we see both consumption and average wealth have a trend of increasing over 60 years. Given that our utility function is in terms of consumption, the investor has the motivation to increase consumption. On the other hand, if the investor consumes too much, his/her wealth tends to go down, and this will result in less wealth to be spent on consumption in the future. Therefore, there exists a trade-off. Overall, an investor's wealth goes up relatively smoothly over the course of time, but there are ups and downs in terms of the trajectory of consumption. We think this fits the reality since a rational investor tends to spend more sometimes as a result of purchasing some big tangible assets, such as a car or house, or health concerns; at other times, an investor spends less money on living expenses. In Figure 3, we further examine the consumption pattern by studying $\eta(t)$. Recall that $\eta(t)$ is the proportion of wealth that an investor spends on consumption. We find that the optimal proportion of consumption $\eta(t)$ is bounded between 0.0134 and 0.0704. The optimal proportion of consumption for a rational investor under the VaR restriction is stable in the long term and would not exceed 8% of the investor's wealth.

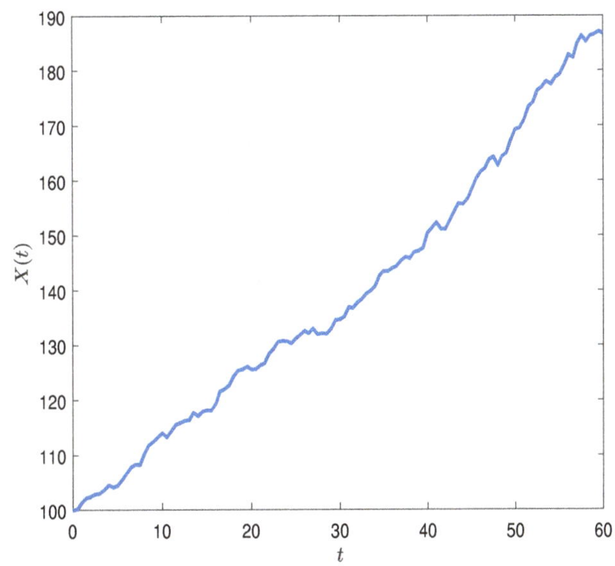

Figure 1. Wealth $X(t)$ as a function of t.

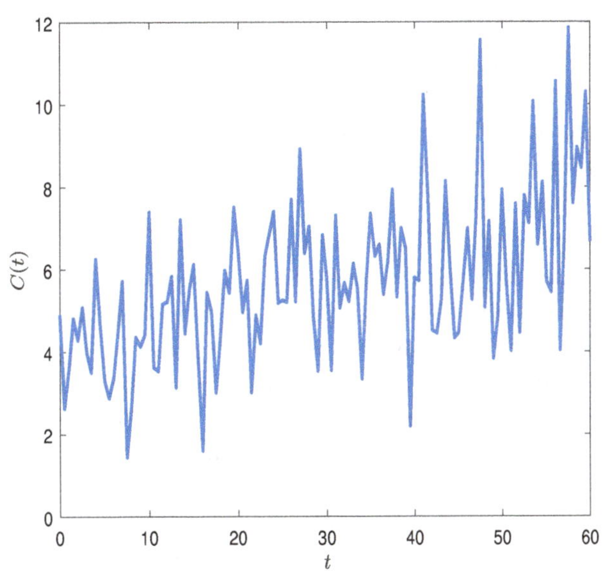

Figure 2. Optimal consumption $C(t)$ as a function of t.

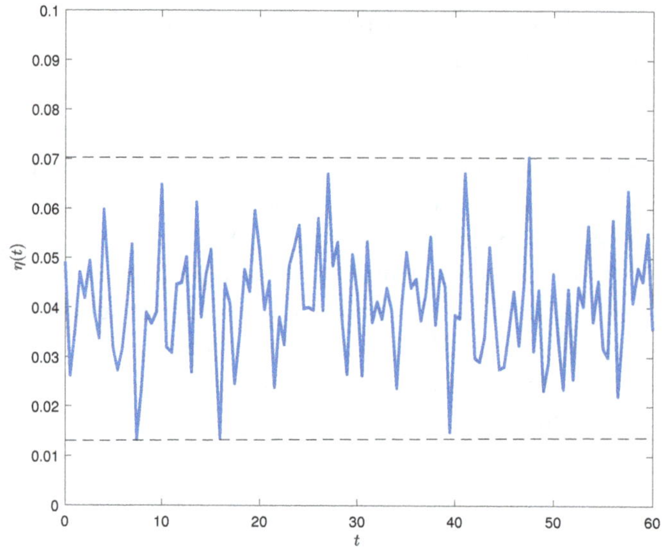

Figure 3. Optimal proportion of consumption $\eta(t)$ as a function of t.

For experts familiar with finance theory, the range of the optimal proportion of consumption might look a bit fishy at first glance since it seems to conflict with the famous frugal 4% consumption rule from the "Trinity study" (Cooley et al. 1998). However, Bengen (1994) showed that the 4% consumption rule is suggested for the first year, and the proportion should be adjusted up or down for inflation every succeeding year. Checking our proposed optimal consumptions, the optimal proportion of consumption takes an average value of 3.775% for the first year. The mean and volatility (standard deviation) of optimal consumption are 4.09% and 1.14%, respectively. Figure 4 shows that 62% of the optimal consumptions fall within [0.0295, 0.0523]. We also notice that 2.48% of the optimal consumptions fall below 0.018, and 3.31% of consumptions are above 0.0637. Thus, we claim that, overall, our numerical results agree with the conclusion of the "Trinity study" well, and the corresponding relative frequencies of large deviations from the "canonical" results are very small. Considering the existing fluctuations in our optimal consumptions, we guess that inflation, the cost of information processing, and random noise could all be contributing factors. That being said, theories from the field of behavioral finance, such as habit formation proposed by Constantinides (1990) and Abel (1990) and the equity risk puzzle discussed by Mehra (2006), could also be underlying driving forces.

Figures 5 and 6 demonstrate the dynamics of optimal proportion of risky assets and optimal attention cost with respect to time. Checking the graphs, we can see that $\pi(t) \in [0.0130, 0.0683]$ and $\alpha(t) \in [0.0078, 0.0747]$. Putting the three control variables together, we see that to maximize the utility function, the investor should put most of his/her wealth in risk-free assets and increase consumption over the course of time so that the wealth can accumulate in a steady way; thus, the investor is able to spend more money on consumption. When the utility function is consumption oriented, there is less incentive for the investor to invest more money in risky assets because of the embedded risk. Thus, the optimal proportion of wealth in the risky asset is not very aggressive.

To see the impact of the VaR restriction, we examined the optimal consumption for a case with and without VaR restrictions with respect to initial wealth X_0. We locked the time to year 1 and 59, respectively, to make comparisons. Figures 7 and 8 reveal the following observations. First, the consumptions in both graphs increase as the initial wealth goes up. Second, investors consume more when there is no restriction. The constraint of VaR serves as a buffer to stop an investor from spending more money. Last but not least, examining the consumption patterns under VaR, we notice that in the early stage of our time window of interest, the consumption under VaR is convex from below as a function of initial wealth. However, the shape becomes slightly concave from below in the end. A possible explanation is that in the beginning, more wealth implies higher consumption, but there is a diminishing marginal utility here, and the investor is risk seeking. However, toward the end of the time horizon, a rational investor will spend as much as possible, as more wealth implies more consumption, and moreover, marginal consumption goes up and the risk aversion part of investor is dominant.

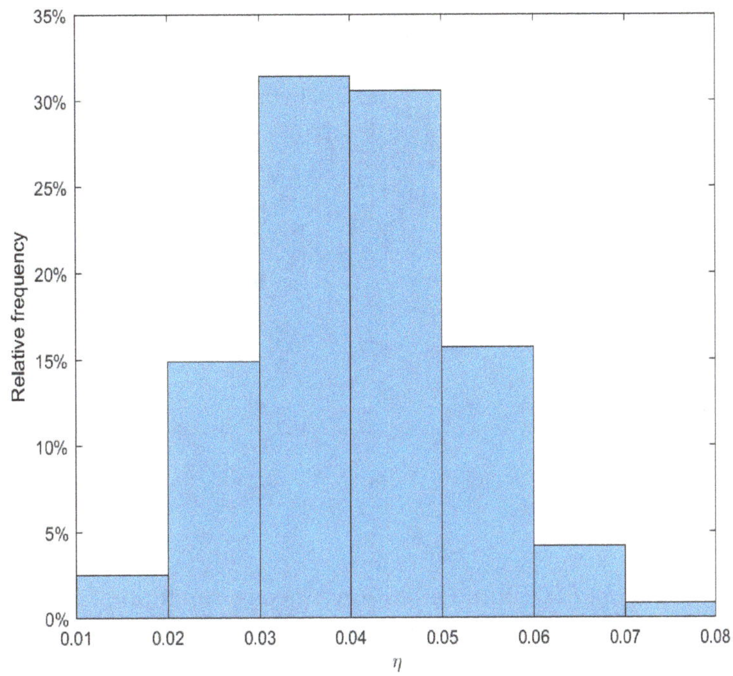

Figure 4. Relative frequency of consumption.

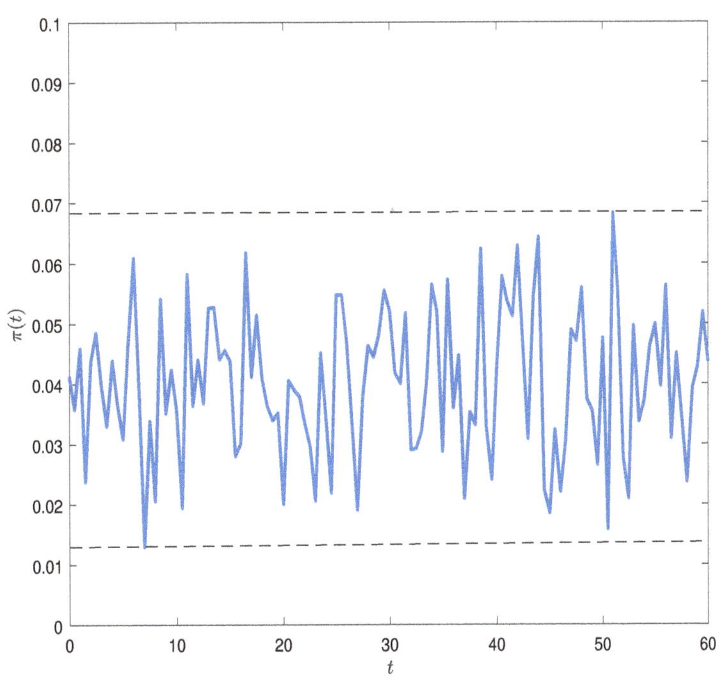

Figure 5. Optimal proportion of risky assets $\pi(t)$ as a function of t.

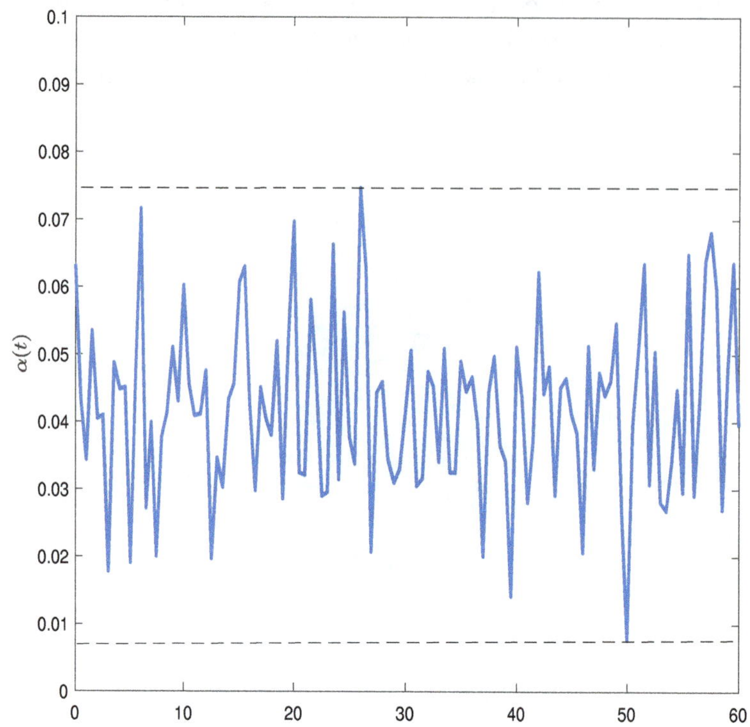

Figure 6. Optimal attention $\alpha(t)$ as a function of t.

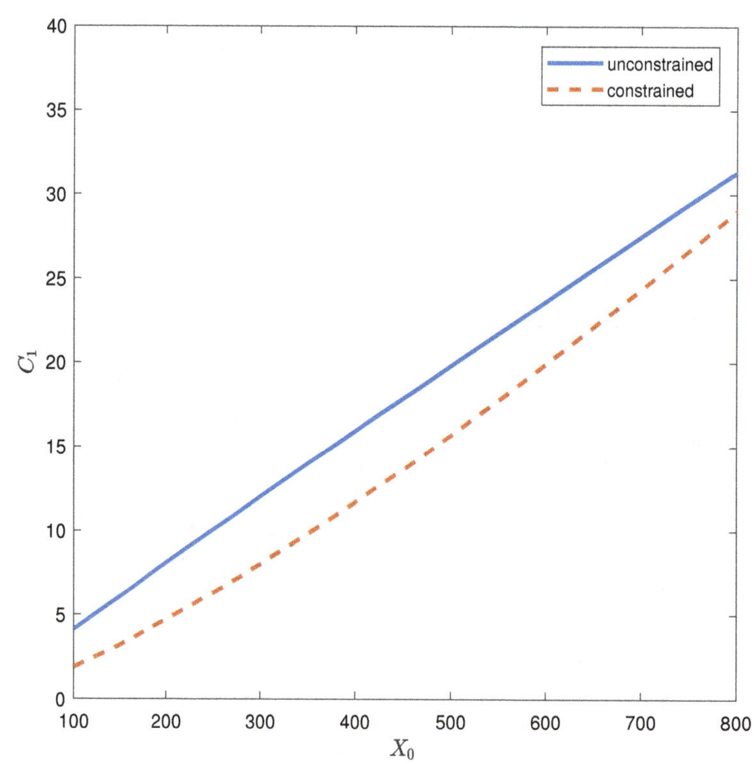

Figure 7. Optimal consumption C at time 1 as a function of initial wealth X_0.

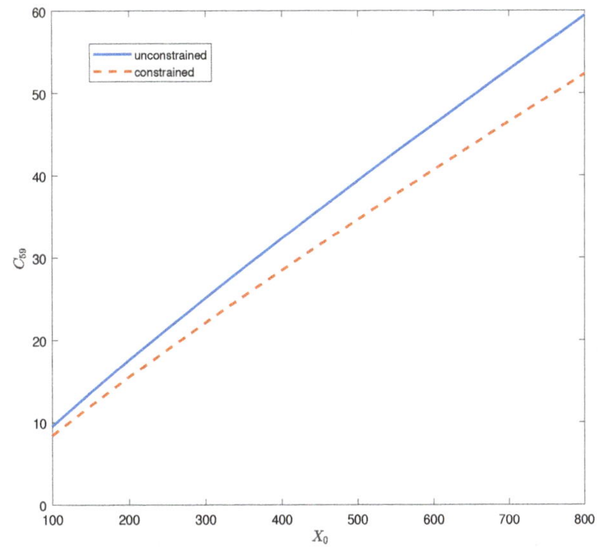

Figure 8. Optimal consumption C at time 59 as a function of initial wealth X_0.

Figure 9 is along the lines of a comparison between the constrained and unconstrained optimization problem, but the focus is on the relationship between the value function and initial wealth. Our numerical result shows that the investor gets a higher utility function when there is no VaR constraint. It is also very interesting to note that the gap between the utility functions is apparent when the initial wealth is small. However, as the initial wealth increases, the gap between the utility functions becomes narrow. In the beginning, the VaR restriction really acts as a restriction because the initial wealth is assumed to be small. Investors will be very careful about their investment strategies and will thus consume conservatively. As the initial wealth increases, while the utility function for the unconstrained case is still higher, it is close to that of the constrained case. It shows that the VaR restriction does not have a substantial influence for a "rich" investor.

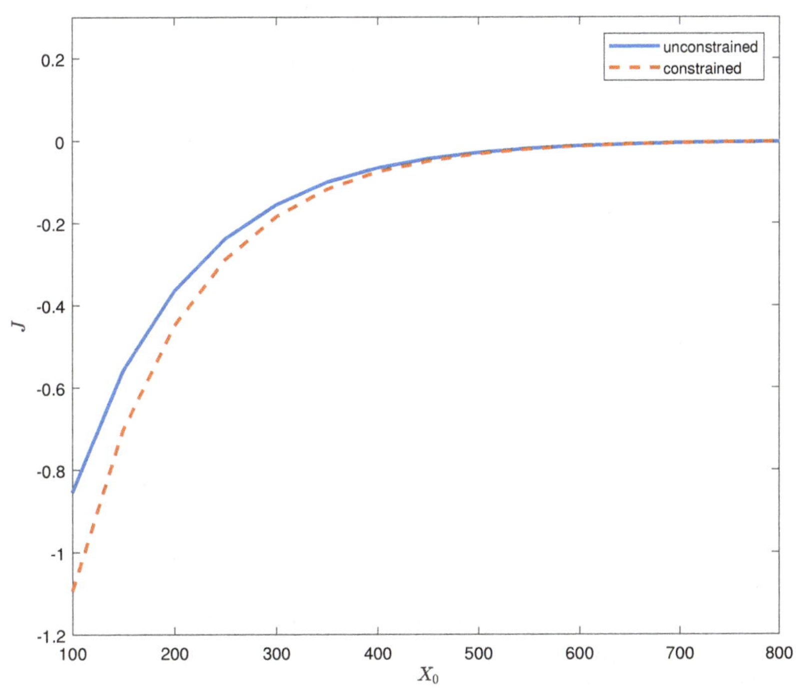

Figure 9. Value function J as a function of initial wealth X_0.

4. Concluding Remarks

In this paper, we present a genetic algorithm to study the optimal consumption and investment strategies for a decision maker whose decision-making is subject to the Value-at-Risk constraint. Because of the partial observability of the return rate of risky assets, the decision maker needs to filter the key economic factors at a cost to maximize the objective function. The observation strength, which requires a trade-off between accuracy and cost, is a control variable to determine. Since solving the high-dimension Hamilton–Jacob–Bellman (HJB) equation analytically is virtually impossible, we developed a genetic algorithm to solve the problem numerically. The numerical simulations yield some interesting observations. In future studies, we can further consider the information-processing capacity constraint of the decision maker. The decision maker has a finite signal-processing capacity to filter the true states with a cost. We can use entropy to quantify the information-processing capacity for decision makers. Luo (2016) analyzed optimal consumption and portfolio strategies with the information-processing capacity constraint. It was shown that the limit imposed by rational inattention has a significant effect on the decision-making process. Together with the Value-at-Risk constraint, the problem becomes more complex and leads to a Hamilton–Jacob–Bellman equation of much higher dimensions. A more advanced algorithm will be studied to tackle the difficulty with high dimensions.

Author Contributions: The authors contributed equally to this work.

Funding: This research was funded by Faculty Research Grant of University of Melbourne.

Acknowledgments: The authors thank three anonymous referees for helpful comments and suggestions that have greatly helped improve the paper and clarify the presentation.

Conflicts of Interest: The authors declare no conflict of interest. The funders had no role in the design of the study; in the collection, analyses, or interpretation of data; in the writing of the manuscript, or in the decision to publish the results.

References

Abel, Andrew B. 1990. Asset prices under habit formation and catching up with the joneses. *The American Economic Review* 80: 38–42. [Crossref]

Abel, Andrew B., Janice C. Eberly, and Stavros Panageas. 2013. Optimal inattention to the stock market with information costs and transactions costs. *Econometrica* 81: 1455–81. [Crossref]

Andrei, Daniel, and Michael Hasler. 2017. Dynamic Attention Behavior Under Return Predictability. Working Paper. Available online: http://www-2.rotman.utoronto.ca/facbios/file/AH3_20170429.pdf (accessed on 22 January 2019).

Bengen, William P. 1994. Determining withdrawal rates using historical data. *Journal of Financial Planning* 1: 14–24. [Crossref]

Brennan, Michael J., and Yihong Xia. 2002. Dynamic asset allocation under inflation. *The Journal of Finance* 57: 1201–38. [Crossref] [CrossRef]

Chen, Shumin, Zhongfei Li, and Kemian Li. 2010. Optimal investment-reinsurance policy for an insurance company with VaR constraint. *Insurance: Mathematics and Economics* 47: 144–53. [Crossref] [CrossRef]

Constantinides, George M. 1990. Habit formation: A resolution of the equity premium puzzle. *Journal of Political Economy* 98: 519–43. [Crossref] [CrossRef]

Cooley, Philip L., Carl M. Hubbard, and Daniel T. Walz. 1998. Retirement savings: Choosing a withdrawal rate that is sustainable. *AAII Journal* 10: 16–21. [Crossref]

Goldberg, David E., and John H. Holland. 1988. Genetic algorithms and machine learning. *Machine Learning* 3: 95–99. [Crossref] [CrossRef]

Huang, Lixin, and Hong Liu. 2007. Rational inattention and portfolio selection. *The Journal of Finance* 62: 1999–2040. [Crossref] [CrossRef]

Kacperczyk, Marcin, Stijn Van Nieuwerburgh, and Laura Veldkamp. 2016. A rational theory of mutual funds' attention allocation. *Econometrica* 84: 571–626. [Crossref] [CrossRef]

Kushner, Harold J., and Paul Dupuis. 2001. *Numerical Methods for Stochastic Control Problems in Continuous Time.* Berlin: Springer.

Liptser, Robert S., and Albert N. Shiryaev. 2007. *Statistics of Random Processes, II: Applications*. Berlin: Springer.

Liu, Baoding, and Ruiqing Zhao. 1998. *Stochastic Programming and Fuzzy Prgramming*. Beijing: Tsinghua University Press.

Luo, Yufei. 2016. Robustly strategic consumption-portfolio rules with informational frictions. *Management Science* 63: 4158–74. [Crossref] [CrossRef]

Maćkowiak, Bartosz, and Mirko Wiederholt. 2015. Business cycle dynamics under rational inattention. *The Review of Economic Studies* 82: 1502–32. [Crossref] [CrossRef]

Mehra, Rajnish. 2006. The equity premium puzzle: A review. *Foundations and Trends in Finance* 2: 1–81. [Crossref] [CrossRef]

Mitchell, Melanie. 1996. *An Introduction to Genetic Algorithms*. Cambridge: MIT Press.

Sadeghi, Javad, Saeid Sadeghi, and Seyed Taghi Akhavan Niaki. 2014. Optimizing a hybrid vendor-managed inventory and transportation problem with fuzzy demand: An improved particle swarm optimization algorithm. *Information Sciences* 272: 126–44. [Crossref] [CrossRef]

Sims, Christopher A. 2003. Implications of rational inattention. *Journal of Monetary Economics* 50: 665–90. [Crossref] [CrossRef]

Sims, Christopher A. 2006. Rational inattention: Beyond the linear-quadratic case. *The American Economic Review* 96: 158–63. [Crossref] [CrossRef]

Steiner, Jakub, Colin Stewart, and Filip Matějka. 2017. Rational inattention dynamics: Inertia and delay in decision-making. *Econometrica* 85: 521–53. [Crossref] [CrossRef]

Yiu, Ka-Fai Cedric. 2004. Optimal portfolios under a value-at-risk constraint. *Journal of Economic Dynamics and Control* 28: 1317–34. [Crossref]

Yiu, Ka-Fai Cedric, Jingzhen Liu, Tak Kuen Siu, and Wai-Ki Ching. 2010. Optimal portfolios with regime switching and value-at-risk constraint. *Automatica* 46: 979–89. [Crossref] [CrossRef]

Yong, Jiongmin, and Xunyu Zhou. 1999. *Stochastic Controls Hamiltonian Systems and HJB Equations*. New York: Springer.

Zhang, Jun, Zhi-hui Zhan, Ying Lin, Ni Chen, Yue-jiao Gong, Jing-hui Zhong, Henry S. H. Chung, Yun Li, and Yu-hui Shi. 2011. Evolutionary computation meets machine learning: A survey. *Computational Intelligence Magazine* 6: 68–75. [Crossref] [CrossRef]

Zhang, Nan, Zhuo Jin, Shuanming Li, and Ping Chen. 2016. Optimal reinsurance under dynamic VaR constraint. *Insurance: Mathematics and Economics* 71: 232–43. [Crossref] [CrossRef]

8

The OFR Financial Stress Index

Phillip J. Monin

Office of Financial Research, 717 14th St NW, Washington, DC 20005, USA; phillip.monin@ofr.treasury.gov

Abstract: We introduce a financial stress index that was developed by the Office of Financial Research (OFR FSI) and detail its purpose, construction, interpretation, and use in financial market monitoring. The index employs a novel and flexible methodology using daily data from global financial markets. Analysis for the 2000–2018 time period is presented. Using a logistic regression framework and dates of government intervention in the financial system as a proxy for stress events, we found that the OFR FSI performs well in identifying systemic financial stress. In addition, we find that the OFR FSI leads the Chicago Fed National Activity Index in a Granger causality analysis, suggesting that increases in financial stress help predict decreases in economic activity.

Keywords: financial stress index; financial stability; financial crises

---

1. Introduction

The history of financial markets demonstrates that financial crises are often followed by large and persistent reductions in real economic activity. The 2007–2009 global financial crisis was a devastating illustration of this. The crisis also made it clear that the modern financial system is global and highly interconnected, and that these interconnections can potentially act as conduits to propagate idiosyncratic shocks across the system in a contagion effect. Because of the potential for negative spillover of financial stress events onto the real economy, accurately measuring financial stress is important to policymakers, who require clear and timely signals of market strains to develop appropriate policy responses to address these events.

Unlike other indicators in the economy such as stock prices or the unemployment rates, financial stress is not directly observed and must instead be estimated. This paper introduces a financial stress index (FSI) developed by the Office of Financial Research (OFR). The OFR FSI is a daily, market-based snapshot of systemic financial stress in global financial markets available to policymakers at the Financial Stability Oversight Council, its member agencies, the financial industry, Congress, and the public. The index distills information embedded in more than 30 indicators into a summary measure of systemic financial stress. It can be decomposed into five categories of indicators or three regions, allowing users to drill down into the drivers of financial stress.[1]

The Dodd-Frank Wall Street Reform and Consumer Protection Act of 2010 mandates the OFR to develop and maintain metrics and reporting systems for risks to financial stability. The law also gives the OFR the responsibility to monitor, investigate, and report on changes in systemwide risk levels and patterns. The OFR FSI complements other financial stability monitoring efforts at the OFR, particularly the Financial System Vulnerabilities Monitor, or FSVM. While the FSVM is intended to provide advanced warning of potential problems, the FSI measures the severity and nature of stress as it occurs. Vulnerabilities can build during periods of low stress. For example, historically

---

1 The OFR Financial Stress Index (OFR FSI) is published after every U.S. trading day by the Office of Financial Research. It is available online at https://www.financialresearch.gov/financial-stress-index/.

high asset valuations can be viewed as a financial stability vulnerability because they suggest that investors have complacent attitudes toward risk. During a time of high asset valuations, stress is likely to be low. However, a sudden and large decline in asset valuations can indicate stress resulting from a shock in investor preferences or risk appetite. Stress and vulnerabilities should therefore be measured separately.

The OFR FSI is distinguished from other FSIs[2] by its global scope, daily frequency, dynamic weighting scheme, transparent and methodical construction, and its ability to be decomposed into indicator categories and regions. Unlike some other FSIs, whose entire time series are re-estimated each time they are updated, the OFR FSI respects the arrow of time. The OFR FSI's value on a given day depends only on information available that day and, once estimated, its value does not change. The OFR FSI's methodology also accommodates input indicators of differing historical timespans. Importantly, as financial markets evolve, indicators that cease to reflect market participants' views about financial stress can be removed and replaced with more appropriate indicators.

The value of the OFR FSI on a given date is proportional to the weighted average of the marginal contributions to financial stress of its constituent indicators. The marginal contribution of an individual indicator to financial stress is its signed standardized value (its value relative to its historical mean, divided by its standard deviation, and signed so that increases in the indicator correspond to increases in financial stress). The weights and the signs of indicators' stress contributions are determined using a dynamic factor model with a single latent factor, which essentially corresponds to the first principal component from a principal component analysis. The index is positive if the (weighted) average stress contribution of the indicators is positive. The index is zero if the average is zero, and negative if the average is negative.

The OFR FSI is constructed in two steps. First, a set of indicators that reflect financial stress is assembled. We define financial stress as disruptions in the typical functioning of financial markets. Symptoms of financial stress are informed by both theory and practice, and include: uncertainty about the fundamental value of financial assets or the behavior of investors; increased asymmetric information; and a decreased willingness to hold risky or illiquid assets (Hakkio and Keeton 2009). Indicators for the index must reflect one or more of these symptoms of stress in a timely manner. In addition, we seek broad and roughly balanced coverage across asset classes and global regions, including representation from U.S.-domiciled financial markets, markets from other advanced economies such as the eurozone and Japan, and emerging markets. The set of indicators is quantitatively screened, and redundant indicators are eliminated. The result of this process is a set of over 30 global financial market indicators, such as implied volatility indexes, yield spreads, valuation measures, and interest rates that are available with varying historical timespans at a daily frequency from publicly available sources.

The second step in the construction of the OFR FSI on a given date is aggregating the set of indicators into a composite index. First, the component indicators are converted to a common unit by taking each indicator, subtracting its mean up until that date, and dividing by its standard deviation. The index is intended to capture systemic financial stress, which occurs when exogenous shocks or contagion effects occur in multiple markets simultaneously. We estimate this simultaneous co-movement using a dynamic factor model with a single latent factor that essentially corresponds to the first principal component. Unlike classical principal component techniques, however, the factor model accommodates indicators of differing historical time spans. This aspect of the methodology means that the set of indicators in the index can change in the future as the financial system evolves. When the next date is estimated, the indicators are re-standardized, and the factor model is re-estimated. As such, the OFR FSI's value depends only on information up until the date on which it is estimated. Unlike some other FSIs, the OFR FSI's past values are not re-estimated each time the model is estimated.

---

2 See Kliesen et al. (2012) and Hatzius et al. (2010) for surveys of other financial stress indexes.

The first-order conditions from the procedure can be used to decompose the index into the marginal contributions of individual indicators to stress. These individual contributions are aggregated into sub-components reflecting the type of indicator. The indicator categories are credit spreads, equity valuation, funding, safe assets, and volatility. These indicator categories are useful for monitoring the drivers of stress. Similarly, the index can be decomposed by region into contributions from U.S. markets, other advanced economies, and emerging markets.

After detailing the construction of the index, we present a summary of its behavior over the 2000–2018 time period. We then discuss specific examples of market monitoring using the OFR FSI. The use cases include the 2007–2009 global financial crisis, the subsequent European sovereign debt crisis, and the recent events of 2018. The index and its decomposition into indicator categories and regions allow us to drill down into the drivers of systemic financial stress, cutting through the clutter of market chatter. Decomposition of the index shows which types of indicators are telegraphing market participants' views of stress. If indicator categories or region categories move together, we get some evidence of a systemic event.

A natural question is whether an FSI actually measures the latent indicator of financial stress. In Section 5, we discuss the empirical properties of the OFR FSI. Using dates of significant government intervention in financial markets as a proxy for financial stress events, we use logistic regression to show that the OFR FSI identifies financial stress periods well and is thus fit for its purpose. We then consider the relationship between financial stress and economic activity. Using the Chicago Fed National Activity Index as a proxy for real economic activity, we use Granger non-causality analysis and conclude that high levels of financial stress help predict decreases in economic activity.

This paper proceeds as follows. The next section provides background on financial stress and financial stress indexes, and distinguishes them from systemic risk indicators. Section 3 describes the construction and interpretation of the OFR FSI. Section 4 illustrates the use of the OFR FSI in OFR monitoring efforts. Section 5 describes empirical properties of the index. Section 6 concludes.

2. Systemic Financial Stress and Financial Stress Indexes

The global financial crisis of 2007–2009 showed that stress events in the financial sector can have severe adverse consequences for real economic activity in terms of output, employment, and welfare. It also underscored the need for policymakers to have accurate and timely signals of financial stress to respond appropriately to mitigate the impact of financial stress events. Since the crisis, policymakers and researchers have become more keenly aware of, and interested in, systemic risk and financial stress.

Financial stress is an unobserved variable in the economy. Several attempts have been made to define and measure it (see Kliesen et al. (2012) and Hatzius et al. (2010) for surveys). Some researchers define financial stress as being directly related to financial market functioning (Carlson et al. 2012; Sandahl et al. 2011). Others define stress indirectly as "systemic risk which has materialized" (Louzis and Vouldis 2013) or as the product of the interactions between vulnerabilities in markets and shocks (Grimaldi 2010, 2011). Although there is yet to be a consensus on what specifically constitutes financial stress or a financial stress event, there are common elements among these notions of stress, and this motivates the following definition: **financial stress refers to disruptions to the normal functioning of financial markets**. The definition is purposely broad, as financial stress can manifest in different ways, and no two stress events are exactly the same. Furthermore, note that financial stress thus defined is not synonymous with materialized systemic risk. Financial stress events can be reflected in some markets but not in others. However, extremely high levels of financial stress likely correlate with truly systemic financial stress events.

Although stress events differ in composition, there are several common economic characteristics of financial stress. Hakkio and Keeton 2009 survey the academic literature and summarize the symptoms of financial stress. According to their framework, financial stress is characterized by the coincident manifestation of one or more of the following:

- **Increased uncertainty about the fundamental value of assets or the behavior of investors.** Volatility may rise when increased uncertainty causes investors to react more strongly to new information. Increased uncertainty can be measured by implied or realized volatility.
- **Increased asymmetry of information.** Asymmetric information can worsen during a stress event if variation in true quality of borrowers or assets increases, or if information is deemed less reliable. Information asymmetries can lead to problems of moral hazard and adverse selection, and to increased borrowing costs and decreased asset prices. Asymmetric information can be measured by increases in credit or funding spreads or decreases in risky asset valuations.
- **Decreased willingness to hold risky assets.** Investors that change their preferences or risk appetite may demand more compensation for holding risky assets. This change may lead to price decreases of risky assets and price increases of safe assets. The change can be measured by decreases in risky asset valuations or increases in safe asset valuations.
- **Decreased willingness to hold illiquid assets.** Investors may become reluctant to hold illiquid assets if demand for liquidity increases in anticipation of unexpected needs for cash. This change may be due to rising volatility, or a perceived deterioration in asset liquidity. The change can be measured by increases in funding spreads.

These symptoms of financial stress are not directly observed in financial market indicators. Instead, financial market indicators that reflect one or more of the above symptoms of stress are collected to monitor stress. A financial stress index is a univariate time series that aggregates the information in these indicators and isolates and measures the level of financial stress.

Financial stress indexes are similar to financial conditions indexes (FCIs). Like FSIs, FCIs combine information from many financial indicators to create a univariate time series that represents conditions in the financial system. The main difference between FSIs and FCIs is in their objectives. The objective of FCIs is to focus on the link between the financial sector and the real economy. Conversely, FSIs are concerned with distress or instability in the financial system without explicit regard for how such distress may manifest in the real economy.

Another principal difference between FSIs and FCIs is in the set of indicators used in their construction. FSIs are generally constructed with market price-based measures. FCIs, on the other hand, are constructed with price-based measures and also include other market characteristics such as flows, trading volume, and stock measures. In practice, there is often considerable overlap between FSIs and FCIs in the sets of indicators included and the construction techniques used. Consequently, there is often considerable overlap in the time series properties of FSIs and FCIs.

A number of FSIs and FCIs have been developed over the past decade or so in the aftermath of the 2007–2009 global financial crisis. Here we only mention a few, and we refer the reader to Kliesen et al. (2012) and Hatzius et al. (2010) for more detailed surveys of various FSIs and FCIs. One of the first FSIs was developed by Illing and Liu (2006) for the Canadian financial market. They aggregate several indicators based on the specification that performs best in crisis times, where such times are identified from surveying policymakers at the Bank of Canada. Notable FSIs that focus on the U.S. financial system have been developed by two regional banks in the Federal Reserve System—the Kansas City Fed Stress Index (Hakkio and Keeton 2009) and the St. Louis Fed Stress Index (Kliesen and Smith 2010). Both FSIs aggregate indicators based on principal components, the notion being that the indicators are picked such that financial stress is manifest when they co-move. Carlson et al. (2012) at the Board of Governors of the Federal Reserve also develop a U.S.-based FSI. Some researchers, particularly in the eurozone, have developed individual FSIs to monitor financial stress in particular countries. Examples include Cardarelli et al. (2011), who created FSIs for 17 advanced economies, Lo Duca and Peltonen (2011), who produced FSIs for 10 advanced and 18 emerging economies, and Duprey et al. (2017), who constructed FSIs for 27 EU member countries and applied a Markov-switching model to endogenously determine high financial stress periods (see also Duprey and Klaus (2017)). Others have constructed FSIs to examine the relationship between financial stress and macroeconomic variables

(Apostolakis and Papadopoulos 2019) or exchange rates (Adam et al. 2018). Vasicek et al. (2017) show that FSIs are difficult to forecast out-of-sample.

Many FCIs have also been developed. Notable examples include the Bloomberg FCI (Rosenberg 2009), which is based on simple arithmetic averaging, and Hatzius et al. (2010) and the Chicago Fed National FCI (Brave and Butters 2011), which both use a dynamic factor model methodology.

Generally, FSIs and FCIs have been constructed in two broad steps. First, a set of observable financial market indicators that reflect stress is assembled. For FSIs, the indicators are nearly universally market-determined prices, reflecting the assumption that markets are the best and quickest aggregators of available information. Common types of indicators included are measures of volatility, credit spreads, funding spreads, and interest rates. After a set of indicators is determined, the second step is to process and aggregate the information contained in these indicators into a single summary measure of stress. Several methods of aggregation are used in the literature. The most common ways are a simple average (Lo Duca and Peltonen 2011), simple averages of sub-indexes (Rosenberg 2009), or by using statistical techniques like principal components analysis (PCA) (Kliesen and Smith 2010; Hakkio and Keeton 2009) or dynamic factor models (Hatzius et al. 2010; Brave and Butters 2011). Some authors take other approaches, such as methods inspired by portfolio theory (Hollo et al. 2012) or logistic regression models based on a pre-defined stress event indicator (Nelson and Perli 2007; Carlson et al. 2012).

The post-crisis environment has also been fertile ground for development of systemic risk indicators, or SRIs. SRIs measure vulnerabilities rather than stress. Examples of these include the conditional value at risk (CoVaR) (Adrian and Brunnermeier 2016), the distressed insurance premium (DIP) (Huang et al. 2012), and the systemic expected shortfall (SES) (Acharya et al. 2017). Like financial stress, systemic risk has no universally accepted definition. Given that the financial system is large, complex, and constantly evolving, a diverse set of approaches and measures is needed to study systemic risk. SRIs such as CoVaR, DIP, SES, and most of the others outlined in the first OFR working paper (Bisias et al. 2012), tend to be institution-specific estimates of the effects of low-probability but consequential, or "tail," market events. Bisias et al. (2012) develops a taxonomy of SRIs, classifying them by focus into macroprudential or microprudential measures and by horizon with respect to risk realization, as contemporaneous or ex-ante measures. As that paper demonstrates, most SRIs are microprudential measures focusing on effects conditional on an event relating to a financial institution. Such measures can be either contemporaneous to risk manifestation or could possibly give early warning signals. In contrast, an FSI is a market-based, macroprudential measure relaying an unconditional, contemporaneous view of market functioning. In other words, an FSI indicates what the state of the financial system is, and an SRI expresses what happens if the state of the financial system contains a specific stress event pertaining to that SRI.

3. Construction and Interpretation of the OFR FSI

The OFR FSI aims to provide a real-time summary measure of the level of financial stress by aggregating the information embedded in a number of market indicators related to stress. Here we detail the indicators included in the index and the way in which we combine them.

3.1. Indicator Selection

The OFR FSI has a transparent and methodical construction. The construction has two steps: indicator selection and indicator aggregation. Indicator selection begins with a survey of the literature and financial market landscape for indicators that reflect one or more of the symptoms of financial stress outlined in the previous section of this paper. After considering the symptoms of stress, we created five distinct indicator categories: credit, equity valuation, funding, safe assets, and volatility. Definitions of these categories appear in Table 1. While the OFR has a statutory mandate to monitor U.S. financial stability, it is important to recognize that stress from foreign markets can migrate to U.S. domestic markets. Accordingly, we consider three regions for classifying indicators: U.S.-centric, other advanced economies (such as the eurozone and Japan), and emerging markets. We require our set of indicators to have broad coverage across major asset classes, the five indicator categories, and the three regions. Moreover, we require each indicator to be—or be directly related to—a market-determined price.

Table 1. OFR FSI indicator category definitions.

Category	Definition
Credit	Contains measures of credit spreads, which represent the difference in borrowing costs for firms of different creditworthiness. In times of stress, credit spreads may widen when default risk increases or credit market functioning is disrupted. Wider spreads may indicate that investors are less willing to hold debt, increasing costs for borrowers to get funding.
Equity valuation	Contains stock valuations from several stock market indexes, which reflect investor confidence and risk appetite. In times of stress, stock values may fall if investors become less willing to hold risky assets.
Funding	Contains measures related to how easily financial institutions can fund their activities. In times of stress, funding markets can freeze if participants perceive greater counterparty credit risk or liquidity risk.
Safe assets	Contains valuation measures of assets that are considered stores of value or have stable and predictable cash flows. In times of stress, higher valuations of safe assets may indicate that investors are migrating from risky or illiquid assets into safer holdings.
Volatility	Contains measures of implied and realized volatility from equity, credit, currency, and commodity markets. In times of stress, rising uncertainty about asset values or investor behavior can lead to higher volatility.

Finally, we combine the qualitative factors with a quantitative test for redundant information. Taking advantage of the fact that the recent history in financial markets contains both a crisis period and periods of tranquility, we use a rolling 500-day pairwise correlation analysis to determine if two indicators substantially produce the same information during both volatile and tranquil periods. If this correlation is consistently high (greater than 0.8 in magnitude) through both the crisis period and bull markets, we consider them to be producing the same information. In the absence of a compelling reason to keep such an indicator in the index, such as for balance across indicator categories, we eliminate such an indicator from the set.

Appendix A contains information about our resulting set of indicators, including source, time span of data, indicator category, economy classification, transformation of the raw data before the aggregation step (to ensure approximate long-run stationarity), and basic summary statistics. All indicators in our set are available at a daily frequency, though this is not a strict requirement for inclusion because the indicator aggregation methodology (see next section) can accommodate indicators of different frequencies, such as weekly or monthly.

3.2. Indicator Aggregation

The 33 indicators used to construct the OFR FSI are chosen to reflect one or more symptoms of financial stress. We assume that financial stress manifests if and when the indicators move together. That is, the extent of the simultaneous co-movement in the indicators reflects systemic financial stress. This suggests that we use the first principal component from a principal components analysis.

We also want to account for relationships among indicators changing over time as the financial system evolves, which suggests a dynamic approach. The financial system may evolve to the point where certain indicators are no longer appropriate for measuring symptoms of financial stress and should be removed and possibly replaced. This is a particularly important aspect of the construction because as the financial system evolves, the set of indicators through which financial stress is manifest can change. For example, currently our set of indicators contains several measures related to the London Interbank Offered Rate (LIBOR) in its funding indicator category. Because of the attempted manipulation of LIBOR during the financial crisis and other problems, work is underway at the OFR and throughout the public and private sectors to develop a LIBOR replacement (ARRC 2017). If such a replacement proves successful and funding market strains are reflected through the new indicator, we will substitute it for LIBOR in the index.

Indicator composition may also change in the future for other reasons. For example, the rise of China as an important financial market over the past decade or so may merit the addition of Chinese indicators that have a sufficient time series and data quality. We may in the future decide that other markets, such as real estate, are worth including in the index, provided we can achieve balance across regions. These and practical data availability considerations suggest the need to accommodate unbalanced panels in our analysis.

Finally, to be useful in real time, a stress measurement on a given date should be measurable with respect to known information on that date. Historical measurements of stress should not depend on information or events that occurred subsequently. All these factors motivate the following approach and estimation method.

We estimate the degree of simultaneous co-movement using a dynamic factor model with a single latent factor, a generalization of classical principal components analysis or PCA. The vector of weights on the indicators from the model shows the direction of highest co-movement or correlation in the data. The vector of weights can be viewed as the single best summary of the correlations in the data. Unlike other PCA-based FSIs, we estimate this weights vector each time the index is calculated, using information available through that date and not information from subsequent dates. Past values of the index are not recomputed. Finally, as in Hatzius et al. (2010), the unbalanced structure of our panel dataset is accommodated by estimating the dynamic factor model using an iterative least squares technique rather than the classical singular value decomposition.

Suppose we want to calculate the OFR FSI on a given date t. Let $\boldsymbol{X} = \boldsymbol{X}(t)$ denote the matrix of the data from the indicators in the index through date t, transformed according to Appendix A, and standardized to have zero mean and unit standard deviation. An indicator is eligible for inclusion on date t if its historical time series goes back at least 500 trading days, which is approximately two years. We consider the following decomposition of the data:

$$X_{is} = w_i * f_s + e_{is}, \qquad (1)$$

where f_s is the unobserved factor common across the indicators, w_i is the unobserved loading of indicator i on this factor, and e_{is} is the residual variation in X_{is}, which is assumed to be uncorrelated across the indicators. Note that X, w, f, and e all depend on the fixed time t, but for ease of exposition, we have dropped the reference to t.

We want to estimate the vector $w = (w_i : i = 1, \ldots, I(t))$ of indicator weights and the vector $f = (f_s : s = 1, \ldots, t)$ of the common factor. Solutions (w,f) of (1) are unique up to a constant, and so without loss of generality we impose the constraint that the vector w has norm one and points in the direction most resembling the expected signs on the indicators (see Appendix A). To estimate (w,f) we follow the approach in Hatzius et al. using least squares (see also Bai and Ng (2008) and Stock and Watson (2002, 2006, 2010)). That is, $\hat{w}$ and $\hat{f}$ solve

$$\text{Minimize} \sum_{is} (X_{is} - w_i * f_s)^2 \text{ over } w_i \text{ and } f_s, \qquad (2)$$

where we only sum over non-null observations of the indicators. This optimization problem is solved using iterative methods.[3] (If the matrix X represented a balanced panel, the solution would be given by

[3] This proceeds as follows: initialize the algorithm with a loading vector w_0 and compute an initial factor $f_0 = w_0^+ X$. Subsequent iterates are computed using $w_n = f_{n-1}^+ X$ and $f_n = w_n^+ X$. We proceed for 200 iterations. We then repeat the analysis 15 times, initializing the vector w_0 in different ways, including taking the first principal component of the largest

classical principal components, i.e., by computing the eigenvectors of the sample correlation matrix.) The value of the OFR FSI on date t is then given by $\hat{f}_t$, the estimated factor evaluated at time t. The decomposition of the OFR FSI into indicator-level contributions and indicator categories follows from the first order condition of (2), namely that

$$\hat{f}' = \hat{w}^{+}\boldsymbol{X} = \frac{\hat{w}'}{\hat{w}'\hat{w}}\boldsymbol{X} = \hat{w}'\boldsymbol{X} = \sum_i \hat{w}_i X_i, \tag{3}$$

where $\hat{w}^{+}$ is the Moore-Penrose pseudoinverse of $\hat{w}$, X_i is the i-th column of $\boldsymbol{X}$ representing the time series of the i-th indicator, and we have used our assumption that the norm of $\hat{w}$ is one. Thus, the OFR FSI decomposes as a sum of contributions over the set of indicators in the index. By summing contributions of indicators in each indicator category, we obtain the subtotals for the credit, equity valuation, funding, safe assets, and volatility indicator categories. Similarly, by summing contributions of indicators in each region, we obtain the subtotals for the United States, other advanced economies, and emerging markets. Note that indicators that are assigned multiple regions have their contributions evenly divided among the assigned regions.

3.3. *The Index and Its Interpretation*

Table 2 provides a decomposition of the OFR FSI on 31 December 2018. The 33 indicators used in the index are listed in their respective indicator categories.[4] The other columns in the table provide each indicator's weight in the loading vector $\hat{w}$ (Coef.) as determined by the dynamic factor model; the value of the indicator on 31 December 2018, standardized with respect to its history up until that time (Data); and the contribution of the indicator to systemic financial stress (Contr.), which is the product of these values. The units of an indicator's standardized value are in the number of standard deviations, and thus, each indicator's weight in the loading vector $\hat{w}$ is naturally interpreted as a sensitivity, that is, as the incremental change in the OFR FSI associated to a one standard deviation increase in the indicator. For example, the coefficient on the Chicago Board Options Exchange Volatility Index, or VIX, on 31 December 2018 was 0.254, and therefore, an increase of one standard deviation in VIX on that date was associated with a 0.254 incremental increase in financial stress, all else being equal. The relationships among the coefficients on the indicators also have important implications about indicators' relative contributions to stress. The coefficient on 31 December 2018 on the 10-year U.S. Treasury note, for example, was −0.105, which in absolute terms is about 40 percent of the coefficient on VIX. This implies that, all else being equal, a one standard deviation decrease in the 10-year Treasury note yield[5] had about 40 percent of the effect on systemic financial stress as a one standard deviation move in the VIX.

The contribution column reports the product of each indicator's weight in the loading vector and its standardized data on 31 December 2018. This value is unitless and is the marginal contribution of the indicator to financial stress. Summing the marginal contributions of the indicators in a given indicator category gives the marginal contribution to financial stress of the category on that date. Similar summing over all the marginal contributions of the indicator categories gives the value of the OFR FSI on that date. An FSI value of zero implies that either all indicators have exactly zero marginal contributions to financial stress or that positive marginal contributions are exactly offset by negative marginal contributions to stress. A necessary but not sufficient condition for this to occur is that each indicator has exactly average performance on the date of the FSI. Positive (negative) values of the FSI

---

subset of balanced panel data, taking the first principal component using a pseudo-correlation matrix constructed by the pairwise correlations using each pair's overlapping sample, and sampling from a random normal vector. We then select the iteration with the smallest sum of squared errors.

4 Descriptions of the indicator categories are in Table 1. Additional information about the indicators in the index, including definitions of the abbreviations used in Table 2, is available in Appendix A.

5 The 10-year Treasury note yield is transformed to be relative to its 250-trading day moving average. See Appendix A.

arise when the positive (negative) marginal contributions outweigh the negative (positive) marginal contributions. For example, the standardized value of VIX on 31 December 2018 was above average, at 0.790, implying a contribution to financial stress of 0.201 on that date. The contribution to stress for the volatility indicator category, equal to −0.326, is computed by summing the marginal contributions of the nine indicators included in the volatility indicator category. Finally, the value of the OFR FSI is computed by summing the marginal contributions of the various risk dimensions, returning 0.268. Examining the marginal contributions of the indicators and indicator categories provides insight on what was driving financial stress on a given date. On 31 December 2018, above average stress in the equity valuation and credit subcategories was balanced by below average stress in the volatility and funding subcategories.

Table 2. Decomposition of the OFR FSI on 31 December 2018.

Indicator Category	Indicator	Coef.	Data	Wgt.	Data *	Contr.	Subtotal
Credit	BaML US Corporate Master (IG) (OAS)	0.241	0.016	0.241	0.016	0.004	
	BaML US High Yield Corporate Master (HY) (OAS)	0.244	−0.114	0.244	−0.114	−0.028	
	BaML Euro Area Corp Bond Index (OAS)	0.160	0.761	0.160	0.761	0.122	
	BaML Euro Area High Yield Bond Index (OAS)	0.230	−0.346	0.230	−0.346	−0.080	
	BaML Japan Corporate (OAS)	0.174	0.697	0.174	0.697	0.122	
	JPMorgan CEMBI Strip Spread	0.209	0.248	0.209	0.248	0.052	
	JPMorgan EMBI Global Strip Spread	0.131	0.100	0.131	0.100	0.013	0.205
Equity Valuation	MSCI Emerging Markets Index (P/B Ratio)	−0.141	−0.618	0.141	0.618	0.087	
	MSCI Europe Index (P/B Ratio)	−0.190	−0.855	0.190	0.855	0.162	
	NIKKEI 225 Index (P/B Ratio)	−0.172	−1.102	0.172	1.102	0.190	
	S&P 500 Index (P/B Ratio)	−0.197	−1.365	0.197	1.365	0.269	0.708
Funding	2-Year EUR/USD Cross-Currency Swap Spread	−0.095	0.244	0.095	−0.244	−0.023	
	2-Year US Swap Spread	0.174	−0.960	0.174	−0.960	−0.167	
	2-Year USD/JPY Cross-Currency Swap Spread	−0.012	−0.484	0.012	0.484	0.006	
	3-Month EURIBOR—EONIA	0.206	−0.579	0.206	−0.579	−0.120	
	3-Month Japanese LIBOR—OIS	0.187	−0.941	0.187	−0.941	−0.176	
	3-Month LIBOR—OIS	0.192	0.407	0.192	0.407	0.078	
	3-Month TED Spread	0.173	0.036	0.173	0.036	0.006	−0.395
Safe Assets	10-Year US Treasury Note (yield)	−0.105	−0.301	0.105	0.301	0.032	
	10-Year German Bond (yield)	−0.095	−0.190	0.095	0.190	0.018	
	Gold/USD Real Spot Exchange Rate	0.033	−0.048	0.033	−0.048	−0.002	
	Japanese Yen/USD Spot Exchange Rate	−0.109	−0.023	0.109	0.023	0.002	
	Swiss Franc/USD Spot Exchange Rate	−0.008	0.191	0.008	−0.191	−0.002	
	US Dollar Index (DXY)	0.050	0.547	0.050	0.547	0.027	0.076
Volatility	CBOE S&P 500 Volatility Index (VIX)	0.254	0.790	0.254	0.790	0.201	
	Dow Jones EURO STOXX 50 Volatility Index (V2X)	0.209	−0.029	0.209	−0.029	−0.006	
	ICE Brent Crude Oil Futures (22-day realized volatility)	0.176	1.518	0.176	1.518	0.267	
	Implied Volatility on 6-Month EUR/USD Options	0.199	−1.052	0.199	−1.052	−0.210	
	Implied Volatility on 6-Month USD/JPY Options	0.161	−0.872	0.161	−0.872	−0.140	
	JPMorgan Emerging Market Volatility Index	0.216	−0.169	0.216	−0.169	−0.037	
	Merrill Lynch Euro Swaptions Volatility Estimate	0.198	−1.696	0.198	−1.696	−0.336	
	Merrill Lynch US Swaptions Volatility Estimate	0.185	−0.922	0.185	−0.922	−0.170	
	NIKKEI Volatility Index	0.208	0.507	0.208	0.507	0.105	−0.326
					OFR FSI		**0.268**

Note: "Coef." provides the indicators' weights $\hat{w}$ in the loading vector of the dynamic factor model; "Data" provides the standardized values $\boldsymbol{X}$ of the indicators on 31 December 2018; "Wgt." is the absolute value of "Coef."; "Data*" is the product of "Data" and the sign of "Coef."; and "Contr." Is the product of "Coef." and "Data" or, equivalently, the product of "Wgt." and "Data*." Sources: Bloomberg Finance L.P., Haver Analytics, OFR analysis.

The information in Table 2 facilitates another interpretation of the OFR FSI: the value of the OFR FSI on a given date is proportional to the weighted average of the standardized values of its constituent indicators. This can be easily seen by examining the Wgt. and Data* columns in Table 2. The Wgt. column is simply the absolute value of the Coef. column, the column of indicator weights from the dynamic factor model. The Data* column is just the standardized value of the indicator on that date, signed to reflect that increases in the indicator correspond to increases in financial stress. The value of the index is then the weighted average, using the weights in Wgt, of these signed standardized values in Data*. The index is positive if the (weighted) average standardized values of the indicators is positive, is zero if this average is zero, and is negative if the average is negative.

Additional interpretation of the OFR FSI can be gained by rewriting it on a given date t as (see (3))

$$FSI_t = \hat{w}^+ X_t = \|X_t\| \cos(\theta_{\hat{w}X_t}),$$

where X_t is the standardized data from date t and $cos(\theta_{\hat{w}X_t})$ is the angle in Euclidean space between the first loading vector $\hat{w}$ and the standardized data vector X_t. This decomposition shows that the FSI is determined by the size $\|X_t\|$ of the standardized data vector X_t and the angle of X_t with the first loading vector $\hat{w}$. For a fixed angle between X_t and $\hat{w}$, the farther the indicators are from their average, the larger the composite size $\|X_t\|$ of the data X_t will be and consequently the larger the' FSI will be. Conversely, for a given deviation of the indicators from their respective means, i.e., for a given $\|X_t\|$, systemic financial stress as reflected in the FSI is maximized when the angle between X_t and $\hat{w}$ is zero, i.e., when X_t is a positive multiple of $\hat{w}$. That is, given a fixed aggregate deviation of the indicators from their means, the FSI is maximized when the relative relationships reflected in the vector $\hat{w}$ across all of the indicators the indicators are maintained. The vector $\hat{w}$ is interpreted as the direction of maximal systemic financial stress. By providing the direction of maximized financial stress, the first loading vector $\hat{w}$ on a given day provides a multidimensional measure of vulnerability in financial markets.

4. Use of the OFR FSI in Market Monitoring

The OFR FSI is plotted from its inception in January 2000 through the end of December 2018 in Figure 1. Several dates of interest are labeled.

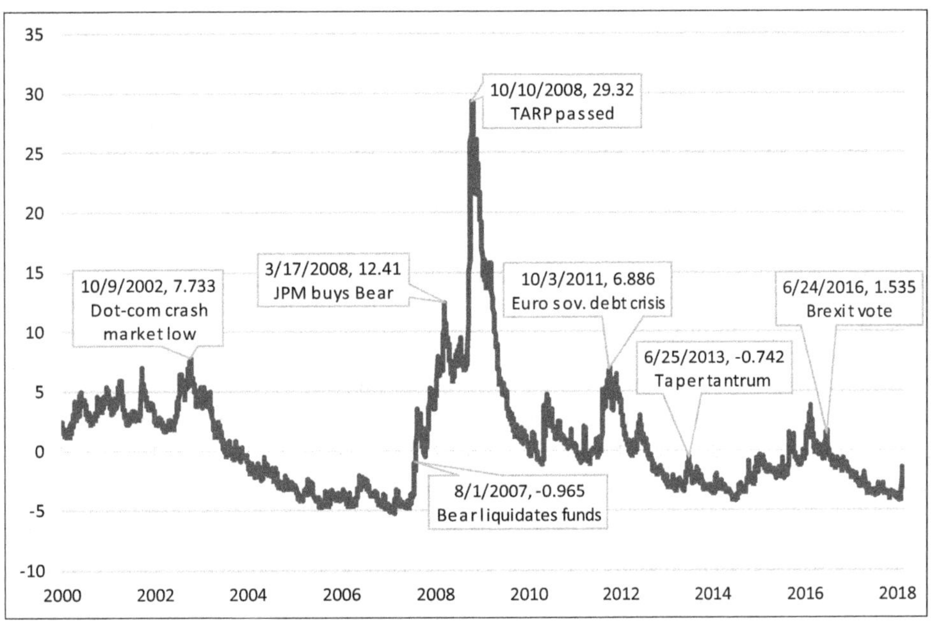

Figure 1. The OFR FSI between January 2000 and December 2018.

The OFR FSI was positive during the bust of the dot-com bubble, before declining into negative territory during the bull market of the mid-2000s. The index increased precipitously in mid-2007 during the beginnings of the global financial crisis; Figure 1 notes the date Bear Stearns liquidated two hedge funds with exposures to subprime mortgages. The OFR FSI continued to increase through March 2008 when JPMorgan Chase & Co. agreed to buy Bear Stearns. Throughout the summer of 2008, the index remained high, and it rose in the fall when Lehman Brothers sought bankruptcy protection. The OFR FSI hit its apex in October and November 2008 after Congress approved the Troubled Asset

Relief Program (TARP). The index eased but remained relatively high through 2009. It increased again during the European sovereign debt crisis of 2010 and 2011. Since then, the OFR FSI has generally declined, with some of its lowest levels since before the crisis occurring during 2018.

Figure 2 shows the index and its decomposition into indicator categories during the 2007–2009 global financial crisis. The OFR FSI started the period at around negative 5, increased steadily through mid-2008 to about 7, and then jumped in the second half of 2007 as the crisis took hold, before declining but still remaining positive during the first half of 2009. Figure 2 shows that stress in each of the five categories was below average until mid-2007, when stress spiked mainly in volatility and funding subcomponents. Stress continued on an upward trend as the credit indicators increased and volatility and funding indicators remained high. Stress from the credit, volatility, funding, and equity valuation categories simultaneously spiked in the fall of 2008, propelling the FSI to its all-time high and illustrating the contagion effect during the global financial crisis.

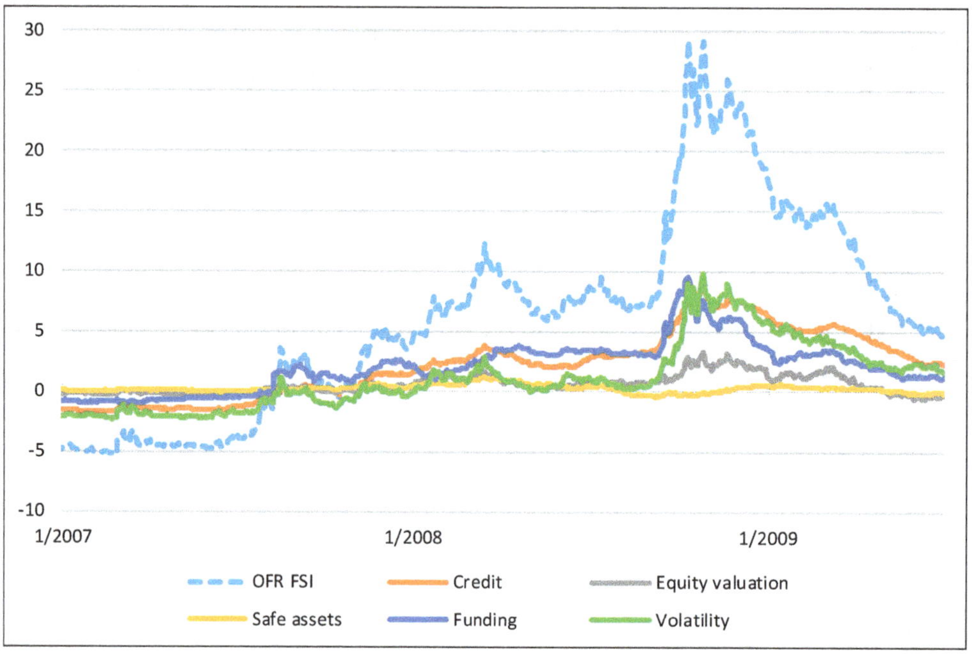

Figure 2. Decomposition of the OFR FSI during the 2007–2009 Global Financial Crisis.

4.1. The European Sovereign Debt Crisis

By 2012, the European sovereign debt crisis was well underway. Bailouts and other government support throughout the global financial crisis of 2007–2009 led to balance sheet strains for many sovereigns, particularly in Europe where some sovereigns were already heavily indebted. Concern over a possible Greek sovereign debt default continued to build in 2009 and 2010, and eventually spread to Portugal, Ireland, and Spain. In late 2010 and early 2011, the EU and International Monetary Fund (IMF) agreed to bailout packages for Greece, Ireland, and Portugal.

Figure 3 depicts the OFR FSI and its indicator categories from April 2011 through May 2013. During late spring and early summer in 2011, market participants became concerned that Greece might become the first country to leave the eurozone. Stress increased slowly during this period from normal levels, except for a short-lived decline in July when the eurozone agreed to a Greece bailout package of over 100 EUR billion to contain potential contagion. However, stress spiked dramatically in August as the result of two events: Standard and Poor's downgraded the credit rating of U.S. sovereign debt for the first time in history, and the European Commission expressed concerns that the sovereign debt crisis was spreading. Italian and Spanish sovereign bond yields rapidly rose as fears of contagion manifested. This increase in stress appeared in all indicator categories of the OFR FSI, particularly the volatility, credit, and funding categories. Figure 4 shows that the eurozone mainly drove the stress increase stress increase, though the U.S. components of the index also contributed, either because of the S&P downgrade or a contagion effect.

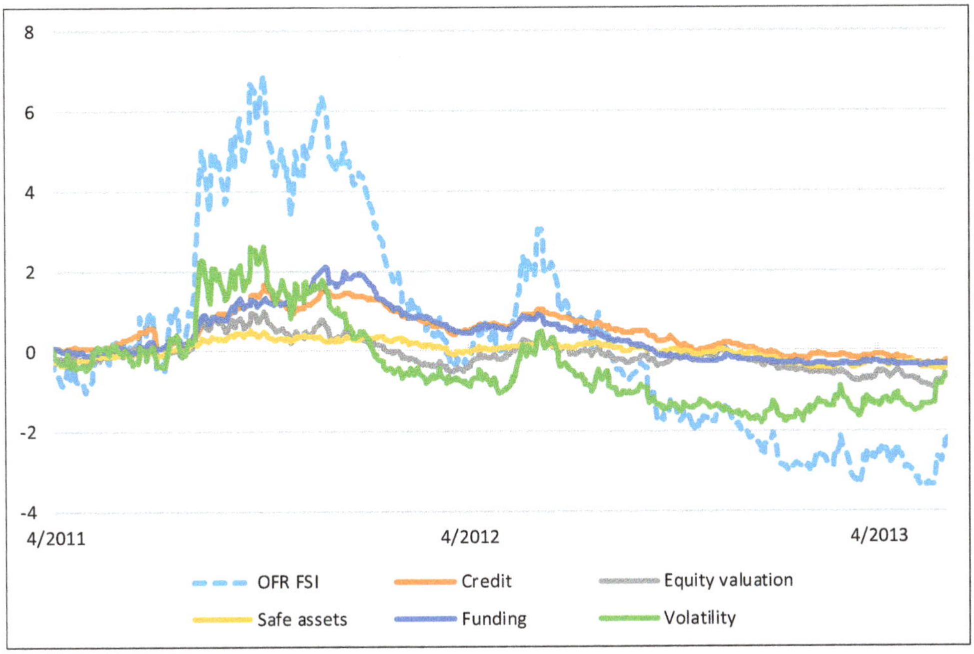

Figure 3. Decomposition of the OFR FSI during European Sovereign Debt Crisis.

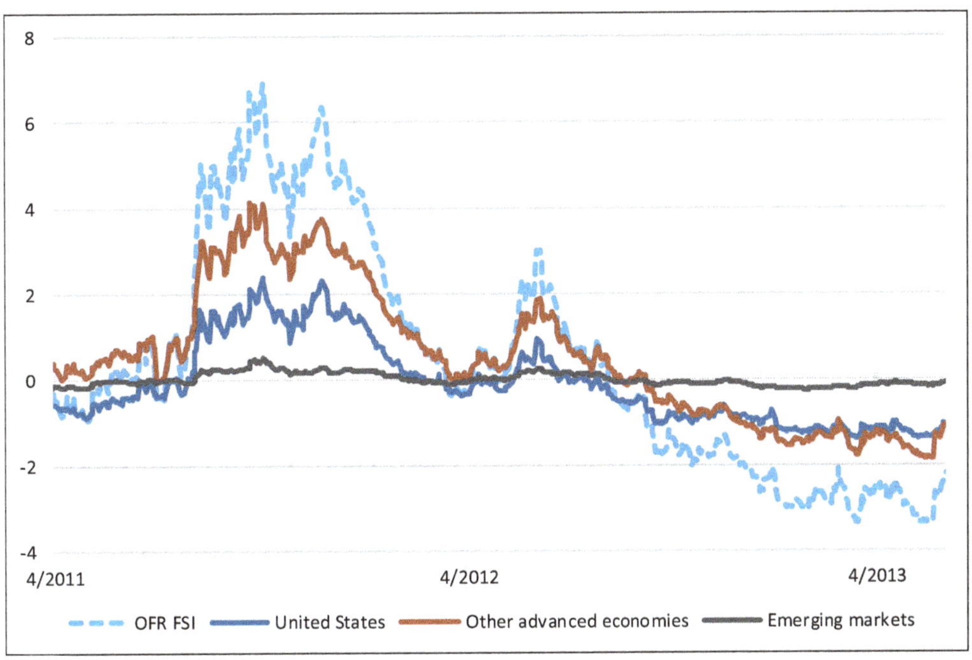

Figure 4. Decomposition of the OFR FSI during European Sovereign Debt Crisis, By Region.

Stress remained high for the next six months as credit ratings were downgraded throughout the eurozone and monetary authorities debated how to stem the crisis. The OFR FSI shows that stress finally abated when Greece received a second bailout. But after trending lower for a few months, stress soared in May due to a Greek election and a large Spanish bank's request for a bailout. Stress declined for the balance of 2012 when Greece formed a new government, the European Central Bank instituted a program promising more bailouts, and German courts allowed Germany's participation in a permanent bailout fund known as the European Stability Mechanism.

4.2. *Financial Stress in 2018*

The OFR FSI shows stress at the beginning of 2018 at its lowest level since the global financial crisis of 2007–2009. Aside from an event in February during which volatility temporarily spiked, stress levels were essentially flat for the first three quarters of 2018 at levels that were well below average. As Figure 5 shows, the low stress was driven mostly by low volatility across global equity, fixed income, currency and commodity markets. Stress contributions from most other categories of the index were also negative. Low stress levels do not necessarily imply low levels of risk. During low stress periods, stress can build up endogenously as the environment may incentivize investors to take on more leverage and reach for yield.[6] Thus, while the OFR FSI suggests that stress levels were low, this does not mean that risk or systemic risk was low. For information about the potential vulnerabilities in the financial system during 2018, we refer the reader to the OFR's Financial System Vulnerabilities Monitor.

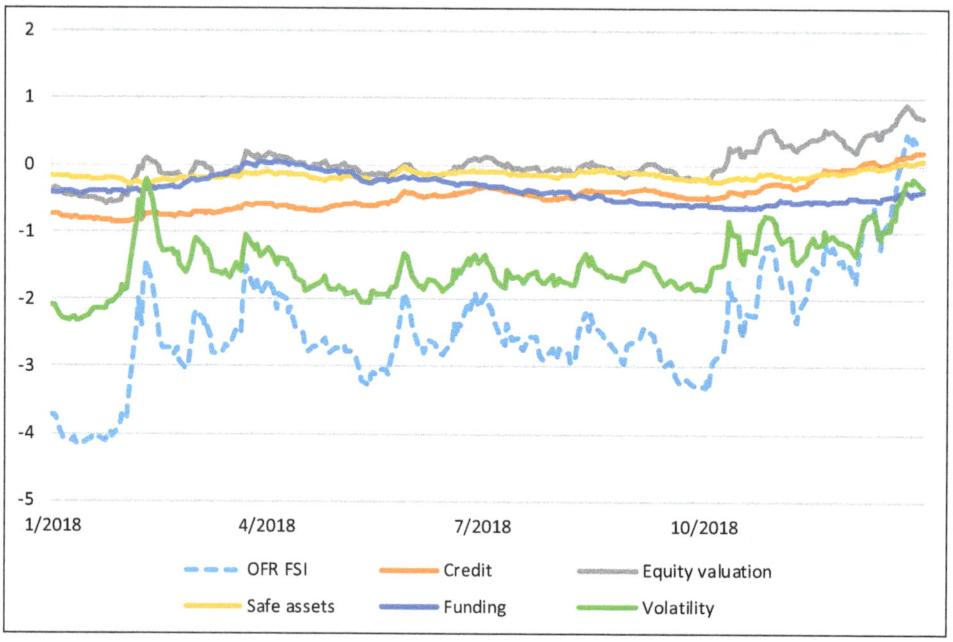

Figure 5. Decomposition of the OFR FSI in 2018.

Financial stress increased dramatically in the fourth quarter of 2018, ending the year at its highest level in more than two years. The increase was most pronounced in the volatility, equity valuation, and credit subcategories of the index. The safe assets category also increased modestly, while the stress contribution from the funding subcategory remained relatively constant at below average levels. These changes reflect the changing risk sentiment in financial markets seen during the quarter. After a rough October and a tepid November, U.S. equities dropped almost 10 percent in December amid much higher market volatility. Credit spreads also widened during the quarter.

5. Stress Identification and the Relationship of Stress to Economic Activity

Previous sections described how the OFR FSI measures systemic financial stress. In this section we aim to empirically test this. This task is challenging because financial stress is a latent indicator in the economy. Following Carlson et al. (2012), we develop a proxy for global financial stress events using dates of significant government intervention. We show that higher values of the OFR FSI are associated with an increased likelihood of a financial stress event, evidence that the index measures financial

---

6 See for example, (OFR Financial Markets Monitor 2017) "The Volatility Paradox: Tranquil Markets May Harbor Hidden Risks."

stress. Next, we examine the relationship between financial stress and real economic activity. We find that higher values of the OFR FSI help predict decreased real economic activity, but not vice-versa. The analysis suggests that the OFR FSI performs well in identifying stress episodes, and that financial stress can have real economic effects.

5.1. Stress Identification Using the OFR FSI

The OFR FSI is designed to be a coincident indicator of stress in the global financial system. A natural question is how well it fulfills its intended purpose. As financial stress is unobserved and subject to interpretation, one challenge in evaluating whether the OFR FSI identifies financial stress periods is the lack of a natural or obvious benchmark for comparison. Some researchers have identified financial stress periods based on opinion (Nelson and Perli 2007; Illing and Liu 2006) while others have identified systemic events as states of abnormal equity returns (Dattels et al. 2010; Arsov et al. 2013). We adapt the approach in Carlson et al. (2012) that identifies U.S. financial stress as periods of "interventions by policymakers that occurred out of concern that troubles at a U.S. financial institution or the impairment in functioning of a U.S. financial market might present systemic risks to financial stability and have negative consequence for economic activity." This approach identifies periods in which institutions or markets as a whole pose enough risk to the stability of the financial system that policymakers are persuaded to intervene. Carlson and coauthors select dates when the Federal Reserve, the Federal Deposit Insurance Corporation, or the Treasury Department interceded directly with an institution or market. The types of interventions are broad and include all actions taken by policymakers to protect market functioning.

In addition to the U.S.-centric intervention dates identified by Carlson et al. (2012), we add an international aspect to assess the global scope intended for the OFR FSI. Specifically, we identify dates in the eurozone starting in 2010 when the European Central Bank, International Monetary Fund, or a eurozone sovereign intervened or implemented policy due to concerns about potential risks to financial stability and spillover effects. Using a Euro crisis timeline compiled by a European think tank (Bruegel 2017), we compile dates since 2010 of intervention in European fiscal matters and financial markets and update the list through August 2017. A complete list of the government intervention dates is in Appendix B.

To test how well the OFR FSI identifies financial stress episodes, we run a logistic regression to assess the performance of the index in stress episodes defined by the intervention dates. The independent variable in the regression is the OFR FSI. The dependent variable, StressEvent, is a binary indicator with a daily frequency that is set at one in the four weeks before and after an intervention takes place, and otherwise set at zero. As in Carlson et al. (2012), we consider stress episodes to extend from four weeks before an intervention date to four weeks after. This captures stress leading up to the intervention, and market reaction and policy implementation following the intervention. The qualitative results of the logistic regression are not sensitive to the choice of window.

Descriptive statistics for the OFR FSI and the StressEvent are in Table 3. Both series are at a daily frequency from the inception of the OFR FSI on 3 January 2000 to 31 August 2017. During this period, the OFR FSI has, on average, been positive, with a mean of 0.76. Approximately one quarter of the daily observations of StressEvent are equal to one, indicating that the system has been experiencing financial stress for approximately one quarter of the sample period.

Table 3. Descriptive statistics for the OFR FSI and StressEvent.

Variable	Mean	Std	25%	50%	75%
OFR FSI	0.76	4.68	−2.64	−0.22	2.95
	Count = 0	Count = 1			
StressEvent	3364	1081			

Note: There are 4445 daily observations for each series from 3 January 2000 to 31 August 2017. Sources: Bloomberg Finance L.P., Bruegel, Carlson et al. (2012), Haver Analytics, OFR analysis.

The logistic regression results are in Table 4. Standard errors for the estimated coefficients were computed using the moving block bootstrap method. We see from the table that the coefficient on the OFR FSI is positive and statistically significant, with a p-value well below 0.0001. The area under the curve of the receiver operator characteristic is 0.76. The results suggest that higher levels of the OFR FSI are associated with being in periods of financial stress. In addition, the odds ratio of 1.31 suggests that the financial system is 1.31 times as likely to be in a stress episode for every one unit increase in the OFR FSI. Finally, the McFadden's pseudo R-squared value of 0.19 suggests that a moderate amount of the variation in StressEvent is explained by the OFR FSI.[7] The analysis confirms the usefulness of the OFR FSI as a coincident indicator of systemic financial stress.

Table 4. Does the OFR FSI identify periods of financial stress?

Dependent Variable: StressEvent				
Variable	**Coef.**	**SE**	***t*-stat**	***p*-Value**
Constant	−1.521	0.044	−34.620	<0.00001
OFR FSI	0.271	0.010	24.270	<0.00001
Odds ratio	1.31			
McF-R2	0.19			
AUC	0.76			

Note: This table reports logistic regression results of StressEvent on the OFR FSI. McF-R2 refers to McFadden's pseudo R-squared value and AUC refers to the area under the Receiver Operator Characteristic. Standard errors are calculated using the moving block bootstrap method. Sources: Bloomberg Finance L.P., Bruegel, Carlson et al. (2012), Haver Analytics, OFR analysis.

5.2. The Relationship of Financial Stress to Real Economic Activity

We have argued that the OFR FSI measures financial stress, a latent indicator in the economy, and have provided statistical evidence that supports this. One of the motivations in measuring financial stress is that it can have adverse real economic effects. This can occur in several ways. In times of increased uncertainty, firms and households may delay or reduce hiring, investment, and spending. Investors may sell riskier investments and buy safer ones, contributing to market illiquidity and increased asymmetric information. All these actions can result in increased borrowing costs and tightened credit standards, leading to a reduction in spending and economic activity (Hakkio and Keeton 2009).

Financial stress, as measured by other FSIs, can forecast declines in economic activity (Apostolakis and Papadopoulos 2019, and Apostolakis and Papadopoulos 2019). Having shown that the OFR FSI is fit for its intended purpose of measuring financial stress, we can empirically test whether increases in financial stress, as measured by the OFR FSI, lead to decreases in economic activity. As in Hakkio and Keeton (2009), we use the Chicago Fed National Activity Index (CFNAI) (Chicago Fed National Activity Index 2016) as a proxy for overall economic activity. The monthly CFNAI is computed as a weighted average of 85 indicators of U.S. national economic activity drawn from four categories: production and income; employment, unemployment, and hours worked; consumption and housing; and sales, orders, and inventories. The CFNAI tracks periods of economic expansion and contraction, and periods of changing inflationary pressure.

Descriptive statistics of the OFR FSI and the CFNAI are in Table 5. To accommodate the monthly frequency of the CFNAI, the OFR FSI is downsampled to a monthly index using the last observation each month. There are 211 monthly observations between January 2000 and July 2017, inclusive. The OFR FSI had an average monthly value of 0.78, which is consistent with an average negative value

[7] McFadden's pseudo R-squared is equal to one minus the ratio of the log-likelihood of the model containing the OFR FSI to that of the model with just a constant. Higher values are thus associated with more variation in StressEvent being explained by the OFR FSI. McFadden (1977) suggests that values above 0.2 indicate "excellent" model fit.

for the CFNAI of −0.29. The OFR FSI has a substantially larger range than the CFNAI and there is a high negative correlation of −0.74 between the two indexes, as expected.

Table 5. Descriptive statistics for the OFR FSI and Chicago Fed National Activity Index.

Variable	Mean	Std	25%	50%	75%
OFR FSI	0.78	4.61	−2.49	−0.22	3.02
CFNAI	−0.29	0.85	−0.51	−0.16	0.19

Note: The OFR FSI is downsampled to a monthly frequency using the last observation for a given month. There are 211 monthly observations. The correlation between the two series is −0.74. Sources: Bloomberg Finance L.P., Haver Analytics, OFR analysis.

We use Granger non-causality analysis to test whether higher values of financial stress help predict decreases in economic activity. This technique involves setting up a regression model where each indicator is regressed on the past values of the other indicator. After properly specifying such a model to account for potential non-stationarity (Toda and Yamamoto 1995), the coefficients on the past values of the independent variable that are statistically significantly different from zero suggest that past values of that variable are helpful for predicting current values of the dependent variable.

The results from our analysis are in Table 6. The top panel reports the results of testing to see whether past values of the OFR FSI help to predict the CFNAI. The null hypothesis of the F-test that lagged values of the OFR FSI are not different from zero is soundly rejected with a p-value less than 0.0001. The coefficient estimates on the lagged values of the OFR FSI are negative. This suggests that decreases in the OFR FSI help to predict increases in the CFNAI. The bottom panel of Table 6 reports the results of whether past values the CFNAI help to predict the OFR FSI. In this case, the null hypothesis that the CFNAI does not Granger cause the OFR FSI cannot be rejected at the 5 percent level. This suggests that past values of the CFNAI do not help to predict the OFR FSI. Overall, the results show that increases in the OFR FSI help predict decreases in the CFNAI (and not vice versa), suggesting that the OFR FSI is useful for predicting reductions in overall economic activity.

Table 6. Does financial stress help predict reductions in economic activity?

Dependent Variable: CFNAI			
Variable	**Coef.**	**SE**	***t*-stat**
OFR FSI (t−1)	−0.036	0.023	−1.521
OFR FSI (t−2)	−0.071	0.035	−2.043
Does the OFR FSI help predict CFNAI?			
Null hypothesis: OFR FSI does not Granger cause the CFNAI			
F-stat	13.30		
p-value	<0.0001		
Dependent Variable: OFR FSI			
Variable	**Coef.**	**SE**	***t*-stat**
CFNAI (t−1)	−0.392	0.212	−1.849
CFNAI (t−2)	0.064	0.200	0.320
Does the CFNAI help predict OFR FSI?			
Null hypothesis: CFNAI does not Granger cause the OFR FSI			
F-stat	1.71		
p-value	0.1835		

Note: Table reports results from Granger non-causality testing performed using method of Toda and Yamamoto (1995). Lag length of 2 determined using the Bayesian Information Criterion. There are 211 monthly observations between January 2000 and July 2017. Sources: Bloomberg Finance L.P., Haver Analytics, OFR analysis.

6. Conclusions

The 2007–2009 global financial crisis showed how severe financial stress events can have devastating real economic consequences. Accordingly, measuring financial stress is of first-order importance to regulators and market participants alike. This paper introduces a new financial stress index, the OFR FSI. The OFR FSI is a daily, market-based snapshot of stress in global financial markets. It distills information from multiple stress categories and regions, offering insight into the drivers of stress. It helps the OFR monitor, compare, and understand financial stress events. The index offers improvements on other FSIs, including its decomposition into stress categories and a dynamic construction that allows for changes in variable composition and cross-asset relationships. Empirical results suggest that the OFR FSI successfully identifies financial stress events and helps predict changes in overall economic activity.

The OFR FSI is an entry point for financial market monitoring, not a sufficient statistic for understanding financial markets or financial stress events. It is a coincident indicator of stress in the financial system, not necessarily a leading indicator or predictor of financial stress events. In these respects, its limitations are analogous to those of body temperature, which provides the physician a summary statistic for a patient's current condition that is correlated with sickness or other maladies but must be considered in tandem with other data to make the correct diagnosis. Similarly, the OFR FSI is considered alongside the OFR's Financial System Vulnerabilities Monitor, and other data sources and factors to produce the OFR's financial stability assessments.

Future research on the OFR FSI mainly concerns the set of its constituent indicators, which is not necessarily fixed. Indeed, the OFR FSI's methodology allows the component list of indicators to change over time as the financial system evolves. For example, the removal of LIBOR as a meaningful reference rate over the next few years may necessitate the replacement of the LIBOR-based indicators currently in the index with other indicators that better reflect funding stress.

Funding: This research received no external funding.

Acknowledgments: An earlier version of the index was developed in collaboration with Thomas Piontek and William Shi. I thank Rebecca McCaughrin, Adam Minson, Kevin Sheppard, seminar participants at the Office of Financial Research, and the Office of Financial Research's Financial Research Advisory Committee members for helpful comments and suggestions. I also thank Jonathan Glicoes for helpful research assistance.

Conflicts of Interest: The author declares no conflict of interest.

Appendix A

Table A1. Variables in the OFR FSI.

Category	Indicator	Region(s)	Source	First Date in FSI	Note	Exp. Sign
Credit	BaML US Corporate Master (IG) (OAS)	US	Haver	1 January 2000	L	Pos.
	BaML US High Yield Corporate Master (HY) (OAS)	US	Haver	1 January 2000	L	Pos.
	BaML Euro Area Corp Bond Index (OAS)	AE	Haver	1 January 2000	L	Pos.
	BaML Euro Area High Yield Bond Index (OAS)	AE	Haver	1 January 2000	L	Pos.
	BaML Japan Corporate (OAS)	AE	Haver	1 January 2000	L	Pos.
	JPMorgan CEMBI Strip Spread	EM	Bloomberg	1 January 2004	L	Pos.
	JPMorgan EMBI Global Strip Spread	EM	Bloomberg	1 April 2003	L	Pos.
Equity Valuation	MSCI Emerging Markets Index (P/B Ratio)	EM	Bloomberg	1 January 2000	LRMA	Neg.
	MSCI Europe Index (P/B Ratio)	AE	Bloomberg	1 February 2001	LRMA	Neg.
	NIKKEI 225 Index (P/B Ratio)	AE	Bloomberg	1 May 2002	LRMA	Neg.
	S&P 500 Index (P/B Ratio)	US	Bloomberg	1 January 2000	LRMA	Neg.
Funding	2-Year EUR/USD Cross-Currency Swap Spread	US, AE	Bloomberg	1 February 2001	L	N/A
	2-Year US Swap Spread	US	Bloomberg	1 January 2000	L	N/A
	2-Year USD/JPY Cross-Currency Swap Spread	US, AE	Bloomberg	1 January 2000	L	N/A
	3-Month EURIBOR—EONIA	AE	Bloomberg, Haver	1 March 2002	L	Pos.
	3-Month Japanese LIBOR—OIS	AE	Bloomberg	1 April 2004	L	Pos.
	3-Month LIBOR—OIS	US	Bloomberg	1 January 2004	L	Pos.
	3-Month TED Spread	US	Bloomberg	1 January 2000	L	Pos.
Safe Assets	10-Year US Treasury Note (yield)	US	Haver	1 January 2000	DMA	Neg.
	10-Year German Bond (yield)	AE	Bloomberg	1 January 2000	DMA	Neg.
	Gold/USD Real Spot Exchange Rate	US, AE, EM	Haver	1 January 2000	LRMA	Pos.
	Japanese Yen/USD Spot Exchange Rate	AE	Haver	1 January 2000	LRMA	N/A
	Swiss Franc/USD Spot Exchange Rate	AE	Haver	1 January 2000	LRMA	N/A
	US Dollar Index (DXY)	US	Bloomberg	1 January 2000	LRMA	N/A

Table A1. *Cont.*

Category	Indicator	Region(s)	Source	First Date in FSI	Note	Exp. Sign
Volatility	CBOE S&P 500 Volatility Index (VIX)	US	Haver	1 January 2000	L	Pos.
	Dow Jones EURO STOXX 50 Volatility Index (V2X)	AE	Bloomberg	1 March 2002	L	Pos.
	ICE Brent Crude Oil Futures (22-day realized vol.)	US, AE, EM	Bloomberg	1 January 2000	L	Pos.
	Implied Volatility on 6-Month EUR/USD Options	US, AE	Bloomberg	1 February 2001	L	Pos.
	Implied Volatility on 6-Month USD/JPY Options	US, AE	Bloomberg	1 January 2000	L	Pos.
	JPMorgan Emerging Market Volatility Index	AE	Bloomberg	1 April 2003	L	Pos.
	Merrill Lynch Euro Swaptions Volatility Estimate	AE	Bloomberg	1 January 2000	L	Pos.
	Merrill Lynch US Swaptions Volatility Estimate	US	Bloomberg	1 January 2000	L	Pos.
	NIKKEI Volatility Index	AE	Bloomberg	1 February 2003	L	Pos.

Key

AE = Advanced economies ex-U.S., e.g., eurozone and Japan	HY = High yield
BaML = Bank of America Merrill Lynch	IG = Investment grade
CBOE = Chicago Board Options Exchange	JPY = Japanese yen
CEMBI = Corporate Emerging Markets Bond Index	LIBOR = London Interbank Offered Rate
EM = Emerging markets	MSCI = Morgan Stanley Capital International
EMBI = Emerging Market Bond Index	OAS = Option-adjusted spread
EONIA = Euro OverNight Index Average	OIS = Overnight indexed swap
EUR = Euro	P/B Ratio = Price-to-book ratio (value-weighted)
EURIBOR = Euro InterBank Offered Rate	USD = U.S. dollar

L = level; DMA = difference of the indicator and its 250-trading day moving average; LRMA = logarithm of the ratio of the indicator to its 250-trading day moving average; All variables are at a daily frequency, using values at market close.

Appendix B

Table A2. Dates of Signficant Government Intervention in Financial Markets.

Date	Intervention
23 September 1998	Federal Reserve coordinates purchase of LTCM by consortium of 12 firms
11 September 2001	Federal Reserve responds to liquidity shortages caused by the physical limitations of 9/11
10 August 2007	Federal Reserve adds $38 billion in reserves and issues a statement reaffirming its commitment to provide liquidity
17 August 2007	Federal Reserve reduces primary credit spread by 50 basis points and allows 30-day term financing
21 August 2007	Federal Reserve reduced minimum fee rate for SOMA securities lending
26 November 2007	Federal Reserve eases terms on SOMA lending
12 December 2007	Federal Reserve announced creation of the TAF
7 March 2008	Federal Reserve announces it is expanding the size of the next two TAF auctions
11 March 2008	Federal Reserve announces the creation of the TSLF
14 March 2008	Federal Reserve lends to Bear Stearns
16 March 2008	Federal Reserve facilitates purchase of Bear Stearns by JPMC and creates PDCF
2 May 2008	Federal Reserve increases the size of TAF auctions
13 July 2008	Federal Reserve authorizes the Federal Reserve Bank of New York to lend to Fannie and Freddie should lending prove necessary
30 July 2008	Federal Reserve extends term lending on TAF to 84 days
7 September 2008	Treasury places Fannie and Freddie into conservatorship and provides liquidity backstops for GSEs
15 September 2008	Federal Reserve expands PDCF eligible assets and conducts two open market operations
16 September 2008	Federal Reserve extends line of credit to AIG
19 September 2008	Federal Reserve announces AMLF and Treasury guarantees MMMFs
28 September 2008	FDIC announces assistance for Wachovia merger and Federal Reserve increase size of TAF
6 October 2008	Federal Reserve further expands size of TAF
7 October 2008	Federal Reserve announces creation of the CPFF
8 October 2008	Federal Reserve decreases fees on SOMA lending
14 October 2008	Treasury announces $250 billion for preferred stock purchases and FDIC announces TLGP
21 October 2008	Federal Reserve announces the creation of the MMIFF

Table A2. *Cont.*

Date	Intervention
23 November 2008	Federal Reserve, Treasury, and FDIC agree to provide Citigroup a package of guarantees, liquidity access, and capital
25 November 2008	Federal Reserve announces the TALF
30 December 2008	Treasury announces the purchase of preferred stock in GMAC
7 January 2009	Federal Reserve expands set of institutions eligible to borrow under the MMIFF
16 January 2009	Treasury, FDIC, and Federal Reserve provide Bank of America with rescue package
30 January 2009	Federal Reserve liberalizes rules related to AMLF
25 February 2009	Federal Reserve, OCC, FDIC, and OTS announce details of the Capital Assistance Program
23 March 2009	Treasury announces the details of the public-partnership investment plan
1 May 2009	Federal Reserve announces the inclusion of the CMBS in the TALF
7 May 2009	Bank stress test results and capital-raising requirements for SCAP firms officially announced
19 May 2009	Federal Reserve further expands collateral eligible under the TALF
2 May 2010	Euro area member states and the IMF announce a three-year program for Greece, totaling €110 billion
9 May 2010	Euro area leaders announce that all the institutions of the euro area, including the ECB, commit to an overhaul of the European macroeconomic surveillance framework. Finance ministers announce the creation of the European Financial Stability Facility
11 May 2010	Federal Reserve agrees with foreign central banks to reestablish temporary dollar swap facilities
29 October 2010	European leaders reach an agreement on the need to set up a permanent crisis mechanism to safeguard the financial stability of the euro area as a whole (the European Stability Mechanism or ESM)
28 November 2010	European leaders and the IMF agree to grant an €85 billion assistance package to Ireland
11 March 2011	Euro area leaders agree to make the EFSF's €440 billion lending capacity fully effective, and to allow the EFSF and ESM to intervene in the primary markets for sovereign debt, as an exception and only in the context of a financial assistance program
17 May 2011	Having received a request from Portugal, the European Council agrees to a financial assistance package totaling €78 billion over three years
21 July 2011	Euro area Heads of State or Government and EU institutions decide on a new package of measures to end the crisis and prevent contagion, including: a new program for Greece, and an agreement hat includes measures to enhance the flexibility of stabilization tolls by allowing the EFSF/ESM to act on the basis of a precautionary program, to intervene in secondary markets, and to finance the recapitalization of financial institutions through loans to governments, including non-program countries
4 August 2011	The ECB reactivates secondary market purchases and starts purchasing Italian and Spanish bonds in an attempt to ease market tensions
6 September 2011	The Swiss Central Bank announces its decision to cap the Swiss franc's euro exchange rate, in an attempt to halt its appreciation
27 October 2011	European leaders agree on another comprehensive package of additional measures, focused on Greece and European firewalls. Leaders also agree to "optimize" the resources of the EFSF by introducing two leverage options, allowing the EFSF's firepower to be multiplied
30 November 2011	The ECB, the Fed, the Bank of Japan, the Bank of England, and the Swiss National Bank announce agreement to enhance their ability to provide liquidity. The agreement involves the extension of these arrangements to February 2013 and the possibility for each of the central banks to provide liquidity support in any of their currencies
8 December 2011	The ECB announces a package of measures to support the banking system, including the long-term refinancing operations
21 February 2012	European leaders agree on the terms for a second rescue program for Greece, with a marginally higher contribution from the private sector
12 March 2012	The Spanish government adopts a new comprehensive package of measures to strengthen the banking sector
9 June 2012	Spain becomes the first country to request financial assistance to recapitalize its banking sector, within the framework of a €100 billion program focused on the banking sector only
25 June 2012	Cyprus formally requests financial assistance form the EU and IMF
30 April 2014	the IMF approves a loan of $17.01 billion to Ukraine under a two-year Stand-by Arrangement in order to support Ukraine's economic reform program
15 January 2015	The Swiss Central Bank abandons its currency cap against the euro as expectations for an ECB quantitative easing program put pressure on the Swiss franc

Table A2. *Cont.*

Date	Intervention
11 March 2015	The IMF approves a new loan of $17.5 billion to Ukraine to stabilize the economy and financial sector, bringing the total bailout package to $40 billion over four years
14 August 2015	Eurozone finance ministers agree to a third Greek bailout package worth €86 billion in exchange for tax hikes and spending cuts
4 August 2016	Bank of England launches four stimulating measures in response to Brexit

Sources: Carlson et al. (2012), Bruegel, OFR analysis.

References

Acharya, Viral V., Lasse H. Pedersen, Thomas Philippon, and Matthew Richardson. 2017. Measuring Systemic Risk. *Review of Financial Studies* 30: 2–47. [CrossRef]

Adam, Tomáš, Soňa Benecká, and Jakub Matějů. 2018. Financial stress and its non-linear impact on CEE exchange rates. *Journal of Financial Stability* 36: 346–60. [CrossRef]

Adrian, Tobias, and Markus K. Brunnermeier. 2016. CoVaR. *American Economic Review* 106: 1705–41. [CrossRef]

Apostolakis, George, and Athanasios P. Papadopoulos. 2019. Financial Stability, Monetary Stability and Growth: A PVAR Analysis. *Open Economies Review* 30: 157–78. [CrossRef]

ARRC. 2017. The ARRC Selects a Broad Repo Rate as its Preferred Alternative Reference Rate. *ARRC: Alternative Reference Rates Committee*. Press Release. June 22. Available online: https://www.newyorkfed.org/arrc/announcements.html (accessed on 23 October 2017).

Arsov, Ivailo, Elie Canetti, Laura E. Kodres, and Srobona Mitra. 2013. Near-Coincident Indicators of Systemic Stress. IMF Working Paper No. 13/115, International Monetary Fund, Washington, DC, USA. May 17.

Bai, Jushan, and Serena Ng. 2008. Large Dimensional Factor Analysis. *Foundations and Trends in Econometrics* 3: 89–163. [CrossRef]

Bisias, Dimitrios, Mark Flood, Andrew W. Lo, and Stavros Valavanis. 2012. A Survey of Systemic Risk Analytics. OFR Working Paper No. 12-01, Office of Financial Research, Washington, DC, USA. January 5.

Brave, Scott A., and R. Butters. 2011. Monitoring Financial Stability: A Financial Conditions Approach. *Economic Perspectives* 35: 22–43.

Bruegel. 2017. Euro Crisis Timeline. Available online: http://www.bruegel.org (accessed on 23 October 2017).

Cardarelli, Roberto, Selim Elekdag, and Subir Lall. 2011. Financial Stress and Economic Contractions. *Journal of Financial Stability* 7: 78–97. [CrossRef]

Carlson, Mark, Kurt Lewis, and William Nelson. 2012. Using Policy Intervention to Identify Financial Stress. Finance and Economics Discussion Series Working Paper 2012-02, Federal Reserve Board, Washington, DC, USA. January 10.

Chicago Fed National Activity Index. 2016. Online Content, December 22. Available online: https://www.chicagofed.org/publications/cfnai/index (accessed on 23 October 2017).

Dattels, Peter, Rebecca McCaughrin, Ken Miyajima, and Jaume Puig. 2010. Can You Map Global Financial Stability? IMF Working Paper No. 2010/145, International Monetary Fund, Washington, DC, USA. June.

Duprey, Thibaut, and Benjamin Klaus. 2017. How to predict financial stress? An assessment of Markov switching models. ECB Working Paper Series No. 2057, European Central Bank, Frankfurt, Germany. May.

Duprey, Thibaut, Benjamin Klaus, and Tuomas Peltonen. 2017. Dating systemic financial stress episodes in EU countries. *Journal of Financial Stability* 32: 30–56. [CrossRef]

Grimaldi, Marianna B. 2010. Detecting and Interpreting Financial Stress in the Euro Area. ECB Working Paper Series No. 1214, European Central Bank, Frankfurt, Germany. June.

Grimaldi, Marianna B. 2011. Up for Count? Central Bank Words and Financial Stress. Sveriges Riksbank Working Paper Series No. 252, Sveriges Riksbank, Stockholm, Sweden. April.

Hakkio, Craig S., and William R. Keeton. 2009. Financial stress: What is it, how can it be measured, and why does it matter? *Economic Review* 94: 5–52.

Hatzius, Jan, Peter Hooper, Frederic S. Mishkin, Kermit L. Schoenholtz, and Mark W. Watson. 2010. Financial Conditions Indexes: A Fresh Look after the Financial Crisis. NBER Working Paper 16150, National Bureau of Economic Research, Cambridge, MA, USA. July.

Hollo, Daniel, Manfred Kremer, and Marco Lo Duca. 2012. CISS—A Composite Indicator of Systemic Stress in the Financial System. ECB Working Paper Series No. 1426, European Central Bank, Frankfurt, Germany. March.

Huang, Xin, Hao Zhou, and Haibin Zhu. 2012. Assessing the systemic risk of a heterogeneous portfolio of banks during the recent financial crisis. *Journal of Financial Stability* 8: 193–205. [CrossRef]

Illing, Mark, and Ying Liu. 2006. Measuring Financial Stress in a Developed Country: An Application to Canada. *Journal of Financial Stability* 2: 243–65. [CrossRef]

Kliesen, Kevin L., and Douglas C. Smith. 2010. Measuring Financial Market Stress. *Federal Reserve Bank of St. Louis National Economic Trends*, January 15.

Kliesen, Kevin L., Michael T. Owyang, and E. Katarina Vermann. 2012. Disentangling Diverse Measures: A Survey of Financial Stress Indexes. *Federal Reserve Bank of St. Louis Review* 94: 369–97. [CrossRef]

Lo Duca, Marco, and Tuomas A. Peltonen. 2011. Macro-Financial Vulnerabilities and Future Financial Stress: Assessing Systemic Risks and Predicting Systemic Events. ECB Working Paper Series No. 1311, European Central Bank, Frankfurt, Germany, March.

Louzis, Dimitrios P., and Angelos T. Vouldis. 2013. A Financial Systemic Stress Index for Greece. ECB Working Paper No 1563, European Central Bank, Frankfurt, Germany. July.

McFadden, Daniel. 1977. *Quantitative Methods for Analyzing Travel Behaviour of Individuals: Some Recent Developments*. Cowles Foundation Discussion Paper No. 474. New Haven: Cowles Foundation for Research in Economics at Yale University, November 22.

Nelson, William R., and Roberto Perli. 2007. Selected Indicators of Financial Stability. *Risk Management and Systemic Risk* 4: 343–72.

OFR Financial Markets Monitor. 2017. The Volatility Paradox: Tranquil Markets May Harbor Hidden Risks. Second Quarter 2017. August 17. Available online: https://www.financialresearch.gov/financial-markets-monitor/2017/08/17/the-volatility-paradox/ (accessed on 23 October 2017).

Rosenberg, Michael. 2009. Financial Conditions Watch: Global Financial Market Trends and Policy. *Bloomberg LLP*, September 11.

Sandahl, Johannes F., Mia Holmfeldt, Anders Rydén, and Maria Strömqvist. 2011. An Index of Financial Stress for Sweden. *Sveriges Riksbank Economic Review* 2: 49–67.

Stock, James H., and Mark Watson. 2002. Macroeconomic Forecasting Using Diffusion Indexes. *Journal of Business & Economic Statistics* 20: 147–62.

Stock, James H., and Mark Watson. 2006. Forecasting with Many Predictors. In *Handbook of Economic Forecasting*. Edited by Graham Elliot, Clive Granger and Allan Timmermann. Amsterdam: Elsevier, chp. 6. pp. 515–54.

Stock, James H., and Mark Watson. 2010. Dynamic Factor Models. In *Oxford Handbook of Economic Forecasting*. Edited by Michael Clements and David Hendry. Oxford: Oxford University Press.

Toda, Hiro Y., and Taku Yamamoto. 1995. Statistical inference in vector autoregressions with possibly integrated processes. *Journal of Econometrics* 66: 225–50. [CrossRef]

Vasicek, Borek, Diana Zigraiova, Marco Hoeberichts, Robert Vermeulen, Katerina Smidkova, and Jakob de Haan. 2017. Leading indicators of financial stress: New evidence. *Journal of Financial Stability* 28: 240–57. [CrossRef]

9

Optimal Portfolio Selection in an Itô–Markov Additive Market

Zbigniew Palmowski [1,*], Łukasz Stettner [2,3] and Anna Sulima [4]

1 Department of Applied Mathematics, Faculty of Pure and Applied Mathematics, Wrocław University of Science and Technology, 50-370 Wrocław, Poland
2 Institute of Mathematics, Polish Academy of Sciences, 00-656 Warsaw, Poland; stettner@impan.pl
3 Vistula University, 02-787 Warsaw, Poland
4 Faculty of Management, Computer Science and Finance, Wrocław University of Economics, 53-345 Wrocław, Poland; anna.sulima@wp.pl
* Correspondence: zbigniew.palmowski@pwr.edu.pl or zbigniew.palmowski@gmail.com

Abstract: We study a portfolio selection problem in a continuous-time Itô–Markov additive market with prices of financial assets described by Markov additive processes that combine Lévy processes and regime switching models. Thus, the model takes into account two sources of risk: the jump diffusion risk and the regime switching risk. For this reason, the market is incomplete. We complete the market by enlarging it with the use of a set of Markovian jump securities, Markovian power-jump securities and impulse regime switching securities. Moreover, we give conditions under which the market is asymptotic-arbitrage-free. We solve the portfolio selection problem in the Itô–Markov additive market for the power utility and the logarithmic utility.

Keywords: Markov additive processes; Markov regime switching market; Markovian jump securities; asymptotic arbitrage; complete market; optimal portfolio

---

1. Introduction

The portfolio selection problem is an important issue in financial mathematics. The problem is to invest an initial wealth in financial assets so as to maximize the expected utility of the terminal wealth. Markowitz (1952) for the first time used the quantitative methods for the optimal portfolio selection problem and proposed the mean-variance approach for portfolio optimization. Explicit solutions for the portfolio selection problem in continuous time were first given by Merton (1971, 1980).

Although Merton's approach produces significant theoretical results, it has some shortcomings coming from daily practice. The first is related to the assumption that the dynamics of a risky asset follows a geometric Brownian motion. Many investigations (e.g., Black et al. (1972) and Merton (1976)) have suggested that this market model cannot describe perfectly some empirical behaviors of financial markets, such as the asymmetry and heavy-tailedness of the distribution of returns of a time-varying volatility. To model this, the stock price driven by a Lévy process is a better choice. The portfolio selection problem on a Lévy market was considered by Niu (2008) and Corcuera et al. (2006).

The second important assumption in the original Black–Scholes–Merton model is that the coefficients are fixed. However, this assumption may not be satisfied over long time period, where structural changes in macroeconomic conditions may occur several times. Therefore, Markov modulated models (otherwise called regime switching) were proposed instead. In such models, the set of model parameters change in time according to a Markov chain, the transitions of which correspond to changes in the state of the economy. Hence, regime switching models describe perfectly structural macroeconomic changes and various business cycles (Zhang 2001). Hamilton (1989) pioneered econometric applications of regime switching models. These models have many applications in finance (Buffington and Elliott 2002; Di Masi et al. 1994; Elliott et al. 2001, 2003, 2005; Goldfeld and Quandt 1973; Guo 2001; Naik 1993; Tong 1978).

There is a growing literature dealing with portfolio optimization problems in markets with non-constant coefficients. Most of these papers assume that the external process is a diffusion process itself, like in the established volatility model of Heston (1993) or in the Ho–Lee and the Vasicek model of Korn and Kraft (2001). Bäuerle and Rieder (2004) and Rieder and Bäuerle (2005) studied the portfolio optimization problem with an observable and an unobservable Markov-modulated drift, respectively. This problem under stochastic volatility was considered by Pham and Quenez (2001) and Fleming and Hernández-Hernández (2003). In contrast to diffusion volatility, Markov chain volatility has the advantage that many portfolio problems have explicit solution. Moreover, a diffusion process can be approximated arbitrarily closely by a continuous-time Markov chain (Kushner and Dupuis 1992).

Portfolio optimization problems have also been studied in financial markets with regime switching. One of the first papers was by Zariphopoulou (1992), who maximized the utility of consumption under proportional transaction costs in a market where stock returns are determined by a continuous-time Markov chain, and established a viscosity property of the value function. The results of Zariphopoulou were extended by many authors, among them Bäuerle and Rieder (2004, 2007), Fontana et al. (2015), Framstad et al. (2004), Zhang and Yin (2004) and Stockbridge (2002). To solve the problem of maximizing the investor's expected utility of terminal wealth, some authors used numerical methods (Sass and Haussmann 2004; Nagai and Runggaldier 2008; Shen et al. 2012; Fu et al. 2014). Zhang et al. (2010) solved the portfolio selection problem without transition cost in a continuous-time Markovian regime switching Black–Scholes–Merton market. They obtained closed-form solutions for the optimal portfolio strategies when utility function is logarithmic or power-type. Similar results for a Black–Scholes market with regime switching were obtained by Liu (2014), Guo et al. (2005) and Sotomayor and Cadenillas (2013). A discrete time set up was also considered by Yin and Zhou (2004). For the mean-variance portfolio selection problem of this type, we refer to Zhou and Yin (2003). Regime switching was also analyzed by Tu (2010) in a Bayesian setting with model uncertainty and parameter uncertainty. He showed that the economic cost of ignoring regime switching can exceed two percent per year. Bae et al. (2014) constructed a program to optimize portfolios in the above mentioned framework and proved that adding Markov modulation improves risk management. Finally, further applications include large investor models Busch et al. (2013) and optimal productmanagement Korn et al. (2017).

In this paper, we consider a market with the prices of financial assets described by Itô–Markov additive processes, which combine Lévy processes and regime switching models. Such a process evolves as an Itô–Lévy process between changes of states of a Markov chain, that is, its parameters depend on the current state of the Markov chain. In addition, a transition of the Markov chain from state i to state j triggers an additional jump. Itô–Markov additive processes are classical in modeling queues, insurance risks, inventories, data communication, finance, environmental problems and in many other applications (Asmussen 2003; Prabhu 1998, chp. 7, and references therein).

The goal of this paper is to construct a general approach of building the optimal portfolio taking into account the asset jumps and possibility of changing environment by considering asset prices modeled by Itô–Markov additive processes. In particular, we assume that the interest rate and the volatility of the financial assets depend on a continuous-time finite-state Markov chain. Thus, our model takes into account two sources of risk: the jump diffusion risk and the regime switching risk. The jump diffusion risk refers to the source of risk due to fluctuations of market prices modeled by a Poisson random measure, while the regime switching risk refers to the source of risk due to transitions of economic conditions.

Due to the presence of these sources of risk, our market model is incomplete. In this paper, we show how to complete the Itô–Markov additive market model by adding Markovian jump securities, Markovian power-jump securities and impulse regime switching securities. Using these securities, all contingent claims can be replicated by a self-financing portfolio. The main idea of completing a Markovian regime switching market is inspired by Corcuera et al. (2005, 2006), Guo (2001), Karatzas et al. (1991), Niu (2008) and Zhang et al. (2012). However, adding the possibility of jumps of underlying markets when Markov chain changes its state produces more complex analysis that one presented in Corcuera et al. (2005, 2006).Moreover, we give conditions for the market to be asymptotic-arbitrage-free, namely, we find a martingale measure under which all the discounted price processes are martingales.

In this paper, we also consider the problem of identifying the optimal strategy that maximizes the expected value of the utility function of the wealth process at the end of some fixed period. The analysis is conducted for the logarithmic and power utility functions. To solve the main problem of determining the optimal portfolio we do not use dynamic programming but the direct differentiation approach.

This paper is organized as follows. In Section 2, we present the dynamics of the price process in an Itô–Markov additive market. In Section 3, we enlarge this market by Markovian jump securities, Markovian power-jump securities and impulse regime switching securities. In Sections 4 and 5, we show that the enlarged market is asymptotic-arbitrage-free and complete. In Section 6, we state the portfolio optimization problem and solve it for the power utility with risk aversion and the logarithmic utility function. Moreover, Section 7 gives a relationship between finite and infinite markets.

2. Market Model

Let $(\Omega, \mathcal{F}, \mathbb{P})$ be a complete probability space and let $\mathbb{T} := [0, T]$, for fixed $0 < T < \infty$, represent the maturity time for all economic activities. On this probability space, we consider the observable and continuous-time Markov chain $J := \{J(t) : t \in \mathbb{T}\}$ with a finite state space. The role of the Markov chain is to ensure that the parameters change according to the market environment and the different states of the Markov chain represent the different states of the economy. For simplicity, we follow the notation of Elliott et al. (1994) and we identify the state space with the standard basis $E := \{\mathbf{e}_1, \ldots, \mathbf{e}_N\}$. Here, $\mathbf{e}_i \in \mathbb{R}^N$ and the jth component of $\mathbf{e}_i$ is the Kronecker delta δ_{ij} for each $i, j = 1, \ldots, N$. Moreover, the Markov chain J is characterized by an intensity matrix $[\lambda_{ij}]_{i,j=1}^N$. The element λ_{ij} is the transition intensity of the Markov chain J jumping from state $\mathbf{e}_i$ to state $\mathbf{e}_j$. We assume $\lambda_{ij} > 0$ for $i \neq j$. Note that $\sum_{j=1}^{N} \lambda_{ij} = 0$, thus $\lambda_{ii} < 0$.

2.1. Risk-Free Asset

Now, we describe the dynamic of the price process of risk-free asset B as follows:

$$\mathrm{d}B(t) = r(t)B(t)\mathrm{d}t, \qquad B(0) = 1. \tag{1}$$

Here, r is the interest rate of B and it is modulated by Markov chain J

$$r(t) := \langle \mathbf{r}, J(t) \rangle = \sum_{i=1}^{N} r_i \langle \mathbf{e}_i, J(t) \rangle,$$

where $\mathbf{r} = (r_1, \ldots, r_N)' \in \mathbb{R}_+^N$ and $\langle \cdot, \cdot \rangle$ is a scalar product in $\mathbb{R}^N$. The value r_i represents the value of the interest rate when the Markov chain is in the state space $\mathbf{e}_i$.

2.2. Risky Asset

We consider the market with risky asset modeled by (non-anticipative) Itô–Markov additive processes.

A process $(J, X) = \{(J(t), X(t)) : t \in \mathbb{T}\}$ on the state space $\{\mathbf{e}_1, \ldots, \mathbf{e}_N\} \times \mathbb{R}$ is a Markov additive process (MAP) if (J, X) is a Markov process and the conditional distribution of $(J(s+t), X(s+t) - X(s))$ for $s, t \in \mathbb{T}$, given $(J(s), X(s))$, depends only on $J(s)$ (Çinlar 1972a, 1972b). Every MAP has a very special structure. It is usually said that X is the additive component and J is the background process representing the environment. Moreover, the process X evolves as a Itô–Lévy process while $J(t) = \mathbf{e}_j$, that is, $X(t) = X^j(t)$ for some Itô–Lévy process $X^j(t)$ with parameters depending on $\mathbf{e}_j$ if $J(t) = \mathbf{e}_j$. In addition, transition of J from $\mathbf{e}_i$ to $\mathbf{e}_j$ triggers a jump of X distributed as $U_n^{(i)}$.

Following Asmussen and Kella (2000), we can decompose the process X as follows:

$$X(t) = \overline{X}(t) + \overline{\overline{X}}(t), \tag{2}$$

where

$$\overline{\overline{X}}(t) := \sum_{i=1}^{N} \Psi_i(t)$$

for

$$\Psi_i(t) := \sum_{n\geq 1} U_n^{(i)} \mathbf{1}_{\{J(T_n-)=\mathbf{e}_i,\, T_n\leq t\}} \tag{3}$$

and for the jump epochs $\{T_n\}$ of J. Here, $U_n^{(i)}$ $(n \geq 1, 1 \leq i \leq N)$ are independent random variables, which are also independent of $\overline{X}$ such that, for every fixed i, the random variables $U_n^{(i)}$ are identically distributed. Note that we can express the process Ψ_i as follows:

$$\Psi_i(t) = \int_0^t \int_{\mathbb{R}} x\, \Pi_U^i(\mathrm{d}s, \mathrm{d}x)$$

for the point measure

$$\Pi_U^i([0,t], \mathrm{d}x) := \sum_{n\geq 1} \mathbf{1}_{\{U_n^{(i)}\in \mathrm{d}x\}} \mathbf{1}_{\{J(T_n)=\mathbf{e}_i,\, T_n\leq t\}}, \quad i = 1, \ldots, N. \tag{4}$$

Moreover, we define the compensated point measure $\bar{\Pi}_U^i(\mathrm{d}t, \mathrm{d}x) := \Pi_U^i(\mathrm{d}t, \mathrm{d}x) - \lambda_i(t)\eta_i(\mathrm{d}x)\mathrm{d}t$ for $\lambda_j(t) := \sum_{i\neq j} \mathbf{1}_{\{J(t-)=\mathbf{e}_i\}}\lambda_{ij}$ and $\eta_i(\mathrm{d}x) = \mathbb{P}(U_n^{(i)} \in \mathrm{d}x)$.

Remark 1. *One can consider jumps $U^{(ij)}$ with distribution depending also on the state $\mathbf{e}_j$ the Markov chain is jumping to by extending the state space to the pairs $(\mathbf{e}_i, \mathbf{e}_j)$ (see Gautam et al. (1999, Thm. 5) for details).*

The first component in the definition in Equation (2) is an Itô–Lévy process and it has the following decomposition (Øksendal and Sulem 2004, p. 5):

$$\overline{X}(t) := \overline{X}(0) + \int_0^t \mu_0(s)\mathrm{d}s + \int_0^t \sigma_0(s)\mathrm{d}W(s) + \int_0^t \int_{\mathbb{R}} \gamma(s-, x)\bar{\Pi}(\mathrm{d}s, \mathrm{d}x), \tag{5}$$

where W denotes the standard Brownian motion independent of J and $\bar{\Pi}(\mathrm{d}t, \mathrm{d}x) := \Pi(\mathrm{d}t, \mathrm{d}x) - \nu(\mathrm{d}x)\mathrm{d}t$ is the compensated Poisson random measure, which is independent of J and W. Furthermore, we define

$$\mu_0(t) := \langle \boldsymbol{\mu}_0, J(t)\rangle = \sum_{i=1}^{N} \mu_0^i \langle \mathbf{e}_i, J(t)\rangle, \tag{6}$$

$$\sigma_0(t) := \langle \boldsymbol{\sigma}_0, J(t)\rangle = \sum_{i=1}^{N} \sigma_0^i \langle \mathbf{e}_i, J(t)\rangle, \tag{7}$$

$$\gamma(t, x) := \langle \gamma(x), J(t)\rangle = \sum_{i=1}^{N} \gamma_i(x) \langle \mathbf{e}_i, J(t)\rangle \tag{8}$$

for some vectors $\boldsymbol{\mu}_0 := (\mu_0^1, \ldots, \mu_0^N)' \in \mathbb{R}^N$, $\boldsymbol{\sigma}_0 := (\sigma_0^1, \ldots, \sigma_0^N)' \in \mathbb{R}_+^N$ with $\sigma_0^j > 0$ and the vector-valued measurable function $\gamma(x) := (\gamma_1(x), \ldots, \gamma_N(x))$. The measure ν is the so-called jump-measure identifying the distribution of the sizes of the jumps of the Poisson measure Π.

The components $\overline{X}$ and $\overline{\overline{X}}$ in Equation (2) are conditionally, on the state of the Markov chain J, independent.

Additionally, we suppose that the Lévy measure satisfies, for some $\varepsilon > 0$ and $\varrho > 0$,

$$\int_{(-\varepsilon,\varepsilon)^c} \exp\left(\varrho|\gamma(s-,x)|\right)\nu(\mathrm{d}x) < \infty, \quad \int_{(-\varepsilon,\varepsilon)^c} \exp(\varrho x)\mathbb{P}(U^{(i)} \in \mathrm{d}x) < \infty, \tag{9}$$

for $i = 1, \ldots, N$. This implies that

$$\int_{\mathbb{R}} |\gamma(s-,x)|^k \nu(\mathrm{d}x) < \infty, \quad \mathbb{E}(U^{(i)})^k < \infty, \quad i = 1, \ldots, N, \ k \geq 2,$$

and that the characteristic function $\mathbb{E}[\exp(kiX)]$ is analytic in a neighborhood of 0. Moreover, X has moments of all orders and the polynomials are dense in $L^2(\mathbb{R}, \mathrm{d}\varphi(t,x))$, where $\varphi(t,x) := \mathbb{P}(X(t) \leq x)$. Itô–Markov additive processes are a natural generalization of Itô–Lévy processes and thus of Lévy processes. Moreover, the structure in Equation (2) explains the used name and can be seen as *Markov-modulated Itô–Lévy process*. Indeed, if $\gamma(s,x) = x$, then X is a Markov additive process. If additionally $N = 1$, then X is a Lévy process. If $U^{(i)} \equiv 0$ and $N > 1$ then X is a Markov modulated Lévy process (Pacheco et al. 2009). If there are no jumps, that is, $\bar{\Pi}(\mathrm{d}s, \mathrm{d}x) = 0$, we have a Markov modulated Brownian motion.

We assume the evolution of the price process of the risky asset S_0 is governed by the Itô–Markov additive process as follows:

$$\begin{cases} \mathrm{d}S_0(t) = S_0(t-)\left[\mu_0(t)\mathrm{d}t + \sigma_0(t)\mathrm{d}W(t) + \int_{\mathbb{R}} \gamma(t-,x)\bar{\Pi}(\mathrm{d}t,\mathrm{d}x) + \sum_{i=1}^{N} \int_{\mathbb{R}} x\bar{\Pi}_U^i(\mathrm{d}t,\mathrm{d}x)\right], \\ S_0(0) = s_0 > 0. \end{cases} \tag{10}$$

To ensure that $S_0(t)$ is non-negative, we additionally assume that

$$\Delta \int_{\mathbb{R}} \gamma(t-,x)\bar{\Pi}(\mathrm{d}t,\mathrm{d}x) > -1, \qquad \Delta \int_{\mathbb{R}} x\bar{\Pi}_U^i(\mathrm{d}t,\mathrm{d}x) > -1, \quad i = 1, \ldots N, \tag{11}$$

where $\Delta Z_t = Z_t - Z_{t-}$ is a jump process related with a processes Z. The last assumption is equivalent to

$$\Delta\Psi_i(t) > -1$$

and it is satisfied when all U^i $(i = 1, \ldots, N)$ have support included in $(-1, +\infty)$. We interpret the coefficient μ_0 defined in Equation (6) as the appreciation rate and σ_0 defined in Equation (7) as the volatility of the risky asset for each $i = 1, \ldots, N$. Similarly, μ_0^i and σ_0^i represent the appreciation rate and the volatility of the risky asset, respectively, when the Markov chain is in state $\mathbf{e}_i$. We assume that

$$\mu_0^i > r_i, \quad i = 1, \ldots, N.$$

Otherwise, stocks would be just a bad investment.

3. Enlarging the Itô–Markov Additive Market

Now, we enlarge the primary market by some financial assets: Markovian jump securities, Markovian power-jump securities and impulse regime switching securities in order to complete the market.

From now, we work with the following filtration on $(\Omega, \mathcal{F}, \mathbb{P})$:

$$\mathcal{F}_t := \mathcal{G}_t \vee \mathcal{N},$$

where $\mathcal{N}$ are the $\mathbb{P}$-null sets of $\mathcal{F}$ and

$$\mathcal{G}_t := \sigma\{J(s), W(s), \Gamma(s), \Pi_U^1([0,s], dx), \ldots, \Pi_U^N([0,s], dx); s \leq t\}$$

for

$$\Gamma(t) := \int_0^t \int_{\mathbb{R}} \gamma(s-, x)\Pi(ds, dx).$$

Note that the filtration $\{\mathcal{F}_t\}_{t\geq 0}$ is right-continuous (Karatzas and Shreve 1998, Prop. 7.7 and also Protter 2005, Thm. 31). By the same arguments as in the proof of Thm. 3.3. of Liao (2004), the filtration $\{\mathcal{G}_t\}_{t\geq 0}$ can be represented as

$$\sigma\{J(s), \overline{X}(s), \Pi_U^1([0,s], dx), \ldots, \Pi_U^N([0,s], dx); s \leq t\}.$$

3.1. Markovian Jump Securities

Let T_n $(n = 1, 2, \ldots)$ denote the jump epochs of the chain J, where $0 < T_1 < T_2 < \ldots$ We observe that the Markov chain J can be represented in terms of a marked point process Φ_j defined by

$$\Phi_j(t) := \Phi([0,t] \times \mathbf{e}_j) = \sum_{n\geq 1} \mathbf{1}_{\{J(T_n)=\mathbf{e}_j,\, T_n\leq t\}}, \quad j = 1, \ldots, N.$$

Note that the process Φ_j describes the number of jumps into state $\mathbf{e}_j$ up to time t. Let ϕ_j be the dual predictable projection of Φ_j (sometimes called the compensator). That is, the process

$$\overline{\Phi}_j(t) := \Phi_j(t) - \phi_j(t), \quad j = 1, \ldots, N, \tag{12}$$

is an $\{\mathcal{F}_t\}$-martingale and it is called the jth Markovian jump martingale. Note that ϕ_j is unique and

$$\phi_j(t) := \int_0^t \lambda_j(s) ds,$$

for

$$\lambda_j(t) := \sum_{i\neq j} \mathbf{1}_{\{J(t-)=\mathbf{e}_i\}} \lambda_{ij}; \tag{13}$$

see Zhang et al. (2012, p. 290).

Now, we consider geometric Markovian jump securities S_j (for $j = 1, \ldots, N$) with evolution of prices described by marked point local martingales as follows:

$$\begin{cases} dS_j(t) = S_j(t-)\left[\mu_j(t)dt + \sigma_j(t-)d\overline{\Phi}_j(t)\right], \\ S_j(0) > 0, \end{cases} \tag{14}$$

where the appreciation rate μ_j and the volatility σ_j are given by

$$\mu_j(t) := \langle \boldsymbol{\mu}_j, J(t)\rangle = \sum_{i=1}^N \mu_j^i \langle \mathbf{e}_i, J(t)\rangle,$$

$$\sigma_j(t) := \langle \boldsymbol{\sigma}_j, J(t)\rangle = \sum_{i=1}^N \sigma_j^i \langle \mathbf{e}_i, J(t)\rangle$$

with $\boldsymbol{\mu}_j := (\mu_j^1, \ldots, \mu_j^N)' \in \mathbb{R}^N$ and $\boldsymbol{\sigma}_j := (\sigma_j^1, \ldots, \sigma_j^N)' \in \mathbb{R}_+^N$.

3.2. Markovian Power-Jump Securities

Following Corcuera et al. (2005), we introduce the power-jump processes

$$X^{(k)}(t) := \sum_{0<s\le t} (\Delta\overline{X}(s))^k, \qquad k \ge 2,$$

where $\Delta\overline{X}(s) = \overline{X}(s) - \overline{X}(s-)$. We set $X^{(1)}(t) = \overline{X}(t)$. The process $X^{(k)}$ is also an Itô–Lévy process with the same jump times as the original process $\overline{X}$ but with their sizes being the kth powers of the jump sizes of $\overline{X}$. From Protter (2005, p. 29), we have

$$\mathbb{E}\big[X^{(k)}(t)|\mathcal{J}_t\big] = \mathbb{E}\Big(\sum_{0<s\le t} (\Delta\overline{X}(s))^k|\mathcal{J}_t\Big) = \int_0^t \int_{\mathbb{R}} \gamma^k(s-,x)\nu(\mathrm{d}x)\mathrm{d}s < \infty, \mathbb{P}-a.e. \quad k \ge 2,$$

for $\mathcal{J}_t := \sigma\{J(s) : s \le t\}$. Hence, the processes

$$\overline{X}^{(k)}(t) := X^{(k)}(t) - \int_0^t \int_{\mathbb{R}} \gamma^k(s-,x)\nu(\mathrm{d}x)\mathrm{d}s, \qquad k \ge 2,$$

are $\{\mathcal{F}_t\}$-martingales (called Teugels martingales of order k; see Schoutens (1999) for details).

We additionally enlarge the market with a series of Markovian kth-power-jump assets $S^{(k)}$ (for $k \ge 2$). The price process of $S^{(k)}$ is described by the stochastic differential equation

$$\begin{cases} \mathrm{d}S^{(k)}(t) = S^{(k)}(t-)\Big[\mu^{(k)}(t)\mathrm{d}t + \sigma^{(k)}(t-)\mathrm{d}\overline{X}^{(k)}(t)\Big], \\ S^{(k)}(0) > 0, \end{cases} \tag{15}$$

where the coefficients are determined by the Markov chain J, namely:

$$\mu^{(k)}(t) := \langle \boldsymbol{\mu}^{(k)}, J(t)\rangle = \sum_{j=1}^N \mu_j^{(k)}\langle \mathbf{e}_j, J(t)\rangle \quad \text{and} \quad \sigma^{(k)}(t) := \langle \boldsymbol{\sigma}^{(k)}, J(t)\rangle = \sum_{j=1}^N \sigma_j^{(k)}\langle \mathbf{e}_j, J(t)\rangle$$

for $\boldsymbol{\mu}^{(k)} := (\mu_1^{(k)}, \ldots, \mu_N^{(k)})' \in \mathbb{R}^N$ and $\boldsymbol{\sigma}^{(k)} := (\sigma_1^{(k)}, \ldots, \sigma_N^{(k)})' \in \mathbb{R}_+^N$. The positivity of these asset prices follow from assumption in Equation (11).

3.3. Impulse Regime Switching Securities

We will also need power martingales related to the second component of X given in Equation (2), namely to $\overline{\overline{X}}$ or to Ψ_i, defined in Equation (3). For $l \ge 1$ and $i = 1, \ldots, N$ we define

$$\Psi_i^{(l)}(t) := \sum_{n\ge1} \Big(U_n^{(i)}\Big)^l \mathbf{1}_{\{J(T_n)=\mathbf{e}_i,\, T_n\le t\}} = \int_0^t \int_{\mathbb{R}} x^l\, \Pi_U^i(\mathrm{d}s, \mathrm{d}x)$$

for Π_U^i given by Equation (4). The compensated version of $\Psi_i^{(l)}$ is called an impulse regime switching martingale if

$$\overline{\Psi}_i^{(l)}(t) := \Psi_i^{(l)}(t) - \mathbb{E}(U_n^{(i)})^l \phi_i(t) = \int_0^t \int_{\mathbb{R}} x^l\, \bar{\Pi}_U^i(\mathrm{d}s, \mathrm{d}x),$$

where $\bar{\Pi}_U^i(\mathrm{d}t, \mathrm{d}x) = \Pi_U^i(\mathrm{d}t, \mathrm{d}x) - \lambda_i(t)\eta_i(\mathrm{d}x)\mathrm{d}t$ for λ_i defined in Equation (13) and $\eta_i(\mathrm{d}x) = \mathbb{P}(U_n^{(i)} \in \mathrm{d}x)$.

We characterize the evolution of impulse regime switching securities $S_i^{(l)}$ as follows:

$$\begin{cases} \mathrm{d}S_i^{(l)}(t) = S_i^{(l)}(t-)\Big[\mu_i^{(l)}(t)\mathrm{d}t + \sigma_i^{(l)}(t-)\mathrm{d}\overline{\Psi}_i^{(l)}(t)\Big], \\ S_i^{(l)}(0) > 0, \end{cases} \tag{16}$$

where the coefficients are determined by the Markov chain J, namely:

$$\mu_i^{(l)}(t) := \langle \boldsymbol{\mu}_i^{(l)}, J(t)\rangle = \sum_{j=1}^{N} \mu_{i,j}^{(l)} \langle \mathbf{e}_j, J(t)\rangle; \quad \sigma_i^{(l)}(t) := \langle \boldsymbol{\sigma}_i^{(l)}, J(t)\rangle = \sum_{j=1}^{N} \sigma_{i,j}^{(l)} \langle \mathbf{e}_j, J(t)\rangle$$

for $\boldsymbol{\mu}_i^{(l)} := (\mu_{i,1}^{(l)}, \ldots, \mu_{i,N}^{(l)})' \in \mathbb{R}^N$ and $\boldsymbol{\sigma}_i^{(l)} := (\sigma_{i,1}^{(l)}, \ldots, \sigma_{i,N}^{(l)})' \in \mathbb{R}_+^N$ ($i = 1, \ldots, N$ and $l \geq 1$). The positivity of these asset prices follow from assumption in Equation (11).

Combining Equations (1), (10), (14)–(16), we get an enlarged Itô–Markov additive market:

$$\begin{cases} dB(t) = r(t)B(t)dt, \\ dS_0(t) = S_0(t-)\left[\mu_0(t)dt + \sigma_0(t)dW(t) + \int_{\mathbb{R}} \gamma(t-,x)\bar{\Pi}(dt,dx) + \sum_{i=1}^{N} \int_{\mathbb{R}} x\bar{\Pi}_U^i(dt,dx)\right], \\ dS_j(t) = S_j(t-)\left[\mu_j(t)dt + \sigma_j(t-)d\overline{\Phi}_j(t)\right], \\ dS^{(k)}(t) = S^{(k)}(t-)\left[\mu^{(k)}(t)dt + \sigma^{(k)}(t-)d\overline{X}^{(k)}(t)\right], \\ dS_i^{(l)}(t) = S_i^{(l)}(t-)\left[\mu_i^{(l)}(t)dt + \sigma_i^{(l)}(t-)d\overline{\Psi}_i^{(l)}(t)\right], \end{cases} \tag{17}$$

for $i, j = 1, \ldots, N$, $k \geq 2$ and $l \geq 1$. Note that this enlarged market has infinitely many securities. In Section 5, we prove that under a new martingale measure this market is complete. Note that μ_j, $\mu^{(k)}$, $\mu_i^{(l)}$, σ_j, $\sigma^{(k)}$ and $\sigma_i^{(l)}$ are artificial parameters and can be changed later.

Following Corcuera et al. (2005), the use of power-jump assets of order two can be motivated by a quadratic variation process (Barndorff-Nielsen and Shephard 2003, 2004) and so-called realized variance. Contracts on realized variance are traded regularly on OTC markets. Typically, a 3rd-power-jump asset measures a kind of asymmetry ("skewness") and a 4th-power-jump process measures extremal movements ("kurtosis"). This type of contracts could be also traded. Moreover, one can construct an insurance contracts against a crash based on 4th-power-jump (or ith-power-jump, $i > 4$) assets. Power-jumps processes appear in other financial-insurance contracts that hedge Lévy jumps as well, e.g., in COS and CDS contracts.

4. Martingale Measure and Asymptotic Arbitrage

Considering a financial market containing an infinite number of assets, Kabanov and Kramkov (1994) introduced the notion of large financial market. This type of market is described by a sequence of market models with a finite number of securities each, also called small markets. Kabanov and Kramkov (1994) introduced an extension of the classical approach to arbitrage theory, namely arbitrage in a large financial market, called asymptotic arbitrage. A deep study of asymptotic arbitrage was carried out by Kabanov and Kramkov (1998) and Björk and Näslund (1998).

In this section we identify a martingale measure in our Itô–Markov additive market and prove that this market model is asymptotic-arbitrage-free.

Let us start with the definition of *asymptotic arbitrage*. Following (Björk and Näslund 1998, Def. 6.1), we say that there is an asymptotic arbitrage opportunity if we have a sequence of strategies such that, for some real number $c > 0$, the value process V^n on a finite market satisfies:

- $V^n(t) \geq -c$ for each $0 < t \leq T$ and for each $n \in \mathbb{N}$;
- $V^n(0) = 0$ for each $n \in \mathbb{N}$;
- $\liminf_{n\to\infty} V^n(T) \geq 0$, $\mathbb{P}$-a.s; and
- $\mathbb{P}(\liminf_{n\to\infty} V^n(T) > 0) > 0$.

Proposition 1 (Björk and Näslund 1998, Prop. 6.1). *If there exists a martingale measure $\mathbb{Q}$ equivalent to $\mathbb{P}$, then the market is asymptotic-arbitrage-free.*

In this paper, we formulate the sufficient condition for absence of asymptotic arbitrage in a form of the existence of a martingale measure. Equivalent conditions for the existence of a so-called separated martingale measure can be found in Cuchiero et al. (2016) who introduced *No Asymptotic Free Lunch with Vanishing Risk* (NALFVR) condition (see also Kreps (1981)).

Now, we find a measure $\mathbb{Q}$ under which the discounted price processes are martingales.

Let $\mathcal{L}^2(W)$ be the set of all predictable, $\{\mathcal{F}_t\}$-adapted processes ξ such that $\mathbb{E}\int_0^T \xi^2(s)\mathrm{d}s < \infty$. Similarly, we define $\mathcal{L}^1(\phi_j)$, that is, $\xi \in \mathcal{L}^1(\phi_j)$ iff ξ is predictable, $\{\mathcal{F}_t\}$-adapted and satisfies $\mathbb{E}\int_0^T |\xi(s)|\lambda_j \mathrm{d}s < \infty$.

Proposition 2 (Boel and Kohlmann 1980, p. 515). *Let $\psi_0 \in \mathcal{L}^2(W)$, $\psi_j \in \mathcal{L}^1(\phi_j)$ for all $j = 1, \ldots, N$ and*

$$\psi_j(s) > -1. \tag{18}$$

Then,

$$\ell(t) := \exp\left[\int_0^t \psi_0(s)\mathrm{d}W(s) - \frac{1}{2}\int_0^t \psi_0^2(s)\mathrm{d}s - \sum_{j=1}^N \int_0^t \psi_j(s)\phi_j(\mathrm{d}s)\right] \tag{19}$$

$$\times \prod_{j=1}^N \prod_{\substack{J(t-)\neq J(t)\\ J(t)=e_j}} (1+\psi_j(t))$$

is a non-negative local martingale. If additionally $\mathbb{E}\ell(t) = 1$, then it is a true martingale.

From now on, we assume that

$$\mathbb{E}\ell(t) = 1. \tag{20}$$

Let $\mathbb{Q}$ be the probability measure defined by the Radon–Nikodym derivative

$$\ell(t) = \left.\frac{\mathrm{d}\mathbb{Q}}{\mathrm{d}\mathbb{P}}\right|_{\mathcal{F}_t}.$$

Then, ℓ, given in Equation (19), is the density process for the new martingale measure $\mathbb{Q}$. By adding a superscript $\mathbb{Q}$, we denote processes observed under this new measure. By a generalized version of Girsanov's theorem for jump-diffusion processes, we have the following theorem:

Theorem 1 (Boel and Kohlmann 1980, p. 517). *The process $\overline{X}$ given in Equation (5) under the new martingale measure $\mathbb{Q}$ has the form*

$$\overline{X}^{\mathbb{Q}}(t) = \int_0^t \sigma_0(s)\mathrm{d}W^{\mathbb{Q}}(s) + \int_0^t \int_{\mathbb{R}} \gamma(s-,x)\overline{\Pi}(\mathrm{d}s,\mathrm{d}x),$$

where

$$W^{\mathbb{Q}}(t) = W(t) - \int_0^t \psi_0(s)\mathrm{d}s$$

is a standard $\mathbb{Q}$-Brownian motion.

Moreover, for $j = 1, \ldots, N$, the process $\overline{\Phi}_j$ given in Equation (12) under the measure $\mathbb{Q}$ is a martingale and takes the form

$$\overline{\Phi}_j^{\mathbb{Q}}(t) = \Phi_j(t) - \int_0^t \Big(1+\psi_j(s)\Big)\phi_j(\mathrm{d}s),$$

that is, the unique predictable projection of Φ_j under $\mathbb{Q}$ is given by

$$\phi_j^{\mathbb{Q}}(t) = \int_0^t \Big(1+\psi_j(s)\Big)\phi_j(\mathrm{d}s).$$

Similarly, for $j = 1, \dots, N$ and $l \geq 1$, the process $\overline{\Psi}_j^{(l)}$ given in Equation (12) under the measure $\mathbb{Q}$ is a martingale and takes the form

$$\overline{\Psi}_j^{(l),\mathbb{Q}}(t) = \Psi_j^{(l)}(t) - \mathbb{E}(U_n^{(i)})^l \phi_j^{\mathbb{Q}}(t).$$

Remark 2. *If ψ_0 and ψ_j $(j = 1, \dots, N)$ are bounded, then $\mathbb{E}\ell(t) = 1$ (see the Novikov condition in Karatzas and Shreve (1998, Cor. 3.5.13, p. 199) and Resnick (2007, Thm. 5.1, p. 135)).*

Note that $\overline{X}^{(k)}$ for $k \geq 2$ do not change their laws under the new measure $\mathbb{Q}$. Moreover, under $\mathbb{Q}$, the price processes are represented as follows:

$$\begin{cases} dB(t) = r(t)B(t)dt, \\ dS_0(t) = S_0(t-)\Big[\Big(\mu_0(t) + \sigma_0(t)\psi_0(t)\Big)dt + \sigma_0(t)dW^{\mathbb{Q}}(t) + \int\limits_{\mathbb{R}} \gamma(t-,x)\bar{\Pi}(dt,dx) + \sum\limits_{i=1}^{N} \int\limits_{\mathbb{R}} x\bar{\Pi}_U^i(dt,dx)\Big], \\ dS_j(t) = S_j(t-)\Big[\Big(\mu_j(t) + \sigma_j(t)\lambda_j(t)\psi_j(t)\Big)dt + \sigma_j(t-)d\overline{\Phi}_j^{\mathbb{Q}}(t)\Big], \\ dS^{(k)}(t) = S^{(k)}(t-)\Big[\mu^{(k)}(t)dt + \sigma^{(k)}(t-)d\overline{X}^{(k)}(t)\Big], \\ dS_i^{(l)}(t) = S_i^{(l)}(t-)\Big[\mu_i^{(l)}(t)dt + \sigma_i^{(l)}(t-)d\overline{\Psi}_i^{(l),\mathbb{Q}}(t)\Big], \end{cases}$$

for $i,j = 1, \dots, N$, $k \geq 2$ and $l \geq 1$. Note that in the above equation we can take $r(t) = r(t-)$, $\mu_j(t) = \mu_j(t-)$ and $\sigma_j(t) = \sigma_j(t-)$ (for $j = 0, 1, \dots, N$). In fact, by stochastic integration by parts, the discounted price processes are governed by

$$\begin{cases} d\tilde{S}_0(t) = \tilde{S}_0(t-)\Big[\Big(\mu_0(t-) + \sigma_0(t-)\psi_0(t) - r(t-)\Big)dt + \sigma_0(t)dW^{\mathbb{Q}}(t) + \int\limits_{\mathbb{R}} \gamma(t-,x)\bar{\Pi}(dt,dx) \\ \quad + \sum\limits_{i=1}^{N} \int\limits_{\mathbb{R}} x\bar{\Pi}_U^i(dt,dx)\Big], \\ d\tilde{S}_j(t) = \tilde{S}_j(t-)\Big[\Big(\mu_j(t-) + \sigma_j(t-)\lambda_j(t)\psi_j(t) - r(t-)\Big)dt + \sigma_j(t-)d\overline{\Phi}_j^{\mathbb{Q}}(t)\Big], \\ d\tilde{S}^{(k)}(t) = \tilde{S}^{(k)}(t-)\Big[\Big(\mu^{(k)}(t) - r(t)\Big)dt + \sigma^{(k)}(t-)d\overline{X}^{(k)}(t)\Big], \\ d\tilde{S}_i^{(l)}(t) = \tilde{S}_i^{(l)}(t-)\Big[\Big(\mu_i^{(l)}(t) - r(t)\Big)dt + \sigma_i^{(l)}(t-)d\overline{\Psi}_i^{(l),\mathbb{Q}}(t)\Big], \end{cases} \tag{21}$$

where $\tilde{S}_0(t) := B^{-1}(t)S_0(t)$, $\tilde{S}_j(t) := B^{-1}(t)S_j(t)$, $\tilde{S}^{(k)}(t) := B^{-1}(t)S^{(k)}(t)$ and $\tilde{S}_i^{(l)}(t) := B^{-1}(t)S_i^{(l)}(t)$. Hence, we require $\tilde{S}_0$, $\tilde{S}_j$, $\tilde{S}^{(k)}$ and $\tilde{S}_i^{(l)}$ to be local martingales (for $i,j = 1, \dots, N$, $k \geq 2$ and $l \geq 1$). A necessary and sufficient condition for this to hold is given by the following equations:

$$\begin{cases} \mu_0(t-) + \sigma_0(t-)\psi_0(t) - r(t-) = 0, \\ \mu_j(t-) + \sigma_j(t-)\lambda_j(t)\psi_j(t) - r(t-) = 0, \\ \mu^{(k)}(t) - r(t) = 0, \\ \mu_i^{(l)}(t) - r(t) = 0, \\ \psi_j(t) > -1, \end{cases} \tag{22}$$

for $i,j = 1, \dots, N$, $k \geq 2$ and $l \geq 1$.

Note that $\lambda_j(t) = 0$ if $J(t-) = \mathbf{e}_j$. Thus, in this case, if $\mu_j^j \neq r_j$, the martingale condition would never be satisfied. Therefore, the discounted price processes of all securities in the enlarged market would not be local martingales under $\mathbb{Q}$. Thus, we have to assume that $\mu_j^j = r_j$ for all $j = 1, \dots, N$

to make the market asymptotic-arbitrage-free. From Equation (22), when $\lambda_j(t) \neq 0$ (i.e., $J(t-) \neq \mathbf{e}_j$), the processes ψ_0 and ψ_j are determined by

$$\begin{cases} \psi_0(t) = \dfrac{r(t-) - \mu_0(t-)}{\sigma_0(t-)}, \\ \psi_j(t) = \dfrac{r(t-) - \mu_j(t-)}{\sigma_j(t-)\lambda_j(t)}, \quad j = 1, \ldots, N, \end{cases} \tag{23}$$

where we assume that

$$r(t-) > \mu_j(t-) - \sigma_j(t-)\lambda_j(t) \tag{24}$$

to satisfy the condition in Equation (18).

Note that ψ_0 and ψ_j $(j = 1, \ldots, N)$ are bounded. Hence, by Remark 2, the density process ℓ is a true martingale. Note that ψ_j $(j = 1, \ldots, N)$ satisfies the assumptions of Proposition 2. We can only determine ψ_j when $J(t-) \neq \mathbf{e}_j$ for $j = 1, \ldots, N$ but this is sufficient to determine the equivalent martingale measure $\mathbb{Q}$. Indeed, if $J(t-) = \mathbf{e}_j$ for $j = 1, \ldots, N$, then $\phi_j(t) = 0$ and ψ_j has no influence on the value of the right side of Equation (19). The above analysis yields the following theorem.

Theorem 2. *Assume that $\mu_j^j = r_j$ for all $j = 1, \ldots, N$ and ψ_0 and ψ_j are given by Equation (23). Then, the discounted price processes of the securities in the enlarged market (Equation (21)) are local martingales under $\mathbb{Q}$ and this market is asymptotic-arbitrage-free.*

From now on, we assume that $\mu_j^j = r_j$ for all $j = 1, \ldots, N$.

5. Asymptotic Completeness of the Enlarged Market

Now, we analyze asymptotic completeness of the enlarged Itô–Markov additive market. A market is said to be complete if each claim can be replicated by a strategy, that is, the claim can be represented as a stochastic integral with respect to the asset prices. We take as class of contingent claims the set $L^2(\Omega, \mathcal{F}, \mathbb{Q})$ of square integrable random variables under the equivalent martingale measure; then, a self-financing strategy is represented as an integrable process and the value of a self-financing portfolio is represented as the stochastic integral of the strategy with respect to the assets. In the case of market models with an infinite number of assets, we define completeness in terms of approximate replication of claims.

For finite market asset, completeness is equivalent to uniqueness of the equivalent martingale measure. In the case of large markets, this property does not occur. Artzner and Heath (1995) constructed a financial market with countably many securities for which there are two equivalent martingale measures under which the market is approximately complete. In the context of a large financial market, Bättig (1999) and Bättig and Jarrow (1999) suggested a definition of completeness that uses neither the notion of arbitrage-free nor equivalent martingale measures. Bättig (1999) constructed an example showing that the existence of an equivalent martingale measure excludes the possibility of replicating a claim, hence proving that the notions of arbitrage-free and completeness could be unrelated to each other in daily practice.

Under $\mathbb{Q}$, the price processes of the securities in the arbitrage-free market have the following representations:

$$\begin{cases} \mathrm{d}B(t) = r(t)B(t)\mathrm{d}t, \\ \mathrm{d}S_0(t) = S_0(t-)\left[r(t)\mathrm{d}t + \sigma_0(t)\mathrm{d}W^{\mathbb{Q}}(t) + \int_{\mathbb{R}} \gamma(t-,x)\bar{\Pi}(\mathrm{d}t,\mathrm{d}x) + \sum_{i=1}^{N} \int_{\mathbb{R}} x\bar{\Pi}_U^i(\mathrm{d}t,\mathrm{d}x)\right], \\ \mathrm{d}S_j(t) = S_j(t-)\left[r(t)\mathrm{d}t + \sigma_j(t-)\mathrm{d}\overline{\Phi}_j^{\mathbb{Q}}(t)\right], \\ \mathrm{d}S^{(k)}(t) = S^{(k)}(t-)\left[r(t)\mathrm{d}t + \sigma^{(k)}(t-)\mathrm{d}\overline{X}^{(k)}(t)\right], \\ \mathrm{d}S_i^{(l)}(t) = S_i^{(l)}(t-)\left[r(t)\mathrm{d}t + \sigma_i^{(l)}(t-)\mathrm{d}\overline{\Psi}_i^{(l),\mathbb{Q}}(t)\right], \end{cases} \tag{25}$$

for $i,j = 1,\ldots,N, k \geq 2$ and $l \geq 1$.

We show that the enlarged market (Equation (25)) is asymptotically complete in the sense that for every square-integrable contingent claim A (i.e., a non-negative square-integrable random variable in $L^2(\Omega,\mathcal{F},\mathbb{Q})$) we can set up a sequence of self-financing portfolios whose final values converge in $L^2(\Omega,\mathcal{F},\mathbb{Q})$ to A.

These portfolios consist of a finite number of risk-free asset, risky asset, kth-power-jump assets, jth geometric Markovian jump security and impulse regime switching securities. We use the following martingale representation property.

Theorem 3 (Palmowski et al. 2018). *Any square-integrable, $\{\mathcal{F}_t\}$-adapted $\mathbb{Q}$-martingale M can be represented as follows:*

$$\begin{aligned} M(t) &= M(0) + \int_0^t h_0(s)\mathrm{d}X^{\mathbb{Q}}(s) + \sum_{j=1}^{N}\int_0^t h_j(s)\mathrm{d}\overline{\Phi}_j^{\mathbb{Q}}(s) + \sum_{k=2}^{\infty}\int_0^t h^{(k)}(s)\mathrm{d}\overline{X}^{(k)}(s) \\ &\quad + \sum_{i=1}^{N}\sum_{l=1}^{\infty}\int_0^t h_i^{(l)}(s)\mathrm{d}\overline{\Psi}_i^{(l),\mathbb{Q}}(s), \end{aligned} \tag{26}$$

where h_0, h_j, $h^{(k)}$ and $h_i^{(l)}$ are predictable processes (for $i,j = 1,\ldots,N, k \geq 2$ and $l \geq 1$).

Remark 3. *The right-hand side of Equation (26) is understood as follows. We take finite sums*

$$\sum_{k=2}^{K}\int_0^t h^{(k)}(s)\mathrm{d}\overline{X}^{(k)}(s) \quad \text{and} \quad \sum_{l=1}^{K}\int_0^t h_i^{(l)}(s)\mathrm{d}\overline{\Psi}_i^{(l),\mathbb{Q}}(s)$$

in $L^2(\Omega,\mathcal{F},\mathbb{Q})$. Since $L^2(\Omega,\mathcal{F},\mathbb{Q})$ is a Hilbert space, the right-hand side of Equation (26) is understood as the limit of the above expressions in $L^2(\Omega,\mathcal{F},\mathbb{Q})$ as $K \to \infty$.

We are ready to prove the main result of this section.

Theorem 4. *The market (Equation (25)) under $\mathbb{Q}$ is asymptotically complete.*

Proof. We consider a square-integrable contingent claim A with maturity T. Let

$$M(t) := E_{\mathbb{Q}}\left[\exp\left(-\int_0^T r(s)\mathrm{d}s\right)A \,\middle|\, \mathcal{F}_t\right]$$

and

$$M^K(t) := M^K(0) + \int_0^t h_0(s)\mathrm{d}X^{\mathbb{Q}}(s) + \sum_{j=1}^{N}\int_0^t h_j(s)\mathrm{d}\overline{\Phi}_j^{\mathbb{Q}}(s) + \sum_{k=2}^{K}\int_0^t h^{(k)}(s)\mathrm{d}\overline{X}^{(k)}(s) \quad (27)$$

$$+ \sum_{i=1}^{N}\sum_{l=1}^{K}\int_0^t h_i^{(l)}(s)\mathrm{d}\overline{\Psi}_i^{(l),\mathbb{Q}}(s).$$

By the martingale representation property given in Theorem 3, we see that

$$\lim_{K\to\infty} M^K(t) = M(t) \quad (28)$$

in $L^2(\Omega, \mathcal{F}, \mathbb{Q})$. For $K \geq 2$, we introduce the sequence of portfolios

$$\theta^K(t) := \left(\alpha^K(t), \beta_0(t), \beta_1(t), \ldots, \beta_N(t), \beta^{(2)}(t), \ldots, \beta^{(K)}(t), \beta_1^{(1)}(t), \ldots, \beta_N^{(K)}(t)\right).$$

We assume that all processes in θ^K are predictable and

$$E_{\mathbb{Q}}\int_0^t (\alpha^K(s))^2\mathrm{d}s < \infty,\ E_{\mathbb{Q}}\int_0^t (\beta_0(s))^2\mathrm{d}\langle S_0\rangle(s) < \infty,\ E_{\mathbb{Q}}\int_0^t (\beta_j(s))^2\mathrm{d}\langle S_j\rangle(s) < \infty, \quad (29)$$

$$E_{\mathbb{Q}}\int_0^t (\beta^{(k)}(s))^2\mathrm{d}\langle S^{(k)}\rangle(s) < \infty,\ E_{\mathbb{Q}}\int_0^t (\beta_i^{(l)}(s))^2\mathrm{d}\langle S_i^{(l)}\rangle(s) < \infty. \quad (30)$$

Here, α^K corresponds to the number of risk-free assets, β_0 is the number of stocks, β_j $(j = 1, \ldots, N)$ is the number of units of the jth geometric Markovian jump security, $\beta^{(k)}$ $(k = 2, \ldots, K)$ is the number of assets $S^{(k)}$, and $\beta_i^{(l)}$ $(i = 1, \ldots, N, l = 1, \ldots, K)$ is the number of assets $S_i^{(l)}$.

We construct the portfolio θ^K as follows:

$$\begin{aligned}
\alpha^K(t) &:= M^K(t-) - \beta_0(t)B^{-1}(t)S_0(t-) - \sum_{j=1}^{N}\beta_j(t)B^{-1}(t)S_j(t-) \\
&\quad - \sum_{k=2}^{K}\beta^{(k)}(t)B^{-1}(t)S^{(k)}(t-) - \sum_{i=1}^{N}\sum_{l=1}^{K}\beta_i^{(l)}(t)B^{-1}(t)S_i^{(l)}(t-), \\
\beta_0(t) &:= h_0(t)B(t)S_0^{-1}(t-), \\
\beta_j(t) &:= \frac{h_j(t)}{\sigma_j(t-)}B(t)S_j^{-1}(t-), \\
\beta^{(k)}(t) &:= \frac{h^{(k)}(t)}{\sigma^{(k)}(t-)}B(t)(S^{(k)})^{-1}(t-), \\
\beta_i^{(l)}(t) &:= \frac{h_i^{(l)}(t)}{\sigma_i^{(l)}(t-)}B(t)(S_i^{(l)})^{-1}(t-).
\end{aligned} \quad (31)$$

Observe that for this choice of portfolio, the moment conditions in Equations (29) and (30) are satisfied, hence all stochastic integrals for this portfolio are well-defined. For example, we prove that

$$E_{\mathbb{Q}}\int_0^t (\beta_0(s))^2\mathrm{d}\langle S_0\rangle(s) < \infty. \quad (32)$$

The proofs of other conditions are similar. To show (32) note that

$$d\langle S_0\rangle(s) = S_0^2(t-)\left[\sigma_0^2(t)\mathrm{d}t + \int_{\mathbb{R}}\gamma^2(t-,x)\overline{\Pi}(dt,\mathrm{d}x) + \sum_{i=1}^{N}\int_{\mathbb{R}}x^2\overline{\Pi}_U^i(dt,\mathrm{d}x)\right]$$

and this condition is equivalent to requirement that

$$\int_0^\infty h_0^2(t)e^{2r(t)}\sigma_0^2(t)\mathrm{d}t < \infty, \qquad \int_0^\infty h_0^2(t)e^{2r(t)}\lambda_i(t)\int_{\mathbb{R}}\gamma^2(t-,x)\nu(\mathrm{d}x)\mathrm{d}t < \infty,$$

$$\int_{\mathbb{R}} x^2\eta_i(\mathrm{d}x)\int_0^\infty h_0^2(t)e^{2r(t)}\lambda_i(t)\mathrm{d}t < \infty.$$

The above conditions follow from Theorem 3 because $\int_0^\infty h_0^2(t)\mathrm{d}t < \infty$. Note that,

$$\begin{aligned}
\Delta M^K(t) &= h_0(t)\Delta X^{\mathbb{Q}}(t) + \sum_{j=1}^N h_j(t)\Delta\overline{\Phi}_j^{\mathbb{Q}}(t) + \sum_{k=2}^K h^{(k)}(t)\Delta\overline{X}^{(k)}(t) + \sum_{i=1}^N\sum_{l=1}^K h_i^{(l)}(t)\Delta\overline{\Psi}_i^{(l),\mathbb{Q}}(t),\\
\Delta S_0(t) &= S_0(t-)\Delta X^{\mathbb{Q}}(t), \qquad (33)\\
\Delta S_j(t) &= S_j(t-)\sigma_j(t-)\Delta\overline{\Phi}_j^{\mathbb{Q}}(t),\\
\Delta S^{(k)}(t) &= S^{(k)}(t-)\sigma^{(k)}(t-)\Delta\overline{X}^{(k)}(t), \quad \Delta S_i^{(l)}(t) = S_i^{(l)}(t-)\sigma_i^{(l)}(t-)\Delta\overline{\Psi}_i^{(l),\mathbb{Q}}(t).
\end{aligned}$$

We claim that $\{\theta^K, K \geq 2\}$ is the sequence of self-financing portfolios which replicates A. Indeed, by Equations (31) and (33), the value V^K of the portfolio θ^K is expressed by

$$\begin{aligned}
V^K(t) &= \alpha^K(t)B(t) + \beta_0(t)S_0(t) + \sum_{j=1}^N \beta_j(t)S_j(t) + \sum_{k=2}^K \beta^{(k)}(t)S^{(k)}(t) + \sum_{i=1}^N\sum_{l=1}^K \beta_i^{(l)}(t)S_i^{(l)}(t)\\
&= M^K(t)B(t) - \Delta M^K(t)B(t) + \beta_0(t)\Delta S_0(t) + \sum_{j=1}^N \beta_j(t)\Delta S_j(t) + \sum_{k=2}^K \beta^{(k)}(t)\Delta S^{(k)}(t)\\
&\quad + \sum_{i=1}^N\sum_{l=1}^K \beta_i^{(l)}(t)\Delta S_i^{(l)}(t) = M^K(t)B(t).
\end{aligned}$$

Thus, the sequence of portfolios $\{\theta^K, K \geq 2\}$ replicates the claim A. We denote

$$\begin{aligned}
G^K(u) &:= \int_0^u \alpha^K(t)\mathrm{d}B(t) + \int_0^u \beta_0(t)\mathrm{d}S_0(t) + \sum_{j=1}^N\int_0^u \beta_j(t)\mathrm{d}S_j(t) \qquad (34)\\
&\quad + \sum_{k=2}^K\int_0^u \beta^{(k)}(t)\mathrm{d}S^{(k)}(t) + \sum_{i=1}^N\sum_{l=1}^K\int_0^u \beta_i^{(l)}(t)\mathrm{d}S_i^{(l)}(t)
\end{aligned}$$

the gain process, i.e., the gains or losses obtained up to time u by following θ^K. We show

$$G^K(u) + M^K(0) = M^K(u)B(u), \qquad (35)$$

which implies that the portfolio is self-financing. Note that, from Equation (28), we have

$$\lim_{K\to\infty} G^K(u) = \lim_{K\to\infty} M^K(u)B(u) - \lim_{K\to\infty} M^K(0) = M(u)B(u) - M(0).$$

Thus, the portfolios with infinitely many assets are self-financing as well. Inserting Equation (31) into Equation (34), we derive

$$
\begin{aligned}
G^K(u) &= \int_0^u M^K(t-)\mathrm{d}B(t) - \int_0^u h_0(t)\mathrm{d}B(t) - \sum_{k=2}^{K}\int_0^u \frac{h^{(k)}(t)}{\sigma^{(k)}(t-)}\mathrm{d}B(t) \\
&- \sum_{j=1}^{N}\int_0^u \frac{h_j(t)}{\sigma_j(t-)}\mathrm{d}B(t) - \sum_{i=1}^{N}\sum_{l=1}^{K}\int_0^u \frac{h_i^{(l)}(t)}{\sigma_i^{(l)}(t-)}\mathrm{d}B(t) + \int_0^u h_0(t)B(t)S_0^{-1}(t-)\mathrm{d}S_0(t) \qquad (36) \\
&+ \sum_{j=1}^{N}\int_0^u \frac{h_j(t)}{\sigma_j(t-)}B(t)S_j^{-1}(t-)\mathrm{d}S_j(t) + \sum_{k=2}^{K}\int_0^u \frac{h^{(k)}(t)}{\sigma^{(k)}(t-)}B(t)(S^{(k)})^{-1}(t-)\mathrm{d}S^{(k)}(t) \\
&+ \sum_{i=1}^{N}\sum_{l=1}^{K}\int_0^u \frac{h_i^{(l)}(t)}{\sigma_i^{(l)}(t-)}B(t)(S_i^{(l)})^{-1}(t-)\mathrm{d}S_i^{(l)}(t).
\end{aligned}
$$

From the martingale representation property given in Theorem 3, the first component of the above sum has the form

$$
\begin{aligned}
\int_0^u M^K(t-)\mathrm{d}B(t) &= \int_0^u \Bigg(M^K(0) + \int_0^{t-} h_0(s)\mathrm{d}X^{\mathbb{Q}}(s) + \sum_{j=1}^{N}\int_0^{t-} h_j(s)\mathrm{d}\overline{\Phi}_j^{\mathbb{Q}}(s) \\
&+ \sum_{k=2}^{K}\int_0^{t-} h^{(k)}(s)\mathrm{d}\overline{X}^{(k)}(s) + \sum_{i=1}^{N}\sum_{l=1}^{K}\int_0^{t-} h_i^{(l)}(s)\mathrm{d}\overline{\Psi}_i^{(l)\mathbb{Q}}(s)\Bigg)\mathrm{d}B(t) \\
&= M^K(0)(B(u)-B(0)) + \int_0^u h_0(s)(B(u)-B(s))\mathrm{d}X^{\mathbb{Q}}(s) + \sum_{j=1}^{N}\int_0^u h_j(s)(B(u)-B(s))\mathrm{d}\overline{\Phi}_j^{\mathbb{Q}}(s) \\
&+ \sum_{k=2}^{K}\int_0^u h^{(k)}(s)(B(u)-B(s))\mathrm{d}\overline{X}^{(k)}(s) + \sum_{i=1}^{N}\sum_{l=1}^{K}\int_0^u h_i^{(l)}(s)(B(u)-B(s))\mathrm{d}\overline{\Psi}_i^{(l),\mathbb{Q}}(s).
\end{aligned}
$$

Now, using Equation (27) and fact that $B(0) = 1$, we can rewrite the above as follows:

$$
\begin{aligned}
\int_0^u M^K(t-)\mathrm{d}B(t) &= M^K(0)(B(u)-B(0)) + B(u)(M^K(u)-M^K(0)) - \int_0^u h_0(s)B(s)\mathrm{d}\overline{X}^{\mathbb{Q}}(s) \\
&- \sum_{j=1}^{N}\int_0^u h_j(s)B(s)\mathrm{d}\overline{\Phi}_j^{\mathbb{Q}}(s) - \sum_{k=2}^{K}\int_0^u h^{(k)}(s)B(s)\mathrm{d}\overline{X}^{(k)}(s) - \sum_{i=1}^{N}\sum_{l=1}^{K}\int_0^u h_i^{(l)}(s)B(s)\mathrm{d}\overline{\Psi}_i^{(l),\mathbb{Q}}(s) \\
&= M^K(u)B(u) - M^K(0) - \int_0^u h_0(s)B(s)\mathrm{d}X^{\mathbb{Q}}(s) - \sum_{j=1}^{N}\int_0^u h_j(s)B(s)\mathrm{d}\overline{\Phi}_j^{\mathbb{Q}}(s) \\
&- \sum_{k=2}^{K}\int_0^u h^{(k)}(s)B(s)\mathrm{d}\overline{X}^{(k)}(s) - \sum_{i=1}^{N}\sum_{l=1}^{K}\int_0^u h_i^{(l)}(s)B(s)\mathrm{d}\overline{\Psi}_i^{(l),\mathbb{Q}}(s).
\end{aligned}
$$

Inserting the above equality into Equation (36), the gain process can be written as:

$$
\begin{aligned}
G^K(u) = M^K(u)B(u) - M^K(0) - \int_0^u h_0(t)B(t)\mathrm{d}X^{\mathbb{Q}}(t) - \sum_{j=1}^{N}\int_0^u h_j(t)B(t)\mathrm{d}\overline{\Phi}_j^{\mathbb{Q}}(t) \\
- \sum_{k=2}^{K}\int_0^u h^{(k)}(t)B(t)\mathrm{d}\overline{X}^{(k)}(t) - \sum_{i=1}^{N}\sum_{l=1}^{K}\int_0^u h_i^{(l)}(t)B(t)\mathrm{d}\overline{\Psi}_i^{(l),\mathbb{Q}}(t) - \int_0^u h_0(t)\mathrm{d}B(t) \\
- \sum_{k=2}^{K}\int_0^u \frac{h^{(k)}(t)}{\sigma^{(k)}(t-)}\mathrm{d}B(t) - \sum_{j=1}^{N}\int_0^u \frac{h_j(t)}{\sigma_j(t-)}\mathrm{d}B(t) - \sum_{i=1}^{N}\sum_{l=1}^{K}\int_0^u \frac{h_i^{(l)}(t)}{\sigma_i^{(l)}(t-)}\mathrm{d}B(t) \\
+ \int_0^u h_0(t)B(t)S_0^{-1}(t-)\mathrm{d}S_0(t) + \sum_{j=1}^{N}\int_0^u \frac{h_j(t)}{\sigma_j(t-)}B(t)S_j^{-1}(t-)\mathrm{d}S_j(t) \\
+ \sum_{k=2}^{K}\int_0^u \frac{h^{(k)}(t)}{\sigma^{(k)}(t-)}B(t)(S^{(k)})^{-1}(t-)\mathrm{d}S^{(k)}(t) + \sum_{i=1}^{N}\sum_{l=1}^{K}\int_0^u \frac{h_i^{(l)}(t)}{\sigma_i^{(l)}(t-)}B(t)(S_i^{(l)})^{-1}(t-)\mathrm{d}S_i^{(l)}(t) \\
= M^K(u)B(u) - M(0).
\end{aligned}
$$

Thus, Equation (35) holds true and the portfolio θ^K is self-financing. □

6. Optimal Portfolio Selection in an Itô–Markov Additive Market

In this section we solve the optimization problem related to identifying the optimal strategy that maximizes the expected value of the utility function of the wealth process at the end of some fixed period. The analysis is conducted for the logarithmic and power utility functions.

Recall that our Itô–Markov additive market is given by Equation (17). Equations (15) and (16) can be rewritten as follows:

$$
\begin{aligned}
\mathrm{d}S^{(k)}(t) &= S^{(k)}(t-)\left[\mu^{(k)}(t)\mathrm{d}t + \int_{\mathbb{R}}\sigma^{(k)}(t-)\gamma^k(t-,x)\bar{\Pi}(\mathrm{d}t,\mathrm{d}x)\right], \\
\mathrm{d}S_i^{(l)}(t) &= S_i^{(l)}(t-)\left[\mu_i^{(l)}(t)\mathrm{d}t + \int_{\mathbb{R}}x^l\sigma_i^{(l)}(t-)\bar{\Pi}_U^i(\mathrm{d}t,\mathrm{d}x)\right]
\end{aligned}
$$

for $i = 1,\ldots,N$, $k \geq 2$ and $l \geq 1$. Note that we consider the price processes with respect the original probability measure $\mathbb{P}$.

We restrict ourselves to self-financing portfolio strategies. Denote by π_0 the proportion of wealth invested in stock. Let π_j $(j = 1,\ldots,N)$, $\pi^{(k)}$ $(k \geq 2)$ and $\pi_i^{(l)}$ $(i = 1,\ldots,N, l \geq 1)$ be the proportions of wealth invested in the jth geometric Markovian jump security S_j, in the Markovian power-jump securities $S^{(k)}$ and in the impulse regime switching securities $S_i^{(l)}$, respectively. The balance of the investor's wealth is invested in the risk-free asset. We denote by $\pi(t) = (\pi_0(t), \pi_1(t),\ldots,\pi_N(t), \pi^{(2)}(t),\ldots,\pi_1^{(1)}(t), \pi_2^{(1)}(t),\ldots)$ a portfolio strategy. We do allow short selling, but we assume that the wealth process is nonnegative at any instant (Teplá 2000).

Let $K < \infty$ be the number of different assets held by the investor in his portfolio. The wealth process R_π^K for the first K assets is governed by the following stochastic differential equation (for $t \in [0,T]$):

$$\begin{aligned}\frac{\mathrm{d}R_\pi^K(t)}{R_\pi^K(t-)} := & \Big(r(t) + \sum_{j=0}^{N} \pi_j(t)(\mu_j(t) - r(t)) + \sum_{k=2}^{K} \pi^{(k)}(t)(\mu^{(k)}(t) - r(t)) \\ & + \sum_{i=1}^{N}\sum_{l=1}^{K} \pi_i^{(l)}(t)(\mu_i^{(l)}(t) - r(t))\Big)\mathrm{d}t + \pi_0(t)\sigma_0(t-)\mathrm{d}W(t) + \sum_{j=1}^{N} \pi_j(t)\sigma_j(t-)\mathrm{d}\overline{\Phi}_j(t) \\ & + \int_{\mathbb{R}} \Big(\pi_0(t)\gamma(t-,x) + \sum_{k=2}^{K} \pi^{(k)}(t)\sigma^{(k)}(t-)\gamma^k(t-,x)\Big)\bar{\Pi}(\mathrm{d}t,\mathrm{d}x) \\ & + \sum_{i=1}^{N}\int_{\mathbb{R}} \Big(x\pi_0(t) + \sum_{l=1}^{K} x^l \pi_i^{(l)}(t)\sigma_i^{(l)}(t-)\Big)\bar{\Pi}_U^i(\mathrm{d}t,\mathrm{d}x).\end{aligned} \tag{37}$$

Note that in Equation (37) we can take $r(t) = r(t-)$, $\mu_j(t) = \mu_j(t-)$ $(j = 0,1,\ldots,N)$, $\mu^{(k)}(t) = \mu^{(k)}(t-)$ $(k \geq 2)$ and $\mu_i^{(l)}(t) = \mu_i^{(l)}(t-)$ $(i = 1,\ldots,N, l \geq 1)$.

Let $\mathcal{A}$ be the class of admissible portfolio strategies π such that π is predictable, $R_\pi^K > 0$, $\int_0^T |\pi(t)|^2 \mathrm{d}t < \infty$ $\mathbb{P}$ – a.s., $\int_{\mathbb{R}} (\pi_0(t)\gamma(t-,x) + \sum_{k=2}^K \pi^{(k)}(t)\sigma^{(k)}(t-)\gamma^k(t-,x))\bar{\Pi}(\mathrm{d}t,\mathrm{d}x) < \infty$, $\int_{\mathbb{R}} \sum_{i=1}^N (x\pi_0(t) + \sum_{l=1}^K x^l \pi_i^{(l)}(t)\sigma_i^{(l)}(t-))\bar{\Pi}_U^i(\mathrm{d}t,\mathrm{d}x) < \infty$ and π satisfies the following convergence: the wealth process R_π^K converges to a process R_π in $L^2(\Omega,\mathcal{F},\mathbb{P})$, where R_π^K is the solution of the SDE in Equation (37) (see Itô's formula in Protter (2005, Thm. 32)), that is,

$$\begin{aligned}R_\pi^K(t) = & R_\pi^K(0)\exp\Bigg[\int_0^t \Big(r(s-) + \sum_{j=0}^{N} \pi_j(s)(\mu_j(s-) - r(s-)) + \sum_{k=2}^{K} \pi^{(k)}(s)(\mu^{(k)}(s) - r(s-)) \\ & + \sum_{i=1}^{N}\sum_{l=1}^{K} \pi_i^{(l)}(s)(\mu_i^{(l)}(s) - r(s-)) - \frac{1}{2}\pi_0^2(s)\sigma_0^2(s-)\Big)\mathrm{d}s \\ & + \int_0^t \pi_0(s)\sigma_0(s-)dW(s) + \sum_{j=1}^{N}\int_0^t \Big(\log(1 + \pi_j(s)\sigma_j(s-)) - \pi_j(s)\sigma_j(s-)\Big)\lambda_j(s)ds \\ & + \int_0^t\int_{\mathbb{R}} \log\Big(1 + \pi_0(s)\gamma(s-,x) + \sum_{k=2}^{K} \pi^{(k)}(s)\sigma^{(k)}(s-)\gamma^k(s-,x)\Big)\bar{\Pi}(\mathrm{d}s,\mathrm{d}x) \\ & + \int_0^t\int_{\mathbb{R}} \Big(\log\Big(1 + \pi_0(s)\gamma(s-,x) + \sum_{k=2}^{K} \pi^{(k)}(s)\sigma^{(k)}(s-)\gamma^k(s-,x)\Big) - \pi_0(s)\gamma(s-,x) \\ & - \sum_{k=2}^{K} \pi^{(k)}(s)\sigma^{(k)}(s-)\gamma^k(s-,x)\Big)\nu(\mathrm{d}x)\mathrm{d}s + \sum_{j=1}^{N}\int_0^t \log(1 + \pi_j(s)\sigma_j(s-))\mathrm{d}\overline{\Phi}_j(s) \\ & + \sum_{i=1}^{N}\int_0^t\int_{\mathbb{R}} \log\Big(1 + x\pi_0(s) + \sum_{l=1}^{K} \pi_i^{(l)}(s)\sigma_i^{(l)}(s-)x^l\Big)\bar{\Pi}_U^i(\mathrm{d}s,\mathrm{d}x) \\ & + \sum_{i=1}^{N}\int_0^t\int_{\mathbb{R}} \Big(\log\Big(1 + x\pi_0(s) + \sum_{l=1}^{K} \pi_i^{(l)}(s)\sigma_i^{(l)}(s-)x^l\Big) - x\pi_0(s) \\ & - \sum_{l=1}^{K} \pi_i^{(l)}(s)\sigma_i^{(l)}(s-)x^l\Big)\lambda_i(s)\eta(\mathrm{d}x)\mathrm{d}s\Bigg].\end{aligned}$$

In other words, for $\pi \in \mathcal{A}$, we require that

$$\lim_{K\to\infty} R_\pi^K(t) = R_\pi(t) \tag{38}$$

in $L^2(\Omega, \mathcal{F}, \mathbb{P})$.

Remark 4. *Note that Equation (38) holds true if*

$$\mathbb{E}_{t,z,i}(R^K_\pi(t))^2 < \infty, \ \ \mathbb{E}_{t,z,i}(R_\pi(t))^2 < \infty,$$

and

$$\mathbb{E}_{t,z,i}\left| \int_0^t \sum_{k=K+1}^{\infty} \pi^{(k)}(s)(\mu^{(k)}(s) - r(s-))\mathrm{d}s \right|^2,$$

$$\mathbb{E}_{t,z,i}\left| \int_0^t \sum_{i=1}^{N} \sum_{l=K+1}^{\infty} \pi_i^{(l)}(s)(\mu_i^{(l)}(s) - r(s-))\mathrm{d}s \right|^2,$$

$$\mathbb{E}_{t,z,i}\left| \int_0^t \int_{\mathbb{R}} \log\left(\frac{1+\pi_0(s)\gamma(s-,x)+\sum_{k=2}^{\infty}\pi^{(k)}(s)\sigma^{(k)}(s-)\gamma^k(s-,x)}{1+\pi_0(s)\gamma(s-,x)+\sum_{k=2}^{K}\pi^{(k)}(s)\sigma^{(k)}(s-)\gamma^k(s-,x)}\right)\bar{\Pi}(\mathrm{d}s,\mathrm{d}x) \right|^2,$$

$$\mathbb{E}_{t,z,i}\left| \int_0^t \int_{\mathbb{R}} \left(\log\left(\frac{1+\pi_0(s)\gamma(s-,x)+\sum_{k=2}^{\infty}\pi^{(k)}(s)\sigma^{(k)}(s-)\gamma^k(s-,x)}{1+\pi_0(s)\gamma(s-,x)+\sum_{k=2}^{K}\pi^{(k)}(s)\sigma^{(k)}(s-)\gamma^k(s-,x)}\right) \right.\right.$$
$$\left.\left. - \sum_{k=K+1}^{\infty} \pi^{(k)}(s)\sigma^{(k)}(s-)\gamma^k(s-,x) \right)\nu(\mathrm{d}x)\mathrm{d}s \right|^2,$$

$$\mathbb{E}_{t,z,i}\left| \int_0^t \int_{\mathbb{R}} \log\left(\frac{1+x\pi_0(s)+\sum_{l=2}^{\infty}\pi_i^{(l)}(s)\sigma_i^{(l)}(s-)x^l}{1+x\pi_0(s)+\sum_{l=2}^{K}\pi_i^{(l)}(s)\sigma_i^{(l)}(s-)x^l}\right)\bar{\Pi}^i_U(\mathrm{d}s,\mathrm{d}x) \right|^2,$$

$$\mathbb{E}_{t,z,i}\left| \sum_{i=1}^{N} \int_0^t \int_{\mathbb{R}} \left(\log\left(\frac{1+x\pi_0(s)+\sum_{l=2}^{\infty}\pi_i^{(l)}(s)\sigma_i^{(l)}(s-)x^l}{1+x\pi_0(s)+\sum_{l=2}^{K}\pi_i^{(l)}(s)\sigma_i^{(l)}(s-)x^l}\right) \right.\right.$$
$$\left.\left. - \sum_{l=K+1}^{\infty} \pi_i^{(l)}(s)\sigma_i^{(l)}(s-)x^l \right)\lambda_i(s)\eta(\mathrm{d}x)\mathrm{d}s \right|^2$$

tend to 0 as $K \to \infty$. Indeed, the convergence of Equation (38) follows directly from our assumptions: from the triangle inequality and the inequality (Fechner 2008)

$$2|\exp(a_1) - \exp(a_2)| \leq |a_1 - a_2||\exp(a_1) + \exp(a_2)|, \ \ a_1, a_2 \in \mathbb{R}.$$

Then, we get

$$\mathbb{E}\,|\,R_\pi(t) - R^K_\pi(t)\,|^2 \leq \mathbb{E}\left|\,\log\frac{R_\pi(t)}{R^K_\pi(t)}\right|^2 \left(\mathbb{E}|R_\pi(t)|^2 + \mathbb{E}|R^K_\pi(t)|^2\right) < \infty$$

and we can use the following equation

$$\begin{aligned}\log\frac{R_\pi(t)}{R^K_\pi(t)} &= \log\frac{R_\pi(0)}{R^K_\pi(0)} + \left[\int_0^t \left(\sum_{k=K+1}^{\infty} \pi^{(k)}(s)(\mu^{(k)}(s) - r(s-))\right.\right. \\ &\quad \left. + \sum_{i=1}^{N}\sum_{l=K+1}^{\infty} \pi_i^{(l)}(s)(\mu_i^{(l)}(s) - r(s-)) - \frac{1}{2}\pi_0^2(s)\sigma_0^2(s-)\right)\mathrm{d}s\end{aligned}$$

$$
\begin{aligned}
&+\int_0^t\int_{\mathbb{R}}\log\left(1+\pi_0(s)\gamma(s-,x)+\sum_{k=2}^{\infty}\pi^{(k)}(s)\sigma^{(k)}(s-)\gamma^k(s-,x)\right)\bar{\Pi}(ds,dx)\\
&-\int_0^t\int_{\mathbb{R}}\log\left(1+\pi_0(s)\gamma(s-,x)+\sum_{k=2}^{K}\pi^{(k)}(s)\sigma^{(k)}(s-)\gamma^k(s-,x)\right)\bar{\Pi}(ds,dx)\\
&+\int_0^t\int_{\mathbb{R}}\Bigg(\log\left(1+\pi_0(s)\gamma(s-,x)+\sum_{k=2}^{\infty}\pi^{(k)}(s)\sigma^{(k)}(s-)\gamma^k(s-,x)\right)\\
&-\sum_{k=K+1}^{\infty}\pi^{(k)}(s)\sigma^{(k)}(s-)\gamma^k(s-,x)\Bigg)\nu(dx)ds\\
&-\int_0^t\int_{\mathbb{R}}\log\left(1+\pi_0(s)\gamma(s-,x)+\sum_{k=2}^{K}\pi^{(k)}(s)\sigma^{(k)}(s-)\gamma^k(s-,x)\right)\nu(dx)ds\\
&+\sum_{i=1}^{N}\int_0^t\int_{\mathbb{R}}\log\left(1+x\pi_0(s)+\sum_{l=1}^{\infty}\pi_i^{(l)}(s)\sigma_i^{(l)}(s-)x^l\right)\bar{\Pi}_U^i(ds,dx)\\
&-\sum_{i=1}^{N}\int_0^t\int_{\mathbb{R}}\log\left(1+x\pi_0(s)+\sum_{l=1}^{K}\pi_i^{(l)}(s)\sigma_i^{(l)}(s-)x^l\right)\bar{\Pi}_U^i(ds,dx)\\
&+\sum_{i=1}^{N}\int_0^t\int_{\mathbb{R}}\Bigg(\log\left(1+x\pi_0(s)+\sum_{l=1}^{\infty}\pi_i^{(l)}(s)\sigma_i^{(l)}(s-)x^l\right)\\
&-\sum_{l=K+1}^{\infty}\pi_i^{(l)}(s)\sigma_i^{(l)}(s-)x^l\Bigg)\lambda_i(s)\eta(dx)ds\\
&-\sum_{i=1}^{N}\int_0^t\int_{\mathbb{R}}\log\left(1+x\pi_0(s)+\sum_{l=1}^{K}\pi_i^{(l)}(s)\sigma_i^{(l)}(s-)x^l\right)\lambda_i(s)\eta(dx)ds\Bigg].
\end{aligned}
$$

Let U denote a utility function of the investor, which is strictly increasing, strictly concave and twice differentiable, that is, $U' > 0$ and $U'' < 0$.

For each $(t,z) \in \mathbb{T} \times \mathbb{R}^+$ and each $i = 1, \dots, N$ we define

$$V^{\pi}(t,z,\mathbf{e}_i) := \mathbb{E}_{t,z,i}[U(R_{\pi}(T))],$$

where $\mathbb{E}_{t,z,i}$ is the conditional expectation given $R_{\pi}(0) = z$ and $J(t) = \mathbf{e}_i$ under $\mathbb{P}$.

The expectation above is understood in the limiting sense, that is, we limit the set of admissible strategies $\mathcal{A}$ to the strategies π such that $\lim_{K\to\infty} \mathbb{E}_{t,z,i}[U(R_{\pi}^K(T))]$ exists and is finite. In other words,

$$\lim_{K\to\infty} \mathbb{E}_{t,z,i}[U(R_{\pi}^K(T))] = \mathbb{E}_{t,z,i}[U(R_{\pi}(T))] < \infty. \tag{39}$$

Then, the value function of the investor's portfolio selection problem is defined by

$$V(t,z,\mathbf{e}_i) := \sup_{\pi\in\mathcal{A}} V^{\pi}(t,z,\mathbf{e}_i) = \sup_{\pi\in\mathcal{A}} \mathbb{E}_{t,z,i}[U(R_{\pi}(T))]. \tag{40}$$

Lemma 1. *Under the assumption in Equation (38), Equation (39) holds true.*

The proof of this Lemma is given in Appendix A.

Our main goal is to identify the value function given in Equation (40). In what follows, we consider two risk-averse utility functions, namely, the logarithmic utility and the power utility.

6.1. Logarithmic Utility

In this subsection, we derive the optimal portfolio strategy in the case of a logarithmic utility function of wealth, namely

$$U(z) = \log(z).$$

Recall that in $\mathcal{A}$ we consider only the strategies for which

$$\lim_{K\to\infty} \mathbb{E}_{t,z,i}\left[\log R^K_\pi(T)\right] = \mathbb{E}_{t,z,i}\left[\log R_\pi(T)\right] < \infty. \tag{41}$$

Theorem 5. *Assume that there exists a solution*

$$\pi^\star(t) := (\pi^\star_0(t), \pi^\star_1(t), \dots, \pi^\star_N(t), \pi^{(2)\star}(t), \pi^{(3)\star}(t), \dots, \pi^{(1)\star}_1(t), \pi^{(1)\star}_2(t), \dots)$$

of the following system of equations (for $i, j = 1, \dots, N$, $k \geq 2$ and $l \geq 1$):

$$\begin{aligned} r(t-) - \mu_0(t-) &= \pi^\star_0(t)\sigma^2_0(t-) + \sum_{i=1}^{N} \frac{r(t-) - \mu^{(1)}_i(t-)}{\sigma^{(1)}_i(t-)} + \int_{\mathbb{R}} \gamma(t-,x)\Bigg(\Big(1 + \pi^\star_0(t)\gamma(t-,x) \\ &\quad + \sum_{k=2}^{\infty} \pi^{(k)\star}(t)\sigma^{(k)}(t-)\gamma^k(t-,x)\Big)^{-1} - 1\Bigg)\nu(dx), \\ \pi^\star_j(t) &= \frac{\mu_j(t-) - r(t-)}{(r(t-) - \mu_j(t-))\sigma_j(t-) + \lambda_j(t)\sigma^2_j(t-)}, \end{aligned} \tag{42}$$

$$\begin{aligned} \frac{r(t-) - \mu^{(k)}(t-)}{\sigma^{(k)}(t-)} &= \int_{\mathbb{R}} \gamma^k(t-,x)\Bigg(\Big(1 + \pi^\star_0(t)\gamma(t-,x) \\ &\quad + \sum_{k=2}^{\infty} \pi^{(k)\star}(t)\sigma^{(k)}(t-)\gamma^k(t-,x)\Big)^{-1} - 1\Bigg)\nu(dx), \\ \frac{r(t-) - \mu^{(l)}_i(t-)}{\sigma^{(l)}_i(t-)} &= \int_{\mathbb{R}} x^l\Bigg(\Big(1 + x\pi^\star_0(t) + \sum_{l=1}^{\infty} \pi^{(l)\star}_i(t)\sigma^{(l)}_i(t-)x^l\Big)^{-1} - 1\Bigg)\lambda_i(t)\eta(dx), \end{aligned}$$

which belongs to $\mathcal{A}$, that is, in particular, satisfies Equations (38) and (41). Then, the optimal portfolio strategy for the portfolio selection problem in Equation (40) with logarithmic utility function of wealth is one of those solutions.

Proof. The conditional expectation of the logarithm of the wealth process has the following form (for $t \in [0, T)$):

$$\begin{aligned} \mathbb{E}_{t,z,i}\left[\log R_\pi(T)\right] &= \log R_\pi(t) + \mathbb{E}_{t,z,i} \int_t^T \Bigg[r(s-) + \sum_{j=0}^{N} \pi_j(s)(\mu_j(s-) - r(s-)) \\ &\quad + \sum_{k=2}^{\infty} \pi^{(k)}(s)(\mu^{(k)}(s) - r(s-)) + \sum_{i=0}^{N}\sum_{l=1}^{\infty} \pi^{(l)}_i(s)(\mu^{(l)}_i(s) - r(s-)) - \frac{1}{2}\pi^2_0(s)\sigma^2_0(s-) \\ &\quad + \sum_{j=1}^{N} \Big(\log\left(1 + \pi_j(s)\sigma_j(s-)\right) - \pi_j(s)\sigma_j(s-)\Big)\lambda_j(s) \\ &\quad + \int_{\mathbb{R}} \Bigg(\log\Big(1 + \pi_0(s)\gamma(s-,x) + \sum_{k=2}^{\infty} \pi^{(k)}(s)\sigma^{(k)}(s-)\gamma^k(s-,x)\Big) \\ &\quad - \pi_0(s)\gamma(s-,x) - \sum_{k=2}^{\infty} \pi^{(k)}(s)\sigma^{(k)}(s-)\gamma^k(s-,x)\Bigg)\nu(dx) \end{aligned}$$

$$+\sum_{i=1}^{N}\int_{\mathbb{R}}\Big(\log\Big(1+x\pi_0(s)+\sum_{l=1}^{\infty}\pi_i^{(l)}(s)\sigma_i^{(l)}(s-)x^l\Big)-x\pi_0(s)-\sum_{l=1}^{\infty}\pi_i^{(l)}(s)\sigma_i^{(l)}(s-)x^l\Big)\lambda_i(s)\eta(\mathrm{d}x)\Big]\mathrm{d}s.$$

Therefore, the optimal value function V can be written as

$$V(t,z,\mathbf{e}_i)=\log(z)+\sup_{\pi\in\mathcal{A}}h_\pi(t,\mathbf{e}_i),$$

where

$$h_\pi(t,\mathbf{e}_i):=\mathbb{E}_{t,z,i}\int_t^T F(\pi_0(s),\pi_1(s),\ldots,\pi_N(s),\pi^{(2)}(s),\ldots,\pi_1^{(1)}(s),\ldots)\mathrm{d}s$$

for

$$\begin{aligned}
F(\pi_0(s),\pi_1(s),\ldots,\pi_N(s),\pi^{(2)}(s),\ldots,\pi_1^{(1)}(s),\ldots)&:=r(s-)+\sum_{j=0}^{N}\pi_j(s)(\mu_j(s-)-r(s-))\\
&+\sum_{k=2}^{\infty}\pi^{(k)}(s)(\mu^{(k)}(s)-r(s-))+\sum_{i=0}^{N}\sum_{l=1}^{\infty}\pi_i^{(l)}(s)(\mu_i^{(l)}(s)-r(s-))-\frac{1}{2}\pi_0^2(s)\sigma_0^2(s-)\\
&+\sum_{j=1}^{N}\Big(\log(1+\pi_j(s)\sigma_j(s-))-\pi_j(s)\sigma_j(s-)\Big)\lambda_j(s)\\
&+\int_{\mathbb{R}}\Big(\log\Big(1+\pi_0(s)\gamma(s-,x)+\sum_{k=2}^{\infty}\pi^{(k)}(s)\sigma^{(k)}(s-)\gamma^k(s-,x)\Big)\\
&-\pi_0(s)\gamma(s-,x)-\sum_{k=2}^{\infty}\pi^{(k)}(s)\sigma^{(k)}(s-)\gamma^k(s-,x)\Big)\nu(\mathrm{d}x)\\
&+\sum_{i=1}^{N}\int_{\mathbb{R}}\Big(\log\Big(1+x\pi_0(s)+\sum_{l=1}^{\infty}\pi_i^{(l)}(s)\sigma_i^{(l)}(s-)x^l\Big)-x\pi_0(s)-\sum_{l=1}^{\infty}\pi_i^{(l)}(s)\sigma_i^{(l)}(s-)x^l\Big)\lambda_i(s)\eta(\mathrm{d}x).
\end{aligned}$$

Thus, to determine the optimal portfolio strategy, it is sufficient to maximize F. Indeed, the maximization of the function $F(\pi_0(s),\pi_1(s),\ldots,\pi_N(s),\pi^{(2)}(s),\ldots,\pi_1^{(1)}(s),\ldots)$ at each time point $s\in[0,T]$ maximizes the integral of F on $[0,T]$. By direct differentiation with respect to $\pi_0,\pi_j,\pi^{(k)},\pi_i^{(l)}$ we obtain conditions (Equation (42)) that the optimal strategies have to satisfy. Observe that, from Equation (9), the integrals

$$\int_{\mathbb{R}}\Big(\log\Big(1+\pi_0(s)\gamma(s-,x)+\sum_{k=2}^{\infty}\pi^{(k)}(s)\sigma^{(k)}(s-)\gamma^k(s-,x)\Big)-\pi_0(s)\gamma(s-,x)$$
$$-\sum_{k=2}^{\infty}\pi^{(k)}(s)\sigma^{(k)}(s-)\gamma^k(s-,x)\Big)\nu(\mathrm{d}x)$$

and (for $i=1,\ldots,N$)

$$\int_{\mathbb{R}}\Big(\log\Big(1+x\pi_0(s)+\sum_{l=1}^{\infty}\pi_i^{(l)}(s)\sigma_i^{(l)}(s-)x^l\Big)-x\pi_0(s)-\sum_{l=1}^{\infty}\pi_i^{(l)}(s)\sigma_i^{(l)}(s-)x^l\Big)\lambda_i(s)\eta(\mathrm{d}x)$$

are well-defined. Hence, by the Leibniz integral rule, we can interchange the above mentioned derivatives and the integrals. □

Remark 5. *We have not been able to prove that a solution of the system in Equation (42) exists and is unique. On a complete Itô–Markov additive market, we have an infinite number of assets, so the optimal portfolio strategy $\pi^\star$ is an infinite dimensional vector. The value function in Equation (40) is understood in the limiting sense and therefore numerically it can be approximated by the finite strategy counterpart. In the case of finite dimensional approximations by Kramkov and Schachermayer (1999, Thm. 2.2), the optimal wealth process exists and is* *unique. Under additional conditions, such as absence of redundant assets, the optimal strategy exists and is unique.*

6.2. Power Utility

In this subsection, we derive the optimal portfolio strategy in the case of the power utility function, namely

$$U(z) = z^{\alpha} \qquad \text{for } \alpha \in (0,1).$$

We assume that, for each $\pi \in \mathcal{A}$,

$$\lim_{K\to\infty} \mathbb{E}_{t,z,i}\big(R_{\pi}^{K}(T)\big)^{\alpha} = \mathbb{E}_{t,z,i}\big(R_{\pi}(T)\big)^{\alpha} < \infty. \tag{43}$$

Theorem 6. *Assume that there exists a solution*

$$\pi^{\star}(t) := (\pi_0^{\star}(t), \pi_1^{\star}(t), \ldots, \pi_N^{\star}(t), \pi^{(2)\star}(t), \pi^{(3)\star}(t), \ldots, \pi_1^{(1)\star}(t), \pi_2^{(1)\star}(t), \ldots)$$

of the following system of equations (for $i, j = 1, \ldots, N$, $k \geq 2$ and $l \geq 1$):

$$\begin{aligned}
r(t-) - \mu_0(t) &= (\alpha-1)\pi_0^{\star}(t)\sigma_0^2(t-) + \sum_{i=1}^{N} \frac{\mu_i^{(1)}(t-) - r(t-)}{\sigma_i^{(1)}(t-)} + \int_{\mathbb{R}} \gamma(t-,x)\Big(\Big(1 + \pi_0^{\star}(t)\gamma(t-,x) \\
&\quad + \sum_{k=2}^{\infty} \pi^{(k)\star}(t)\sigma^{(k)}(t-)\gamma^k(t-,x)\Big)^{\alpha-1} - 1\Big)\nu(\mathrm{d}x), \\
\pi_j^{\star}(t) &= \frac{\left(1 - \frac{\mu_j(t-) - r(t-)}{\lambda_i(t)\sigma_j(t-)}\right)^{\frac{1}{\alpha-1}} - 1}{\sigma_j(t-)}, \\
r(t-) - \mu^{(k)}(t) &= \int_{\mathbb{R}} \sigma^{(k)}(t-)\gamma^k(t-,x)\Big(\Big(1 + \pi_0^{\star}(t)\gamma(t-,x) \\
&\quad + \sum_{k=2}^{\infty} \pi^{(k)\star}(t)\sigma^{(k)}(t-)\gamma^k(t-,x)\Big)^{\alpha-1} - 1\Big)\nu(\mathrm{d}x), \\
r(t-) - \mu_i^{(l)}(t) &= \int_{\mathbb{R}} \sigma_i^{(l)}(t-)x^l\Big(\Big(1 + x\pi_0^{\star}(t) + \sum_{l=1}^{\infty} \pi_i^{\star(l)}(t)x^l\sigma_i^{(l)}(t-)\Big)^{\alpha-1} - 1\Big)\lambda_i(t)\eta(\mathrm{d}x)\mathrm{d}t,
\end{aligned} \tag{44}$$

which belongs to $\mathcal{A}$, that is, in particular, it satisfies Equations (38) and (43). Then, the optimal portfolio strategy for the portfolio selection problem in Equation (40) with power utility function of wealth is one of those solutions.

Proof. From Itô's formula (see Protter (2005, Thm. 32)) for the power utility function of wealth, we obtain (for $s \in [t,T]$ and $t \in [0,T]$)

$$\begin{aligned}
(R_{\pi}(T))^{\alpha} - (R_{\pi}(t))^{\alpha} &= \int_t^T \alpha(R_{\pi}(s))^{\alpha}\Big(r(s-) + \sum_{j=0}^{N} \pi_j(s)(\mu_j(s-) - r(s-)) + \sum_{k=2}^{\infty} \pi^{(k)}(s)(\mu^{(k)}(s) - r(s-)) \\
&\quad + \sum_{i=0}^{N}\sum_{l=1}^{\infty} \pi_i^{(l)}(s)(\mu_i^{(l)}(s) - r(s-))\Big)\mathrm{d}s + \int_t^T \alpha(R_{\pi}(s))^{\alpha}\pi_0(s)\sigma_0(s-)\mathrm{d}W(s) \\
&\quad + \int_t^T \frac{1}{2}\alpha(\alpha-1)(R_{\pi}(s))^{\alpha}\pi_0^2(s)\sigma_0^2(s-)\mathrm{d}s + \sum_{j=1}^{N}\int_t^T \Big((R_{\pi}(s) + R_{\pi}(s)\pi_j(s)\sigma_j(s-))^{\alpha} - (R_{\pi}(s))^{\alpha}\Big)\mathrm{d}\overline{\Phi}_j(s) \\
&\quad + \sum_{j=1}^{N}\int_t^T \Big((R_{\pi}(s) + R_{\pi}(s)\pi_j(s)\sigma_j(s-))^{\alpha} - (R_{\pi}(s))^{\alpha} - \alpha(R_{\pi}(s))^{\alpha}\pi_j(s)\sigma_j(s-)\Big)\lambda_j(s)\mathrm{d}s
\end{aligned}$$

$$+\int_t^T\int_{\mathbb{R}}\Bigg(\Big(R_\pi(s-)+R_\pi(s)\Big(\pi_0(s)\gamma(s-,x)+\sum_{k=2}^{\infty}\pi^{(k)}(s)\sigma^{(k)}(s-)\gamma^k(s-,x)\Big)\Big)^{\alpha}$$
$$-(R_\pi(s-))^{\alpha}-\alpha(R_\pi(s-))^{\alpha}\Big(\pi_0(s)\gamma(s-,x)+\sum_{k=2}^{\infty}\pi^{(k)}(s)\sigma^{(k)}(s-)\gamma^k(s-,x)\Big)\Bigg)\nu(\mathrm{d}x)\mathrm{d}s$$
$$+\int_t^T\int_{\mathbb{R}}\Bigg(\Big(R_\pi(s-)+R_\pi(s)\Big(\pi_0(s)\gamma(s-,x)+\sum_{k=2}^{\infty}\pi^{(k)}(s)\sigma^{(k)}(s-)\gamma^k(s-,x)\Big)\Big)^{\alpha}-(R_\pi(s-))^{\alpha}\Bigg)\bar{\Pi}(\mathrm{d}s,\mathrm{d}x)$$
$$+\sum_{i=1}^{N}\int_t^T\int_{\mathbb{R}}\Bigg(\Big(R_\pi(s-)+R_\pi(s)\Big(x\pi_0(s)+\sum_{l=1}^{\infty}x^l\pi_i^{(l)}(s)\sigma_i^{(l)}(s-)\Big)\Big)^{\alpha}-(R_\pi(s-))^{\alpha}$$
$$-\alpha(R_\pi(s-))^{\alpha}\Big(x\pi_0(s)+\sum_{l=1}^{\infty}x^l\pi_i^{(l)}(s)\sigma_i^{(l)}(s-)\Big)\Bigg)\lambda_i(s)\eta(\mathrm{d}x)\mathrm{d}s$$
$$+\sum_{i=1}^{N}\int_t^T\int_{\mathbb{R}}\Bigg(\Big(R_\pi(s-)+R_\pi(s)\Big(x\pi_0(s)+\sum_{l=1}^{\infty}x^l\pi_i^{(l)}(s)\sigma_i^{(l)}(s-)\Big)\Big)^{\alpha}-(R_\pi(s-))^{\alpha}\Bigg)\bar{\Pi}_U^i(\mathrm{d}s,\mathrm{d}x).$$

From this and Equation (40), the value function is given by

$$\begin{aligned}V(t,z,\mathbf{e}_i) \;=\;& z^{\alpha}+\sup_{\pi\in\mathcal{A}}\mathbb{E}_{t,z,i}\int_t^T z^{\alpha}\Bigg[\alpha\Big(r(s-)+\sum_{j=0}^{N}\pi_j(s)(\mu_j(s-)-r(s-))+\sum_{k=2}^{\infty}\pi^{(k)}(s)(\mu^{(k)}(s)-r(s-))\\
&+\sum_{i=0}^{N}\sum_{l=1}^{\infty}\pi_i^{(l)}(s)(\mu_i^{(l)}(s)-r(s-))+\frac{1}{2}(\alpha-1)\pi_0^2(s)\sigma_0^2(s-)\Big)\\
&+\sum_{j=1}^{N}\Big((1+\pi_j(s)\sigma_j(s-))^{\alpha}-1-\alpha\pi_j(s)\sigma_j(s-)\Big)\lambda_j(s)\\
&+\int_{\mathbb{R}}\Bigg(\Big(1+\pi_0(s)\gamma(s-,x)+\sum_{k=2}^{\infty}\pi^{(k)}(s)\sigma^{(k)}(s-)\gamma^k(s-,x)\Big)^{\alpha}\\
&-1-\alpha\Big(\pi_0(s)\gamma(s-,x)+\sum_{k=2}^{\infty}\pi^{(k)}(s)\sigma^{(k)}(s-)\gamma^k(s-,x)\Big)\Bigg)\nu(\mathrm{d}x)\\
&+\sum_{i=1}^{N}\int_{\mathbb{R}}\Bigg(\Big(1+x\pi_0(s)+\sum_{l=1}^{\infty}x^l\pi_i^{(l)}(s)\sigma_i^{(l)}(s-)\Big)^{\alpha}-1\\
&-\alpha\Big(x\pi_0(s)+\sum_{l=1}^{\infty}x^l\pi_i^{(l)}(s)\sigma_i^{(l)}(s-)\Big)\Bigg)\lambda_i(s)\eta(\mathrm{d}x)\Bigg]\mathrm{d}s.\end{aligned}$$

By direct differentiation with respect to each strategy, this supremum is attained if the strategies satisfy the system in Equation (44). Observe that, from Equation (9), the integrals

$$\int_{\mathbb{R}}\Bigg(\Big(1+\pi_0(s)\gamma(s-,x)+\sum_{k=2}^{\infty}\pi^{(k)}(s)\sigma^{(k)}(s-)\gamma^k(s-,x)\Big)^{\alpha}$$
$$-1-\alpha\Big(\pi_0(s)\gamma(s-,x)+\sum_{k=2}^{\infty}\pi^{(k)}(s)\sigma^{(k)}(s-)\gamma^k(s-,x)\Big)\Bigg)\nu(\mathrm{d}x)$$

and (for $i=1,\dots,N$)

$$\int_{\mathbb{R}}\Bigg(\Big(1+x\pi_0(s)+\sum_{l=1}^{\infty}x^l\pi_i^{(l)}(s)\sigma_i^{(l)}(s-)\Big)^{\alpha}-1-\alpha\Big(x\pi_0(s)+\sum_{l=1}^{\infty}x^l\pi_i^{(l)}(s)\sigma_i^{(l)}(s-)\Big)\Bigg)\lambda_i(s)\eta(\mathrm{d}x)$$

are well-defined. Hence, by the Leibniz integral rule, we can interchange the derivatives and integrals. □

Remark 6. *We have not been able to prove that a solution of Equation (44) exists and is unique. However, if we consider a finite market, then this solution exists and is unique and must be the optimal portfolio by Kramkov and Schachermayer (1999, Thm. 2.2). In $\pi_j^*(t)$, one can observe the dependence of this strategy on Sharpe ratio.*

Remark 7. *If the prices of assets in the Black–Scholes–Merton market are described by processes without jumps (that is, $\bar{\Pi}(\mathrm{d}t,\mathrm{d}x) = 0$ and $\bar{\Pi}_U^i(\mathrm{d}t,\mathrm{d}x) = 0$), then we obtain closed-form solutions to the optimal portfolio selection problem in Equation (40) for the logarithmic and power utilities (Zhang et al. 2010). In addition, the value function in the primary market is the same as in the enlarged market, while in our market this does not occur.*

7. Optimal Portfolio Selection in the Original Market

In this section, we find conditions for optimal portfolio strategies in the original market, i.e., in the market with one risk-free asset and one share.

Let $\tilde{\pi}_0$ be the proportion of wealth invested in share S_0 in the original market. Then, the corresponding wealth process, denoted as $R^{\tilde{\pi}_0}$, is given by the stochastic differential equation

$$\begin{aligned}\frac{\mathrm{d}R_{\tilde{\pi}_0}(t)}{R_{\tilde{\pi}_0}(t-)} &:= \Big(r(t-) + \tilde{\pi}_0(t)\big(\mu_0(t-) - r(t-)\big)\Big)\mathrm{d}t + \tilde{\pi}_0(t)\sigma_0(t-)\mathrm{d}W(t) \\ &\quad + \tilde{\pi}_0(t)\int_{\mathbb{R}}\gamma(t-,x)\bar{\Pi}(\mathrm{d}t,\mathrm{d}x) + \tilde{\pi}_0(t)\sum_{i=1}^{N}\int_{\mathbb{R}}x\bar{\Pi}_U^i(\mathrm{d}t,\mathrm{d}x).\end{aligned}$$

Let $\mathcal{A}_0$ be the class of admissible portfolio strategies $\tilde{\pi}_0$ such that $\tilde{\pi}_0$ is predictable, $\{\mathcal{F}_t\}$-adaptable and satisfies the condition $\int_t^T |\tilde{\pi}_0(s)|^2\mathrm{d}s < \infty, \mathbb{P}-\text{a.s.}$ Similar to the definition of the value function in the enlarged market, we define the value function in the original incomplete market as

$$V_0(t,z,\mathbf{e}_i) := \sup_{\tilde{\pi}_0\in\mathcal{A}_0} \mathbb{E}_{t,z,i}\big[U(R^{\tilde{\pi}_0}(T))\big]. \tag{45}$$

We assume $\mathbb{E}_{t,z,i}\big[U(R_{\tilde{\pi}_0}(T))\big] < \infty$ for $i = 1,\ldots,N$.

First, we consider the logarithmic utility function. We have

$$\begin{aligned}\mathbb{E}_{t,z,i}\big[\log R_{\tilde{\pi}_0}(T)\big] &= \log z + \mathbb{E}_{t,z,i}\int_t^T\Big[r(s-) + \tilde{\pi}_0(s)\big(\mu_0(s-) - r(s-)\big) - \frac{1}{2}\tilde{\pi}_0^2(s)\sigma_0^2(s-) \\ &\quad + \int_{\mathbb{R}}\Big(\log\big(1+\tilde{\pi}_0(s)\gamma(s-,x)\big) - \tilde{\pi}_0(s)\gamma(s-,x)\Big)\nu(\mathrm{d}x) \\ &\quad + \sum_{i=1}^{N}\int_{\mathbb{R}}\Big(\log\big(1+x\tilde{\pi}_0(s)\big) - x\tilde{\pi}_0(s)\Big)\lambda_i(s)\eta(\mathrm{d}x)\Big]\mathrm{d}s,\end{aligned}$$

that is, for the logarithmic utility, the value function V_0 can be written as follows:

$$\begin{aligned}V_0(t,z,\mathbf{e}_i) &= \log z + \sup_{\tilde{\pi}_0\in\mathcal{A}_0}\mathbb{E}_{t,z,i}\int_t^T\Big[r(s-) + \tilde{\pi}_0(s)\big(\mu_0(s-) - r(s-)\big) - \frac{1}{2}\tilde{\pi}_0^2(s)\sigma_0^2(s-) \\ &\quad + \int_{\mathbb{R}}\Big(\log\big(1+\tilde{\pi}_0(s)\gamma(s-,x)\big) - \tilde{\pi}_0(s)\gamma(s-,x)\Big)\nu(\mathrm{d}x) \\ &\quad + \sum_{i=1}^{N}\int_{\mathbb{R}}\Big(\log\big(1+x\tilde{\pi}_0(s)\big) - x\tilde{\pi}_0(s)\Big)\lambda_i(s)\eta(\mathrm{d}x)\Big]\mathrm{d}s.\end{aligned}$$

From Equation (9), the integrals

$$\int_{\mathbb{R}}\Big(\log\big(1+\tilde{\pi}_0(s)\gamma(s-,x)\big) - \tilde{\pi}_0(s)\gamma(s-,x)\Big)\nu(\mathrm{d}x)$$

and (for $i = 1, \dots, N$)

$$\int_{\mathbb{R}} \Big(\log\left(1 + x\tilde{\pi}_0(s)\right) - x\tilde{\pi}_0(s) \Big) \lambda_i(s)\eta(\mathrm{d}x)$$

are well-defined. Hence, by the Leibniz integral rule, we can differentiate the above integrals with respect to $\tilde{\pi}_0$. The above supremum is attained if $\tilde{\pi}_0$ solves the equation

$$\mu_0(s-) - r(s) - \sigma_0^2(s-)\tilde{\pi}_0(s) + \int_{\mathbb{R}} \left(\frac{\gamma(s-,x)}{1 + \tilde{\pi}_0(s)\gamma(s-,x)} - \gamma(s-,x) \right) \nu(\mathrm{d}x) \\ + \sum_{i=1}^{N} \int_{\mathbb{R}} \left(\frac{x}{1 + x\tilde{\pi}_0(s)} - x \right) \lambda_i(s)\eta(\mathrm{d}x) = 0. \tag{46}$$

In the case of the power utility, the value function V_0 can be written as

$$\begin{aligned} V_0(t,z,\mathbf{e}_i) \;=\; & z^\alpha + \sup_{\tilde{\pi}_0 \in \mathcal{A}_0} \mathbb{E}_{t,z,i} \int_t^T \Bigg[\alpha z^\alpha \Big(r(s-) + \tilde{\pi}_0(s)\big(\mu_0(s-) - r(s-)\big) + \frac{1}{2}(\alpha - 1)\tilde{\pi}_0^2(s)\sigma_0^2(s-) \Big) \\ & + \int_{\mathbb{R}} z^\alpha \Big(\Big(1 + \tilde{\pi}_0(s)\gamma(s-,x)\Big)^\alpha - 1 - \alpha\tilde{\pi}_0(s)\gamma(s-,x) \Big) \nu(\mathrm{d}x) \\ & + \sum_{i=1}^{N} \int_{\mathbb{R}} z^\alpha \Big(\Big(1 + x\tilde{\pi}_0(s)\Big)^\alpha - 1 - \alpha x\tilde{\pi}_0(s) \Big) \lambda_i(s)\eta(\mathrm{d}x) \Bigg] \mathrm{d}s. \end{aligned}$$

Note that, from Equation (9), the integrals

$$\int_{\mathbb{R}} z^\alpha \Big(\Big(1 + \tilde{\pi}_0(s)\gamma(s-,x)\Big)^\alpha - 1 - \alpha\tilde{\pi}_0(s)\gamma(s-,x) \Big) \nu(\mathrm{d}x)$$

and (for $i = 1, \dots, N$)

$$\int_{\mathbb{R}} z^\alpha \Big(\Big(1 + x\tilde{\pi}_0(s)\Big)^\alpha - 1 - \alpha x\tilde{\pi}_0(s) \Big) \lambda_i(s)\eta(\mathrm{d}x)$$

are well-defined. By direct differentiation in Equation (47) with respect to $\tilde{\pi}_0$, we get

$$\mu_0(s-) - r(s) - (\alpha - 1)\sigma_0^2(s-)\tilde{\pi}_0(s) + \int_{\mathbb{R}} \Big(\gamma(s-,x)\big(1 + \tilde{\pi}_0(s)\gamma(s-,x)\big)^{\alpha-1} - \gamma(s-,x) \Big) \nu(\mathrm{d}x) \\ + \sum_{i=1}^{N} \int_{\mathbb{R}} \Big(x\big(1 + x\tilde{\pi}_0(s)\big)^{\alpha-1} - x \Big) \lambda_i(s)\eta(\mathrm{d}x) = 0. \tag{47}$$

Lemma 2. *The solutions of Equations (46) and (47) are optimal strategies for the portfolio selection problem in Equation (45) for the logarithmic and power utilities, respectively.*

Proof. We prove that solutions of Equations (46) and (47) are optimal portfolio strategies; their existence was proved by Kramkov and Schachermayer (1999). Let $\tilde{\pi}_0^\varepsilon := \tilde{\pi}_0 + \varepsilon$ be a perturbed portfolio strategy for $\varepsilon > 0$.

We define the value function V_0^ε related to the strategy $\tilde{\pi}_0^\varepsilon$ (Fouque et al. 2017a, 2017b; Mokkhavesa and Atkinson 2002) as follows:

$$V_0^\varepsilon(t,z,\mathbf{e}_i) := \sup_{\tilde{\pi}_0^\varepsilon \in \mathcal{A}_0} \mathbb{E}_{t,z,i}\big[U(R_{\tilde{\pi}_0^\varepsilon}(T))\big].$$

In the case of the logarithmic utility,

$$\begin{aligned} V_0^\varepsilon(t,z,\mathbf{e}_i) &= \log z + \sup_{\tilde{\pi}_0\in\mathcal{A}_0} \mathbb{E}_{t,z,i} \int_t^T \Big[r(s-) + (\tilde{\pi}_0(s)+\varepsilon)\big(\mu_0(s-)-r(s-)\big) - \frac{1}{2}(\tilde{\pi}_0(s)+\varepsilon)^2\sigma_0^2(s-) \\ &+ \int_{\mathbb{R}} \Big(\log\big(1+(\tilde{\pi}_0(s)+\varepsilon)\gamma(s-,x)\big) - (\tilde{\pi}_0(s)+\varepsilon)\gamma(s-,x) \Big)\nu(\mathrm{d}x) \\ &+ \sum_{i=1}^N \int_{\mathbb{R}} \Big(\log\big(1+x(\tilde{\pi}_0(s)+\varepsilon)\big) - x(\tilde{\pi}_0(s)+\varepsilon) \Big)\lambda_i(s)\eta(\mathrm{d}x) \Big] \mathrm{d}s, \end{aligned}$$

and for the power utility,

$$\begin{aligned} V_0^\varepsilon(t,z,\mathbf{e}_i) &= z^\alpha + \sup_{\tilde{\pi}_0\in\mathcal{A}_0} \mathbb{E}_{t,z,i} \int_t^T \Big[\alpha z^\alpha \Big(r(s-) + (\tilde{\pi}_0(s)+\varepsilon)\big(\mu_0(s-)-r(s-)\big) \\ &+ \frac{1}{2}(\alpha-1)(\tilde{\pi}_0(s)+\varepsilon)^2\sigma_0^2(s-) \Big) \\ &+ \int_{\mathbb{R}} z^\alpha \Big(\Big(1+(\tilde{\pi}_0(s)+\varepsilon)\gamma(s-,x)\Big)^\alpha - 1 - \alpha(\tilde{\pi}_0(s)+\varepsilon)\gamma(s-,x) \Big)\nu(\mathrm{d}x) \\ &+ \sum_{i=1}^N \int_{\mathbb{R}} z^\alpha \Big(\Big(1+x(\tilde{\pi}_0(s)+\varepsilon)\Big)^\alpha - 1 - \alpha x(\tilde{\pi}_0(s)+\varepsilon) \Big)\lambda_i(s)\eta(\mathrm{d}x) \Big] \mathrm{d}s. \end{aligned}$$

Note that $\tilde{\pi}_0$ is a portfolio strategy that maximizes the value function, so $\frac{\partial}{\partial\varepsilon}V_0^\varepsilon\Big|_{\varepsilon=0} = 0$. Calculating this derivative for V_0^ε in both cases, we get Equations (46) and (47).

Thus, the optimal portfolio strategies solve these equations. The existence and uniqueness of the optimal strategies follows from Kramkov and Schachermayer (1999). In that paper, the main assumption concerns the utility function, which has to have asymptotic elasticity strictly less than 1, that is,

$$\overline{\lim_{z\to\infty}} \frac{zU'(z)}{U(z)} < 1.$$

Note that the power and logarithmic utilities satisfy this condition. □

Remark 8. *In a general semi-martingale market model, Goll and Kallsen (2000, 2003) obtained the optimal solution explicitly in terms of semi-martingale characteristics of the price process for the logarithmic utility.*

Author Contributions: Methodology, Z.P. and Ł.S.; Formal Analysis, A.S., Z.P. and Ł.S.; Investigation, A.S., Z.P. and Ł.S.; Writing—Original Draft Preparation, A.S.; Writing—Review and Editing, A.S., Z.P. and Ł.S.; Visualization, A.S.; Supervision, Z.P. and Ł.S.; Project Administration, Z.P. and Ł.S.; and Funding Acquisition, Z.P.

Funding: This paper was supported by the National Science Centre under the grant 2016/23/B/HS4/00566 (2017–2020).

Acknowledgments: Anna Sulima would like to thank Monique Pontier (Université Paul Sabatier, Toulouse) for plenty of helpful suggestions that improved this paper.

Conflicts of Interest: The authors declare no conflict of interest. The funders had no role in the design of the study; in the collection, analyses, or interpretation of data; in the writing of the manuscript, or in the decision to publish the results.

Appendix A

Proof of Lemma 1. We define
$$U_M(z) := U(z)\mathbf{1}_{\{z:|U(z)|\le M\}}.$$

The convergence of R_π^K to R_π in $L^2(\Omega,\mathcal{F},\mathbb{P})$ given in Equation (38) implies the convergence in probability of R_π^K to R_π as $K\to\infty$ (see Jacod and Protter (2004, Thm. 17.2)).

Thus, for the bounded and continuous function U_M given above, we have

$$\lim_{K\to\infty}\mathbb{E}_{t,z,i}\big[U_M(R_\pi^K(T))\big]=\mathbb{E}_{t,z,i}\big[U_M(R_\pi(T))\big] \tag{A1}$$

(see Jacod and Protter (2004, Thm. 18.1)). Note that

$$\mathbb{E}_{t,z,i}\big[U(R_\pi^K(T))\big]=\mathbb{E}_{t,z,i}\big[U_M(R_\pi^K(T))\big]+\mathbb{E}_{t,z,i}\big[U(R_\pi^K(T))\mathbf{1}_{\{R_\pi^K(T):|U(R_\pi^K(T))|>M\}}\big]. \tag{A2}$$

From the concavity of U, it follows that $U(z)\le b+cz$ for each $z\ge 0$ and some real $b,c\ge 0$. Thus, the second term on the right-hand side of Equation (A2) satisfies

$$\mathbb{E}_{t,z,i}\big[U(R_\pi^K(T))\mathbf{1}_{\{R_\pi^K(T):|U(R_\pi^K(T))|>M\}}\big] \;\le\; b+c\,\mathbb{E}_{t,z,i}\big[R_\pi^K(T)\mathbf{1}_{\{R_\pi^K(T):|U(R_\pi^K(T))|>M\}}\big].$$

Now, we prove that

$$\lim_{K\to\infty}\mathbb{E}_{t,z,i}\big[R_\pi^K(T)\mathbb{I}^K(T)\big]=\mathbb{E}_{t,z,i}\big[R_\pi(T)\mathbb{I}(T)\big], \tag{A3}$$

where
$$\mathbb{I}^K(T):=\mathbf{1}_{\{R_\pi^K(T):|U(R_\pi^K(T))|>M\}}\ \text{ and }\ \mathbb{I}(T):=\mathbf{1}_{\{R_\pi(T):|U(R_\pi(T))|>M\}}.$$

Note that

$$\begin{aligned}
&\mathbb{E}_{t,z,i}\big|R_\pi^K(T)\mathbb{I}^K(T)-R_\pi(T)\mathbb{I}(T)\big|\\
&\le\Big[\mathbb{E}_{t,z,i}\big(R_\pi^K(T)-R_\pi(T)\big)^2\Big]^{\frac12}\Big[\mathbb{E}_{t,z,i}\big(\mathbb{I}(T)\big)\Big]^{\frac12}\\
&\quad+\Big[\mathbb{E}_{t,z,i}\big(R_\pi(T)\big)^2\Big]^{\frac12}\Big[\mathbb{E}_{t,z,i}\big(\mathbb{I}(T)-\mathbb{I}^K(T)\big)^2\Big]^{\frac12}\\
&\quad+\Big[\mathbb{E}_{t,z,i}\big(R_\pi^K(T)\big)^2\Big]^{\frac12}\Big[\mathbb{E}_{t,z,i}\big(\mathbb{I}^K(T)-\mathbb{I}(T)\big)^2\Big]^{\frac12}\\
&\quad+\Big[\mathbb{E}_{t,z,i}\big(R_\pi(T)\big)^2\Big]^{\frac12}\Big[\mathbb{E}_{t,z,i}\big(\mathbb{I}^K(T)-\mathbb{I}(T)\big)^2\Big]^{\frac12}.
\end{aligned} \tag{A4}$$

Indeed, from the triangle inequality, we obtain

$$\begin{aligned}
&\mathbb{E}_{t,z,i}\big|R_\pi^K(T)\mathbb{I}^K(T)-R_\pi(T)\mathbb{I}(T)\big|\\
&\le\ \mathbb{E}_{t,z,i}\big|R_\pi^K(T)\mathbb{I}^K(T)-R_\pi^K(T)\mathbb{I}(T)\big|+\mathbb{E}_{t,z,i}\Big|R_\pi^K(T)\mathbb{I}(T)-R_\pi(T)\mathbb{I}^K(T)\Big|\\
&\quad+\mathbb{E}_{t,z,i}\Big|R_\pi(T)\mathbb{I}^K(T)-R_\pi(T)\mathbb{I}(T)\Big|.
\end{aligned} \tag{A5}$$

Moreover, using Hölder's inequality, we get

$$\mathbb{E}_{t,z,i}\Big|R_\pi^K(T)\mathbb{I}^K(T)-R_\pi^K(T)\mathbb{I}(T)\Big|\le\Big[\mathbb{E}_{t,z,i}\big(R_\pi^K(T)\big)^2\Big]^{\frac12}\Big[\mathbb{E}_{t,z,i}\big(\mathbb{I}^K(T)-\mathbb{I}(T)\big)^2\Big]^{\frac12} \tag{A6}$$

and

$$\mathbb{E}_{t,z,i}\left|R_\pi(T)\mathbb{I}^K(T) - R_\pi(T)\mathbb{I}(T)\right| \le \left[\mathbb{E}_{t,z,i}(R_\pi(T))^2\right]^{\frac{1}{2}}\left[\mathbb{E}_{t,z,i}(\mathbb{I}^K(T) - \mathbb{I}(T))^2\right]^{\frac{1}{2}}. \tag{A7}$$

Finally, from the triangle inequality and Hölder's inequality, we derive

$$\begin{aligned} &\mathbb{E}_{t,z,i}\left|R_\pi^K(T)\mathbb{I}(T) - R_\pi(T)\mathbb{I}^K(T)\right| \\ \le\ &\left[\mathbb{E}_{t,z,i}(R_\pi^K(T) - R_\pi(T))^2\right]^{\frac{1}{2}}\left[\mathbb{E}_{t,z,i}(\mathbb{I}(T))\right]^{\frac{1}{2}} \\ &+ \left[\mathbb{E}_{t,z,i}(R_\pi(T))^2\right]^{\frac{1}{2}}\left[\mathbb{E}_{t,z,i}(\mathbb{I}(T) - \mathbb{I}^K(T))^2\right]^{\frac{1}{2}}. \end{aligned} \tag{A8}$$

Combining Equations (A5)–(A8), we get the inequality in Equation (A4).

Now, we prove that

$$\mathbb{I}^K \to \mathbb{I} \tag{A9}$$

in $L^2(\Omega, \mathcal{F}, \mathbb{P})$ as $K \to \infty$.

First, we verify this convergence in probability. Indeed, for any $\varepsilon > 0$, there exists $\delta > 0$ such that

$$\begin{aligned} \mathbb{P}(|\mathbb{I}^K(T) - \mathbb{I}(T)| > \varepsilon) &= \mathbb{P}(\{U(R_\pi^K(T)) > M, U(R_\pi(T)) < M\} \cup \{U(R_\pi^K(T)) < M, U(R_\pi(T)) > M\}) \\ &\le \mathbb{P}(|U(R_\pi^K(T)) - U(R_\pi(T))| > \delta). \end{aligned}$$

The right-hand side of the above inequality tends to zero as $K \to \infty$, since the convergence in probability of R_π^K to R_π yields the convergence in probability of $U(R_\pi^K)$ to $U(R_\pi)$ (see Jacod and Protter (2004, Thm. 17.5)).

Moreover, we have

$$\mathbb{I}^K(T) \le 1,$$

thus $\{\mathbb{I}^K\}_{K=2}^\infty$ is uniformly integrable and

$$\lim_{K\to\infty} \mathbb{I}^K(T) = \mathbb{I}(T)$$

in $L^2(\Omega, \mathcal{F}, \mathbb{P})$ (see Gut (2005, Thm. 4.5, p. 216 and Thm. 5.4, p. 221)). This completes the proof of Equation (A9).

By Equations (38) and (A9), the right-hand side of the inequality in Equation (A4) tends to 0 as $K \to \infty$. This completes the proof of Equation (A3).

From Equation (A3), it follows that

$$\overline{\lim_{K\to\infty}}\, \mathbb{E}_{t,z,i}\left[U(R_\pi^K(T))\mathbf{1}_{\{R_\pi^K(T):|U(R_\pi^K(T))|>M\}}\right]$$

is well-defined. Thus, as $M \to \infty$, the second term on the right-hand side of Equation (A2) tends to zero. Moreover, the first term converges to $\mathbb{E}_{t,z,i}\left[U(R_\pi(T))\right]$ by (A1). This completes the proof. □

References

Artzner, Philippe, and David Heath. 1995. Approximate completeness with multiple martingale measures. *Mathematical Finance* 5: 1–11.

Asmussen, Søren. 2003. *Applied Probability and Queues*, 2nd ed; Berlin and Heidelberg: Springer.

Asmussen, Søren, and Offer Kella. 2000. Multi-dimensional martingale for Markov additive processes and its applications. *Advances in Applied Probability* 32: 376–80. [CrossRef]

Bae, Geum, Woo Chang Kim, and John M. Mulvey. 2014. Dynamic asset allocation for varied financial markets under regime switching framework. *European Journal of Operational Research* 234: 450–58. [CrossRef]

Barndorff-Nielsen, Ole E., and Neil Shephard. 2003. Realised power variation and stochastic volatility models. *Bernoulli* 9: 243–65. [CrossRef]

Barndorff-Nielsen, Ole E., and Neil Shephard. 2004. *Financial Volatility: Stochastic Volatility and Lévy Based Models*. Cambridge: Cambridge University Press.

Bättig, Robert. 1999. Completeness of securities market models-an operator point of view. *Annals of Applied Probability* 9: 529–66. [CrossRef]

Bättig, Robert, and Robert A. Jarrow. 1999. The second fundamental theorem of asset pricing: A new approach. *The Review of Financial Studies* 12: 1219–35. [CrossRef]

Bäuerle, Nicole, and Ulric Rieder. 2004. Portfolio optimization with Markov-modulated stock prices and interest rates. *IEEE Transactions on Automatic Control* 49: 442–47. [CrossRef]

Bäuerle, Nicole, and Ulric Riede. 2007. Portfolio optimization with jumps and unobservable intensity process. *Mathematical Finance* 17: 205–24. [CrossRef]

Björk, Tomas, and Bertil Näslund. 1998. Diversified portfolios in continuous time. *European Financial Review* 1: 361–87. [CrossRef]

Black, Fischer, Michael C. Jensen, and Myron Scholes. 1972. Some Empirical Tests, Studies in the Theory of Capital Markets. In *Studies in the Theory of Capital Markets*. Edited by M. Jensen. New York: Praeger, pp. 79–121.

Boel, René, and Michael Kohlmann. 1980. Semimartingale models of stochastic optimal control, with applications to double Martingales. *SIAM Journal on Control and Optimization* 18: 511–33. [CrossRef]

Buffington, John, and Robert J. Elliott. 2002. American options with regime switching. *International Journal of Theoretical and Applied Finance* 5: 497–514. [CrossRef]

Busch, Michael, Ralf Korn, and Frank Thomas Seifried. 2013. Optimal consumption and investment for a large investor: An intensity-based control framework. *Mathematical Finance* 23: 687–717. [CrossRef]

Çinlar, Erhan. 1972a. Markov additive processes: I. *Zeitschrift Wahrscheinlichkeitstheorie und verwandte Gebiete* 24: 85–93. [CrossRef]

Çinlar, Erhan. 1972b. Markov additive processes: II. *Zeitschrift Wahrscheinlichkeitstheorie und verwandte Gebiete* 24: 95–121. [CrossRef]

Corcuera, José Manuel, Joao Guerra, David Nualart, and Wim Schoutens. 2006. Optimal investment in a Lévy market. *Applied Mathematics and Optimization* 53: 279–309. [CrossRef]

Corcuera, José Manuel, David Nualart, and Wim Schoutens. 2005. Completion of a Lévy market by power-jump assets. *Finance and Stochastics* 9: 109–27. [CrossRef]

Cuchiero, Christa, Irene Klein, and Josef Teichmann. 2016. A new perspective on the fundamental theorem of asset pricing for large financial markets. *Theory of Probability and its Applications* 60: 561–79. [CrossRef]

Di Masi, Giovanni Battista, Yuri M. Kabanov, and Wolfgang J. Runggaldier. 1994. Mean variance hedging of options on stocks with Markov volatility. *Theory of Probability and Applications* 39: 173–81. [CrossRef]

Elliott, Rogemar J., Lakhdar Aggoun, and John B. Moore. 1994. *Hidden Markov Models: Estimation and Control*. Berlin: Springer.

Elliott, Rogemar J., Leunglung Chan, and Tak Kuen Siu. 2005. Option pricing and esscher transform under regime switching. *Annals of Finance* 1: 423–32. [CrossRef]

Elliott, Rogemar J., William C. Hunter, and Barbara M. Jamieson. 2001. Financial signal processing: A self calibrating model. *International Journal of Theoretical and Applied Finance* 4: 567–84. [CrossRef]

Elliott, Rogemar J., W. P. Malcolm, and Allanus H. Tsoi. 2003. Robust parameter estimation for asset price models with Markov modulated volatilities. *Journal of Economic Dynamics and Control* 27: 1391–409. [CrossRef]

Fechner, Włodzimierz. 2008. Some inequalities connected with the exponential function. *Archivum Mathematicum (Brno)* 44: 217–22.

Fleming, Wendell H., and Daniel Hernández-Hernández. 2003. An optimal consumption model with stochastic volatility. *Finance and Stochastics* 7: 245–62. [CrossRef]

Fontana, Claudio, Bernt Øksendal, and Agnès Sulem. 2015. Market viability and martingale measures under partial information. *Methodology and Computing in Applied Probability* 17: 15–39. [CrossRef]

Fouque, Jean-Pierre, Andrew Papanicolaou, and Ronnie Sircar. 2017a. Perturbation Analysis for Investment Portfolios Under Partial Information with Expert Opinions. *SIAM Journal on Control and Optimization* 55: 1534–66. [CrossRef]

Fouque, Jean-Pierre, Ronnie Sircar, and T. Zariphopoulou. 2017b. Portfolio optimization and stochastic volatility asymptotics. *Mathematical Finance* 27: 704–45. [CrossRef]

Framstad, Nils Chr., Bernt Øksendal, and Agnes Sulem. 2004. Sufficient stochastic maximum principle for the optimal control of jump diffusions and applications to finance. *Journal of Optimization Theory and Applications* 121: 77–98. [CrossRef]

Fu, Jun, Jiaqin Wei, and Hailiang Yang. 2014. Portfolio optimization in a regime-switching market with derivatives. *European Journal of Operational Research* 233: 184–92. [CrossRef]

Gautam, Natarajan, Vidyadhar Kulkarni, Zbigniew Palmowski, and Tomasz Rolski. 1999. Bounds for fluid models driven by semi-Markov inputs. *Probability in Engineering and Information Sciences* 13: 429–75. [CrossRef]

Goldfeld, Stephen M., and Richard E. Quandt. 1973. A Markov model for switching regressions. *Journal of Econometrics* 1: 3–16. [CrossRef]

Goll, Thomas, and Jan Kallsen. 2000. Optimal portfolios for logarithmic utility. *Stochastic Processes and their Applications* 89: 31–48. [CrossRef]

Goll, Thomas, and Jan Kallsen. 2003. A complete explicit solution to the log-optimal portfolio problem. *The Annals of Applied Probability* 13: 774–99.

Guo, Xin. 2001. Information and option pricings. *Quantitative Finance* 1: 38–44. [CrossRef]

Guo, Xin, Jianjun Miao, and Erwan Morellec. 2005. Irreversible investments with regime shifts. *Journal of Economic Theory* 122: 37–59. [CrossRef]

Gut, Allan. 2005. *Probability: A Graduate Course*. New York: Springer.

Hamilton, James D. 1989. A new approach to the economics analysis of non-stationary time series. *Econometrica* 57: 357–84. [CrossRef]

Heston, Steven. 1993. A closed-form solution for options with stochastic volatility with applications to bond and currency options. *Review of Financial Studies* 6: 327–43. [CrossRef]

Jacod, Jean, and Philip Protter. 2004. *Probability Essentials*, 2nd ed. Berlin and Heidelberg: Springer.

Kabanov, Yuri, and Dmitry Kramkov. 1994. Large financial markets: Asymptotic arbitrage and contiguity. *Probability Theory and Its Applications* 39: 222–29. [CrossRef]

Kabanov, Yuri, and Dmitry Kramkov. 1998. Asymptotic arbitrage in large financial markets. *Finance and Stochastics* 2: 143–72. [CrossRef]

Karatzas, Ioannis, John P. Lehoczky, Steven E. Shreve, and Gan-Lin Xu. 1991. Martingale and duality methods for utility maximization in an incomplete market. *SIAM Journal on Control and Optimization* 29: 702–30. [CrossRef]

Karatzas, Ioannis, and Steven E. Shreve. 1998. *Brownian Motion and Stochastic Calculus*. Berlin, Heidelberg and New York: Springer.

Korn, Ralf, Yaroslav Melnyk, and Frank Thomas Seifried. 2017. Stochastic impulse control with regime-switching dynamics. *European Journal of Operational Research* 260: 1024–42. [CrossRef]

Korn, Ralf, and H. Kraft. 2001. A stochastic control approach to portfolio problems with stochastic interest rates. *SIAM Journal on Control and Optimization* 40: 1250–69. [CrossRef]

Kramkov, Dmitry, and Walter Schachermayer. 1999. The asymptotic elasticity of utility functions and optimal investment in incomplete markets. *Annals of Applied Probability* 9: 904–50. [CrossRef]

Kreps, David M. 1981. Arbitrage and equilibrium in economies with infinitely many commodities. *Journal of Mathematical Economics* 8: 15–35. [CrossRef]

Kushner, Harold J., and Paul G. Dupuis. 1992. *Numerical Methods for Stochastic Control Problems in Continuous Time*. New York: Springer.

Liao, Ming. 2004. *Lévy Processes in Lie Groups*. Cambridge Tracts in Mathematics. Cambridge: Cambridge University Press, vol. 162.

Liu, Ruihua. 2014. Optimal investment and consumption with proportional transaction costs in regime-switching model. *Journal of Optimization Theory and Applications* 163: 614–41. [CrossRef]

Markowitz, Harry M. 1952. Portfolio selection. *The Journal of Finance* 7: 77–91.

Merton, Robert C. 1971. Optimal consumption and portfolio rules in a continuous time model. *Journal of Economic Theory* 3: 373–413. [CrossRef]

Merton, Robert C. 1976. Option pricing when underlying stock returns are discontinuous. *Journal of Financial Economics* 3: 125–44. [CrossRef]

Merton, Robert C. 1980. On estimating the expected return on the market. *Journal of Financial Economics* 8: 323–61. [CrossRef]

Mokkhavesa, Sutee, and Colin Atkinson. 2002. Perturbation solution of optimal portfolio theory with transaction costs for any utility function. *IMA Journal of Management Mathematics* 13: 131–51. [CrossRef]

Nagai, Hideo, and Wolfgang J. Runggaldier. 2008. PDE Approach to Utility Maximization for Market Models with Hidden Markov Factors. In *Seminar on Stochastic Analysis, Random Fields and Applications V, Progress in Probability*. Edited by R. C. Dalang, M. Dozzi and F. Russo. Basel: Birkhuser Verlag, vol. 59, pp. 493–506.

Naik, Vasanttilak. 1993. Option valuation and hedging strategies with jumps in the volatility of asset returns. *Journal of Finance* 48: 1969–84. [CrossRef]

Niu, Liqun. 2008. Some stability results of optimal investment in a simple Lévy market. *Insurance Mathematics Economics* 42: 445–52. [CrossRef]

Øksendal, Bernt, and Agnès Sulem. 2004. *Applied Stochastic Control of Jump Diffusions*. Berlin and Heidelberg: Springer.

Pacheco, António, Loon Ching Tang, and Narahari U. Prabhu. 2009. *Markov-Modulated Processes and Semigenerative Phenomena*. Hackensack: World Scientific.

Palmowski, Zbigniew, Łukasz Stettner, and Anna Sulima. 2018. A note on chaotic and predictable representations for Itô-Markov additive processes. *Stochastic Analysis and Applications* 36: 622–38. [CrossRef]

Pham, Huyên Pham, and Marie-Claire Quenez. 2001. Optimal portfolio in partially observed stochastic volatility models. *The Annals of Applied Probability* 11: 210–38. [CrossRef]

Prabhu, Narahari U. 1998. *Stochastic Storage Processes: Queues, Insurance Risk, Dams, and Data Communication*, 2nd ed. Berlin and Heidelberg:Springer.

Protter, Philip E. 2005. *Stochastic Integration and Differential Equations: A New Approach*, 2nd ed. Berlin: Springer.

Resnick, Sidney I. 2007. *Heavy-Tail Phenomena. Probabilistic and Statistical Modeling*. New York: Springer.

Rieder, Ulrich, and Nicole Bäuerle. 2005. Portfolio optimization with unobservable markov-modulated drift process. *Journal of Applied Probability* 42: 362–78. [CrossRef]

Sass, Jörn, and Ulrich G. Haussmann. 2004. Optimizing the terminal wealth under partial information: The drift process as a continuous time markov chain. *Finance and Stochastics* 8: 553–77. [CrossRef]

Schoutens, Wim. 1999. *Stochastic Processes and Orthogonal Polynomials*. Lecture Notes in Statistics. New York: Springer, vol. 146.

Shen, Yang, and Tak Kuen Siu. 2012. Asset allocation under stochastic interest rate with regime switching. *Economic Modelling* 29: 1126–36. [CrossRef]

Sotomayor, Luz R., and Abel Cadenillas. 2013. Stochastic impulse control with regime switching for the optimal dividend policy when there are business cycles, taxes and fixed costs. *Stochastics: An International Journal of Probability and Stochastic Processes* 85: 707–22. [CrossRef]

Stockbridge, Richard. 2002. Portfolio optimization in markets having stochastic rates. In *Lecture Notes in Control and Information Sciences: Stochastic Theory and Control*. Edited by B. Pasik-Duncan. Berlin: Springer, vol. 280, pp. 447–58.

Teplá, Lucie. 2000. Optimal portfolio policies with borrowing and shortsale constraints. *Journal of Economic Dynamics and Control* 24: 1623–39. [CrossRef]

Tong, Howell. 1978. *Threshold Models in Non-linear Time Series Analysis*. Berlin: Springer.

Tu, Jun. 2010. Is regime switching in stock returns important in asset allocations? *Management Science* 56: 1198–215. [CrossRef]

Yin, George, and Xun Yu Zhou. 2004. Markowitz's mean-variance portfolio selection with regime switching: From discrete-time models to their continuous-time limits. *IEEE Transactions on Automatic Control* 49: 349–60. [CrossRef]

Zariphopoulou, Thaleia. 1992. Investment-consumption models with transaction fees and markov-chain parameters. *SIAM Journal on Control and Optimization* 30: 613–36. [CrossRef]

Zhang, Xin, Robert J. Elliott, Tak Kuen Siu, and Junyi Guo. 2012. Markovian regime-switching market completion using additional Markov jump assets. *IMA Journal of Management Mathematics* 23: 283–305. [CrossRef]

Zhang, Qing. 2001. Stock trading: An optimal selling rule. *SIAM Journal on Control and Optimization* 40: 64–87. [CrossRef]

Zhang, Xin, Tak Kuen Siu, and Qingbin Meng. 2010. Porfolio selection in the enlarged Markovian regime-switching market. *SIAM Journal on Control and Optimization* 48: 3368–88. [CrossRef]

Zhou, Xun Yu, and George Yin. 2003. Markowitz's Mean-Variance Portfolio Selection with Regime Switching: A Continuous Time Model. *SIAM Journal on Control and Optimization* 42: 1466–82. [CrossRef]

Zhang, Qing, and George Yin. 2004. Nearly-optimal asset allocation in hybrid stock investment models. *Journal of Optimization Theory and Applications* 121: 197–222. [CrossRef]

10

Phase-Type Models in Life Insurance: Fitting and Valuation of Equity-Linked Benefits

Søren Asmussen [1,*], Patrick J. Laub [2] and Hailiang Yang [3]

1 Department of Mathematics, Aarhus University, 8000 Aarhus, Denmark
2 Institut de Science Financière et d'Assurances, Université Lyon 1, 69007 Lyon, France; patrick.laub@univ-lyon1.fr
3 Department of Statistics & Actuarial Science, Hong Kong University, Hong Kong 999077, China; hlyang@hku.hk
* Correspondence: asmus@math.au.dk

Abstract: Phase-type (PH) distributions are defined as distributions of lifetimes of finite continuous-time Markov processes. Their traditional applications are in queueing, insurance risk, and reliability, but more recently, also in finance and, though to a lesser extent, to life and health insurance. The advantage is that PH distributions form a dense class and that problems having explicit solutions for exponential distributions typically become computationally tractable under PH assumptions. In the first part of this paper, fitting of PH distributions to human lifetimes is considered. The class of generalized Coxian distributions is given special attention. In part, some new software is developed. In the second part, pricing of life insurance products such as guaranteed minimum death benefit and high-water benefit is treated for the case where the lifetime distribution is approximated by a PH distribution and the underlying asset price process is described by a jump diffusion with PH jumps. The expressions are typically explicit in terms of matrix-exponentials involving two matrices closely related to the Wiener-Hopf factorization, for which recently, a Lévy process version has been developed for a PH horizon. The computational power of the method of the approach is illustrated via a number of numerical examples.

Keywords: generalized Coxian distribution; EM algorithm, guaranteed minimum death benefit; high-water benefit; jump diffusion, matrix-analytic methods; reserves; Wiener-Hopf factorization

---

1. Introduction

A random variable (r.v.) τ is phase-type (PH) with representation $(\boldsymbol{\alpha}, \boldsymbol{T})$ if it is distributed as the lifetime $\inf\{t \geq 0 : J_t = \dagger\}$ of a killed (terminating) time-homogenous Markov process $J = \{J_t\}_{t\geq 0}$ with $p < \infty$ states, initial distribution $\boldsymbol{\alpha}$ (a row vector), and generator $\boldsymbol{T}$, where $\dagger$ is an additional absorbing state. PH distributions originate from queueing theory and the work of A.K. Erlang, A. Jensen and M.F. Neuts. However, in recent decades, they have found numerous applications to different areas. The main reason for this is that many calculations that are explicit for exponential distributions are often computationally tractable with PH assumptions and that, in addition, PH distributions are dense so that a given distribution F on $[0, \infty)$ can be approximated arbitrarily well by a PH distribution provided one takes p large enough. For surveys of the theory and applications, see (Asmussen 2003; Asmussen and Albrecher 2010; Bladt and Nielsen 2017). The present paper is concerned with some applications to life insurance, an area where PH distributions have been far less employed than in the related areas of non-life insurance. There are many papers in ruin theory that assume that claim sizes are PH distributed; see (Cai and Li 2005b) and the review paper (Bladt 2005). Some papers assume that the claim time is PH distributed; see (Stanford et al. 2000).

(Zadeh et al. 2014) considered disability insurance using a PH model. (Zadeh and Stanford 2016) studied credibility theory using PH distributions. In finance, PH distributions have also been used extensively. For example, (Asmussen et al. 2004) considered option pricing under an exponential phase-type Lévy model; (Cai and Li 2005a) dealt with applications of PH distributions to risk measures; and (Egami and Yamazaki 2014) considered PH approximations of Lévy models. On the contrary, the only references of applications of PH distributions to life insurance we know of are (Lin and Liu 2007) and (Zadeh et al. 2014).

The motivation for the present study is some valuation problems of equity-linked products in life insurance considered in Gerber et al. (2012, 2013, 2015) (GSY). Let $\tau = \tau_x$ be the remaining lifetime of an insured of age x when signing the contract, then the payment of this class of benefits has the form $\Psi(\overline{S}_\tau, S_\tau)$ where S_t is the price at time t of some stock or stock index and $\overline{S}_t = \max_{v \le t} S_t$ the running maximum. An example of such a benefit is the guaranteed minimum death benefit (GMDB) $\max(S_\tau, K)$, but there are many others; see the list in Section 4. Defining X_t as $X_t = \log(S_t/S_0)$, $M_t = \overline{X}_t$ as the running maximum of X, and $D_t = M_t - X_t$ as the displacement from the maximum, we then have:

$$\Psi(\overline{S}_\tau, S_\tau) = \Phi(M_\tau, D_\tau) \qquad \text{where } \Phi(m,d) = \Psi(S_0 e^m, S_0 e^{m-d}) \tag{1}$$

(note that $X_t = M_t - D_t$), and the fair value of the benefit is the expected discounted payment.

A widely-used model (Cont and Tankov 2004) assumes that $X = \{X_t\}_{t \ge 0}$ is a Lévy process, and the key vehicle in GSY for the computations for such expectations is the classical Wiener-Hopf factorization:

Lemma 1. *For a Lévy process X_t and an independent exponential time τ, the r.v.'s $M_\tau = \max_{0 \le s \le \tau} X_s$ and $D_\tau = M_\tau - X_\tau$ are independent. Further,*

$$D_\tau \stackrel{d}{=} -\underline{X}_\tau = -\min_{0 \le s \le \tau} X_s\,.$$

For the geometric Brownian motion model where X is a Brownian motion (BM) with drift, M_τ and D_τ both have an exponential distribution, and for more general jump diffusions, a number of computational procedures have been developed (see Section 5 for references). In GSY, they approximate the density/tail of τ_x by a linear combination of exponential terms, which allows them to reduce the computations to simple integrations using Lemma 1.

The approximation of the distribution of τ_x by a linear combination of exponential terms in GSY uses an ad hoc optimization procedure. The main problem there is that it is very difficult to make the linear combination of exponential densities to be a density function; in particular, very often, in the tail part, the linear combination of exponential densities can be negative. Since, in the application to valuing equity-linked insurance products, the distribution at the tail part plays an important role, this motivated us to consider using the PH distribution to approximate the future lifetime distribution. For PH distributions, more classical statistical methods using maximum likelihood have, however, been developed (Asmussen et al. 1996), and in view of the denseness of PH distributions and the fact that they have proven a computationally-tractable generalization of the exponential distribution in other settings, a natural idea is therefore to use a PH approximation τ to τ_x. The first step in implementing this for pricing equity-linked benefits is to develop a version of the Wiener-Hopf factorization for the case where τ is PH and independent of X. This has been done in a companion paper (Asmussen and Ivanovs 2019), and the contribution of the present paper is to provide the further steps such as PH fitting of human mortality and computations of prices of equity-linked benefits for BM and jump diffusions.

2. Preliminaries

The vector of killing rates of a PH$(\boldsymbol{\alpha}, \boldsymbol{T})$ r.v. τ is given by $\boldsymbol{t} = -\boldsymbol{T}\boldsymbol{1}$, where $\boldsymbol{1}$ is a column vector with all entries equal to one. The density is $\boldsymbol{\alpha}e^{\boldsymbol{T}z}\boldsymbol{t}$, and the tail $\mathbb{P}(\tau > z)$ is $\boldsymbol{\alpha}e^{\boldsymbol{T}z}\boldsymbol{1}$. Here, the exponential $e^{\boldsymbol{R}}$ of a matrix is defined as $\sum_0^\infty \boldsymbol{R}^n/n!$. We shall often use formulas like:

$$\int_a^b e^{\boldsymbol{R}x}\,dx = \boldsymbol{R}^{-1}(e^{\boldsymbol{R}b} - e^{\boldsymbol{R}a}) = (e^{\boldsymbol{R}b} - e^{\boldsymbol{R}a})\boldsymbol{R}^{-1}, \quad \int_0^\infty e^{\boldsymbol{R}x}\,dx = -\boldsymbol{R}^{-1},$$

that are immediate analogues of standard formulas for univariate exponentials. For example, taking $\boldsymbol{R} = -s\boldsymbol{I} + \boldsymbol{T}$ gives the Laplace transform $\mathbb{E}[e^{-s\tau}]$ as $\boldsymbol{\alpha}(s\boldsymbol{I} - \boldsymbol{T})^{-1}\boldsymbol{t}$. Of course, the existence of $\boldsymbol{R}^{-1}$ has to be verified, which for a PH generator $\boldsymbol{R} = \boldsymbol{T}$ is a standard fact.

The subclass of generalized Coxian (GC) distributions will play a particular role. Here, the states are run through in lexicographical order, with exponential (λ_i) holding time in state i, and it is possible to enter or exit from any state (see Figure 1), where q_i is the probability of exit after a visit to i and $r_i = 1 - q_i$ the probability of going to the next state. The structure of Coxian distributions is similar, except that only State 1 can be entered so that $\alpha_1 = 1$. Coxian distributions are in particular used in (Lin and Liu 2007) and (Zadeh et al. 2014).

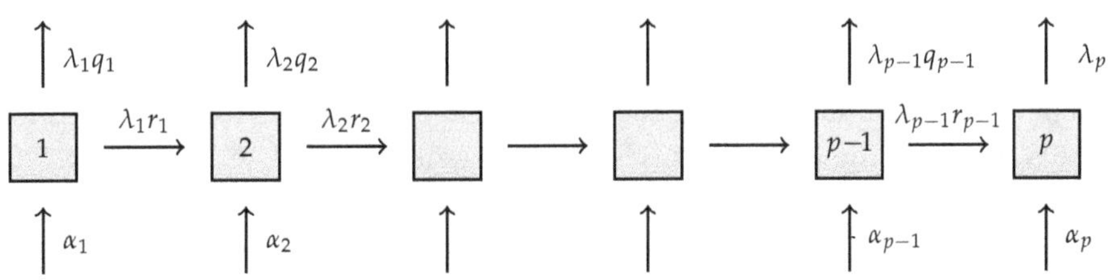

Figure 1. A GC distribution.

Remark 1. Though computational tractability and denseness are the main reasons for the popularity of PH distributions, other advantages have also sometimes been advocated. For example, whereas in the majority of examples, the PH modeling is purely descriptive, there are others where attempts have been made to give the Markov states a physical meaning like in compartment models and, in the life insurance context, in (Lin and Liu 2007) and (Zadeh et al. 2014). This makes the number p of phases quite large there, of order 200, whereas we have taken the descriptive point of view. The fit obviously becomes better when increasing p, but how good it needs to be depends very much on what it will be used for. In this paper, we consider the valuation problem, that is to calculate the net premium (expected discounted payoff) for equity-linked insurance products, and our numerical examples will show that taking $p = 50$ will be sufficient for the precision one needs in this context.

3. PH Fits of Human Mortality Data

The distribution of human lifetimes of course varies somewhat according to the period where the data were collected, geographical and social conditions, etc., but the basic shapes are much alike. We have therefore concentrated on a single example, the illustrative life table in Appendix 2A of (Bowers et al. 1997). The form of the distribution, as illustrated via the number of deaths in consecutive years, is given in Figure 2.

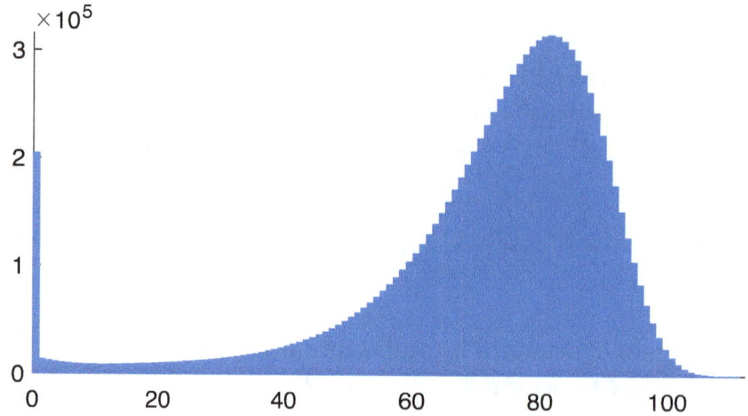

Figure 2. Life table data.

We use an EM algorithm to fit various types of phase-type distributions to this life table. This idea was originally developed in (Asmussen et al. 1996), with the case of censored data and other implementation details given in (Olsson 1996). Olsson (Olsson 1998) has written a C implementation of this algorithm called EMpht, which is available online. The overwhelming computational burden is in the E step, where many complicated integrals involving matrix exponentials must be evaluated. This is done approximately by converting the problem into a system of ODEs, which are approximately solved via a Runge-Kutta method. While the original C implementation is still very adequate for creating fits with a small number of phases p, it can be improved upon for larger p.

We wrote a new implementation using the Julia language. It allows for the E step to be evaluated in three different ways: (i) using an ODE solver (as in (Asmussen et al. 1996; Olsson 1996)), (ii) using quadrature methods, and (iii) using the uniformization method of Okamura et al. Okamura et al. (2011a, 2011b). We used this last method to generate the fits found later in this paper; the code we used to create the figures below will be made available online (Asmussen et al. 2019). Each fit was given one hour execution time restricted to one thread on the processor Intel(R) Xeon(R) CPU E5-2698 v4 @ 2.20 GHz. The EM algorithm could have been terminated much earlier without a major difference to the quality of the fits, but as we were comparing the various values of p, we wanted to ensure no individual fit was judged poorly for simply being stuck in a local maxima.

The PH representation in terms of $\boldsymbol{\alpha}, \boldsymbol{T}$ is heavily overparameterized. There is an abundance of sets $\boldsymbol{\alpha}, \boldsymbol{T}$ that leads to the same distribution. Consider, e.g., the PH with $\boldsymbol{\alpha} = \frac{1}{p}\mathbf{1}^{\mathsf{T}}$ (where ^{T} stands for transposition) and where $\boldsymbol{T}$ is a diagonal matrix with $(-1, -2, \ldots, -p)$ on the diagonal (i.e., a hyperexponential distribution). If the diagonal elements in $\boldsymbol{T}$ are permuted in any of the $p!$ possibilities, then the distribution is unchanged. This example indicates that the maximum ℓ^* of the likelihood function ℓ is attained at several parameter values so that the choice of the initial parameter set will determine which one is found by the EM algorithm. The presence of local maxima with values $< \ell^*$ cannot be excluded, but we are not aware of serious cases where the EM algorithm has been stuck in one of these.

In life insurance calculations, the relevant lifetime is not the overall one τ_0, but rather the remaining lifetime $\tau = \tau_x$ of the insured at the time when he/she signs the contract. That is, if the age of the insured at that time is x, the relevant distribution is that of $\tau_0 - x$ given $\tau_0 \geq x$. As a typical example, we took $x = 35$ and fitted PH distributions with various structure and various numbers p of phases. Note that while we fit the distribution of $\tau_0 - x$, which starts at zero, in the following, we plot τ_0 given $\tau_0 \geq x$ (i.e., the x axes begin at $x = 35$ and not zero).

As a first illustration, we fit both a general structure PH and a generalized Coxian (GC) one with $p = 20$ phases. The results are in Figure 3, with the densities of the fitted PH distributions in the left panel together with the data and the corresponding hazard rates in the right panel.

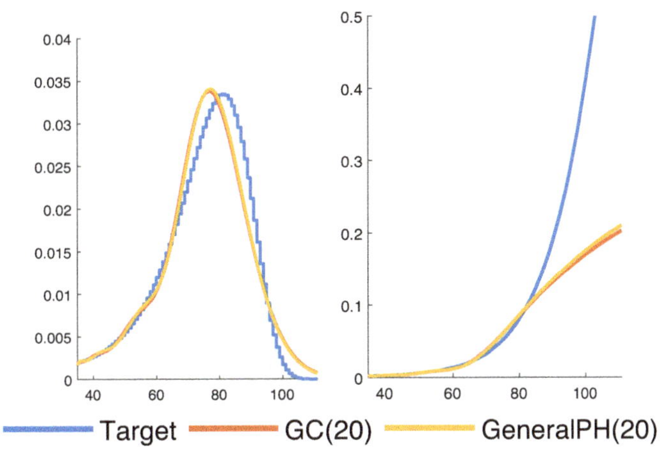

Figure 3. Probability density functions and hazard rate functions for the life table and phase-type (PH) fits using the general and the generalized Coxian (GC) structures with $p = 20$ phases.

The fits of the two structures are almost identical (but the shape of the density is somewhat off the data, which indicates that a larger valuer of p could be appropriate). The general structure leads to a system of ODEs of dimension $q = p^2 + p$, whereas the corresponding number for GC is only $q = 2p - 1$. Due to this curse of dimensionality and the marginal differences of the fits, we have only considered GC structures for higher values of p

Figure 4 shows GC fits for $p = 35$ and $p = 40$. As expected, $p = 40$ improves upon $p = 35$.

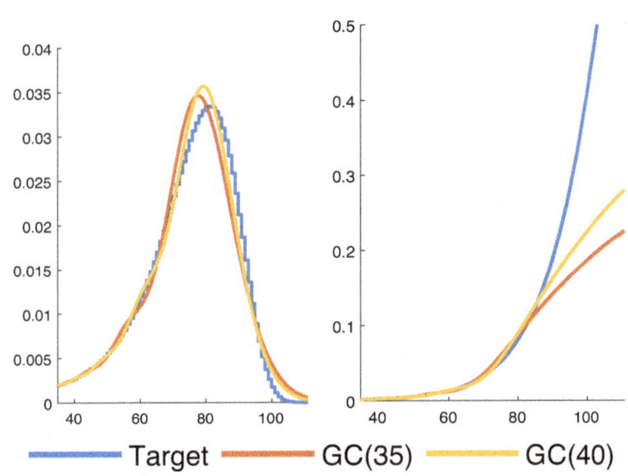

Figure 4. Probability density functions and hazard rate functions for the life table and phase-type fits using the generalized Coxian structures with $p = 35, 40$ phases.

In Figure 5, we complement Figure 4 by plots of the tails. Such plots are frequently used to illustrate the quality of fits, but in our minds, a good agreement is not an argument in itself: two tails may come out quite similar in a comparison even if the shapes of the densities are rather different. Finally, Figure 6 gives GC fits with $p = 50, 75, 100$.

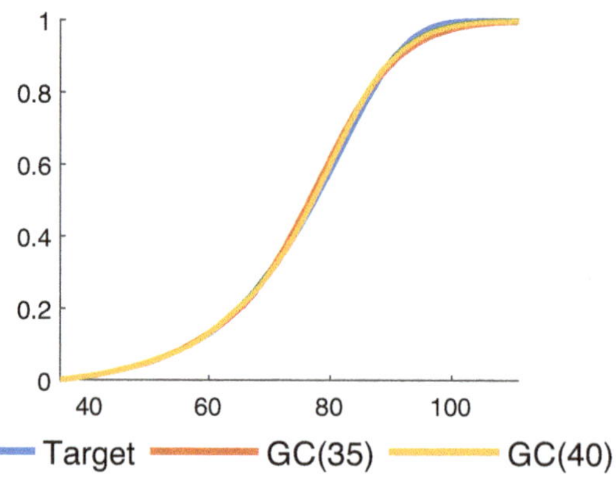

Figure 5. Tails of the life table and GC fits with $p = 35, 40$ phases.

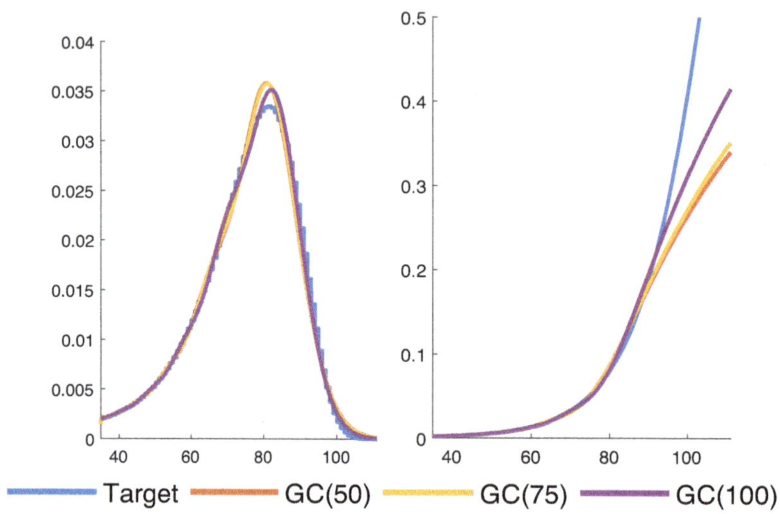

Figure 6. Probability density functions and hazard rate functions for the life table and GC fits with $p = 50, 75, 100$ phases.

Which value of p should one then work with? There exists hardly a single criterion for answering such questions, i.e., assessing the quality of the fits to the data. Some concerns may be aesthetic, such as avoiding negative values of the density (cf. Appendix A below), support outside the obvious range of the data (cf. kernel estimates), or an excessive number of parameters (as is the case for most PH fits as compared to, e.g., the classical Gompertz-Makeham fit of life table data). Other concerns may have to do with the features of the distribution which are considered especially important, be it the overall shape of the density (caught well by maximum likelihood), the cumulative distribution function (c.d.f.), although c.d.f.'s may look close even for rather different distributions, the tail (where maximum likelihood fails and other tools such as the Hill estimator may be more appropriate), the hazard rate (as showing up in numerous life insurance contexts), or the behavior in a more narrow range (cf. a life insurance contract signed at the start of employment and running up to the time of retirement). For the present purposes and related ones like applications in queueing and insurance risk, the main point is, however, that PH fitting is not done for its own sake, but for the purpose of facilitating some calculation, here of the prices of equity-linked products, in queueing, say of waiting time characteristics, etc. In the rest of the paper, we therefore study the performance of the PH approach and the various fits and return to a discussion of the issue in the concluding Section 8.

4. Valuation of Benefits

The main application of the results in this paper is valuing equity-linked insurance products, in particular GMDBs in various deferred annuities. The time of payment of this kind of product is at the time τ of death of the policyholder, often denoted τ_x, where x is his/her age at $t = 0$ when he/she signs the contract. The amount of the payment depends on the price S_τ of a stock (or stock index) at that time and possibly also on the history of the stock price as, e.g., in (1). There are many different products (benefit functions) in the market. One example is the GMDB with benefit function being:

$$\Psi(\overline{S}_\tau, S_\tau) = \max(S_\tau, K) = S_\tau + [K - S_\tau]_+, \tag{2}$$

where K is the guaranteed amount, e.g., $K = 0.9S_0$. The second term on the right-hand side (r.h.s.) of (2) is the payoff of a life-contingent put option. Another popular product is the so-called high-water benefit (HWB) with the payoff function being:

$$\Psi(\overline{S}_\tau, S_\tau) = \overline{S}_\tau.$$

Another form of the HWB function is:

$$\Psi(\overline{S}_\tau, S_\tau) = \max(a\overline{S}_\tau, S_\tau)$$

where $0 < a < 1$. Since:

$$\max(a\overline{S}_\tau, S_\tau) = S_\tau + \max(a\overline{S}_\tau - S_\tau, 0), \tag{3}$$

the second term on the r.h.s. of (3) is the payoff of a life-contingent fractional lookback option.

In practice, the policyholders can withdraw. Note that the payment of the GMDB can be written as the payoff of a put option (plus a share of underlying stock). When the stock price rises, put options become less valuable; hence, policies may lapse. This motivates considering the benefit function:

$$\Psi(\overline{S}_\tau, S_\tau) = I_{\{\overline{S}_\tau < H\}}[K - S_\tau]_+,$$

where $I_{\{.\}}$ is the indicator function and H is a "barrier". This is a barrier option payoff form.

Since we can approximate the distribution of τ_x by a PH distribution, the valuation problem becomes calculating:

$$\mathbb{E}[\mathrm{e}^{-\delta\tau}\Psi(\overline{S}_\tau, S_\tau)], \tag{4}$$

where δ denotes a discounting factor and τ is PH r.v. One example is to take δ as the force of interest, but the company may want to use a lower δ in its technical reserve to ensure a conservative pricing.

5. The Factorization: Implementation for Jump Diffusions

Our basic assumption is that X is a jump diffusion with Brownian parameters μ, σ^2, upward jumps at rate λ_1 and with a $\mathrm{PH}(p_1, \boldsymbol{\alpha}_1, \boldsymbol{T}_1)$ distribution of the sizes, and similar parameters $\lambda_2, p_2, \boldsymbol{\alpha}_2, \boldsymbol{T}_2$ for the downward jumps.

We will first need to introduce the equivalent time-reversed PH representation $(\boldsymbol{\alpha}^*, \boldsymbol{T}^*)$ of τ. It is obtained by considering:

$$J_t^* = \begin{cases} J_{(\tau-t)-}, & \text{if } t < \tau, \\ \dagger, & \text{otherwise.} \end{cases}$$

It turns out (Asmussen 2003, III.5) that J^* is a terminating time-homogeneous Markov process with initial distribution $\boldsymbol{\alpha}^*$ and generator $\boldsymbol{T}^*$ given by:

$$\boldsymbol{\alpha}^* = \mathbb{E}\tau \cdot \boldsymbol{t}^\mathsf{T}\boldsymbol{\Delta}_\nu, \quad \boldsymbol{T}^* = \boldsymbol{\Delta}_\nu^{-1}\boldsymbol{T}^\mathsf{T}\boldsymbol{\Delta}_\nu, \tag{5}$$

where $\boldsymbol{\Delta}_\nu$ denotes the diagonal matrix with the positive vector $\boldsymbol{\nu} = -\boldsymbol{\alpha}\boldsymbol{T}^{-1}$ on the diagonal. To see this, consider a doubly-infinite stationary Markovian arrival process (Asmussen 2003, XI.1) with generator $\boldsymbol{T} + \boldsymbol{D}$, where $\boldsymbol{D} = \boldsymbol{t}\boldsymbol{\alpha}$ gives the rates of phase changes with arrivals, and note that the corresponding stationary distribution of the phase process is proportional to $\boldsymbol{\nu}$. Now, just use the standard time reversion for non-killed Markov processes. Considering, for the ease of exposition, the case $\delta = 0$ of no discounting, the form of the factorization identity of (Asmussen and Ivanovs 2019) that is most convenient for our purposes is then:

$$\mathbb{P}(M_\tau \in \mathrm{d}x, D_\tau \in \mathrm{d}y) = \sum_{k=1}^{p} \frac{1}{c_k} \mathbb{P}^*_{\boldsymbol{\alpha}}(M_\tau \in \mathrm{d}x, J_{\overline{\sigma}_\tau} = k) \mathbb{P}^*_{\boldsymbol{\alpha}^*}(M_\tau \in \mathrm{d}y, J_{\overline{\sigma}_\tau} = k), \tag{6}$$

where $\mathbb{P}^*$ is the probability measure where τ is generated by the time-reversed representation and X evolves as $-X$ did under $\mathbb{P}$, $\overline{\sigma}_\tau$ is the time at which the maximum is attained, and $c_k = \mathbb{P}_{\boldsymbol{\alpha}}(J_{\overline{\sigma}_\tau} = k) = \mathbb{P}^*_{\boldsymbol{\alpha}^*}(J_{\overline{\sigma}_\tau} = k)$.

The distributions of M_τ, D_τ are particularly simple if X is BM(μ, σ^2) and τ exponential (λ). In fact, they are then exponential with rates ρ^+, respectively ρ^-, where:

$$\rho^{\pm} = \mp \frac{\mu}{\sigma^2} + \sqrt{\frac{\mu^2}{\sigma^4} + \frac{2\lambda}{\sigma^2}}.$$

If more generally, $X(t)$ is a jump diffusion with both up- and down-ward PH jumps, there is an abundance of results and algorithms giving the distributions in various representations or their Laplace transforms. See, among others, (Bean et al. 2005; Breuer 2008; Dieker and Mandjes 2011; Horváth and Telek 2017; Jacobsen 2005; Jiang and Pistorius 2008; Lewis and Mordecki 2008; Mordecki 2002; Pistorius 2006). The most appropriate form for our purposes is that for (computable) matrices $\boldsymbol{U}, \boldsymbol{U}^*$ of dimension $p(1+p_1) \times p(1+p_1)$, respectively $p(1+p_2) \times p(1+p_2)$, one has:

$$\mathbb{P}_i(M_\tau \in \mathrm{d}x,\ J_{\overline{\sigma}} = k) = \boldsymbol{e}_i^{\mathsf{T}} \mathrm{e}^{\boldsymbol{U}x} \boldsymbol{e}_k \cdot u_k \tag{7}$$

$$\mathbb{P}^*_j(M_\tau \in \mathrm{d}y, J_{\overline{\sigma}_\tau} = k) = \boldsymbol{e}_j^{\mathsf{T}} \mathrm{e}^{\boldsymbol{U}^* y} \boldsymbol{e}_k \cdot u_k^* \tag{8}$$

where u_k, u_k^* are the kth element of the vectors $-\boldsymbol{U}\boldsymbol{e}$, respectively $-\boldsymbol{U}^*\boldsymbol{e}$; this occurs already in (Asmussen 1995), as well as several later sources, but we have in fact used a new and (we feel) somewhat more straightforward approach; see Appendix B.

Multiplying (7), (8) by α_i, respectively α_j^* and summing over i, j, the factorization (6) then takes the form:

$$\mathbb{P}(M_\tau \in \mathrm{d}x, D_\tau \in \mathrm{d}y) = \sum_{k=1}^{p} r_k \cdot \boldsymbol{\alpha} \mathrm{e}^{\boldsymbol{U}x} \boldsymbol{e}_k \cdot \boldsymbol{\alpha}^* \mathrm{e}^{-\boldsymbol{U}^* y} \boldsymbol{e}_k$$

where $r_k = u_k u_k^* / c_k$. The modification with discounting is explained in Section 4 of (Asmussen and Ivanovs 2019) and becomes:

$$\mathbb{E}[\mathrm{e}^{-\delta\tau}; M_\tau \in \mathrm{d}x, D_\tau \in \mathrm{d}y] = \sum_{k=1}^{p} r_k \cdot \boldsymbol{\alpha} \mathrm{e}^{\boldsymbol{U}_\delta x} \boldsymbol{e}_k \cdot \boldsymbol{\alpha}^* \mathrm{e}^{-\boldsymbol{U}_\delta^* y} \boldsymbol{e}_k \tag{9}$$

where $\boldsymbol{U}_\delta$, $\boldsymbol{U}_\delta^*$ are calculated as $\boldsymbol{U}, \boldsymbol{U}^*$ with $\boldsymbol{T}$ replaced by $\boldsymbol{T} - \delta \boldsymbol{I}$ (here, the r_k remain unchanged, i.e., u_k, u_k^* and c_k are computed for the case $\delta = 0$). This can be rewritten in matrix form as follows:

Corollary 1. (i) *For* $x, y \geq 0$,

$$\mathbb{E}[\mathrm{e}^{-\delta\tau}; M_\tau \in \mathrm{d}x, D_\tau \in \mathrm{d}y] = \boldsymbol{\alpha} \mathrm{e}^{\boldsymbol{U}_\delta x} \boldsymbol{\Delta}_r \mathrm{e}^{\boldsymbol{U}_\delta^{*\mathsf{T}} y} \boldsymbol{\alpha}^{*\mathsf{T}} = \boldsymbol{\alpha}^* \mathrm{e}^{\boldsymbol{U}_\delta^* y} \boldsymbol{\Delta}_r \mathrm{e}^{\boldsymbol{U}_\delta^{\mathsf{T}} x} \boldsymbol{\alpha}^{\mathsf{T}};$$

(ii) *For functions* f *and* g,

$$\mathbb{E}\left[\mathrm{e}^{-\delta\tau} f(M_\tau) g(D_\tau)\right] = \boldsymbol{\alpha} F_{\boldsymbol{U}_\delta} \boldsymbol{\Delta}_r G_{\boldsymbol{U}_\delta^*}^{\mathsf{T}} \boldsymbol{\alpha}^{*\mathsf{T}} = \boldsymbol{\alpha}^* G_{\boldsymbol{U}_\delta^*} \boldsymbol{\Delta}_r G_{\boldsymbol{U}_\delta}^{\mathsf{T}} \boldsymbol{\alpha}^{\mathsf{T}}$$

where F_{U_δ}, $G_{U_\delta^*}$ *are the matrices* $\int_0^\infty f(x)\mathrm{e}^{U_\delta x}\,\mathrm{d}x$, *respectively* $\int_0^\infty g(y)\mathrm{e}^{U_\delta^* y}\,\mathrm{d}y$.

Proof. Since $\alpha^*\mathrm{e}^{-U_\delta^* y}e_k \in \mathbb{R}^1$, it may be replaced by its transpose $e_k^{\mathsf{T}}\mathrm{e}^{-U_\delta^{*\mathsf{T}} y}\alpha^{*\mathsf{T}}$ in (9), and this gives the first identity in (i); the second follows by transposition. Part (ii) then follows by integration. □

For computations, the matrix form rather than the sum form is convenient for keeping the code short and transparent, and in many software packages like MATLAB, it also is faster. In a number of our examples, the matrices F_U, G_{U^*} come out in a simple form, avoiding integration. Here is a first example:

Example 1. For the HWB, we need to compute:

$$\mathbb{E}\big[\mathrm{e}^{-\delta\tau}\max(a\overline{S}_\tau, S_\tau)\big] = S_0\mathbb{E}\big[\mathrm{e}^{-\delta\overline{\tau}}\mathrm{e}^{M_\tau}\cdot\mathrm{e}^{-\delta\underline{\tau}}\max(a,\mathrm{e}^{-D_\tau})\big]. \tag{10}$$

Thus (assuming $S_0 = 1$ w.l.o.g.), we have $f(x) = \mathrm{e}^x$, $g(y) = \max(a, \mathrm{e}^{-y})$ in Part (ii) of Corollary 1, and we get:

$$\begin{aligned} F_{U_\delta} &= \int_0^\infty \mathrm{e}^x\mathrm{e}^{U_\delta x}\,\mathrm{d}x = -(I+U_\delta)^{-1}, \\ G_{U_\delta^*} &= a\int_{-\log a}^\infty \mathrm{e}^{U_\delta^* y}\,\mathrm{d}y + \int_0^{-\log a}\mathrm{e}^{-y}\mathrm{e}^{U_\delta^* y}\,\mathrm{d}y \\ &= -a\mathrm{e}^{-U_\delta^*\log a}U_\delta^{*-1} + (I - a\mathrm{e}^{-U_\delta^*\log a})(I-U_\delta^*)^{-1}. \end{aligned}$$

◇

Corollary 2. *Define* $S_\delta = \int_0^\infty \mathrm{e}^{U_\delta y}\Delta_r\mathrm{e}^{U_\delta^{*\mathsf{T}} y}\,\mathrm{d}y$. *Then:*

$$\mathbb{E}[\mathrm{e}^{-\delta\tau}; X_\tau \in \mathrm{d}x] = \begin{cases} \alpha\mathrm{e}^{U_\delta x}S_\delta\alpha^{*\mathsf{T}} & \text{for } x > 0 \\ \alpha^*\mathrm{e}^{-U_\delta^* x}S_\delta^{\mathsf{T}}\alpha^{\mathsf{T}} & \text{for } x < 0. \end{cases}$$

Proof. For $x > 0$, we have:

$$\mathbb{E}[\mathrm{e}^{-\delta\tau}; X_\tau \in \mathrm{d}x] = \int_0^\infty \mathbb{E}[\mathrm{e}^{-\delta\tau}; M_\tau \in \mathrm{d}x + y, D_\tau \in \mathrm{d}y],$$

and so, the result follows immediately by Part (ii) of Corollary 1. The proof for $x < 0$ is similar; one only has to note that if S_δ^* is defined as S_δ with U_δ and U_δ^* interchanged, then $S_\delta^* = S_\delta^{\mathsf{T}}$. □

Remark 2. The distribution of X_τ restricted to $(0,\infty)$ is in fact (defective) PH, but in general, with a different generator $\widetilde{U}$ than $U = U_0$ (for this one would have needed that $S_\delta\alpha^{*\mathsf{T}}$ be proportional to $-Ue$). This follows from the general fact that if $\alpha, s \geq 0$ and T is a phase generator, but possibly $s \neq -Te$, then $\alpha\mathrm{e}^{Tx}s = \widetilde{\alpha}\mathrm{e}^{\widetilde{T}x}\widetilde{t}$ where:

$$\widetilde{\alpha} = \alpha\Delta_v,\ \ \widetilde{T} = \Delta_v^{-1}T\Delta_v,\ \ \widetilde{t} = -\widetilde{T}e = \Delta_v^{-1}s \ \text{ with } v = -T^{-1}s,$$

and here, $\widetilde{T}$ is a phase generator; all needed positivity properties follow from S_δ and $-T^{-1}$ being non-negative.

Similar remarks apply to the negative part of X_τ. These observations may be seen as an extension to jump diffusions at PH times of the standard fact that Brownian motion at an independent exponential time has a two-sided exponential distribution (often called the Laplace distribution). A similar result for matrix-exponential distributions is on p. 478 of (Bladt and Nielsen 2017), but is in terms of Laplace transforms rather than densities.

Example 2. For the GMDB, the price is (taking $S_0 = 1$):

$$\mathbb{E}[e^{-\delta\tau}\max(S_\tau, K)] = K\mathbb{E}[e^{-\delta\tau}; X_\tau \le \log K] + \mathbb{E}[e^{-\delta\tau + X_\tau}; X_\tau > \log K].$$

In the most common case $K < S_0$, the first term equals:

$$K\int_{-\infty}^{\log K} \alpha^* e^{-U_\delta^* x} S_\delta^\mathsf{T} \alpha^\mathsf{T}\, dx = -K\alpha^* U_\delta^{*-1} e^{-U_\delta^* \log K} S_\delta^\mathsf{T} \alpha^\mathsf{T}$$

when $S_0 = 1$, whereas the second is:

$$\int_{\log K}^{0} e^x \alpha^* e^{-U_\delta^* x} S_\delta^\mathsf{T} \alpha^\mathsf{T}\, dx + \int_0^\infty e^x \alpha e^{U_\delta x} S_\delta \alpha^{*\mathsf{T}}\, dx$$
$$= \alpha^*(I - U_\delta^*)^{-1}(I - Ke^{-U_\delta^* \log K}) S_\delta^\mathsf{T} \alpha^\mathsf{T} - \alpha(I + U_\delta)^{-1} S_\delta \alpha^{*\mathsf{T}}.$$

◇

Example 3. The calculation of reserves:

$$V_t = \mathbb{E}\big[e^{-\delta(\tau - t)}\Phi(M_\tau, D_\tau)\,\big|\, X_s, 0 \le s \le t, \tau > t\big]$$

is closely related to price calculations. However, the details may be somewhat more cumbersome since for a fixed t, the expressions for M_τ, D_τ have two components, the quantities $m_0 = \max_{s \le t} X_s$ and $d_0 = m_0 - X_t$, which are known at time t, and the unknown random ones:

$$m_1 = \max_{t \le s < \tau}(X_s - X_t), \quad d_1 = m_1 - x_1 \text{ where } x_1 = X_\tau - X_t.$$

In terms of these and the relations:

$$\begin{aligned} M_\tau &= \max(m_0, x_0 + m_1), \\ D_\tau &= \max(m_0, x_0 + m_1) - x_0 - x_1 = \max(d_0, d_1) - x_1 \\ &= [d_0 - m_1]^+ + d_1, \end{aligned}$$

we can write $\Phi(M_\tau, D_\tau) = \widetilde{\Phi}(m_1, d_1)$, where:

$$\widetilde{\Phi}(x, y) = \Phi(\max(m_0, x_0 + x), [d_0 - x]^+ + y).$$

Since the conditional distribution of $\tau - t$ given $\tau > t$ is PH(α_t, T) where $\alpha_t = \alpha e^{Tt}/\alpha e^{Tt} e$, this gives:

$$V_t = \int_0^\infty \int_0^\infty \widetilde{\Phi}(x, y) \alpha_t e^{U_\delta x} \Delta_r e^{U_\delta^{*\mathsf{T}} y} \alpha^{*\mathsf{T}}\, dy\, dx \tag{11}$$

(note that for the reversal, we need not calculate α^* by replacing α by α_t in (5), but can use the same α^* for all t, cf. Section 2.2 of (Asmussen and Ivanovs 2019)).

Example 4. For the GMDB, we have:

$$\Phi(M_\tau, D_\tau) = \max(K, e^{X_\tau}) = \max(K, e^{x_0 + x_1}) = e^{x_0}\max(\widetilde{K}, e^{x_1})$$

where $\widetilde{K} = Ke^{-x_0}$. Combining with Remark 2, we therefore arrive at the same expression as in Example 2 when $Ke^{-x_0} \le 1$, only with K replaced by $\widetilde{K}$ and α by α_t. The case $Ke^{-x_0} > 1$ may arise by randomness, but is just a minor modification.

Example 5. The details for the HWB reserves are somewhat more complicated than for the GMDB. Here, one needs to consider $e^{M_\tau}\max(a, e^{-D_\tau})$, corresponding to:

$$\widetilde{\Phi}(x,y) = \exp\{\max(m_0, x_0+m_1)\}\max(a, \exp\{-[d_0-m_1]^+ - d_1\}.$$

One approach (potentially the easier one) may be simply to insert in (11) and do the two-dimensional numerical integration. However, in fact, one can reduce to a one-dimensional numerical integration similar to Corollary 2. To this end, note that $e^{M_\tau}\max(a, e^{-D_\tau})$ after simple derivations comes out as:

$$\begin{cases} e^{x_0+m_1}a & \text{if } m_1 > d_0,\ d_1 > -\log a, & (12a)\\ e^{x_0+m_1-d_1} & \text{if } m_1 > d_0,\ d_1 \le -\log a, & (12b)\\ e^{m_0}a & \text{if } m_1 \le d_0,\ d_0-m_1+d_1 > -\log a, & (12c)\\ e^{m_0}e^{-d_0+m_1-d_1} & \text{if } m_1 \le d_0,\ d_0-m_1+d_1 \le -\log a. & (12d)\end{cases}$$

of these four possibilities, (12d) (and to a slightly lesser extent, (12c)) is the most complicated one with which to deal. The contribution to the reserve from (12c) is zero if $m_0 < d_0 + \log a$, since then, the defining region is empty. Otherwise, it becomes:

$$e^{-\delta t+m_0-d_0}\int_{m_0+\log a}^{d_0}\int_0^{x-d_0-\log a} e^{x-y}\boldsymbol{\alpha}_t e^{\boldsymbol{U}_\delta x}\boldsymbol{\Delta}_r e^{\boldsymbol{U}_\delta^{*\mathsf{T}} y}\boldsymbol{\alpha}^{*\mathsf{T}}\,dy\,dx$$

which after two integrations reduces to an expression, which, though complicated, only involves known matrices and their exponentials, except that:

$$\boldsymbol{S}_\delta(b,c) = \int_b^c e^{\boldsymbol{U}_\delta x}\boldsymbol{\Delta}_r e^{\boldsymbol{U}_\delta^{*\mathsf{T}} x}\,dx$$

is left to be determined by numerical integration. ◊

6. Numerical Examples

For the underlying stock price process $S_t = S_0e^{X_t}$, the most popular model is the geometric Brownian motion model. Since this model cannot capture the asymmetric leptokurtic features and the volatility smile, many modified models have been proposed in the literature; one of these is the jump diffusion model, cf. (Kou 2002). Empirical studies show that the daily return distribution tends to have larger kurtosis than the distribution of monthly returns, and the jump diffusion model can capture this feature; see (Das and Foresi 1996). As an illustrative example, we suppose that the yearly interest rate is $r = 3\%$ and the yearly volatility $\sigma = 0.25$. The jumps follow a compound Poisson process with upward jump rate $\lambda_1 = 3$ with the jump sizes being exponential with rate $\nu_1 = 50$ (mean 1/50) and downward jump rate $\lambda_2 = 2$ with jump size being exponential with rate $\nu_2 = 30$. When considering the valuation of an insurance product alone, it is not necessary to use a risk-neutral valuation approach. However, since in our setting, the underlying involves an equity, it is natural to use an equivalent martingale measure $\mathbb{Q}$, defined by the requirement $\log \mathbb{E}_{\mathbb{Q}} e^{X(1)} = r$. This does not define $\mathbb{Q}$ uniquely since the market is incomplete due to the jumps and the mortality risk. Our choice was to let the parameters $\sigma^2, \lambda_1, \lambda_2, \nu_1, \nu_2$ remain unchanged, which gives the risk-neutral Brownian drift as:

$$\mu = r - \frac{\sigma^2}{2} - \frac{\lambda_1}{\nu_1 - 1} + \frac{\lambda_2}{\nu_2+1}.$$

For the illustrative example, we have:

$$\mu = 0.03 - \frac{0.25^2}{2} - \frac{3}{50-1} + \frac{2}{30+1} = 0.002042.$$

It is left to compute the $\boldsymbol{U}_\delta, \boldsymbol{U}_\delta^*$. Writing:

$$\boldsymbol{U} = \boldsymbol{U}(\boldsymbol{T}, \mu, \sigma^2, \lambda_1, \lambda_2, \nu_1, \nu_2)$$

we obtain:

$$\boldsymbol{U}^* = \boldsymbol{U}(\boldsymbol{T}^*, -\mu, \sigma^2, \lambda_2, \lambda_1, \nu_2, \nu_1), \quad \boldsymbol{U}_\delta = \boldsymbol{U}(\boldsymbol{T} - \delta \boldsymbol{I}, \mu, \sigma^2, \lambda_1, \lambda_2, \nu_1, \nu_2),$$

and thus, it suffices to consider $\boldsymbol{U}$. Essentially, two types of algorithms are available. One set is based on finding roots in the complex plane of equations of the form $\kappa(s) = a$ where $\kappa(s) = \log \mathbb{E}e^{sX(1)}$ is the Lévy exponent of X. The other uses fixed-point equations of the form $\boldsymbol{U} = \psi(\boldsymbol{U})$ and iteration, $\boldsymbol{U} = \lim_{n\to\infty} \boldsymbol{U}_n$, with $\boldsymbol{U}_n = \psi(\boldsymbol{U}_{n-1})$ and $\boldsymbol{U}_0$ suitably chosen.

We give a few examples of previous algorithms of both types in Appendix B. When implementing these with τ having one of the GC representations fitted in Section 3, our experience was that the root-finding method was only feasible for a rather small number p of phases. More precisely, for $p = 50$ or $p = 75$, meaningless results were produced, with warnings of the matrix $\boldsymbol{H}$ being close to singular. This is understandable since many eigenvalues of the relevant matrices are almost identical. Since the iterative algorithms ran without problems also for large values of p, we have therefore concentrated on these. In fact, we have developed a new iterative algorithm, which may be simpler than previous ones. It is presented in Appendix B, but for now, we concentrate on some numerical examples.

Example 6. In Figure 7, we have plotted the marginal densities of M_τ, D_τ, and X_τ.

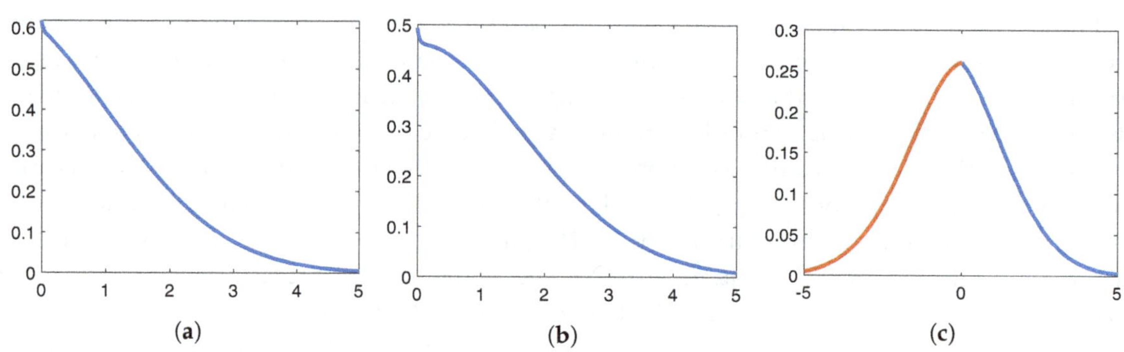

Figure 7. Densities of (**a**) M_τ, (**b**) D_τ, and (**c**) X_τ.

Example 7. Figure 8 gives the joint distribution of M_τ and D_τ (computed by Corollary 1) for our jump diffusion with the parameters given above.

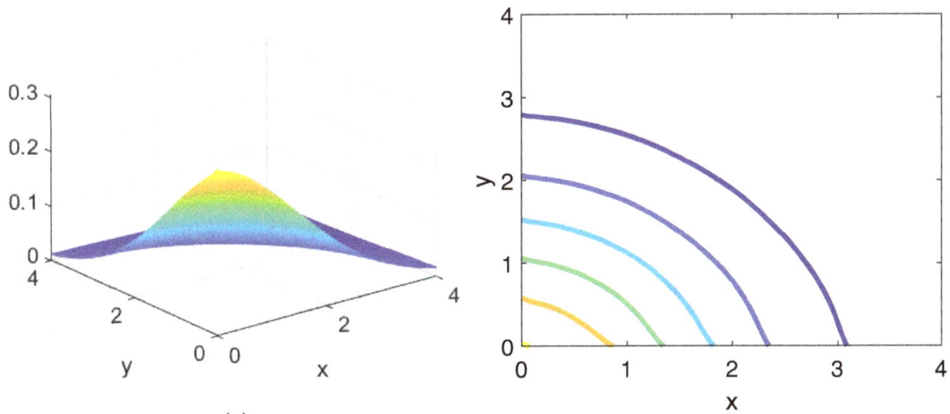

(a)

(b)

Figure 8. Joint distribution of M_τ and D_τ. The joint density is in the left panel and a contour plot in the right.

Example 8. To consider the sensitivity of the algorithms to the value p of chosen phases for τ, we took $\delta = r = 0.03$ or 0.00 and computed the price (10) for $p = 20, 35, 40, 50, 75, 100$ and the GC fits presented in Section 3 for two products, the HWB with $a = 0.85$ and the GMDB with $K = 0.85$; the relevant formulas are available from Examples 1 and 2. The results are in Table 1. We also complemented with a Monte Carlo simulation estimate with an associated 95% confidence interval based on $R = 10^6$ replications, where τ was generated from the discrete life table distribution with an additional randomization within the year.

Table 1. Price estimates for $\delta = r$ and varying p. HWB, high-water benefit; GMDB, guaranteed minimum death benefit.

p	20	35	40	50	75	100	Monte Carlo
HWB, $\delta = r = 0$	2.703	2.703	2.704	2.704	2.704	2.704	2.665 ± 0.008
HWB, $\delta = r = 0.03$	1.698	1.699	1.699	1.699	1.699	1.699	1.680 ± 0.008
GMDB, $\delta = r = 0$	1.468	1.468	1.468	1.468	1.468	1.468	1.467 ± 0.008
GMDB, $\delta = r = 0.03$	1.080	1.080	1.079	1.079	1.079	1.079	1.079 ± 0.010

A related question is how varying different fits can be for a fixed p due to issues such as non-uniqueness of PH representations and possibly local maxima of the likelihood. We illustrate this point in Table 2, which is a parallel of Table 1. We fix p at 50, but use five different initial values (seeds) for the EM algorithm, all allowed the same running time. The fitted densities are in Figure 9.

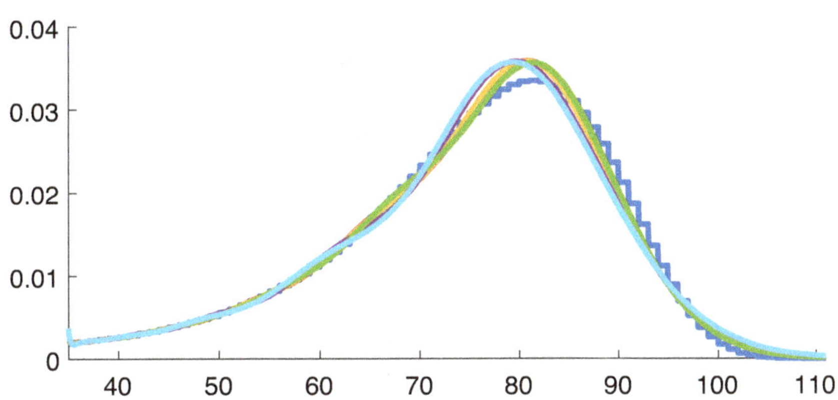

Figure 9. Fitted densities for five different seeds (against the life table data).

Our conclusion is that the differences are too minor to be of any concern, and certainly, using a single fit with $p \geq 50$ will produce acceptable results. Insisting on more than 2–3-digit precision in price estimates does not make sense due to issues such as model uncertainty and that payments will be adjusted later via bonus and dividend arrangements.

Table 2. Price estimates for $\delta = r$ and varying seeds.

Seed	**1**	**2**	**3**	**4**	**5**	**Monte Carlo**
HWB, $\delta = r = 0$	2.704	2.704	2.703	2.702	2.704	2.665 ± 0.008
HWB, $\delta = r = 0.03$	1.699	1.699	1.699	1.698	1.699	1.680 ± 0.008
GMDB, $\delta = r = 0$	1.468	1.468	1.468	1.467	1.468	1.467 ± 0.008
GMDB, $\delta = r = 0.03$	1.079	1.079	1.079	1.078	1.080	1.079 ± 0.010

The programming was done in MATLAB on a 2014 MacBook Air with a 1.4 GHz Intel Core i5 processor. As an example of execution times, MATLAB's tic-toc command reported approximately two seconds for each HWB or GMDB value using the PH methodology. The figures for the Monte Carlo values were much higher, approximately 30,000 replications per minute (recall that 10^6 replications were used). The programming is very simple, with the main effort lying in writing a routine for computing $\boldsymbol{U}$ for a given set of input parameters. This amounted to 50 lines of code in our implementation. Given this ease, we did some further price computations, even if our aim here is not to illustrate pricing aspects, but rather the computational ones.

Example 9. We first consider varying the discount rate δ, but not the force of interest r, cf. the remarks following (4) (that in particular motivate taking $\delta \le r$). The results for the HWB are in Table 3 and show the expected picture, that the price is decreasing in the discount rate.

Table 3. HWB price estimates for $r = 0.03$ and varying δ.

δ	**0.00**	**0.01**	**0.02**	**0.03**
Price	6.24	3.99	2.58	1.70

Example 10. The next example is discounting with the force of interest, i.e., taking $r = \delta$ and varying r. The numerical values are in Table 4, and the picture is again that the price is decreasing in $r = \delta$. The intuition is less clear-cut here, since the Brownian drift μ is increasing and thus pulls in the opposite direction.

Table 4. HWB price estimates for varying $r = \delta$.

$r = \delta$	**0.00**	**0.01**	**0.02**	**0.03**	**0.05**
Price	2.70	2.23	1.92	1.70	1.44

Example 11. Next, we give an illustration of a feature of the factorization: if τ is exponential, then M_τ and D_τ are independent. cf. Lemma 1. In the PH case, there is dependence caused by the common value of $\overline{\tau} = k$. How does this influence the price? A numerical illustration is in Table 5, where the entries are the ratios between the correct price with dependence and the incorrect one computed assuming independence, i.e., as:

$$\begin{aligned}
&\mathbb{E}\mathrm{e}^{-\delta\overline{\tau}}\mathrm{e}^{M_\tau} \cdot \mathbb{E}\mathrm{e}^{-\delta\underline{\tau}}\max(a,\mathrm{e}^{-D_\tau}) \\
&\quad= \int_0^\infty \mathrm{e}^x \boldsymbol{\alpha}\mathrm{e}^{\boldsymbol{U}_\delta x}\boldsymbol{u}\,\mathrm{d}x \cdot \left(a\int_{-\log a}^\infty \boldsymbol{\alpha}^*\mathrm{e}^{\boldsymbol{U}_\delta^* y}\boldsymbol{u}^*\,\mathrm{d}y + \int_0^{-\log a}\mathrm{e}^{-y}\boldsymbol{\alpha}^*\mathrm{e}^{\boldsymbol{U}_\delta^* y}\boldsymbol{u}^*\,\mathrm{d}y\right) \\
&\quad= -\boldsymbol{\alpha}(\boldsymbol{I}+\boldsymbol{U}_\delta)^{-1}\boldsymbol{u}\Big(-a\,\boldsymbol{\alpha}^*\mathrm{e}^{-\boldsymbol{U}_\delta^*\log a}\boldsymbol{U}_\delta^{*-1}\boldsymbol{u}^* + \boldsymbol{\alpha}^*(\boldsymbol{I}-a\mathrm{e}^{-\boldsymbol{U}_\delta^*\log a})(\boldsymbol{I}-\boldsymbol{U}_\delta^*)^{-1}\boldsymbol{u}^*\Big).
\end{aligned}$$

The other settings are as in Table 3. Table 5 shows that in some cases, dependence indeed influences the price quite a bit.

Table 5. Ratios between prices with and without dependence.

δ	**0.00**	**0.01**	**0.02**	**0.03**	**0.05**
Ratio	0.97	0.88	0.78	0.68	0.51

Example 12. As a follow-up of Example 3, we finally consider the evaluation of reserves. Two paths of the jump diffusion were simulated, and the reserve was calculated for each value of t using the formulas of Examples 3, 4 and 5. The results are given in the graphs of Figure 10. The upper panel gives the stock price $S_{a-35} = \mathrm{e}^{X_{a-35}}$ (assuming $S_{35} = 1$) and the lower one the ratio $V_{a-35}/\mathrm{e}^{X_{a-35}}$ as function of the age a of the insured.

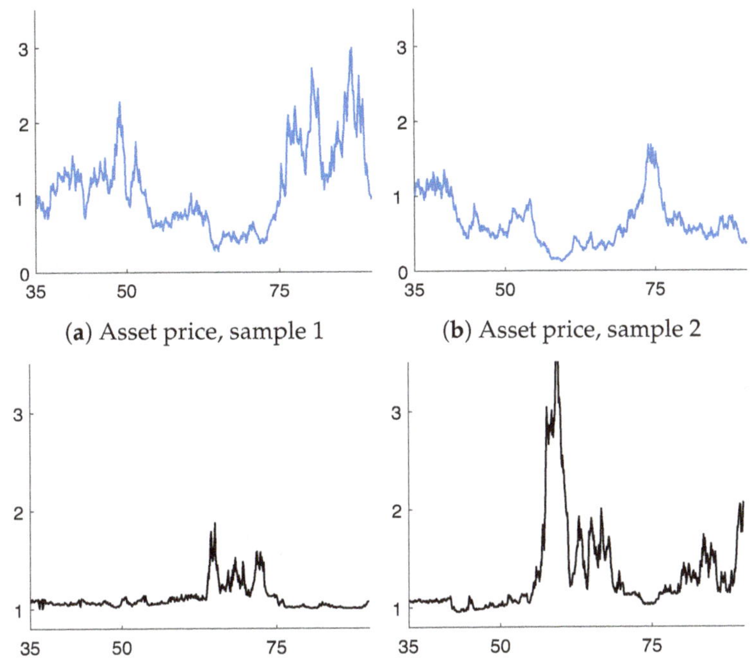

(**a**) Asset price, sample 1 (**b**) Asset price, sample 2

(**c**) Reserve/asset price, sample 1 (**d**) Reserve/asset price, sample 2

Figure 10. Asset price paths and excess ratio of associated GMDB reserves.

When $\delta = r$,

$$\begin{aligned} V_t &= \mathbb{E}\big[\mathrm{e}^{-\delta(\tau-t)}\max(K,\mathrm{e}^{X_\tau})\,\big|\,\tau > t, X_t\big] \\ &\geq \mathbb{E}\big[\mathrm{e}^{-\delta(\tau-t)}\mathrm{e}^{X_\tau})\,\big|\,\tau > t, X_t\big] \;=\; \mathrm{e}^{X_t} \end{aligned}$$

because of the martingale property. Hence, the ratio in the lower panel should always be at least one. This is also confirmed from the figure, as well as the expectation that the ratio should be close to one when X_t is large.

In the calculations, we used the fact that α^* and $\boldsymbol{U}^*$ need not be recalculated for each t, cf. the remarks following (11). This gave a substantial speed-up.

7. Erlangization and Extrapolation

A multitude of papers in finance, insurance, and queuing theory explore the idea of Erlangization or Canadization, that is approximation of a deterministic time T by an Erlang(q) time $E = E_{q,q/T}$ with the same mean. Here, q is the number of stages and q/T is the rate, so that $E_{q,q/T}$ is the sum of q mean T/q exponential r.v.'s. This idea has various applications: explicit identities (see, e.g., (Asmussen et al. 2002; Carr 1998; Stanford et al. 2005)); this is used in (Kuznetsov et al. 2011) together with the traditional Wiener-Hopf factorization to provide an algorithm simulating (M_E, X_E)

to approximate (M_T, X_T) and as a numerical tool for calculating $f(T)$ as the limit of $\mathbb{E}f(E_{q,q/T})$ (or just $f(E_{q,q/T})$) under suitable continuity conditions on f; see, e.g., (Asmussen et al. 2002; Carr 1998; Leung et al. 2015). This last procedure uses the fact that $E_{q,q/T}$ converges in probability to T as $q \to \infty$. In (Asmussen et al. 2002), it is combined with extrapolation, which is based on the asymptotics:

$$\mathbb{E}f(E_{q,q/T}) = f(T) + \frac{C}{q} + O(q^{-2}) \tag{13}$$

valid for f smooth and some $C = C(f)$. This C is typically not available, but (13) suggests eliminating C by estimating $f(T)$ using:

$$q\mathbb{E}f(E_{q,q/T}) - (q-1)\mathbb{E}f(E_{(q-1),q/T}) \tag{14}$$

which converges to $f(T)$ at the improved rate $O(q^{-2})$. The numerical examples of (Asmussen et al. 2002) indicate that often, calculations with q set as small as 2–4 will give very good precision.

The relevance for the present purposes is that the time horizon of many life insurance contracts is not the remaining lifetime τ of the insured, but rather $T \wedge \tau$, where T is a fixed deterministic number. For example, when the age of the insured is 35 at the time of underwriting, $T = 45$ corresponds to contract expiry at age 80 if the insured is still alive. Some calculations can be found in Section 10 of (Gerber et al. 2012) for τ exponential and a call or put option, but rely heavily on this particular structure. For our life insurance applications, it is crucial that $E_{q,q/T} \wedge \tau$ is again PH when $E_{q,q/T}$ and τ are independent. The details involve the Kronecker product $\otimes$ and sum $\oplus$ so that:

$$\boldsymbol{A} \oplus \boldsymbol{B} = \boldsymbol{A} \otimes \boldsymbol{I} + \boldsymbol{I} \otimes \boldsymbol{B}, \quad (\boldsymbol{A} \oplus \boldsymbol{B})(\boldsymbol{v} \otimes \boldsymbol{h}) = \boldsymbol{A}\boldsymbol{v} \otimes \boldsymbol{h} + \boldsymbol{v} \otimes \boldsymbol{B}.$$

For two Markov process generators, the Kronecker sum is the generator of independent versions, and so, $E_{q,q/T} \wedge \tau$ is PH with generator $\boldsymbol{E} \oplus \boldsymbol{T}$ of dimension $nq \times nq$ where $\boldsymbol{E} = \boldsymbol{E}_{q,q/T}$ is the PH generator of $E_{q,q/T}$. Written out with lexicographical order of the states:

$$\boldsymbol{E} \oplus \boldsymbol{T} = \begin{pmatrix} \boldsymbol{T} - \beta\boldsymbol{I} & \beta\boldsymbol{I} & \boldsymbol{0} & \cdots & \boldsymbol{0} & \boldsymbol{0} \\ \boldsymbol{0} & \boldsymbol{T} - \beta\boldsymbol{I} & \beta\boldsymbol{I} & \cdots & \boldsymbol{0} & \boldsymbol{0} \\ \vdots & & & \ddots & & \cdots \\ \boldsymbol{0} & \boldsymbol{0} & \boldsymbol{0} & \cdots & \boldsymbol{T} - \beta\boldsymbol{I} & \beta\boldsymbol{I} \\ \boldsymbol{0} & \boldsymbol{0} & \boldsymbol{0} & \cdots & \boldsymbol{0} & \boldsymbol{T} - \beta\boldsymbol{I} \end{pmatrix}.$$

Example 13. We consider a HWB or GMDB contract signed at age 35 of the insured and expiring at the time τ of death or at age 70, whatever comes first. We took $r = \delta = 3\%$ and used the GC fit with $p = 50$, leading to the numerical values given in Table 6; in comparison, Monte Carlo simulation with $R = 50{,}000$ replications gave the 95% confidence interval 1.636 ± 0.034 for the HWB and 1.097 ± 0.029 for the GMDB.

Table 6. Erlangized price estimates.

q	HWB Simple	HWB Extrapolated	GMDB Simple	GMDB Extrapolated
1	1.523	1.523	1.092	1.092
2	1.583	1.642	1.097	1.102
3	1.606	1.652	1.097	1.099
4	1.618	1.655	1.097	1.096
5	1.626	1.657	1.097	1.095
6	1.631	1.658	1.096	1.095
7	1.635	1.658	1.096	1.094
8	1.638	1.659	1.096	1.094
9	1.640	1.659	1.096	1.094
10	1.642	1.659	1.095	1.094

The extrapolation is done via (14), with the required smoothness being obvious for the GMDB. For the HWB, $d \mapsto \max(a, e^{-d})$ is not smooth at $d = -\log a$, but some rough heuristics (that we omit) suggest that (13) remains in force for this special f. Certainly, extrapolation appears to produce sensible results also for the GMDB. In both cases, it seems that $q = 4$–6 is enough to obtain sufficiently precise estimates, whereas without extrapolation, one would need at least $q = 10$. This is a considerable improvement upon simple Erlangization, since the dimension of the matrices in the computations (where inversion is the heavy part) is $2pq$. This means that for $p = 50$, one would need to invert matrices of dimension 400 when $q = 4$, but 1000 when $q = 10$, and since the inversion of an $n \times n$ matrix has complexity n^3 (or slightly less with sophisticated methods), this corresponds to reducing computation time by a factor of about $2.5^3 = 15.6$.

8. Conclusions

In this paper, we have considered pricing calculations for life insurance products like the guaranteed minimum death benefit and the high-water benefit. The payout occurs at the death time τ of the insured, and its size is linked to an asset price S either via its current value S_τ or to features of its past evolution during the time of the contract such as the maximum $\overline{S}_\tau$.

The key observation is that for the most popular model of S, an exponential jump diffusion, the distributions of S_τ and/or $\overline{S}_\tau$ are available when the jumps and τ are phase-type. This has long been known in the geometric Brownian motion setting without jumps when τ is exponential and is essentially just the Wiener-Hopf factorization of Brownian motion. There is also an extensive literature for PH jumps, and for τ itself being PH, the relevant Wiener-Hopf factorization has recently been developed in (Asmussen and Ivanovs 2019).

The program thus involves two steps, first fitting a PH distribution of τ to lifetime data and next implementing the pricing calculations.

The shape of lifetime data with a steep decline after the mode makes the fitting of PH distributions non-trivial, necessitating the number p of phases to be relatively high. However, we already made the points that a good fit is one that produces reliable estimates of the prices of the life insurance products, and that giving more than 2–3-digit precision in price estimates does not make sense due to issues such as uncertainty about the model and its parameters (think, e.g., of longevity risk) and bonus/dividend arrangements. We found $p = 50$ to be more than sufficient in the sense of providing appropriate accuracy of the calculated price of life insurance products and could well have worked with smaller values. An alternative is developed in GSY, to use matrix-exponentials fitted at a selected number of points, but we show in Appendix A that this approach has its pitfalls.

Fitting of so high-dimensional PH distributions is slow, though we developed in part some new software giving substantial speed-up. However, given this step has been passed, pricing calculations are both very easy to program and run very fast, also compared to Monte Carlo simulation, and this may be the main advantage of our approach. A limitation is of course that we need the pay-out to be of the form (1), and there are many products for which this is not the case. Alternatives such as Monte Carlo simulation and traditional methods based on Thiele-type differential equations may then be more suitable. Therefore, we do not claim the superiority of our own approach for all purposes, but have rather tried to clarify its advantages and disadvantages.

Author Contributions: Conceptualization and methodology, S.A. and H.Y.; software and validation, S.A. and P.J.L.; writing–original draft preparation, all authors; writing–review and editing, P.J.L.

Funding: Hailiang Yang was funded by Research Grants Council of the Hong Kong Special Administrative Region (Project No. HKU 17305018). Patrick J. Laub conducted this research with the support of the ANR under the "Investments for the Future" program and the support of DAMI—Data Analytics and Models for Insurance—Chair under the aegis of the Fondation du Risque, a joint initiative by UCBL (Université Lyon 1, SAF EA2429) and BNP Paribas Cardif.

Acknowledgments: We are grateful to Jevgenijs Ivanovs for useful discussions and comments.

Conflicts of Interest: The authors declare no conflict of interest. The funders had no role in the design of the study; in the collection, analyses, or interpretation of data; in the writing of the manuscript; nor in the decision to publish the results.

Appendix A. Fits Using Sum-of-Exponentials

We here briefly reinspect the approach of (Siu et al. 2015) for fitting a distribution with tail of the form:

$$\overline{F}_{\boldsymbol{a},\boldsymbol{b}}(t) = \sum_{i=1}^{\ell} a_i e^{-b_i t}$$

to lifetime data where $\boldsymbol{a}$ is the vector $(a_1, \dots, a_\ell)$ (some a_i may be negative) and similarly for $\boldsymbol{b}$. Such a tail is of matrix-exponential form, meaning $\overline{F}(t) = \boldsymbol{a}e^{\boldsymbol{\Delta}t}\boldsymbol{s}$ for suitable $\boldsymbol{a}, \boldsymbol{\Delta}, \boldsymbol{s}$ (not restricted to the Markov process interpretation in PH tails). In fact, the only restriction is that $\boldsymbol{\Delta}$ must be diagonalizable. We refer to (Bladt and Nielsen 2017) for further background on matrix-exponential distributions.

In (Siu et al. 2015), the vectors $\boldsymbol{a}$ and $\boldsymbol{b}$ are found by minimizing:

$$\sum_{t=1}^{n} \left({}_t p_x - \overline{F}_{\boldsymbol{a},\boldsymbol{b}}(t)\right)^2 \tag{A1}$$

for some fixed ℓ and n, where ${}_t p_x$ is the survival probability (derived from the life table) of a person aged x surviving until age $x + t$. In other words, they minimize the mean squared error between the empirical and theoretical survival probabilities at ages $x, x+1, \dots, x+n$.

In (Siu et al. 2015), the values $x = 30$ and $n = 25$ are used as examples, and so, the age span considered begins at 30 and goes until 55. We fit this type of approximation to our life table with similar parameters and plotted the resulting densities; we used $\ell = 10$ exponential terms, the same as in (Siu et al. 2015), but we set the starting age as $x = 35$ rather than $x = 30$.

The relevant ages for life insurance are often greater than 60 years old, and so, we create a sequence of fits with $n = 25, 50, 75$ (shown in Figures A1 and A2a) to try to approximate accurately an increasing portion of the life table. For each fit, we plot time across the whole age range of 35–110, even though one cannot expect a sum-of-exponentials fit to be accurate outside of the time period $t \in (x, x+n)$.

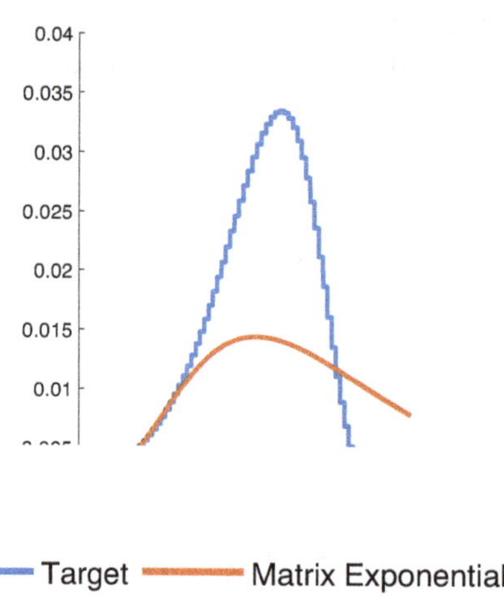

Figure A1. Sum-of-exponentials fits in age range 35–60.

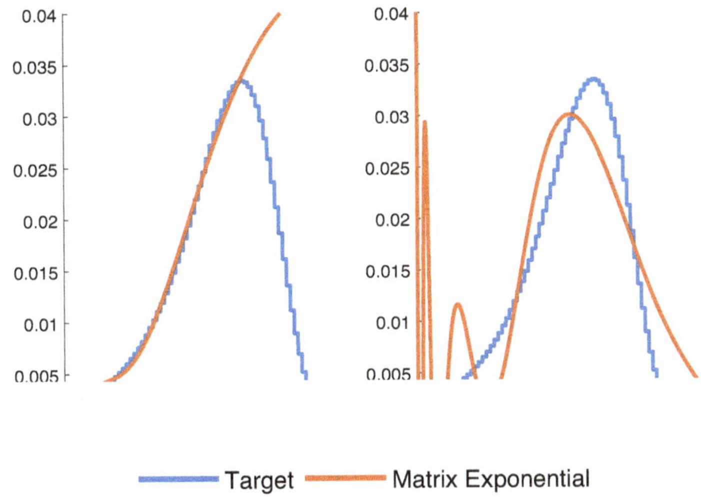

(a) (b)

Figure A2. Sum-of-exponentials fits in age ranges 35–85 (left) and 35–110 (right).

In Figures A1 and A2a, the fits are fine in the selected age range $(x, x+n)$, but fail miserably beyond. This is not necessarily a drawback if the fit has been made for the pricing of a product where $x+n$ is the upper limit of the relevant age range. The picture in Figure A2b is more rough, but presumably repairable by increasing ℓ beyond $\ell = 10$. Another phenomenon that is observed is the possibility of densities that are negative and exhibit weird oscillations. This is seen most markedly in Figure A2b.

This behavior is a result of the fitting criterion (A1), which only pays attention to the selected grid $x, x+1, \ldots, x+n$, and not to what goes on in between the grid points.

Appendix B. Algorithms for Computing U

As an example of the root-finding algorithms, we state the following particularly simple example, which is a special case of Corollary 5.2 of (Asmussen 1995):

Proposition A1. *Assume X is BM(μ, σ^2) and that τ is GC, as in Figure 1. Then,* $\mathbb{P}_i(M_\tau \in \mathrm{d}y;\, J_{\overline{\sigma}} = k) = \boldsymbol{e}_i^\top \mathrm{e}^{\boldsymbol{U}y} \boldsymbol{e}_k \,\mathrm{d}y$ *where:*

$\boldsymbol{U} = \boldsymbol{H}\boldsymbol{\Delta}_{-\boldsymbol{s}}\boldsymbol{H}^{-1}$;
$\boldsymbol{s}$ is the vector with elements $s_j = -\mu/\sigma^2 + \sqrt{\mu^2/\sigma^4 + 2\lambda_j/\sigma^2}$;
$\boldsymbol{H}$ is the matrix with columns $\boldsymbol{h}_1, \ldots, \boldsymbol{h}_n$;
$\boldsymbol{h}_j$ is the eigenvector of $\boldsymbol{T} + \lambda_j \boldsymbol{I}$ corresponding to eigenvalue zero, with elements h_{ij} given by $h_{ij} = 0$ for $i > j$, $h_{1j} = 1$ and:

$$h_{ij} = \prod_{k=1}^{i-1} \frac{\lambda_k - \lambda_j}{\lambda_k q_k} \quad \text{for } 1 < i \leq j.$$

In particular, $\mathbb{P}(J_{\overline{\sigma}} = k) = -\boldsymbol{\alpha}\boldsymbol{U}^{-1}\boldsymbol{e}_k \cdot u_k$ *where u_k is the kth element of* $-\boldsymbol{U}\boldsymbol{e}$.

Remark A1. For a GC distribution, the characteristic polynomial, its roots, and the eigenvalues are explicit because of the upper triangular form of the generator matrix. This may of course be a curiosity in the computer age, and it is probably faster to code the program of Proposition A1 via matrix software than to use the explicit formulas. However, continuing in the same vein, note that not only is the determinant of an upper triangular matrix explicit, but also the inverse. Indeed, let $\boldsymbol{k}$ be the vector of diagonal elements of $\boldsymbol{H}$ and write $\boldsymbol{H} = \boldsymbol{\Delta}_{\boldsymbol{k}}(\boldsymbol{I} + \boldsymbol{N})$, i.e., $\boldsymbol{N} = \boldsymbol{\Delta}_{1/\boldsymbol{k}}(\boldsymbol{H} - \boldsymbol{I})$. Then, $\boldsymbol{N}$ is nilpotent and:

$$\boldsymbol{H}^{-1} = (\boldsymbol{I} - \boldsymbol{N})^{-1}\boldsymbol{\Delta}_{1/\boldsymbol{k}} = \sum_{k=1}^{n-1}(-1)^k \boldsymbol{N}^k \boldsymbol{\Delta}_{1/\boldsymbol{k}}\,.$$

The iterative algorithms are hardly simpler for the GC case than for a general PH structure. An example (Theorem 4.1 of (Asmussen 1995)) follows.

Proposition A2. *Assume X is BM(μ, σ^2) and that τ is PH$(\boldsymbol{\alpha}, \boldsymbol{T})$. Define $\lambda_i = -T_{ii}$,*

$$\omega_i = -\mu/\sigma^2 + \sqrt{\mu^2/\sigma^4 + 2\lambda_j/\sigma^2}\,, \qquad \eta_i = \mu/\sigma^2 + \sqrt{\mu^2/\sigma^4 + 2\lambda_j/\sigma^2}\,.$$

Then, $\boldsymbol{U}$ is the solution of the fixed-point problem $\boldsymbol{U} = \psi(\boldsymbol{U})$ where $\psi(\boldsymbol{V})$ is the matrix whose i^{th} row is the ith row of the matrix:

$$\frac{2}{\sigma^2}(\boldsymbol{\Delta}_\lambda + \boldsymbol{T})(\eta_i \boldsymbol{I} - \boldsymbol{V})^{-1} - \boldsymbol{\Delta}_\omega\,.$$

Further, $\boldsymbol{U} = \lim_{n\to\infty} \boldsymbol{U}_n$ with $\boldsymbol{U}_n = \psi(\boldsymbol{U}_{n-1})$ and $\boldsymbol{U}_0 = -\boldsymbol{\Delta}_\omega$.

In our numerical examples, we have used an algorithm that is somewhat related, but also contains some genuinely new ideas. It is applicable to more general models than jump diffusions and thereby also in other application areas than life insurance. For this reason, the details will be provided elsewhere, and we give here only a very brief outline. The basic idea is illustrated in Figure A3, which contains a realization of the jump diffusion X up to the PH time τ. The underlying Markov process has two states, blue B and red R for τ, two cyan C and magenta M for the upward jumps, and one green G for the downward ones. The phases when X is at a maximum are shown in the left-hand vertical bar and have four possible states B, R, CB, MB, CR, MR with legends given in the upper right corner.

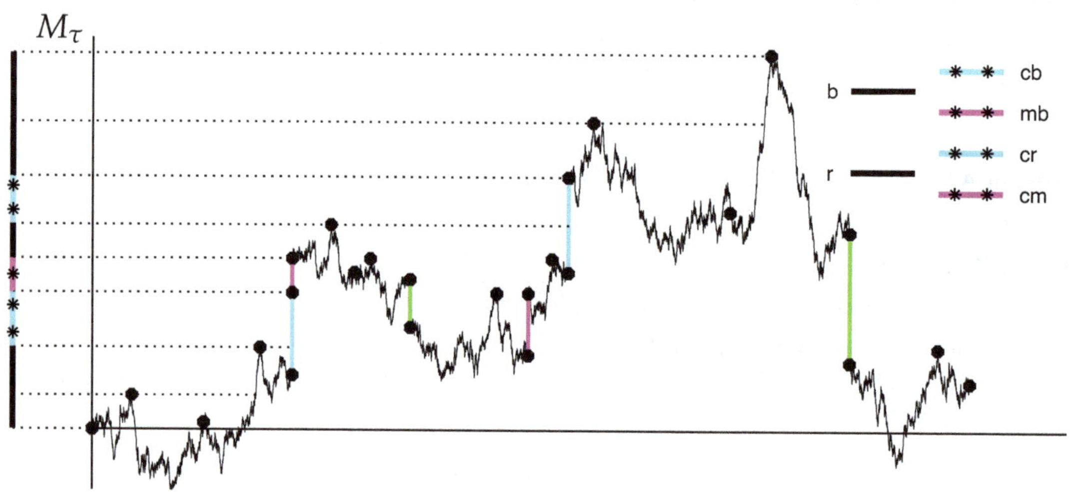

Figure A3. Jump diffusion and embedded Markov random walk.

The basic observation for the algorithm is that this process $\xi(x)$ of phases at maxima x (and thereby, the overall maximum M_τ) is the same as for the embedded discrete time killed Markov random walk marked by black dots. Its values are the values in the graph of X either at the start of a Brownian segment, just before the end, or at the maximum, or at phase changes in jumps. Here, the graph of X is understood to comprise the vertical parts from jumps, and Brownian segments are separated either by state changes in the Markov process underlying the phase horizon τ, or by jumps. The generator $\boldsymbol{U}$ of ξ is then shown to satisfy a certain fixed-point equation that is solved iteratively.

Computationally, the main effort in each step is to invert a matrix $\boldsymbol{U}_n$ whose dimension is the number $p(1+p^+)$ of states of ξ.

References

Asmussen, Søren. 1995. Stationary distributions for fluid flow models with or without brownian noise. *Stochastic Models* 11: 21–49. [CrossRef]

Asmussen, Søren. 2003. Applied Probability and Queues. In *Stochastic Modelling and Applied Probability Series*, 2nd ed. Berlin: Springer, vol. 51.

Asmussen, Søren, and Hansjörg Albrecher. 2010. Ruin Probabilities. In *Advanced Series on Statistical Science and Applied Probability*, 2nd ed. Singapore: World Scientific, vol. 14.

Asmussen, Søren, Florin Avram, and Martijn R. Pistorius. 2004. Russian and american put options under exponential phase-type lévy models. *Stochastic Processes and Their Applications* 109: 79–111. [CrossRef]

Asmussen, Søren, Florin Avram, and Miguel Usabel. 2002. Erlangian approximations for finite-horizon ruin probabilities. *ASTIN Bulletin* 32: 267–81. [CrossRef]

Asmussen, Søren, and Jevgenijs Ivanovs. 2019. A factorization of a Lévy process over a phase-type horizon. *Stochastic Models*. accepted. [CrossRef]

Asmussen, Søren, Patrick J. Laub, and Hailiang Yang. 2019. Online accompaniment for "Phase-Type Models in Life Insurance: Fitting and Valuation of Equity-Linked Benefits". Available online: https://github.com/Pat-Laub/PhaseTypeLifeInsurance (accessed on 4 February 2019).

Asmussen, Søren, Olle Nerman, and Marita Olsson. 1996. Fitting phase-type distributions via the EM algorithm. *Scandinavian Journal of Statistics* 23: 419–41.

Bean, Nigel G., Małgorzata M. O'Reilly, and Peter G. Taylor. 2005. Algorithms for return probabilities for stochastic fluid flows. *Stochastic Models* 21: 149–84. [CrossRef]

Bladt, Mogens. 2005. A review on phase-type distributions and their use in risk theory. *ASTIN Bulletin* 35: 145–67. [CrossRef]

Bladt, Mogens, and Bo Friis Nielsen. 2017. *Matrix-Exponential Distributions in Applied Probability*. Berlin: Springer.

Bowers, Newton L., Hans U. Gerber, James C. Hickman, Donald A. Jones, and Cecil J. Nesbitt. 1997. *Actuarial Mathematics*, 2nd ed. Schaumburg: The Society of Actuaries.

Breuer, Lothar. 2008. First passage times for Markov additive processes with positive jumps of phase type. *Journal of Applied Probability* 45: 779–99. [CrossRef]

Cai, Jun, and Haijun Li. 2005a. Conditional tail expectations for multivariate phase type distributions. *Journal of Applied Probability* 42: 810–25. [CrossRef]

Cai, Jun, and Haijun Li. 2005b. Multivariate risk model of phase type. *Insurance: Mathematics and Economics* 36: 137–52. [CrossRef]

Carr, Peter. 1998. Randomization and the american put. *The Review of Financial Studies* 11: 597–626. [CrossRef]

Cont, Rama, and Peter Tankov. 2004. *Financial Modelling with Jump Processes*. London: Chapman & Hall, CRC.

Das, Sanjiv Ranjan, and Silverio Foresi. 1996. Exact solutions for bond and option prices with systematic jump risk. *Review of Derivatives Research* 1: 7–24. [CrossRef]

Dieker, Antonius B., and Michel Mandjes. 2011. Extremes of markov-additive processes with one-sided jumps, with queueing applications. *Methodology and Computing in Applied Probability* 13: 221–67. [CrossRef]

Egami, Masahiko, and Kazutoshi Yamazaki. 2014. Phase-type fitting of scale functions for spectrally negative Lévy processes. *Journal of Computational and Applied Mathematics* 264: 1–22. [CrossRef]

Gerber, Hans U., Elias S. W. Shiu, and Hailiang Yang. 2012. Valuing equity-linked death benefits and other contingent options: A discounted density approach. *Insurance: Mathematics and Economics* 51: 73–92. [CrossRef]

Gerber, Hans U., Elias S. W. Shiu, and Hailiang Yang. 2013. Valuing equity-linked death benefits in jump diffusion models. *Insurance: Mathematics and Economics* 53: 615–23. [CrossRef]

Gerber, Hans U., Elias S. W. Shiu, and Hailiang Yang. 2015. Geometric stopping of a random walk and its application to valuation of equity-linked death benefits. *Insurance: Mathematics and Economics* 64: 313–25.

Horváth, Gábor, and Miklós Telek. 2017. Matrix-analytic solutions of infinite, finite and level-dependent second-order fluid queues. *Queueing Systems: Theory and Applications* 87: 325–43. [CrossRef]

Jacobsen, Martin. 2005. The time to ruin for a class of markov additive risk process with two-sided jumps. *Advances in Applied Probability* 37: 963–92. [CrossRef]

Jiang, Zhengjun, and Martijn R. Pistorius. 2008. On perpetual american put valuation and first-passage in a regime-switching model with jumps. *Finance and Stochastics* 12: 331–55. [CrossRef]

Kou, Steven G. 2002. A jump diffusion model for option pricing. *Management Science* 48: 1086–101. [CrossRef]

Kuznetsov, Alexey, Andreas E. Kyprianou, Juan C. Pardo, and Kees van Schaik. 2011. A Wiener–Hopf Monte Carlo simulation technique for Lévy processes. *The Annals of Applied Probability* 21: 2171–90. [CrossRef]

Leung, Tim, Kazutoshi Yamazaki, and Hongzhong Zhang. 2015. An analytic recursive method for optimal multiple stopping: Canadization and phase-type fitting. *International Journal of Theoretical and Applied Finance* 18: 31. [CrossRef]

Lewis, Alan L., and Ernesto Mordecki. 2008. Wiener-Hopf factorization for Lévy processes having positive jumps with rational transforms. *Journal of Applied Probability* 45: 118–34. [CrossRef]

Lin, X. Sheldon, and Xiaoming Liu. 2007. Markov aging process and phase-type law of mortality. *North American Actuarial Journal* 11: 92–109. [CrossRef]

Mordecki, Ernesto. 2002. The distribution of the maximum of a Lévy process with positive jumps of phase-type. *Theory of Stochastic Processes* 8: 309–16.

Okamura, Hiroyuki, Tadashi Dohi, and Kishor S. Trivedi. 2011a. Improvement of expectation-maximization algorithm for phase-type distributions with grouped and truncated data. *Applied Stochastic Models in Business and Industry* 29: 141–56. [CrossRef]

Okamura, Hiroyuki, Tadashi Dohi, and Kishor S. Trivedi. 2011b. A refined EM algorithm for PH distributions. *Performance Evaluation* 68: 938–54. [CrossRef]

Olsson, Marita. 1996. Estimation of phase-type distributions from censored data. *Scandinavian Journal of Statistics* 23: 443–60.

Olsson, Marita. 1998. The Empht-Programme. Available online: http://home.math.au.dk/asmus/dl/EMusersguide.ps (accessed on 4 February 2019).

Pistorius, Martijn R. 2006. On maxima and ladder processes for a dense class of Lévy process. *Journal of Applied Probability* 43: 208–20. [CrossRef]

Siu, Chi Chung, Sheung Chi Yam, and Hailiang Yang. 2015. Valuing equity-linked deaths benefits in a regime-switching framework. *ASTIN Bulletin* 45: 355–95. [CrossRef]

Stanford, David A., Guy Latouche, Douglas G. Woolford, Dennis Boychuk, and Alek Hunchak. 2005. Erlangized fluid queues with application to uncontrolled fire perimeter. *Stochastic Models* 21: 631–42. [CrossRef]

Stanford, David A., Krzysztof J. Stroiński, and Karen Lee. 2000. Ruin probabilities based at claim instants for some non-Poisson claim processes. *Insurance: Mathematics and Economics* 26: 251–67. [CrossRef]

Zadeh, Amin Hassan, Bruce L. Jones, and David A. Stanford. 2014. The use of phase-type models for disability insurance calculations. *Scandinavian Actuarial Journal* 8: 714–28. [CrossRef]

Zadeh, Amin Hassan, and David A. Stanford. 2016. Bayesian and Bühlmann credibility for phase-type distributions with a univariate risk parameter. *Scandinavian Actuarial Journal* 2016: 338–55. [CrossRef]

11

Multivariate Risk-Neutral Pricing of Reverse Mortgages under the Bayesian Framework

Jackie Li [1,*], Atsuyuki Kogure [2] and Jia Liu [1]

[1] Department of Actuarial Studies and Business Analytics, Macquarie University, Macquarie Park, NSW 2109, Australia; jacie.liu@mq.edu.au

[2] Faculty of Business Administration, Tokyo Keizai University, Tokyo 185-8502, Japan; atsuyuki.kogure@gmail.com

* Correspondence: jackie.li@mq.edu.au

Abstract: In this paper, we suggest a Bayesian multivariate approach for pricing a reverse mortgage, allowing for house price risk, interest rate risk and longevity risk. We adopt the principle of maximum entropy in risk-neutralisation of these three risk components simultaneously. Our numerical results based on Australian data suggest that a reverse mortgage would be financially sustainable under the current financial environment and the model settings and assumptions.

Keywords: reverse mortgage; house price risk; interest rate risk; longevity risk; risk-neutralisation; principle of maximum entropy; Bayesian modelling

---

1. Introduction

A reverse mortgage allows the owner of a home property to make a loan based on the value of the property while keeping the right to stay in the property for life. If the homeowner dies or moves out, the sale proceeds of the property are used to pay back the loan as well as the accumulated interest. In Australia, each product usually has a no-negative-equity guarantee such that the total final payment is no more than the sale value of the mortgaged property. Seniors and retirees can use a reverse mortgage to unlock their home equity and obtain extra funding to pay for their living expenses and other needs. Under the ageing population and the common problem of being asset-rich-cash-poor[1], reverse mortgages represent a financially feasible solution for millions of households. This market has been growing quite steadily in Australia[2].

Providers of reverse mortgages encounter a wide range of market, insurance and business risks. It is of utmost importance to assess these different risks adequately in pricing and reserving. Generally speaking, the main ones are house price risk, interest rate risk, longevity risk and other types of business risks. First, if the homeowner lives longer than anticipated, the exposure and thus the chance of the property value dropping below the accumulated loan balance would be increased. Second, the house price and the interest rate fluctuate over time and are subject to economic cycles, leading to uncertainty in the financial outcomes. Moreover, there are various types of common business issues such as fraud, legal risk and operational risk.

---

[1] The average balance in superannuation of those Australians who were aged 60 to 64 was merely AUD$214,897 in 2015–2016, but the amount required to achieve a "comfortable retirement" is estimated to be AUD$640,000 for couples and AUD$545,000 for singles (https://www.superannuation.asn.au/).

[2] The reverse mortgage industry revenue in Australia has grown by about 0.9% p.a. in the last five years (https://www.ibisworld.com.au/).

In the literature of pricing reverse mortgages, many of the authors assumed a fixed interest rate and allowed for either longevity risk or house price risk or both (e.g., Debón et al. 2013; Ji et al. 2012; Kogure et al. 2014). A few took all of the house price risk, interest rate risk and longevity risk into account but used different pricing methods for these three risks separately (e.g., Wang et al. 2008; Lee et al. 2012). In this article, we suggest a Bayesian approach to include all the three risk components in a more consistent manner. Particularly, we adopt the maximum entropy approach (Kogure and Kurachi 2010; Li 2010) in risk-neutralisation, which has some potential advantages over the other pricing methods such as the Esscher transform and Wang transform. It is more flexible in terms of being able to incorporate more than one market price, allowing the use of different simulation methods, and pricing multiple risk factors within the same framework. Moreover, Bayesian modelling offers a number of desirable features. One can estimate the mortality structure and the time series process more coherently in a single step, rather than the usual two separate steps in most of the previous mortality projection work. It is relatively straightforward to deal with missing values, which can be an important issue when the market is not fully developed and only limited data are available. Other reference information may also be incorporated into the priors to assist in parameter estimation. Finally, both process error and parameter error (uncertainty in estimating parameters), and possibly model error (uncertainty in choosing between models), can readily be allowed for in the Bayesian modelling process.

The remaining parts are presented as follows. Section 2 sets forth the concept of applying the principle of maximum entropy in pricing reverse mortgages. Section 3 introduces the Bayesian models we adopt for modelling house price risk, interest rate risk and longevity risk. Section 4 discusses the numerical results of a hypothetical example based on Australian data and provides the analysis. Section 5 gives the concluding remarks.

2. Pricing Mechanism

Let X be the random value of a risk factor at time T, $f(x)$ be its real-world probability density function (pdf), $h_i(X)$ be the random payoff of the ith security at time T, v_i be the time-0 market price of that security and r be the risk-free interest rate. Under the principle of maximum entropy, the risk-neutral pdf $f^*(x)$ is obtained by minimising the Kullback–Leibler information criterion $\int f^*(x)\ln\frac{f^*(x)}{f(x)}dx$, subject to the constraints $\int f^*(x)dx = 1$ and $(1+r)^{-T}\int h_i(x)f^*(x)dx = v_i$ for $i = 1, 2, \ldots, m$. This pricing method has several advantages. Firstly, any number m of market prices can be embedded into the constraints in principle. This property is suitable for the currently developing and illiquid life market. Secondly, different simulation and bootstrapping methods (e.g., Li 2014a) can readily be implemented under this method. It allows one to avoid complex derivations and facilitates implementation in practice. Thirdly, this method can be applied to multiple risk factors simultaneously. This treatment is arguably more consistent or coherent than the way of arbitrarily applying different risk-neutral measures to different risk factors, which is usually seen in the literature. Finally, there are both theoretical arguments and empirical evidence supporting the use of this pricing method. For instance, the maximum entropy principle is closely related to the expected utility hypothesis, and this measure can produce prices similar to Black–Scholes ones in a simulated environment based on the Black–Scholes model settings (e.g., Li 2010).

In the next two sections, we use Bayesian modelling to generate n random scenarios with equal real-world probability $\pi_j = 1/n$ for $j = 1, 2, \ldots, n$. Accordingly, we utilise the discrete form of the maximum entropy principle, in which the Kullback–Leibler information criterion becomes $\sum_{j=1}^{n}\pi_j^*\ln\frac{\pi_j^*}{\pi_j}$ and the constraints are $\sum_{j=1}^{n}\pi_j^* = 1$ and $(1+r)^{-T}\sum_{j=1}^{n}h_{i,j}\,\pi_j^* = v_i$. The term π_j^* represents the risk-neutral probability and $h_{i,j}$ is the jth simulated payoff of the ith security at time T. The Lagrange expression is stated as:

$$\mathcal{L}=\sum_{j=1}^{n}\pi_j^*\ln\frac{\pi_j^*}{\pi_j}-\lambda(\sum_{j=1}^{n}\pi_j^*-1)-\sum_{i=1}^{m}\gamma_i((1+r)^{-T}\sum_{j=1}^{n}h_{i,j}\,\pi_j^*-v_i),$$

in which λ and γ_i are the Lagrange multipliers. To find the risk-neutral probabilities π_j^* which minimise the Kullback–Leibler information criterion, all the partial derivatives of the Lagrange expression are first set to zero:

$$\frac{\partial \mathcal{L}}{\partial \pi_j^*} = \ln \frac{\pi_j^*}{\pi_j} + 1 - \lambda - \sum_{i=1}^{m} \gamma_i (1+r)^{-T} h_{i,j} = 0,$$

$$\frac{\partial \mathcal{L}}{\partial \lambda} = -(\sum_{j=1}^{n} \pi_j^* - 1) = 0,$$

$$\frac{\partial \mathcal{L}}{\partial \gamma_i} = -((1+r)^{-T} \sum_{j=1}^{n} h_{i,j}\, \pi_j^* - v_i) = 0.$$

The last two equations are just the two constraints, while the first one can be expressed as:

$$\pi_j^* = \pi_j \exp(-1 + \lambda + \sum_{i=1}^{m} \gamma_i (1+r)^{-T} h_{i,j}).$$

Since $\sum_{j=1}^{n} \pi_j^* = 1$, the following can be deduced:

$$\sum_{j=1}^{n} \pi_j^* = \exp(-1+\lambda) \sum_{j=1}^{n} \pi_j \exp(\sum_{i=1}^{m} \gamma_i (1+r)^{-T} h_{i,j}) = 1,$$

$$\exp(-1+\lambda) = \frac{1}{\sum_{j=1}^{n} \pi_j \exp(\sum_{i=1}^{m} \gamma_i (1+r)^{-T} h_{i,j})},$$

$$\pi_j^* = \frac{\pi_j \exp(\sum_{i=1}^{m} \gamma_i (1+r)^{-T} h_{i,j})}{\sum_{j=1}^{n} \pi_j \exp(\sum_{i=1}^{m} \gamma_i (1+r)^{-T} h_{i,j})} = \frac{\exp(\sum_{i=1}^{m} \gamma_i (1+r)^{-T} h_{i,j})}{\sum_{j=1}^{n} \exp(\sum_{i=1}^{m} \gamma_i (1+r)^{-T} h_{i,j})}. \tag{1}$$

The Lagrange multipliers γ_i and so the risk-neutral probabilities π_j^* can then be obtained by incorporating Equation (1) into the market price constraints $(1+r)^{-T} \sum_{j=1}^{n} h_{i,j}\, \pi_j^* = v_i$ and using numerical optimisation to solve the resulting equations[3].

The derivation above is based on one risk factor and can readily be extended to multiple risk factors. For instance, the following equation can be used when all of the house price risk, interest rate risk and longevity risk are integrated into pricing a reverse mortgage:

$$\pi_j^* = \frac{\exp(\sum_{i=1}^{m} \gamma_i\, pv_{i,j})}{\sum_{j=1}^{n} \exp(\sum_{i=1}^{m} \gamma_i\, pv_{i,j})}, \tag{2}$$

where $pv_{i,j}$ is the simulated time-0 present value of the ith security in the jth scenario. The value of each security is a function of one or two or all of the three risk factors. Note that the underlying discount rate can be treated as stochastic in this more generalised setting.

3 For the numerical results in Section 4, we have empirically verified the minimisation of the information criterion by testing several other randomly picked values of risk-neutral probabilities and checking whether the numerically optimised values do represent the minimum. Another theoretical way to verify the minimisation is to compute the bordered Hessian matrix and apply the second derivative test for an extrema of a Lagrange expression. However, this approach is impractical for our analysis as the dimension of the matrix is too large.

3. Bayesian Modelling

Consider a person aged x who has purchased a reverse mortgage at time 0. Let L_t be the outstanding loan balance and P_t be the mortgaged property's market value at time t. Suppose the loan interest rate is constant at l p.a. and so $L_t = L_0 \exp(lt)$. When the borrower dies between time $t-1$ and time t, the loan is terminated and the lender receives a lump sum of $\min(L_t, P_t) = L_t - \max(L_t - P_t, 0)$ at time t[4]. In effect, $\max(L_t - P_t, 0)$ refers to the potential payoff to the homeowner from the no-negative-equity guarantee, which can be viewed as a put option written on the house price with a moving strike price. For a large portfolio of borrowers[5] from the same birth cohort with homogenous house price growth experience and mortality improvement, define I_t as the future percentage of this group who die between time $t-1$ and time t. The lender then receives $\min(L_t, P_t)\ I_t$ at $t = 1, 2, 3, \ldots$ on average per borrower. Denote $r_{0,t}$ as the risk-free rate per annum covering time 0 to time t. The time-0 expected present value of the reverse mortgage per capita is $\mathrm{E}^*[\sum_t \exp(-r_{0,t}\ t) \min(L_t, P_t)\ I_t]$ under the risk-neutral measure. The reverse mortgage is financially viable for the lender if this expected present value is larger than the initial loan size L_0. Note that there are three stochastic variables in this formula: $r_{0,t}$ (interest rate risk), P_t (house price risk) and I_t (longevity risk), which require proper modelling to allow for their uncertainties. It is assumed that longevity risk and market risks are real-world independent.

We set $I_t = (1 - q_{x,0})(1 - q_{x+1,1}) \ldots (1 - q_{x+t-2,t-2}) q_{x+t-1,t-1}$, in which $q_{x,t}$ is the mortality rate that a life aged x at time t dies during the next year. Assuming the force of mortality $\mu_{x,t}$ remains unchanged within every age–time cell and it is equal to the central death rate $m_{x,t}$, it can be deduced that $q_{x,t} = 1 - \exp(-m_{x,t})$. We use the well-known Lee and Carter (1992) model $\ln m_{x,t} = \alpha_x + \beta_x\ \kappa_t$, where α_x describes the overall age schedule and β_x measures the age-sensitivity of the log central death rate to the mortality index κ_t[6]. We assume the number of deaths $D_{x,t} \sim \mathrm{Poisson}(e_{x,t}\ m_{x,t})$ with $e_{x,t}$ as the central exposed to risk, and the random walk with drift $\kappa_t = \mu + \kappa_{t-1} + \varepsilon_t$ for the mortality index, in which μ is the drift and $\varepsilon_t \sim \mathrm{N}(0, \sigma_\varepsilon^2)$. Under the Bayesian framework, following Kogure et al. (2009) and Li (2014b), we set the priors $\alpha_x \sim \mathrm{N}(0, \sigma_\alpha^2)$, $\beta_x \sim \mathrm{N}(\frac{1}{no.\ of\ ages}, \sigma_\beta^2)$, $\mu \sim \mathrm{N}(\mu_0, \sigma_\mu^2)$ and $\sigma_\varepsilon^{-2} \sim \mathrm{Gamma}(a, b)$[7]. The major step is to obtain the posterior distribution of the unknown quantities and parameters given the dataset, using $f(\theta|D) \propto f(D|\theta) f(\theta)$. However, the derivation of an explicit solution of the posterior density is intractable for the models being used here. Therefore, we utilise the Markov chain Monte Carlo (MCMC) method to simulate random samples based on a Markov chain which has its stationary distribution equivalent to the required posterior distribution. These random samples are then put into Equations (1) or (2) to compute the risk-neutral probabilities.

To cope with the autocorrelations and cross-correlations found in the house price growth rates[8] and interest rates, we adopt the vector autoregressive process, VAR(p):

$$\begin{pmatrix} g_{t+1,t} \\ r_{t+1,t} \end{pmatrix} = \begin{pmatrix} \phi_1^{(0)} \\ \phi_2^{(0)} \end{pmatrix} + \begin{pmatrix} \phi_{1,1}^{(1)} & \phi_{1,2}^{(1)} \\ \phi_{2,1}^{(1)} & \phi_{2,1}^{(1)} \end{pmatrix} \begin{pmatrix} g_{t,t-1} \\ r_{t,t-1} \end{pmatrix} + \begin{pmatrix} \phi_{1,1}^{(2)} & \phi_{1,2}^{(2)} \\ \phi_{2,1}^{(2)} & \phi_{2,1}^{(2)} \end{pmatrix} \begin{pmatrix} g_{t-1,t-2} \\ r_{t-1,t-2} \end{pmatrix} + \ldots + \begin{pmatrix} \phi_{1,1}^{(p)} & \phi_{1,2}^{(p)} \\ \phi_{2,1}^{(p)} & \phi_{2,1}^{(p)} \end{pmatrix} \begin{pmatrix} g_{t-p+1,t-p} \\ r_{t-p+1,t-p} \end{pmatrix} + \begin{pmatrix} v_{t+1} \\ \omega_{t+1} \end{pmatrix}$$

---

4 For convenience, we assume that the repayment is settled at the end of the year of death.

5 We assume that the reverse mortgage portfolio is very large and so sampling error due to individual uncertainty (non-systematic longevity risk) is negligible.

6 In Bayesian modelling, all the unknown parameters are treated as random variables, and so in theory there is no identifiability issue and parameter constraints are not needed. But we realise that our simulation algorithm converges much more slowly if there is no constraint. Hence, we set the two constraints $\sum_x \beta_x = 1$ and $k_0 = c$, along the line of the initial Lee–Carter model.

7 The variances σ_α^2 and σ_β^2 are set as the sample variances of the estimated α_x and β_x over age times 10; a is set to be 2.1; b is set to be 1.1 times the sample variance of the estimated $\kappa_t - \kappa_{t-1}$ over time; μ_0 and σ_μ^2 are computed from the sample mean and its standard error of the estimated $\kappa_t - \kappa_{t-1}$. These values are largely chosen to represent vague prior knowledge.

8 Due to the existence of autocorrelations and cross-correlations, the widely used assumption of the geometric Brownian motion is not suitable here.

where $g_{t+1,t} = \ln(P_{t+1}/P_t)$, ϕ's are the autoregressive coefficients and $(\nu_t, \omega_t)'$ are bivariate normal with zero mean. As stated in Rosenberg and Young (1999), autoregressive processes are more straightforward to implement in a Bayesian setting compared to moving-average processes. If the order p of the autoregressive terms is high enough, the modelling results would be similar to a given autoregressive moving-average process. We set the prior of ϕ's as multivariate normal with zero mean, and the prior of the inverse covariance matrix of $(\nu_t, \omega_t)'$ distributed as Wishart[9].

In the MCMC simulation process, we discard the starting 5000 iterations in order to eliminate the impact of the initial values and collect 1000 sample paths afterwards. As shown in the Appendix A, the resulting autocorrelations between successive MCMC samples of each variable are minimal, which suggest that the extent of convergence is adequate in our computations. We apply the Bayesian software WinBUGS (Spiegelhalter et al. 2003) to perform the MCMC simulation via Gibbs sampling. The fundamental idea is to sequentially generate samples from the distribution of each variable conditional on all the other variables. Li (2014b) provided some examples of writing WinBUGS codes for projection and simulation of future death rates.

4. Analysis of Modelling Results

We obtain Australian male mortality data from the Human Mortality Database (Human Mortality Database HMD) for a period of 40 years from 1975 to 2014 and an age range of 65 to 99. Figure 1 exhibits the central death rates across age for each decade. It can be seen that generally there has been a continual mortality improvement over time. The extent appears to be more significant at ages 80 and above in the most recent period. Figure 2 presents the estimated Lee–Carter mortality index, which is decreasing mostly linearly across time, and its projected central values (sample means) and the corresponding 95% prediction intervals from the MCMC simulation. Figure 3 displays the simulated density functions of the future survival probabilities from age 65 (at time 0) to ages 75, 85 and 95.

We collect the quarterly residential property price index values (calculated as a weighted average of eight capital cities) from the Australian Bureau of Statistics (ABS) for the period 2003 to 2018. We also obtain the 3-month bank accepted bills yields from the Reserve Bank of Australia (RBA) for the same period. Note that the property price index (a price-based index) is taken as a proxy, as each property is unique by nature itself and is infrequently traded. Figure 4 shows that the overall property market in Australia has experienced significant growth over the past sixteen years. Despite this major trend, the house prices do not simply increase linearly but move in some forms of cycles. The quarterly growth rates during the period actually range widely from −2.2% to 5.4%. The figure also demonstrates the cyclical interest rate movements for the period and the broad level has decreased from above 5% p.a. to around 2% p.a. of late. Figure 5 illustrates that there are significant sample autocorrelations and cross-correlations in between the time series of the house price growth rates and interest rates. A bivariate autoregressive process can be adopted to capture these time-dependent patterns. After examining the sample partial autocorrelation matrices and the sample cross-correlation matrices, we notice that a VAR(5) process (i.e., a maximum lag of five quarters) appears to fit the data reasonably well and the corresponding residuals do not have significant time-varying patterns in general, as shown in Figure 6. The sample autocorrelations of the squared residuals are also found to be insignificant and so a GARCH-type model for conditional heteroscedasticity is not required here. Figure 7 plots the simulated density functions of the future quarterly house price growth rates and interest rates after 10, 20 and 30 years.

---

9 The inverse covariance matrix of ϕ's is assumed as Wishart with a degree of freedom of $4p + 4$. The inverse covariance matrix of $(\nu_t, \omega_t)'$ is assumed as Wishart with a degree of freedom of 4. The small degrees of freedom are selected to represent vague prior knowledge.

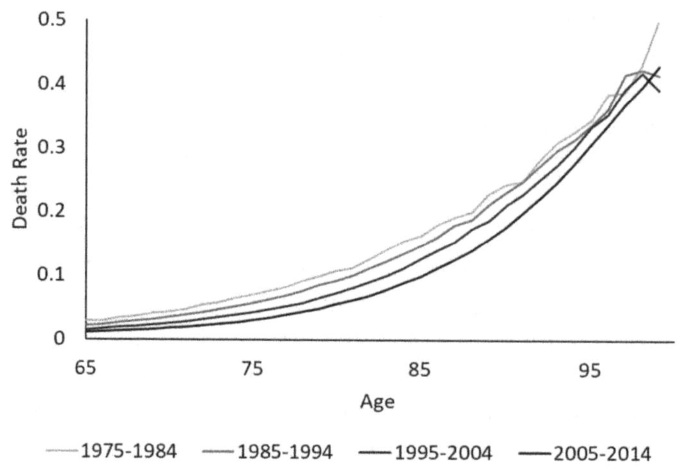

Figure 1. Australian male central death rates for 1975 to 2014.

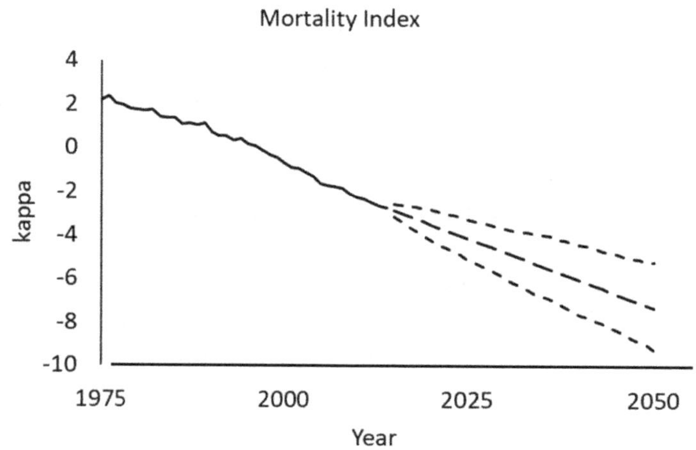

Figure 2. Bayesian Lee–Carter mortality index for 1975 to 2014 (solid line) and projected values with 95% prediction intervals for 2015 to 2050 (dashed and dotted lines).

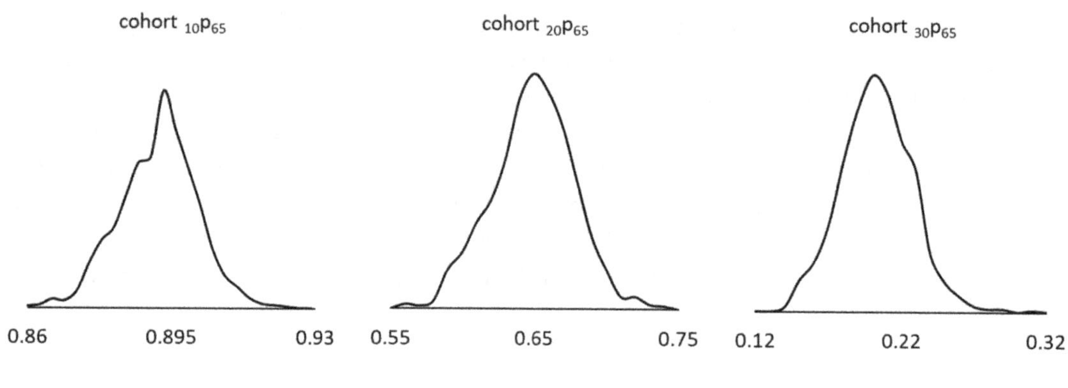

Figure 3. Simulated density functions of future survival probabilities of the cohort aged 65 (at the start of 2019) for 10, 20 and 30 years.

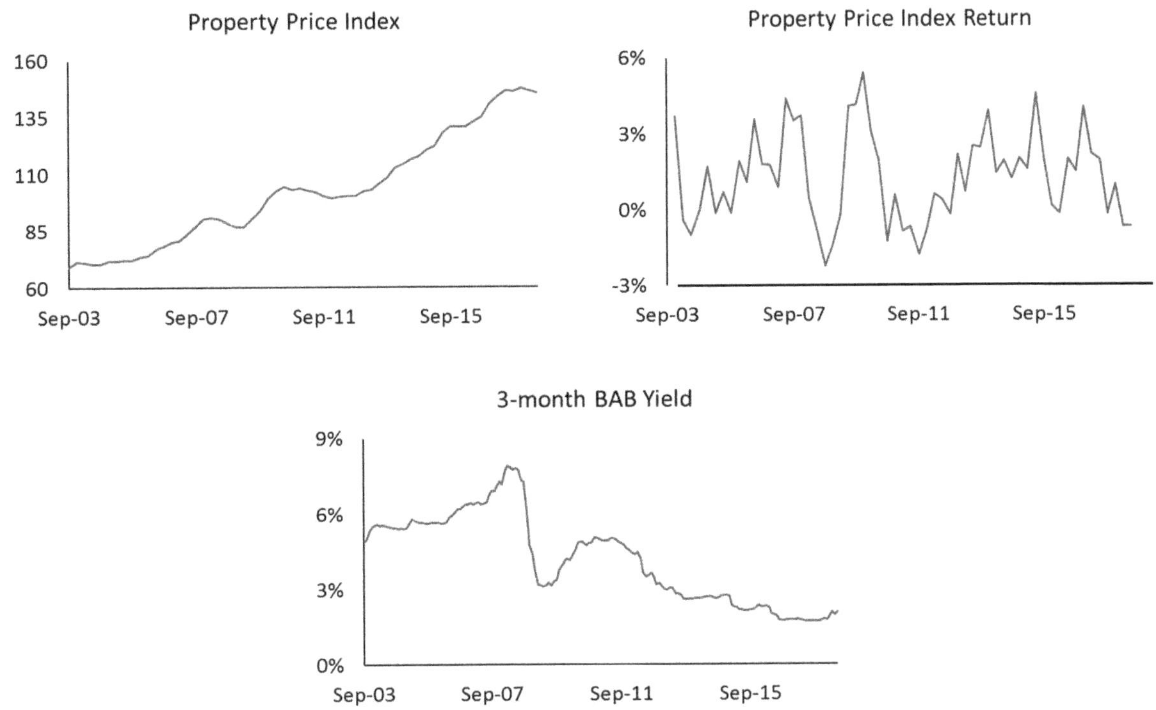

Figure 4. Australian quarterly residential property price index values (weighted average of Sydney, Melbourne, Brisbane, Adelaide, Perth, Hobart, Darwin and Canberra) and growth rates, and 3-month bank accepted bills yields, from September 2003 to June 2018.

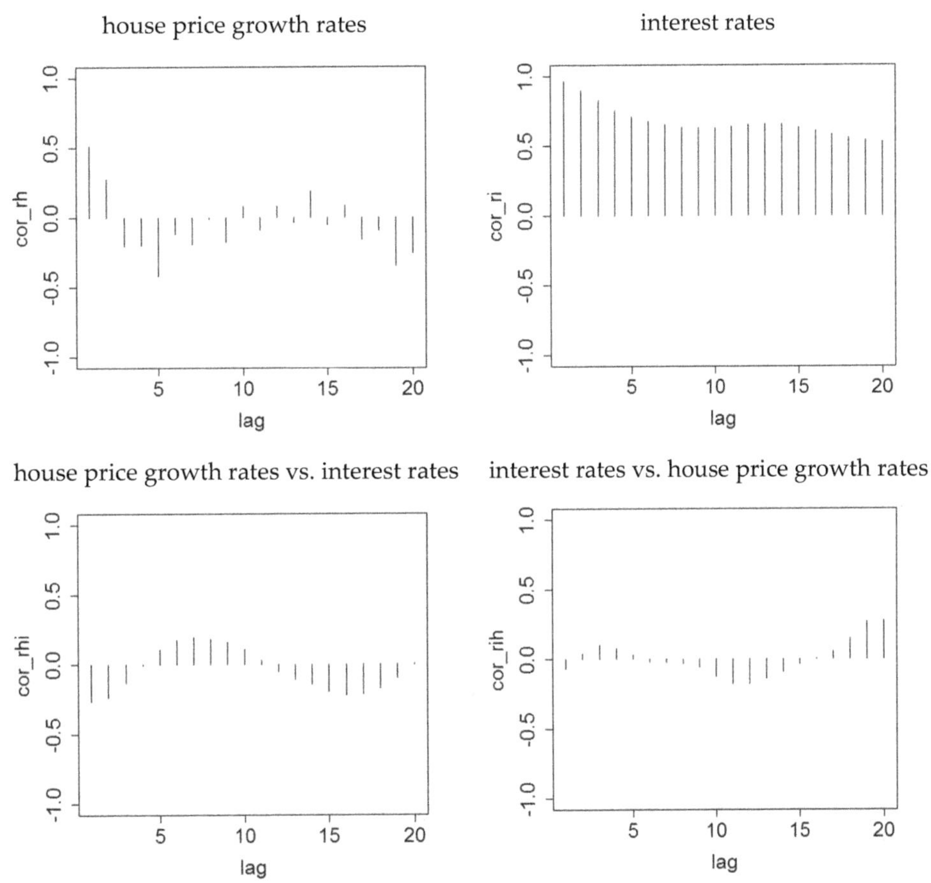

Figure 5. Sample autocorrelations and cross-correlations of house price growth rates and interest rates.

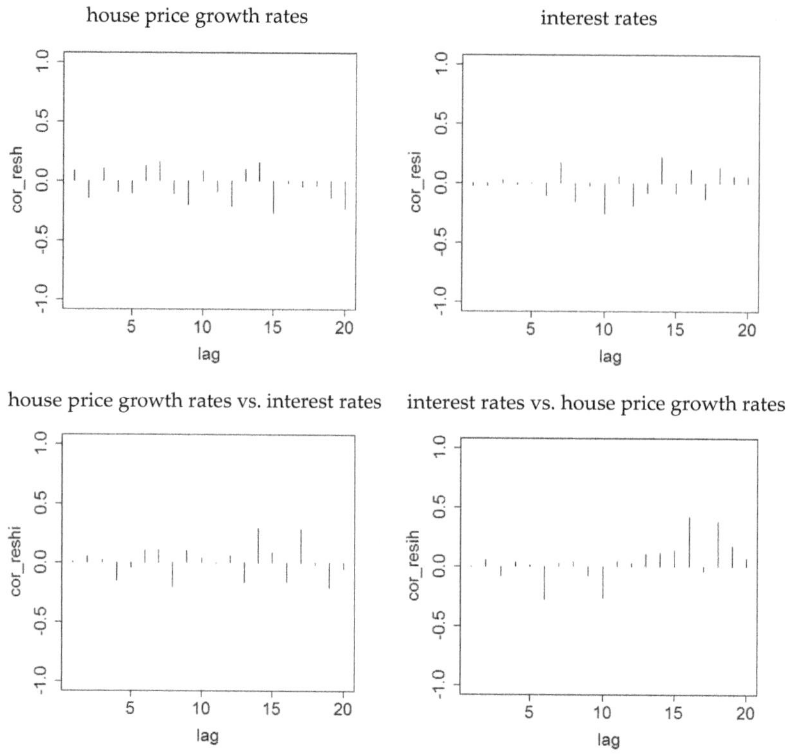

Figure 6. Sample autocorrelations and cross-correlations of residuals after fitting VAR(5).

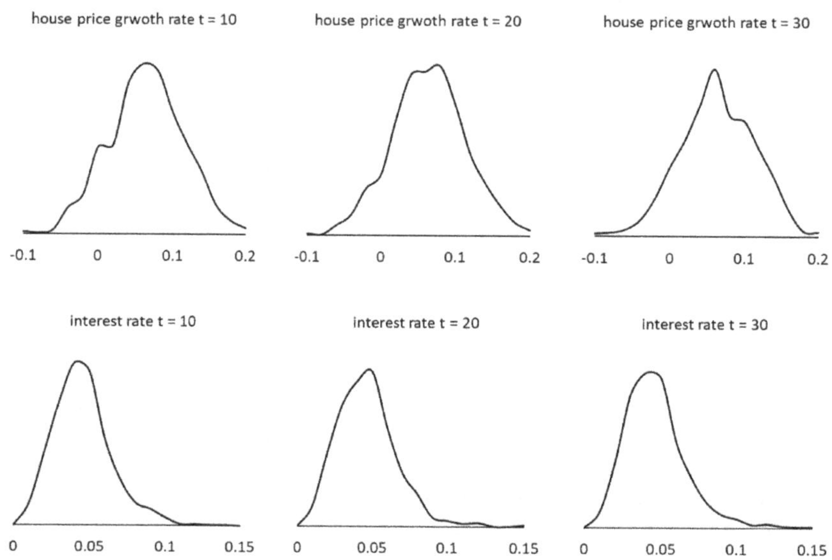

Figure 7. Simulated density functions of future house price growth rates and interest rates after 10, 20 and 30 years (from the start of 2019).

Since the Australian annuity market is very thin, we use the mortality investigation reports published by the Institute of Actuaries of Australia[10] and the underlying improvement rates to deduce the annuity market price. We also take the ABS property price index as the house market price, and collect the latest Australian government bond price in the market. These market prices are substituted into the constraints as noted in Section 2. Figure 8 exhibits the resulting risk-neutral probabilities.

[10] It is now called the Actuaries Institute and the website is www.actuaries.asn.au.

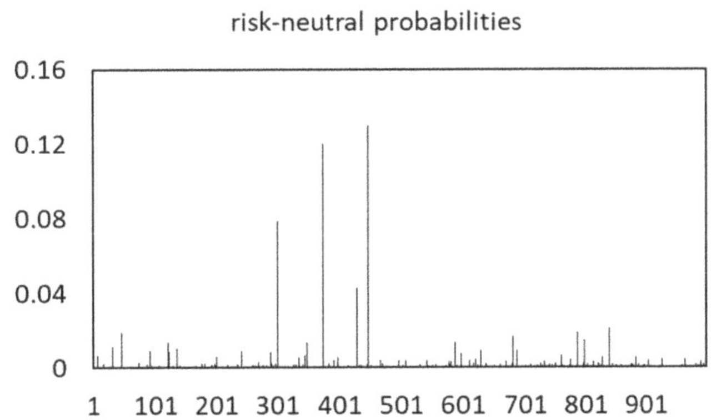

Figure 8. Risk-neutral probabilities calculated from simulated values and market price constraints.

Suppose the valuation date (t = 0) is as at the start of 2019 and P_0 = 550,000[11]. We consider an individual aged 65 or 75 entering into a reverse mortgage contract with a loan-to-value (LTV) ratio of 10%, 20%, . . . , or 100%, i.e., L_0 = 55,000, 110,000, . . . , or 550,000, and l = 1%, 2%, . . . , or 10% p.a[12]. These are a total of 200 cases in which we examine the calculated market prices of the reverse mortgage based on the different terms being offered.

Tables 1 and 2 give the (risk-neutral) expected present values of the reverse mortgage under various loan interest rates and LTV ratios. When the loan interest rate is 1% or 2% p.a., the initial loan size is larger than the expected present value, and the reverse mortgage is then financially infeasible for the lender. As the loan interest rate rises, the reverse mortgage value increases and the contract becomes more feasible for the lender. But this effect is lesser if the LTV ratio is higher, because under the no-negative-equity guarantee, the embedded put option is worth more when there is a higher chance for the market value of the mortgaged property to be lower than the accumulated loan balance. In the current market, the loan interest rate is above 6% p.a. for reverse mortgages (see Table 3), which is 1% to 2% higher than for a standard home loan, and the LTV ratio is around 20% (30%) for a borrower aged 65 (75). The figures in Tables 1 and 2 pinpoint that the reverse mortgage products presently offered are financially viable from the providers' perspective.

To further differentiate the outcomes, we also examine the percentage differences between the expected present value and the initial loan size in each case. Ignoring expenses (e.g., commissions, distribution costs), in Tables 1 and 2, those cases incurring a loss are shaded as dark grey; the offers that generate a less than 10% profit are noted as medium grey; those giving 10% to 50% of profit are highlighted as light grey; and all the other cases with more than 50% gain are not shaded. It seems that the current providers are actually overly conservative in designing their products (the range of which is circled) and the existing market offers tend to be too expensive. There appears to be some room for Australian banks and insurers to provide more attractive products by increasing the LTV ratio, decreasing the loan interest rate or delivering more flexible solutions. As noted in Australian Securities and Investments Commission (Australian Securities and Investments Commission ASIC), however, the current market is highly concentrated with the largest four lenders accounting for 92% of new approved loans during 2013 to 2017. The lenders imposed limits on the maximum LTV ratio which were lower than the levels prescribed in the enhanced consumer protections. There may also be a barrier for lenders to enter the market such as the capital requirement and the difficulty accessing wholesale funding after the global financial crisis. Besides improving the protection for customers' interests, the government can actually consider giving more incentives for the industry to supply

---

11 The national median home price in Australia is AUD$552,141 as of 31 August 2018. (https://edge.alluremedia.com.au/uploads/businessinsider/2018/09/CoreLogic-home-value-index-August-2018-table.jpg).

12 The analysis can readily be extended to a floating loan interest rate, which can be set as the risk-free rate plus a spread. Accordingly, there would be some offsetting between the loan interest rate and the discounting. There may then be less interest rate risk and the calculated reverse mortgage price may be lower. We leave this interesting option for future research.

reverse mortgage products (e.g., the US Home Equity Conversion Mortgage program managed by the Department of Housing and Urban Development). More education and promotion can also be used to increase the public awareness of these products in an ageing society.

Table 1. Expected present values of the reverse mortgage under different loan interest rates and loan-to-value (LTV) ratios for a homeowner aged 65.

r\LTV	**10%**	**20%**	**30%**	**40%**	**50%**	**60%**	**70%**	**80%**	**90%**	**100%**
Size	**55**	**110**	**165**	**220**	**275**	**330**	**385**	**440**	**495**	**550**
1%	36	73	109	145	181	218	254	290	326	360
2%	45	90	135	180	224	269	314	358	400	435
3%	56	112	168	224	280	335	390	439	476	504
4%	70	141	211	281	351	418	469	503	530	549
5%	89	178	266	355	433	484	521	547	563	572
6%	113	226	338	432	491	530	555	569	576	579
7%	145	289	413	487	531	556	569	576	579	580
8%	187	362	468	523	552	566	574	578	580	580
9%	242	423	506	543	561	571	576	579	580	580
10%	306	468	528	553	566	573	577	579	580	580

Table 2. Expected present values of the reverse mortgage under different loan interest rates and LTV ratios for a homeowner aged 75.

r\LTV	**10%**	**20%**	**30%**	**40%**	**50%**	**60%**	**70%**	**80%**	**90%**	**100%**
Size	**55**	**110**	**165**	**220**	**275**	**330**	**385**	**440**	**495**	**550**
1%	44	88	131	175	219	263	307	350	393	430
2%	50	100	149	199	249	299	349	398	441	473
3%	57	114	171	228	285	341	397	445	481	509
4%	65	131	196	261	326	390	443	484	515	538
5%	75	151	226	301	374	433	481	517	542	557
6%	87	174	261	346	416	472	513	541	558	565
7%	101	203	303	388	455	503	535	554	564	567
8%	118	236	344	426	486	525	548	560	566	567
9%	139	275	383	459	508	537	553	562	566	567
10%	163	313	417	484	523	544	556	563	567	568

Table 3. Current reverse mortgage loan interest rates in Australia.

Bank	**Interest Rate (p.a.)**
Bankwest	6.42%
Commonwealth Bank	6.52%
Heartland Seniors Finance	6.54%
Heritage Bank	6.29%
P&N Bank	6.24%

Note: These figures were collected from https://www.finder.com.au/reverse-mortgages on 28 November 2018.

5. Concluding Remarks

Our proposed Bayesian multivariate risk-neutral pricing method has been shown to be very flexible in dealing with multiple risks and setting market price constraints. It gives a more coherent treatment of the various steps and components, compared to the other earlier approaches on pricing reverse mortgages. The results of our case study further suggest that a reverse mortgage provider in Australia can operate in a sustainable manner, under the current financial environment and the model settings and assumptions.

There are a number of areas which require future research. While we have focused on a plain vanilla type of reverse mortgage, there are other features that are worth studying such as joint lives, multiple decrements and a variety of other product designs (e.g., income payments, variable loan interest rate, capital protection and long-term care). Relevant prior information can be put into the modelling process and the resulting impact can be investigated. One can also replace the Lee–Carter model and the VAR process with other models and compare the corresponding results. Furthermore, model uncertainty can further be integrated by setting prior probabilities on a few pre-selected model choices and then deriving their posterior distributions.

Author Contributions: Methodology, J.L. (Jackie Li), A.K. and J.L. (Jia Liu); Valuation, J.L. (Jackie Li) and J.L. (Jia Liu); Analysis, J.L. (Jackie Li), A.K. and J.L. (Jia Liu); Writing, J.L. (Jackie Li), A.K. and J.L. (Jia Liu).

Funding: This research received no external funding.

Conflicts of Interest: The authors declare no conflict of interest.

Appendix A

As shown below, the autocorrelations between successive WinBUGS samples of each variable are negligible. It appears that the level of convergence is adequate in our simulations. The Monte Carlo errors are only around 1% of the sample standard deviations, which further confirm sufficient convergence. Different initial values are also tested and the corresponding simulated results are similar.

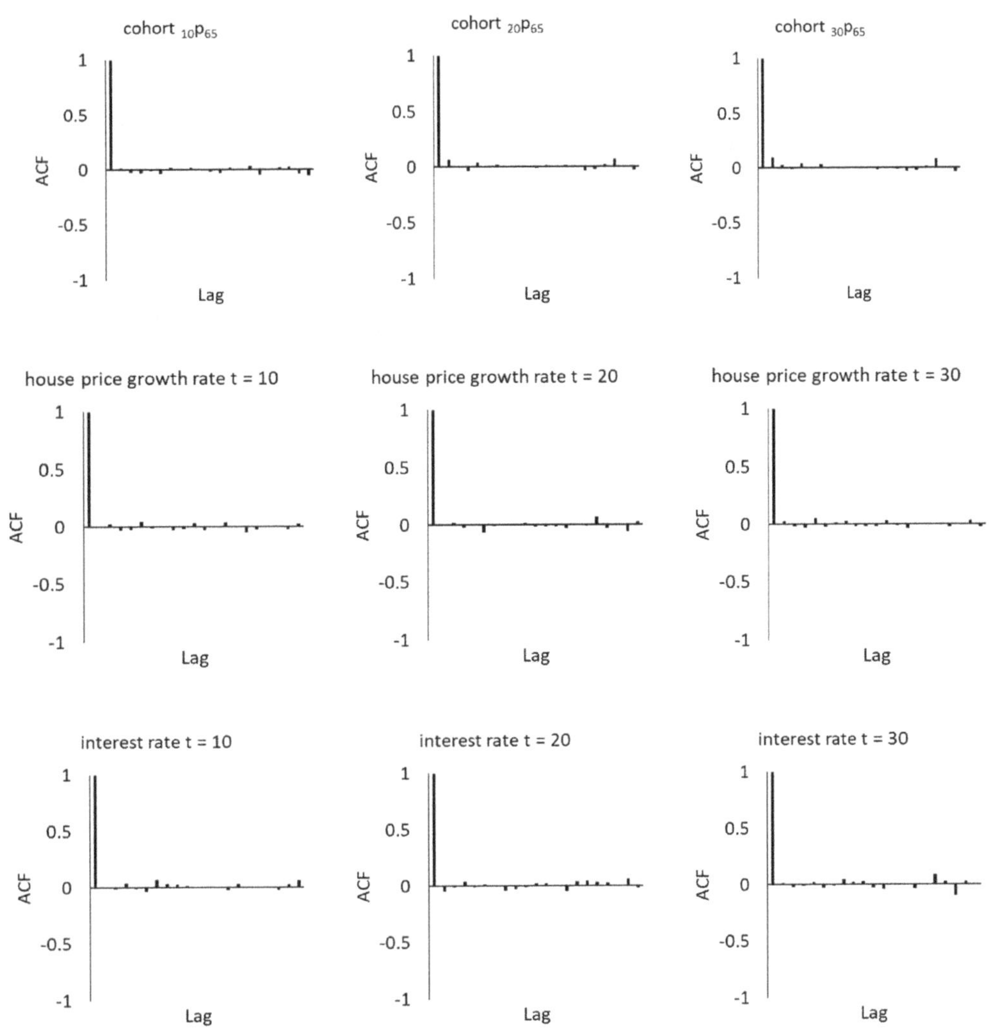

Figure A1. Sample autocorrelations between successive Markov chain Monte Carlo (MCMC) samples of future survival probabilities, house price growth rates and interest rates.

References

Australian Securities and Investments Commission (ASIC). 2018. *Review of Reverse Mortgage Lending in Australia.* Report 586. Sydney: ASIC.

Debón, Ana, Francisco Montes, and Ramón Sala-Garrido. 2013. Pricing reverse mortgages in Spain. *European Actuarial Journal* 3: 23–43. [CrossRef]

Human Mortality Database (HMD). 2018. University of California, Berkeley (USA) and Max Planck Institute for Demographic Research (Germany). Available online: https://www.mortality.org/ (accessed on 26 September 2018).

Ji, Min, Mary Hardy, and Johnny Siu-Hang Li. 2012. A semi-Markov multiple state model for reverse mortgage terminations. *Annals of Actuarial Science* 6: 235–57. [CrossRef]

Kogure, Atsuyuki, and Yoshiyuki Kurachi. 2010. A Bayesian approach to pricing longevity risk based on risk-neutral predictive distributions. *Insurance: Mathematics and Economics* 46: 162–72. [CrossRef]

Kogure, Atsuyuki, Kenji Kitsukawa, and Yoshiyuki Kurachi. 2009. A Bayesian comparison of models for changing mortalities toward evaluating longevity risk in Japan. *Asia-Pacific Journal of Risk and Insurance* 3: 1–21. [CrossRef]

Kogure, Atsuyuki, Jackie Li, and Shinichi Kamiya. 2014. A Bayesian multivariate risk-neutral method for pricing reverse mortgages. *North American Actuarial Journal* 18: 242–57. [CrossRef]

Lee, Ronald D., and Lawrence R. Carter. 1992. Modeling and forecasting U.S. mortality. *Journal of the American Statistical Association* 87: 659–71. [CrossRef]

Lee, Yung-Tsung, Chou-Wen Wang, and Hong-Chih Huang. 2012. On the valuation of reverse mortgages with regular tenure payments. *Insurance: Mathematics and Economics* 51: 430–41. [CrossRef]

Li, Johnny Siu-Hang. 2010. Pricing longevity risk with the parametric bootstrap: A maximum entropy approach. *Insurance: Mathematics and Economics* 47: 176–86. [CrossRef]

Li, Jackie. 2014a. A quantitative comparison of simulation strategies for mortality projection. *Annals of Actuarial Science* 8: 281–97. [CrossRef]

Li, Jackie. 2014b. An application of MCMC simulation in mortality projection for populations with limited data. *Demographic Research* 30: 1–47. [CrossRef]

Rosenberg, Marjorie A., and Virginia R. Young. 1999. A Bayesian approach to understanding time series data. *North American Actuarial Journal* 3: 130–43. [CrossRef]

Spiegelhalter, David, Andrew Thomas, Nicky Best, and Dave Lunn. 2003. WinBUGS User Manual. Available online: https://www.mrc-bsu.cam.ac.uk/wp-content/uploads/manual14.pdf (accessed on 24 January 2019).

Wang, Liang, Emiliano A. Valdez, and John Piggott. 2008. Securitization of longevity risk in reverse mortgages. *North American Actuarial Journal* 12: 345–71. [CrossRef]

Permissions

All chapters in this book were first published in RISK, by MDPI; hereby published with permission under the Creative Commons Attribution License or equivalent. Every chapter published in this book has been scrutinized by our experts. Their significance has been extensively debated. The topics covered herein carry significant findings which will fuel the growth of the discipline. They may even be implemented as practical applications or may be referred to as a beginning point for another development.

The contributors of this book come from diverse backgrounds, making this book a truly international effort. This book will bring forth new frontiers with its revolutionizing research information and detailed analysis of the nascent developments around the world.

We would like to thank all the contributing authors for lending their expertise to make the book truly unique. They have played a crucial role in the development of this book. Without their invaluable contributions this book wouldn't have been possible. They have made vital efforts to compile up to date information on the varied aspects of this subject to make this book a valuable addition to the collection of many professionals and students.

This book was conceptualized with the vision of imparting up-to-date information and advanced data in this field. To ensure the same, a matchless editorial board was set up. Every individual on the board went through rigorous rounds of assessment to prove their worth. After which they invested a large part of their time researching and compiling the most relevant data for our readers.

The editorial board has been involved in producing this book since its inception. They have spent rigorous hours researching and exploring the diverse topics which have resulted in the successful publishing of this book. They have passed on their knowledge of decades through this book. To expedite this challenging task, the publisher supported the team at every step. A small team of assistant editors was also appointed to further simplify the editing procedure and attain best results for the readers.

Apart from the editorial board, the designing team has also invested a significant amount of their time in understanding the subject and creating the most relevant covers. They scrutinized every image to scout for the most suitable representation of the subject and create an appropriate cover for the book.

The publishing team has been an ardent support to the editorial, designing and production team. Their endless efforts to recruit the best for this project, has resulted in the accomplishment of this book. They are a veteran in the field of academics and their pool of knowledge is as vast as their experience in printing. Their expertise and guidance has proved useful at every step. Their uncompromising quality standards have made this book an exceptional effort. Their encouragement from time to time has been an inspiration for everyone.

The publisher and the editorial board hope that this book will prove to be a valuable piece of knowledge for researchers, students, practitioners and scholars across the globe.

List of Contributors

Maria Elena De Giuli
Department of Economics and Management, University of Pavia, 27100 Pavia PV, Italy

Alessandro Greppi
Zurich Investment Life, 20159 Milan MI, Italy

Marina Resta
School of Social Sciences, Department of Economics and Business Studies, University of Genova, 16126 Genova GE, Italy

Wanbing Zhang and Peibiao Zhao
School of Science, Nanjing University of Science and Technology, Nanjing 210094, China

Sisi Zhang
Securities Co., Ltd., Beijing 102627, China

Rui Zhou
Department of Economics, University of Melbourne, Parkville, VIC 3010, Australia

Guangyu Xing
Manulife-Sinochem, Shanghai 200121, China

Min Ji
Department of Mathematics, Towson University, Towson, MD 21252, USA

Hui Ye and Anthony Bellotti
Department of Mathematics, Imperial College London, London SW7 2AZ, UK

Shi Chen and Wenyu Yao
School of Economics, Southwestern University of Finance and Economics, Chengdu 611130, China

Jyh-Horng Lin
Department of International Business, Tamkang University, New Taipei City 25137, Taiwan

Fu-Wei Huang
Department of Management Sciences, Tamkang University, New Taipei City 25137, Taiwan

Ranjit Singh
Department of Management Studies, Indian Institute of Information Technology, Allahabad 211012, India

Jayashree Bhattacharjee
Department of Business Administration, Assam University, Silchar 788011, India

Zhuo Jin
Centre for Actuarial Studies, Department of Economics, The University of Melbourne, Melbourne, VIC 3010, Australia

Zhixin Yang and Quan Yuan
Department of Mathematical Sciences, Ball State University, Muncie, IN 47306, USA

Phillip J. Monin
Office of Financial Research, 717 14th St NW, Washington, DC 20005, USA

Zbigniew Palmowski
Department of Applied Mathematics, Faculty of Pure and Applied Mathematics, Wrocław University of Science and Technology, 50-370Wrocław, Poland

Łukasz Stettner
Institute of Mathematics, Polish Academy of Sciences, 00-656Warsaw, Poland; Vistula University, 02-787Warsaw, Poland

Anna Sulima
Faculty of Management, Computer Science and Finance, Wrocław University of Economics, 53-345 Wrocław, Poland

Søren Asmussen
Department of Mathematics, Aarhus University, 8000 Aarhus, Denmark

Patrick J. Laub
Institut de Science Financière et d'Assurances, Université Lyon 1, 69007 Lyon, France

Hailiang Yang
Department of Statistics & Actuarial Science, Hong Kong University, Hong Kong 999077, China

Jackie Li and Jia Liu
Department of Actuarial Studies and Business Analytics, Macquarie University, Macquarie Park, NSW 2109, Australia

Atsuyuki Kogure
Faculty of Business Administration, Tokyo Keizai University, Tokyo 185-8502, Japan

Index

www.ingramcontent.com/pod-product-compliance
Lightning Source LLC
LaVergne TN
LVHW060556210926
848485LV00005B/1323